SIX SCOTTISH COURTLY AND CHIVALRIC POEMS, INCLUDING LYNDSAY'S *SQUYER MELDRUM*

MIDDLE ENGLISH TEXTS SERIES

The Middle English Texts Series are scholarly texts designed for research and classroom use. Its goal is to make available to teachers, scholars, and students texts that occupy an important place in the literary and cultural canon but have not been readily available in print and online editions. The series does not include those authors, such as Chaucer, Langland, or Malory, whose English works are normally in print in good student editions. The focus is, instead, upon Middle English literature adjacent to those authors that are needed for doing research or teaching. The editions maintain the linguistic integrity of the original work but within the parameters of modern reading conventions. The texts are printed in the modern alphabet and follow the practices of modern capitalization, word formation, and punctuation. Manuscript abbreviations are silently expanded, and *u/v* and *j/i* spellings are regularized according to modern orthography. Yogh (ȝ) is transcribed as *g, gh, y,* or *s,* according to the sound in Modern English spelling to which the medieval pronunciation corresponds; thorn (þ) and eth (ð) are transcribed as *th.* Distinction between the second person pronoun and the definite article is made by spelling the one *thee* and the other *the,* and final *-e* that receives full syllabic value is accented (e.g., *charité*). Hard words, difficult phrases, and unusual idioms are glossed either in the right margin or at the foot of the page. Explanatory and textual notes appear at the end of the text, often along with a glossary. The editions include short introductions on the history of the work, its merits and points of topical interest, and brief working bibliographies.

This series is published in association with the University of Rochester.

Medieval Institute Publications is a program of
The Medieval Institute, College of Arts and Sciences

WESTERN MICHIGAN UNIVERSITY

SIX SCOTTISH COURTLY AND CHIVALRIC POEMS, INCLUDING LYNDSAY'S *SQUYER MELDRUM*

Edited by

Rhiannon Purdie and Emily Wingfield

TEAMS • Teaching Association for Medieval Studies • University of Rochester

MEDIEVAL INSTITUTE PUBLICATIONS
Western Michigan University
Kalamazoo

Copyright © 2018 by the Board of Trustees of Western Michigan University

Printed and bound by CPI Group (UK) Ltd, Croydon, CR0 4YY

**Library of Congress Cataloging-in-Publication Data
are available from the Library of Congress.**

ISBN: 978-1-58044-332-6 (paperback)
ISBN: 978-1-58044-342-5 (hardback)

P 5 4 3 2 1

CONTENTS

# ACKNOWLEDGMENTS

Rhiannon:

I would first of all like to thank Emily for bringing both her scholarship and her formidable work-ethic to this project: without her this edition could have been many more years in the making, as well as being much the poorer. I am also extremely grateful to Janet Hadley Williams for her generously detailed read-through of all of the *Meldrum* material: any remaining errors or infelicities in this section are, needless to say, entirely my own. I would also like to thank Michael Brown and Roger Mason for reading parts of the "historical" sections (with particular thanks to Roger for details of late-medieval anti-football legislation), and to Katie Stevenson for patiently fielding questions on squires and heraldry. I must also thank Cynthia Neville and Kathy Cawsey for inviting me to give a paper on *Squyer Meldrum* to the Stokes Seminar series at Dalhousie University (March 11, 2016): perceptive questions from this audience helped me through an interpretative crux, and I hope that if any of them read the results here, they will be pleased to recognize the changes they helped to effect. Tremendous thanks are due to Russell Peck and Pamela Yee at METS — to Russell for the warm encouragement to propose this volume in the first place, and to both for the extraordinary amount of work they have put into polishing it and seeing it through. I would also like to extend heartfelt thanks to staff editors Kyle Huskin, Alison Harper, Ashley Conklin, and Emily Lowman for the care and extra hours they put into the edition. I can safely say I have never had my work read with such minute attention before (and I still can't decide if I liked it).

My half of this project would never have been brought to such a timely conclusion without the support of the US–UK Fulbright Commission, whose Visiting Scholar award in 2016 allowed me to spend a semester at the University of Rochester's fabulous Robbins Library. Staff at Robbins were unfailingly helpful and welcoming, in particular Rosemary Paprocki. I am also grateful to the National Endowment for the Humanities (NEH) for its long-standing funding of METS, and without which this publication would not be possible. The School of English at St Andrews, headed by Professor Gill Plain, have been supportive in every possible way, both personally and professionally. I would also like to thank: staff in the Special Collections department of the National Library of Scotland; Special Collections staff at Edinburgh Central Library; Neil Dickson at Stirling Council Archives; David Oswald at Aberdeen Central Library, and Richard Foster at Winchester College Library, all of whom allowed me access to prints of Lyndsay's work, or to materials related to Lyndsay, or patiently answered questions about their holdings.

Finally, I would like to thank my family: Neale, who was not only willing to become a single parent for the four months I spent at Rochester, but who actually *suggested* the idea (and generously strove to hide his dismay when I took him up on it), and Isaac and Russell, who wait uncomplainingly for each book to be finished as they make themselves baked beans and pot noodles for dinner, only to find that another book is queuing up behind it.

Emily:

First and foremost, I would like to thank Rhiannon for inviting me to take part in this edition, and for all of the support she has shown me since initially acting as my external examiner back in 2010. In addition, my thanks to the School of English, Drama, American & Canadian Studies at the University of Birmingham; Sally Baggott, Priscilla Bawcutt, Erika Graham-Goering, David Griffith, Elizabeth L'Estrange, Alasdair MacDonald, Sally Mapstone, Rebecca Marsland, Joanna Martin, Kate McClune, Tricia McElroy, Nicola Royan and Claude Thiry for their advice and comments (plus translations and proof-reading); as well as the librarians at the Bibliothèque Royale, Brussels; the Bodleian Library; Edinburgh University Library; the National Library of Scotland; National Records of Scotland; and the Parker Library (Corpus Christi, Cambridge). I would also like to thank the students of the medieval reading group at the University of Birmingham for helping me notice a mistake — and offering a new reading of the *Balletis*. Work on this edition began prior to the birth of my daughter in 2015 and continued on and off during and after my maternity leave. I am therefore grateful to Sophie, for slowly getting the hang of daytime napping, and to Paul and my parents for helping me out when I needed to return to my desk; I cannot thank them enough for the love and support they have shown me over the last two years. I am also very grateful to the staff at the Middle English Texts Series, in particular Russell Peck and Pamela Yee, for their sharp observations and insightful comments — as well as to the NEH for their generous sponsorship of METS. Any errors that remain are my own responsibility (or — I like to pretend — the result of 'baby brain' and a protracted lack of sleep!).

As its title suggests, this volume brings together six poems on courtly and chivalric themes from late medieval Scotland. Three of these are anonymous and date from the fifteenth century: the *Balletis of the Nine Nobles* (c. 1438–47); *Complaint for the Death of Margaret, Princess of Scotland* (c. 1445–60); and the *Talis of the Fyve Bestes* (c. 1480–1520). The other three items — the *Answer to the Kingis Flyting* (c. 1535–36), *The Historie of Squyer Meldrum*, and its appended *Testament of Squyer Meldrum* (both re-dated here to c. 1540–47) — were all written in the first half of the sixteenth century by the poet and herald Sir David Lyndsay (c. 1486–1555), who had a prominent career at the court of James V. All six poems have been researched, edited, and interpreted anew: the *Complaint* and *Balletis* are here presented for the first time as a scholarly edition.

Despite the obvious differences between them in terms of date and authorship, our six Scottish pieces exist very much in dialogue with one another and offer new ways of thinking about notions of courtly and chivalric literature. The latest author, Sir David Lyndsay, can even be seen to represent in himself the core values and concerns of the poems in this collection. In October 1542 he was officially appointed Lyon king of arms, and in the same year he completed an illustrated armorial register, i.e., a formal register of the coats of arms of Scottish families, which he expanded to include key foreign nobles and even some literary figures.[1] As J. K. McGinley has observed, "[s]trikingly, the text of the armorial register is almost entirely composed in the vernacular, indicating a strong commitment on Lyndsay's part to championing the authority of his mother tongue even for such an official and ceremonial purpose."[2] Lyndsay's interest in, and knowledge of, wider vernacular literary traditions is evident throughout the register. He thus includes "the armys off ye nyne maist nobill," those figures from Biblical, Classical, and earlier medieval history (Alexander, Julius Caesar, Joshua, David, Judas Maccabeus, Arthur, Charlemagne, and Godfrey of Bouillon) who form the subject of the *Balletis of the Nine Nobles*, edited here.[3] Alongside the arms of James I's wife, Joan Beaufort (d. 1445), the Armorial mentions their daughter Margaret, who was "spousit with ye dalphyne of france"; this is the princess Margaret whose death is lamented in the *Complaint* edited here. In terms of genre, the latter poem anticipates Lyndsay's own *Deploratioun of the Deith of Quene Magdalene*, written on the occasion of the

---

[1] Now NLS Advocates MS 31.4.3. For an accessible version, see *Fac-Simile of an Ancient Heraldic Manuscript*, ed. Laing.

[2] *ODNB*, "Lyndsay, Sir David (c. 1486–1555)."

[3] *Fac-Simile of an Ancient Heraldic Manuscript*, ed. Laing, pp. 7–10. Lyndsay also cites Hector, Arthur, Julius Caesar, and Alexander amongst heroes whose legends he told to the young King James (*The Dreme*, ed. Hadley Williams, lines 32–35).

death of James V's first wife, Madeleine de Valois (1520–37),[4] and also (in less serious form) *The Testament of Squyer Meldrum* edited here.

A primary meaning of *court* is the entourage of a monarch or a powerful noble, and the place of residence, temporary or otherwise, of such an entourage.[5] (The related sense of *court* as a seat of justice or administration is less relevant here.) The *court* has a much broader cultural significance than this, however. Antony Hasler has described it recently as "a political institution with a firm location in history," but also "a term describing a loose set of attitudes and values . . . the court of our imagining is inescapably multiple: political institution, symbolic focus, literary trope."[6] The range of meaning for the adjective *courtly* is broader still. Although the *Oxford English Dictionary* retains a sense of connection to a royal or noble court with its senses, "Of, pertaining to, or connected with the Court," and "of persons (or their manners): Having the manners or breeding befitting the Court; polished, refined, or a high-bred courtesy" (all of which senses are relevant to the poems edited here), the *Dictionary of the Older Scottish Tongue* offers a simpler primary definition of "Courtly, courteous; refined, elegant," with no direct link to the person or place of the King.[7] The two poems in the present collection which are "courtly" in the most literal sense are of course the *Complaint for the Death of Margaret* and Lyndsay's *Answer to the Kingis Flyting*, with their direct connections to the royal courts of Scotland and France. Yet even here, the *Complaint* can also be seen to apply royal and governmental structures metaphorically to Death's "duellyng" (line 10), to the "parliament" where we will each "ansuere" after death (lines 144–45), and to the manner in which God governs the Earth. Elsewhere, there are two courts in the *Talis of the Fyve Bestes*, but the imagined splendor of the lion-king's court is undercut by the far less royal roost over which the cock "bair the governans" (line 172). Lyndsay's brief comic *Flyting*, meanwhile, is courtly in the most baldly literal sense of being written about, and to, the king, and yet the startlingly coarse language of some of its lines — such as the moment Lyndsay describes his king as "Ay fukkand lyke ane furious fornicatour" (line 49) — is probably the last thing that comes to most readers' minds when they think of "courtly poetry."

Like his Scottish poetic forebear, William Dunbar, Sir David Lyndsay was a court poet. Although he was employed for diplomatic and administrative rather than poetic services, he nevertheless wrote *from within* about the royal court in whose employ he spent much of his adult life, and we might therefore profitably study him alongside fifteenth-century writers from south of the border such as John Skelton (c. 1460–1529), Stephen Hawes (b. c. 1474, d. before 1529), Sir Thomas Wyatt (c. 1503–42), and Henry Howard, earl of Surrey (1516/17–47). Lyndsay's very public career at court means that we have a great deal of

---

[4] *Selected Poems*, ed. Hadley Williams, pp. 101–08.

[5] See *OED court* (n.), sense II. Mapstone's now-classic challenge, "Was there a Court Literature in Fifteenth-Century Scotland?" focuses on this primary sense of "court." She concludes that, with very few exceptions (the *Complaint* edited here being one of them), the royal court had relatively little influence on the Scots literature of this century, which she demonstrates to have been largely of provincial origin, where origins can be traced at all.

[6] Hasler, *Court Poetry*, p. 2.

[7] The constitution of the International Courtly Literature Society likewise emphasizes this broader range of meaning with its stated remit "to promote the study of courts and *court-related cultures*, with particular reference to the written records of medieval Europe" (italics ours).

contextual information to aid in the interpretation of his poems, but the origins of the three poems from the fifteenth century are far less certain. There is nothing in the limited evidence available to suggest that the *Balletis of the Nine Nobles* or *Talis of the Fyve Bestes* were written by writers connected to the court. *The Complaint for the Death of Princess Margaret* is a more complicated case, despite its royal subject. Its author is unknown, as is the author of the Latin chronicle in which it appears; it is not clear whether Latin chronicler and Scots poet are the same person. The chronicler reveals, however, that he became familiar with Margaret whilst spending time at the French court where she resided, and the same is most probably true of the *Complaint*'s author. We know that Margaret formed part of a royal and female literary coterie at the French royal court and that she associated therein with administrators who — like Lyndsay — combined careers as court servants with writing of poetry. As such, this volume brings together several kinds of court literature, but all remain firmly *of*, albeit not always from, the court in terms of their values and concerns.

The other adjective used in the title to this volume — "chivalric" — has a slightly different status in that, as Richard Kaeuper points out:

> . . . the very term *chivalry* was continually and confidently spoken and written throughout half a medieval millennium. Not all the terms we employ as modern scholars studying those centuries can make this claim to reality in the society they are meant to describe.[8]

Medieval writers may have used the term with confidence, but this still does not make it particularly easy to define. Both Richard Kaeuper and Maurice Keen stress its firm connection to "the martial world of the mounted warrior."[9] The term "chivalry" can refer most literally to knightly deeds of valor or the collective body of knights themselves,[10] but it also "cannot be divorced from aristocracy, because knights commonly were men of high lineage: and from the middle of the twelfth century on it very frequently carries ethical or religious overtones."[11] Most broadly, chivalry can be said to consist of "the clusters of general principles and practices that most knights accepted and could aspire to follow" as well as the enduring fundamental values to be found within such principles and practices.[12] This last is what "chivalric literature" encodes, explores, or interrogates. In texts such as the *Balletis of the Nine Nobles*, *Talis of the Fyve Bestes*, and the *Squyer Meldrum* poems we see as much questioning of chivalric values as we do emulation. Robert Bruce is, for instance, explicitly offered as a Tenth Worthy in the *Balletis*, but in ending with a riddle addressed to a plural audience — "Yhe gude men at thir balletis redis, / Demis ye quha dochtiast was in dedis" (lines 61–62) — the poem invites and remains open to a variety of answers. *The Talis of the Fyve Bestes* tackle questions of proper princely or chivalric conduct through tales of such figures as Alexander the Great (one of the *Nine Nobles* described in the *Balletis*) or Scottish national hero William Wallace. Writing in the sixteenth century, Sir David Lyndsay

---

[8] Kaeuper, *Medieval Chivalry*, p. 7. For a specifically Scottish study, see Stevenson, *Chivalry and Knighthood in Scotland*.

[9] Keen, *Chivalry*, p. 2.

[10] Kaeuper, *Medieval Chivalry*, p. 9.

[11] Keen, *Chivalry*, p. 2.

[12] Kaeuper, *Medieval Chivalry*, p. 11.

uses the by-then faintly archaic form of medieval metrical romance to extol, but ultimately question the chivalric virtues represented by Squire Meldrum.

Notions of "courtly" and "chivalric" start to coalesce the further one moves away from their more literal senses, with the values and ideals that each was held to represent lending themselves to much wider application. One expression of this is the theme of "good governance." In recent years it has become a critical commonplace to see Older Scots literature as being particularly concerned with good governance, both of the self and others, and it certainly does play a prominent part in the texts edited here.[13] Lyndsay's *Historie of Squyer Meldrum*, for instance, opens (lines 1–10) with a traditional summary of the writer's role as preserver of reputations both good and ill.[14] In drawing attention to literature's ability to provide cautionary tales (albeit slightly tongue in cheek here) Lyndsay presents the reading and writing of literature as an ethical activity requiring the application of correct and careful moral judgement, and this impulse can be seen even more clearly in the way that he adapts the comic flyting form in his *Answer to the Kingis Flyting* in order to offer the hot-blooded young king a gentle warning against excessive sexual promiscuity.[15] This ethical or advisory role is even more prominent in the earlier texts in this volume, whether they engage with fictional characters or real historical figures. The *Complaint for the Death of Princess of Margaret* presents the daughter of James I as a model of female and specifically royal good behavior, while the text as a whole offers broader social commentary and advice on how best to govern others. The *Balletis of the Nine Nobles* presents the Nine Worthies as models of the kind of chivalric behavior emulated by Lyndsay's Squire Meldrum. Throughout the *Talis of the Fyve Bestes* we are invited to scrutinize the behavior of characters who prove unable to set public duty above private desire, while Lyndsay touches on this same theme by highlighting the quiet virtue of Meldrum's later years, when public service as a sheriff-depute and as a doctor have taken the place of more glamorous chivalric exploits.

The theme of good governance is itself bound up with another theme found at the heart of these texts: independence and sovereignty, which can be approached from a personal or national perspective. National sovereignty is at the core of the *Talis of the Fyve Bestes* in "The Hartis Tale"'s account of the Scottish national hero William Wallace's career and posthumous ascent to heaven, and in "The Baris Tale"'s narration of Alexander's failed attempt to conquer the city of Lapsat, which notably echoes the sentiments and vocabulary of medieval Scotland's key political document, the 1320 *Declaration of Arbroath*. The *Balletis of the Nine Nobles*, meanwhile, offers the Scottish King Robert Bruce as an additional and implicitly superior "Worthy," whilst the *Complaint for the Death of Princess Margaret* documents the exemplary role the young princess played in a crucial political alliance. Lyndsay is careful to set Meldrum's chivalric adventures in his *Historie* against the sober

---

[13] The seminal work is Mapstone, "Advice to Princes Tradition." See also *Premodern Scotland*, eds. Martin and Wingfield.

[14] Well-known examples of the same trope include lines 1–32 of Barbour's *Bruce* and lines 1–7 of Henryson's *Orpheus and Eurydice*; see also the note to these lines of the *Historie*.

[15] Lyndsay also engages with the theme in his Armorial, where he goes to some lengths to justify his inclusion of the arms of forfeited families; one reason is so that "nobill mene" can "behald and . . . consider ye causs" of the crimes and "tak exempill to eschew in tyme cumyng sic exorbitant transgressionis aganis yair princis" (*Fac-Simile of an Ancient Heraldic Manuscript*, ed. Laing, p. 66).

background of Scotland's rumbling conflict with Henry VIII's England, whether in English-held Carrickfergus in Ireland, or on the battlefields of France, with whom Scotland was allied. Meldrum is positioned, and indeed positions himself, as a singular representative of Scottish sovereignty and martial prowess, a quasi-national hero, and his implicit parallel to William Wallace is underlined by the many allusions in the *Historie* to Hary's *Wallace*.[16] His fortune takes a turn for the worse, however, when (like his literary models Arthur and Lancelot) he fails to maintain independence and sovereignty in the much more private matter of love.

In this volume, we set out to introduce the writing of Sir David Lyndsay and his anonymous poetic forebears to a new audience, and to offer more advanced scholars freshly and/or uniquely edited Older Scots texts on a wide range of courtly and chivalric themes. The fifteenth-century anonymous poems *Balletis of the Nine Nobles*, *The Complaint on the Death of Margaret, Princess of Scotland*, and *The Talis of the Fyve Bestes* were edited by Emily Wingfield, and Lyndsay's *Answer to the Kingis Flyting* and the *Historie* and *Testament of Squyer Meldrum* were edited by Rhiannon Purdie.

READING OLDER SCOTS

Before setting out a brief guide to some of the distinctive features of Older Scots as they appear in the six poems edited here, it would be as well to explain the term "Older Scots" itself.[17] "Scots" as it is now used refers to the descendant of Old Northumbrian (the northernmost dialect of Old English) spoken in Scotland. Until the very end of the fifteenth century, Scottish writers of what we *now* call "Scots" referred to this vernacular as "Inglis," i.e., English, the better to distinguish it from the Gaelic language. (Although the Gaelic language itself was more often called *Erse*, i.e., "Irish," the term "Scottis" was often used to describe the Gaelic-speaking peoples in the west of Scotland,[18] so confusion could result).[19] It was only from the beginning of the sixteenth century that the term "Scottis" gained currency for the Old English-derived language we now call Scots. Its adoption was encouraged by prominent writers such as Gavin Douglas who, in his Prologue to his Older Scots translation of Virgil's *Aeneid*, apologized for having to use "Sum bastard Latyn, French or Inglys oyss [usage], / Quhar scant was Scottis — I had nane other choys" (Some false Latin, French or English usage, where Scots was scarce — I had no other choice).[20] As for "Older Scots," this is the term used to describe Scots from its beginnings to 1700 by the standard dictionary covering early Scots usage, the *Dictionary of the Older Scottish Tongue* (*DOST*). A. J. Aitken, the most prominent twentieth-century scholar of Scots and a senior editor of *DOST*, subdivided this lengthy period into "Pre-literary Scots" (i.e., before the c. 1375 appearance of Barbour's *Bruce*), "Early Scots" (1375–1450), and "Middle Scots"

---

[16] See notes to the *Historie*, lines 102–03, 633, 691–98, 710–848, 856, and 1055.

[17] See Macafee and Aitken, "History of Scots to 1700," and Corbett, McClure, and Stuart-Smith, "A Brief History of Scots," pp. 1–12.

[18] See *DOST scottis* (adj.), sense 2.

[19] See Smith, *Linguistic Reader*, p. 8, and McClure, "Scottis, Inglis, Suddroun," pp. 53–55.

[20] *Eneados*, ed. Coldwell, 2:6, lines 117–18.

(1450–1700).[21] The labeling of the eras of Scots language and literature is thus difficult to align with that of English language and literary periods, and confusion can result. While most people would be happy enough to label the *Talis of the Fyve Bestis* (dating from the turn of the fifteenth and sixteenth centuries) as a "Middle Scots" text, they may balk at having to apply the different label of "Early Scots" to the earlier fifteenth-century *Balletis of the Nine Nobles* edited here, especially when linguistic differences are scarcely apparent to a non-expert. They may be similarly confused to learn that Sir David Lyndsay's poems from the 1520–50s are still held to be written in "Middle Scots," although the works of his contemporaries in England — Skelton, Wyatt, and Surrey, for example — are universally considered to be in Early Modern English. It is for this reason that the misleading term "Middle Scots" has been falling out of fashion in recent scholarship in favor of the non-divisive "Older Scots," the term championed by *DOST*. "Older Scots" (OSc) is thus the term used throughout the present volume.

Reading Older Scots can present a challenge to the unwary reader who, perhaps flushed with confidence from reading some Middle English, turns to Older Scots expecting something similar. Since all of the texts edited here are presented with generous marginal glosses, the problem of unfamiliar vocabulary is minimized. But a knowledge of some of the distinctive spelling conventions of Scots will greatly ease the reading experience, as will some awareness of key differences between the pronunciation (and therefore spellings) of words common to southern Middle English and Older Scots (readers familiar with northern varieties of Middle English may, on the other hand, feel quite at home reading Older Scots). Beyond these two categories, there are a few common words which are either distinctively Scots, or have unexpected alternative senses in Scots. The following is by no means a comprehensive description of the characteristics of Older Scots; it is merely a list of key features intended to ease the reading of the six glossed poems edited here.[22]

Vowels

OSc *a, ai* / MdnE *o*

> Middle and Modern English long *o* corresponds to Older Scots long *a*: *ane, anis, ga, hale, mare, na, twa* (one, once, go, whole, more, no, two). That this is a difference of pronunciation is confirmed by rhymes such as the "Unicornis Tale," *schame; hame* (shame; home, lines 225–26).

OSc *u, ui* / MdnE *oo, ou*

> Middle and Modern English long *oo* or *ou* corresponds to Older Scots *u*: *gude* (good), *blude* (blood); *pure* (poor); *bukis* (books).

---

[21] Aitken, *Concise Scots Dictionary*, p. xiii (slightly updated by Macafee in "History of Scots to 1700," §1.1.3).

[22] For more comprehensive discussion of these and other distinctive features of Older Scots, see Macafee and Aitken, "History of Scots to 1700," §3 "Characteristics of Older Scots"; and Smith, *Linguistic Reader*, pp. 18–50 and Appendix: "The First Hundred Words." See also Parkinson, "Henryson's Language," in his Introduction to *Complete Works*, pp. 12–25.

OSc diacritic -i-

> Vowel length in Older Scots is sometimes indicated by a final -e as in Middle English usage, e.g., *mare* "more," but as in Northern Middle English, Older Scots might instead use a diacritic *i*, e.g., *baith* (both); *wait* (know, corresponding to Middle English *wot, wote*); *raid* (pa.t. rode); *loif* (glorify); *boist* (boast); *oist* (host); *pruif* (prove); *forsuith* (forsooth). The use of diacritic -i- to mark vowel length becomes increasingly common in the sixteenth century, and is a regular feature of the Lyndsay poems edited here.

OSc *i/y*

> Note that, as in Middle English, vowels *i* and *y* are used interchangeably in spelling.

Consonants

OSc *Quh-* for MdnE *Wh-*

> This reflects the aspirated pronunciation that still obtains in most dialects of Modern Scots: *quhilk* (which); *quha, quham, quhais* (who, whom, whose, where it is combined with OSc long *a* as described above; see also the variant form *quhome* whom); *quhat* (what); *quhen* (when); *quhar, quhare, quhair* (where); *quhy* (why); *quhether* (whether); *quhill* (until).

OSc medial *-ch-* for MdnE *-gh-*

> This consonant was always pronounced in Older Scots, as it still is in broad Scots (i.e., more strongly dialectal Scots) today: *micht* (might); *knicht* (knight); *brocht* (brought); *faucht* (fought); *fechtand* (fighting; see below on the present participle ending *-and*).

OSc *s-* or *sch-* for MdnE *sh-*

> *Sch-* was the standard OSc spelling for this consonant, e.g., *schaw* (show); *schort* (short); *schip* (ship); *scheild* (shield); *schure* (pa.t. sheared); *flesche* (flesh); *worschipe* (worship).

> It was also habitually used for certain words such as *schir* (sir), perhaps reflecting a more aspirated pronunciation.

> On the other hand, modal verbs *sal, suld* (shall, should) are normally spelled with a single *s-*.

OSc *f* for MdnE *v*

> This would seem to reflect a genuine unvoiced pronunciation: *leif* (leave); *greif* (grieve); *luif/luf/luffe, luiffit/luffit/lufit, luifferis* (love, loved, lovers); *haf* (have); *gaf* (gave); *remuf* (remove); *resaif* (receive).

Noun and Verb Endings

Both singular *and* plural verbs, 2nd and 3rd person, normally end with *-is* (sometimes *-es* or *-s*) in the present tense; see the final couplet of the *Balletis*:

> *Yhe gude men at thir balletis <u>redis</u>,* (present plural)
>
> *<u>Demis</u> ye quha dochtiast was in dedis* (imperative plural)
>
> (You good men who read these verses, / judge who was the most valiant)

-is, -it, -in: unstressed endings are most often written with *-i-*:

> Plural or genitive nouns: *richtis* (rights); *bemis* (beams); *wyfis* (wives or wife's); *mennis* (men's).
>
> Past tense or weak past participles with *-it*: *lichtit* (lighted); *passit* (passed); *lukit* (looked); *unrekkynit* (unreckoned, uncounted).
>
> Strong past participles with *-in*: *takin* (taken); *gevin* (given); *cassin* (cast).

Present participles normally end in *-and* (beside occasional *-ing*, as in MdnE)

> E.g., *syngand* (singing); *fechtand* (fighting); *haifand* (having).
>
> Note that the verbal noun normally ends in *-ing*, e.g., *his departing* (his departing/departure)

Common Words

aganis, egaynis (prep.) against
ay (adv.) always, ever
als (adv., conj.) also, as
at (rel. pron., conj.) that, which, who
aucht (num.) eight
awin (adj.) own
bot (prep., adv., conj.) but, except, only
but (prep.) without
couth (aux. v.) could (but also sometimes used for simple past tense, e.g., *my leg couth bleid*; my leg did bleed, *Fyve Bestes* line 236)

deed, dede, deid (n.) death
gang (v.) go
gar, ger (v.); *gart* (pa.t.) make [something happen]
gif (conj.) if
hes (v.) has, had (sing. and pl.)
hie (adj., adv.) high
hir (pron.) her
ilk (adj.) every
intil, intill (prep.) in, into
ma (adv.) more
maist (adj.) most
mon (v.) must
nocht (n.) nothing
nocht (adv.) not
our (prep.) over, above
quhill (conj.) until (not "while")
richt (adv.) very
scho (pron.) she
sen (prep. and conj.) since, after
sex (num.) six
sik (adj.) such
syn (adv.) then, afterwards
swa (adv. and conj.) so, thus
tan (p.p.) taken
thir (dem. pl.) these
thocht (conj.) although
til, till (prep.) to
yhe (pron.) ye (MdnE "you")
wald (v.) would
wes (pa.t.) was, were (sing. and pl.)
war (pa.t. or subj.) were

INTRODUCTION TO THE *BALLETIS OF THE NINE NOBLES*

The *Balletis of the Nine Nobles* (*NIMEV* 1181) is an early to mid-fifteenth-century Scottish text in the Nine Worthies tradition.[1]

THE NINE WORTHIES TRADITION

The Nine Worthies tradition was first formulated in *Les Voeux du Paon*, an originally independent poem composed c. 1310–12 by Jacques de Longuyon.[2] *Les Voeux* was the most common of the French Alexander poems and survives in over thirty manuscripts, where it is often appended to the *Roman d'Alexandre*, or interpolated within Branch III of that romance. Together with another French Alexander poem, *Le Fuerre de Gadres*, *Les Voeux* was also translated into Scots c. 1438; the two parts of the poem are known as "The Forray of Gaderis" and "Avowis of Alexander," and the complete c. 14,500-line "buik of the most noble and valiant Conquerour Alexander the grit" (*NIMEV* 3923) (hereafter *Octosyllabic Alexander / OA*) survives uniquely in a printed edition of c. 1580 produced by the Edinburgh printer, Alexander Arbuthnet (*STC* 321.5).[3] In the late nineteenth and early twentieth century several attempts were made to ascribe the *Octosyllabic Alexander* to John Barbour, author of *The Bruce* (c. 1375–76), but this attribution is no longer accepted.

One of most central characters in *Les Voeux* is Porrus, eldest son of the Indian king, Clarus. During the final Great Battle of Epheson, the narrator focuses on Porrus' bravery and, to better illustrate this, suspends narrative action and compares Porrus to the Nine Worthies. They comprise three pagans (Hector of Troy, Alexander the Great, and Julius

---

[1] I briefly discussed the Scottish Nine Worthies tradition in my monograph: *The Trojan Legend in Medieval Scottish Literature*. I am grateful to Boydell & Brewer for allowing me to here reproduce and expound upon a small amount of material from this book.

[2] The listing together of some of the Nine Worthies did occur in early texts and they had also long been recognized as fitting subjects for romance, but they first appeared together in *Les Voeux*. On the tradition and its development, see Höltgen, "Die 'Nine Worthies'"; Schroeder, *Der Topos der Nine Worthies*; Schroeder, "The Nine Worthies: A Supplement"; "Texts Illustrative of 'The Nine Worthies,'" ed. Gollancz; Loomis, "Verses on the Nine Worthies"; Turville-Petre, "The Nine Worthies in the *Parliament of the Thre Ages*"; Cropp, "Les Vers Sur Les Neuf Preux"; Bellon-Méguelle, *Du Temple de Mars à la Chambre de Vénus*, pp. 489–96.

[3] *Buik of Alexander*, ed. Ritchie. Ritchie edits the Scots poem in parallel with the French original. All citations from *Les Voeux* and "The Avowis" will be from this edition, under the collective short title *Alexander*.

Caesar); three Jews (Joshua, David, and Judas Maccabeus); and three Christians (King Arthur, Charlemagne, and Godfrey of Bouillon).[4]

The Nine Worthies tradition subsequently became increasingly popular across medieval art, drama, and literature, and was used either to represent a chivalric or monarchical ideal, or alternatively as an exemplum of the vanity of all earthly things. Short verse and prose catalogues of the Worthies were commonly written onto flyleaves and spare spaces in manuscripts,[5] whilst tableaux of the heroes formed part of royal entrances and civic pageants as mirrors of prowess and good rule to be emulated by their monarchical audience. The Worthies also formed the subject of tapestries, wall paintings, and woodcuts, where their images were often accompanied by verses in which each hero presented himself in a short first person account.[6] A tradition of heraldry associated with each Worthy developed, as did a corresponding set of female Worthies, although the latter never gained as fixed a form as its male counterpart. It also became common to append a tenth Worthy to the traditional nine, most often a notable national hero, and in Scotland that hero was Robert I (1274–1379), otherwise known as Robert the Bruce.

Robert I was first compared to a number of the Nine Worthies in John Barbour's *The Bruce* (c. 1375–76). Barbour here uses the Nine Worthies tradition to negotiate the difficulties of Bruce's murder of his political opponent, John Comyn (d. 1306). In murdering Comyn at the high altar of Greyfriars' monastery in Dumfries, Bruce committed a heinous crime for which subsequent Brucean ideology had to account. In order to exculpate his hero from this sacrilegious act of homicide, Barbour neutralizes Bruce's crime by instead emphasizing Comyn's act of betrayal, and he prefaces the murder scene with a digression on the dangers of treason, "Bot off all thing wa worth tresoun" (1.515–68, quotation on line 515).[7] Within this digression, Barbour compares Bruce to Alexander, Julius Caesar, and Arthur, three of the Nine Worthies who also fell victim to treachery. He also opens his account by comparing Comyn's betrayal of Bruce to the treachery which brought about the downfall of Troy (1.521–28). This comparison implies that Comyn's treachery of Bruce is to be read as a betrayal of the entire Scottish nation and that Bruce himself is to be aligned with the Trojan king, Priam. Bruce is, however, ultimately shown to be superior to Priam, as well as to Alexander, Julius Caesar, and Arthur, since he avoids their fate: "ik herd neuer in romanys tell / Off man sa hard frayit as wes he / Yat efterwart com to sic bounte" (2.46–48).

Bruce is aligned for the second time with the Nine Worthies in a twelfth-century illuminated copy of the Vulgate Bible from north-east France, once belonging to Sweetheart Abbey, Kirkudbright (now Princeton University Library, Garrett MS 27). On an otherwise blank folio (fol. 365v) we find written in a hand of c. 1380 the following Latin lines: *Ector,*

---

[4] For a more extensive analysis of the *OA* Nine Worthies tradition see Wingfield, *Trojan Legend*, pp. 65–70.

[5] Scottish examples include two catalogues in the *Book of the Dean of Lismore* (Edinburgh, National Library of Scotland, Advocates' MS 72.1.37). See Mackechnie, *Catalogue of Gaelic Manuscripts in Selected Libraries*, 1:185–86, nos. 171 and 201.

[6] A Scottish example is the ceiling of Crathes Castle. See Bath, *Renaissance Decorative Painting in Scotland*, pp. 185–90; Hargreaves, "The Crathes Ceiling Inscriptions."

[7] Barbour, *Barbour's Bruce*, ed. McDiarmid and Stevenson. All subsequent citations are taken from this edition.

Alexander, Julius, Josue, David, Machabeus, / Arthurus, Carulus, et postremus Godofrydus — / Robertus rex Scotorum denus est in numero meliorum.[8] This instance of the Nine Worthies tradition appears to position King Robert I authoritatively as a Tenth Worthy. Directly opposite the blank folio on which these lines are written, however, is the Prologue to the Book of Joshua. The Prologue begins with an historiated initial depicting a shield held in the mouth of a monster, designed to illustrate the arms of the Balliol family. The juxtaposition of Latin text proposing Bruce as a Tenth Worthy alongside an image that aligns the Balliol family with Joshua and the Israelites recalls the rival claims for the Scottish crown of Robert I's grandfather and John Balliol during the Great Cause and subsequent Wars of Independence.[9] It also recalls the famous 1320 letter of Scottish barons to Pope John XXII, known as the Declaration of Arbroath. This document was written to counter the increasing hostility of the papacy against the Scottish king, Robert I, and has been interpreted both as an essentially diplomatic document and as a political manifesto asserting Scottish independence and sovereignty. In it, the early Scots are paralleled with the Israelites and their leaders with Moses, Joshua, and Judas Maccabeus: Scottish ancestors are said to have journeyed from Egypt "twelve hundred years after the people of Israel crossed the Red Sea" and Robert Bruce is "like another Maccabeus or Joshua."[10]

Bruce appears as a Tenth Worthy for the third time in the anonymous *Balletis of the Nine Nobles* (edited here), which survives amongst a collection of extraneous material in four manuscripts of Walter Bower's *Scotichronicon* (c. 1441–47) — a history of the Scottish people from their mythological origins to the murder of James I of Scotland in 1437 and minority of his son, James II — and also in an abbreviation of that chronicle begun in 1521 by a canon of St Andrews, John Law.[11] These five manuscript witnesses are discussed in further detail below.

THE *BALLETIS* AND ITS SOURCES

The *Balletis* offers an abbreviated version of the Nine Worthies passage in the French *Les Voeux* and Scots "Avowis." It omits all of the summative material which concludes and prefaces each group of three Worthies in these latter texts and consists of 62 lines, or rather ten stanzas of six lines (rhyming *aabbcc*)[12] — one being devoted to each of the Nine Worthies and Robert Bruce — plus a final couplet addressing the audience: "Yhe gude men at thir balletis redis, / Demis ye quha dochtiast was in dedis" (lines 61–62).[13]

---

[8] This phrase proves difficult to translate accurately as *denus* is not a standard form, but a rough paraphrase would be "Hector . . . [etc.] Robert King of Scots is tenth in the number of our betters [i.e., the tenth worthy]."

[9] Higgitt, "Manuscripts and Libraries in the Diocese of Glasgow."

[10] *Declaration of Arbroth*, ed. Fergusson and trans. Borthwick.

[11] Bower, *Scotichronicon*, ed. Watt; Laing, "De Cronicis Scotorum Brevia by John Law." See also Durkan, "St Andrews in John Law's Chronicle"; Drexler, "The Extant Abridgements of Walter Bower's 'Scotichronicon.'"

[12] The poem is metrically irregular. Lines have anywhere between 8 and 11 syllables with no discernable pattern.

[13] Examples of such summative material include linked passages between the accounts of the Worthies (e.g., "Of thir thre Iowes we find it writ, / The auld Testament witnesis it, / They did sa mekle that commonly / All men thame lufis generally, / And, as I trow, sall lufe thame ay, / Euermare quhill

Detailed comparison of the *Balletis* with "The Avowis" and *Les Voeux*, documented in the explanatory notes, demonstrates that the *Balletis'* author knew both the Scots translation and the French original and drew on each text for his or her own composition. Particular echoes or influence of "The Avowis" on the *Balletis* are apparent at lines 2, 5, 11, 12, 16, 22, 28, 36, 43, and 45–46; these echoes either have no counterpart in, or do not correspond as closely to, the original Nine Worthies passage in *Les Voeux*. In reporting the details of Hector's conquests, however, the *Balletis* author reports that Hector slew "ammirallis a hunder and mare" (line 3). This detail is not in "The Avowis" but it is present in the original French where Hector *[o]cist . . . / . . . amiraus et contes, ce croi je, plus de .C.* (*Alexander*, 4:403, lines 7492–93). Similarly, instead of killing "mony ane fell pagan," as in "The Avowis" (*Alexander*, 4:404, line 9961), in the *Balletis* David kills "Filestens at felon was" (line 26). The adjective *felon* occurs only in the French (*Et maint felon payen fist venir a noiant*, *Alexander*, 4:404, line 7532). Furthermore, only in "The Avowis" is Godfrey of Bouillon king of Jerusalem for "ane ōeir and mare" (*Alexander*, 4:406, line 10009); in the *Balletis* (line 54) and *Les Voeux* (*Alexander*, 4:406, line 7572) he reigns for just one year. Such details therefore indicate that the *Balletis* author worked from and had access to the original French *Les Voeux* as well as the Scots translation.

Further details demonstrate that the author also worked from other vernacular sources. The *Balletis* stanza on Arthur is, for instance, notably different from that in *Les Voeux* and "The Avowis," with the exception of the detail that Arthur killed more than one giant (compare "Avowis," *Alexander*, 4:405, line 9991 and *Les Voeux*, *Alexander*, 4:405, line 7556). Other details of this stanza appear to stem either directly or indirectly from Geoffrey of Monmouth's account of Arthur's enemy, Lucius, in his *Historia Regum Britanniae* (c. 1136). Geoffrey and the *Balletis* author both describe Lucius as a "procuratour," whereas he appears elsewhere, for instance in the *Alliterative Morte Arthure* (ed. Benson, lines 554, 1293) or Barbour's *Bruce* (1.555), as an "emperour."

The *Balletis'* description of Arthur may furthermore owe something to Andrew of Wyntoun's *Original Chronicle* (c. 1408–24), book 5, chapter 13 (ed. Amours). In a well known passage where Wyntoun discusses the enigmatic poet "Huchon of þe Aule Reale" (MS Cotton, 4:21–27, lines 4279–360, quotation from line 4279), he spends some time discussing whether Lucius should be called "emperoure." He clarifies that Huchon in fact states that "Lucyus Hyberyus in his dayis / Was of þe hee state procuratoure" (4:23, lines 4302–03).

The *Balletis* was, finally, also influenced by Barbour's *Bruce*. A number of parallels between the two poems were listed by the *Octosyllabic Alexander*'s editor, R. L. Graeme Ritchie, in a bid to prove common authorship.[14] They include stock phrases such as "throu hard feichtingis," "at was ferli," "discumfit," "stalwart stour," "hard batel," and "Throu Goddis grace." Such phrases were very much the stock-in-trade of late fourteenth- and early

---

domisday" (*Alexander*, 4:404, lines 9941–46)). The *Balletis* author also omits certain extra information provided about each character, such as the background note that Hector took on the leadership of the Trojan forces "Quhen Menelayus the mychty King / Assegit in Troy the King Priant / For Elene . . ." (*Alexander*, 4:402, lines 9900–02).

[14] *Buik of Alexander*, ed. Ritchie, 1:cxxxiv–cli, cliv–vi. Ritchie attributed the *OA* to Barbour, arguing that the former poem's internal date of 1438 was a scribal error. Common authorship is no longer accepted. The *OA* and *Bruce* are in conscious dialogue, but this does not necessitate common authorship. See further Wingfield, "The Manuscript and Print Contexts of Older Scots Romance," pp. 26–40.

fifteenth-century Scottish verse; better correspondences between the two poems are instead those episodes in *The Bruce* where Barbour himself engages with the Nine Worthies and aligns his heroes with them, such as the treason digression prefacing Bruce's murder of Comyn (discussed above), or the comparison of the poem's second hero, James Douglas, to Hector of Troy (1.395–96).

The stanza on Julius Caesar in the *Balletis* is particularly close to the lines on him in the treason digression in *The Bruce*. In the *Balletis*, "Julius Cesar wan halili / The ilis of Grece and al Surry; / Affrike, arab, Bretan wan he, / [. . . .] / He was the first was emperor" (lines 13–18). In *The Bruce*, "Iulius Cesar als, yat wan / Bretane and Fraunce as dowchty man, / Affryk Arrabe Egipt Surry / And all Evrope halyly, / [. . .] / Off Rome wes fryst maid emperour" (1.537–42). The same verb, "wan," is used in both texts, as well as the qualifying adverb "halili." The list of places conquered is also strikingly similar, as well as the comment that Caesar was the first emperor.

Finally, the closing *demande* in the *Balletis* has a parallel in *The Bruce*. After Bruce has single-handedly fought against a large number of men of Galloway, the narrator compares his prowess to that of Tydeus who single-handedly killed fifty men (6.181–286). He asks firstly, "Ōe yat yis redys, cheys yhe / Quheyer yat mar suld prysit be / Ye king [. . .] / Or Thedeus," and secondly, "Now demys quheyer mar lowing / Suld Thedeus haiff or ye king" (6.271–77, 285–86).

THE *BALLETIS*: LITERARY ANALYSIS

As already noted, the *Balletis* consists of thirty couplets plus a coda of two lines. Six lines (three couplets) are allotted to each of the Nine Worthies and a further six are given to Robert Bruce. The poem presents the career of each Worthy — describing them variously as "nobil," "geantill," and "michti" — and it focuses on their martial victories and prowess, in particular on the number of people and places that they kill or conquer. Verbs and phrases such as "throu hard feichtingis," "slew," "wan," "stalwart stour," and "conquirit" are, furthermore, repeated throughout the poem to emphasize the similarities of each Worthy. The opening stanza thus describes how:

> Hector of Troy throu hard feichtingis
> In half thrid yeris slew xix kingis,
> And ammirallis a hunder and mare,
> With smal folk at unrekkynnit war;
> He slew so fele at was ferli,
> Quham Achiles slew tresnabili.
> (lines 1–6)

The final stanza on Robert Bruce, which echoes and distills the previous verses, reads:

> Robert the Brois throu hard feichting
> With few vencust the michti Kyng
> Of Ingland, Edward, twyse in ficht,
> At occupide his realme but richt;
> At sumtyme was set so hard
> At had nocht sex til him toward.
> (lines 55–60)

The nomenclature "Robert the Brois" (line 55) echoes "Hector of Troy" (line 1) and "Charles of France" (line 43) but replaces a national name with a family name and thus ensures that Bruce, like Hector and Charlemagne, is associated with the dynasty to which he belonged and for which he fought, and also that his family name becomes inextricably linked with the nation, Scotland. Bruce's achievement of victory "throu hard feichting" (line 55) moreover recalls the similar victories "throu hard feichtingis" of Hector (line 1), Alexander (line 8), and Godfrey (line 53), whilst his triumph "With few" men (line 56) recalls Hector's victory "With smal folk" (line 4) and Judas Maccabeus' fighting "ane egaynis ten" (line 36). Such verbal parallels ensure that Bruce is on a par with the heroes of classical, biblical, and Christian past.

The close juxtaposition of the stanza on Bruce with the closing *demande* (quoted above) might, furthermore, imply that it is Bruce who is to be chosen as "dochtiast . . . in dedis" (line 62). The *Balletis* arguably presents the Scottish king as the culmination of the previous nine heroes — his role in history appears predetermined, his dynasty is legitimized, and he is presented as part of a line of succession that has its origins in Troy — and therefore makes in succinct form the point made more diffusely and implicitly in Barbour's *Bruce*, namely that Robert I stands amongst the Nine Worthies and may even be superior to them.

His superiority is further stressed by one interesting difference between Bruce and the majority of the Worthies. Many of the other heroes are depicted as conquerors or colonizers: Alexander wins "al landis under the firmament" (line 9) but still desires more land; Julius Caesar triumphs in Greece, Syria, Africa, Arabia, and Britain; Joshua conquers the lands of the 31 kings he defeats; and Arthur, Charlemagne, and Godfrey continue this trend, conquering much of Europe and engaging in holy war. (Indeed, such is the repeated emphasis on this aspect of each hero's career that approaching the poem from a post-colonial lens would be an interesting future line of enquiry.) By contrast, Bruce successfully defends his realm from the unjust onslaughts of a would-be colonizer; Scotland's worthy is signally in no danger of here being associated with the morally questionable acquisition of other lands (whereas in book 14 of *The Bruce* he is uncomfortably associated with his brother, Edward's, Irish Campaign).

The *Balletis'* companion text, Bower's *Scotichronicon*, appears to support a reading of Bruce as the superior Worthy. The chronicle thus deals at some length with the reign of Robert Bruce, and Bower emphasizes his role as savior and champion of the Scottish nation. Seeing the suffering of his people, Bruce was "moved inwardly with heartfelt sorrow, and like a second Maccabeus (*tamquam alter Machabeus*)"; he endured "unbearable burdens" in order to "free his fellow country-men."[15] Bower also repeatedly suggests that no one can comprehend the sufferings which Bruce endured on behalf of his people, and proposes that there will be found "none in the regions of the world to be his equals."[16] In addition, he draws upon the Nine Worthies tradition itself when proposing in a supplementary genealogy that Robert I "was proclaimed as eleventh [Worthy] after Godfrey of Boulogne."[17]

---

[15] Bower, *Scotichronicon*, ed. Watt, 6:301, lines 30–33.

[16] Bower, *Scotichronicon*, ed. Watt, 6:319, line 32.

[17] The genealogy is found in the *Liber Extravagens*, a supplementary book composed after the main *Scotichronicon*. The reference to Bruce as eleventh rather than tenth Worthy is simply a scribal error. See "Liber Extravagens," line 41, in Bower, *Scotichronicon*, ed. Watt, 9:94–95.

There are, furthermore, five illustrations in the principal witness of the *Scotichronicon* (Cambridge, Corpus Christi College, MS 171) that support the *Balletis'* positioning of Robert I.[18] In the fifth and final image (fol. 265r), which depicts the Battle of Bannockburn, we see Bruce, as we do in the *Balletis*, in the midst of "hard feichting" (line 55), vanquishing "the michti Kyng / Of Ingland, Edward" (lines 56–57) and his army. This image of Bruce also concludes the manuscript's succession of images, just as the stanza on Bruce comes at the end of the *Balletis*. In the latter poem, Bruce is to be read as the most recent in a line of descent stretching back to Hector; in the *Scotichronicon* illustrations he is similarly traced back through the Scottish kings Alexander III and Malcolm Canmore to the founders of the Scottish race, Gaythelos and Scota. In vernacular verse and visual image Bruce is therefore presented as the natural, legitimate successor to Scotland's original founding fathers.

There are, however, other passages in the *Scotichronicon* which complicate this interpretation, in particular the chapters on Bruce's death and burial (book 13, chapters 13 and 14). The latter contains a long anonymous Latin poem in which Robert I is compared to a whole host of heroes, including six of the Nine Worthies, and several other main figures from the Trojan war: Priam, Achilles, Ajax, Ulysses, and Aeneas. Bruce is described as a "radiant light" (line 69), a "mirror" (line 71), and "rule for conduct" (lines 71–72) and an analogy is also drawn between the king and certain items of jewelry — he has a "bracelet for the arms" (line 74) and "an ear-ring in the ear of the upright" (line 75), for instance. The poem then ends with an *ubi sunt* passage that reflects on the transience of earthly life and concludes with the sobering statement: "exalted office means nothing at the end of one's days" (line 83). The passing of Bruce is thus presented here as a supreme example of the mortality and transience of all earthly beings and their power, and such thematic emphasis alerts us to what remains unspoken in the *Balletis*. There, the wheel of fortune is entirely absent. The *Balletis* never once mentions the death of any of its heroes, and whilst its sequence of Worthies sweeps across a large chronological period, the poem seemingly neutralizes any sense of temporal change and earthly transience. It neutralizes, also, the history of Scotland after Bruce's death. That period, which saw another Bruce-Balliol conflict for the Scottish throne and further Anglo-Scots hostility, is recounted elsewhere in Bower's *Scotichronicon*, but it is not mentioned at all in the *Balletis*.

And yet, one might argue that poem's closing *demande* is itself designed in part to alert us to such absences. It is easy to miss the fact that this final riddle is addressed to "gude men" in the plural (line 61), but once this point is noted, we could suggest that, far from unequivocally positioning Bruce as the Tenth Worthy, the poem in fact invites and remains open to a variety of answers. The plurality of its intended audience reminds us, moreover, that judgment of human worth is subjective to each individual, place and time, and accordingly that the appendage of Robert Bruce as the Tenth Worthy is subjective both to Scotland's own unique history and to one interpretation of that history. In short, we might read the closing riddle of the *Balletis* not just as a further championing of Brucean ideology but also in part as a warning of the hermeneutical risks involved in attempting to position a national figure, in particular a monarch, as the Tenth Worthy.

---

[18] These images portray the voyage of Scotland's mythological founding figures, Gaythelos and Scota, and their followers from Egypt (fol. 14r); the meeting of Malcolm and Macduff, thane of Fife (fol. 88r); the inauguration of King Alexander III (fol. 206r); the funeral of Alexander III (fol. 225v); and the Battle of Bannockburn (fol. 265r). See further Higgitt, "Decoration and Illustration."

DATE, AUTHORSHIP, AND MATERIAL CONTEXTS

Having discussed the poem's sources and themes, it remains to consider its date, authorship, and material contexts in further detail. As briefly noted above, the poem survives amongst a collection of extraneous material in four manuscripts of the *Scotichronicon* by Walter Bower, and also in John Law's abbreviation of that chronicle, begun in 1521:

- Cambridge, Corpus Christi College, MS 171, fol. 371r (MS C)
- Darnaway Castle, Forres, Donibristle MS, fol. 433v (MS D)[19]
- Edinburgh, National Records of Scotland, MS GD 45/26/48, fol. 420v (MS B)
- Edinburgh, University Library, MS 186, fol. 434r (MS E)
- Edinburgh, University Library, MS Dc.7.63., fols. 155v–56r (John Law's abbreviation of Bower's *Scotichronicon*)

MS D, dated 1471–72, was copied from MS C for Simon Finlay, chaplain of the altar of St. Michael in St. Giles' Cathedral, Edinburgh.[20] MS B, dated 1481, was copied from MS D by the professional scribe, Magnus Makculloch, and rubricated by James Gray.[21] The copyist of MS E, dated 1510, had access to MS C, but mainly copied from MS D.[22] The transmission of the *Balletis* to MSS D, B, and E thus stemmed directly from MS C, or indirectly from MS C through MS D. For that reason, MS C is chosen as the copytext for this edition.

The Dictionary of the Older Scottish Tongue has dated the *Balletis* to c. 1440 based upon its first surviving appearance in MS C. This manuscript of the *Scotichronicon* has been described as a "fair copy developing into a working copy intended for the library of Inchcolm Abbey" where Bower was abbot.[23] Watt further suggests that "the main text was probably written by a scribe under Bower's direction at Inchcolm in the mid-1440s before marginal additions [including the *Balletis*] were being made by 1447 at [the] latest."[24] The *Balletis' terminus ad quem* is therefore most likely to be 1447. Its *terminus a quo* must be 1438, the date of the Scottish translation of *Les Voeux* from which the poem so clearly derives. The *Balletis* cannot, therefore, have been composed by John Barbour, author of *The Bruce*, as Ritchie suggested, since Barbour is thought to have died in or around 1395. It might, however, have been composed by the *OA* author, as proposed by Craigie.[25] This unknown author definitely knew and had access to *Les Voeux*, his or her own "Avowis," and Barbour's *Bruce*; parallels between *The Bruce* and *OA* which were once seen as so extensive as to warrant numerous explanations

---

[19] Since this manuscript remains in private hands it is most easily accessed via a microfilm in St Andrews University Library (ms38423/10/3).

[20] Bower, *Scotichronicon*, ed. Watt, 9:187–88.

[21] Bower, *Scotichronicon*, ed. Watt, 9:188–89; Lyall, "Books and Book-Owners in Fifteenth-Century Scotland," pp. 245–46.

[22] Bower, *Scotichronicon*, ed. Watt, 9:191–92.

[23] Bower, *Scotichtonicon*, ed. Watt, 9:149.

[24] Bower, *Scotichronicon*, ed. Watt, 9:149.

[25] Craigie, ed. "The 'Ballet of the Nine Nobles'," pp. 359–65. Matthew P. McDiarmid attributed the *Balletis* to Hary, author of *The Wallace* (c. 1476–78) but its date of composition is too early for Hary's authorship. See *Hary's Wallace*, ed. McDiarmid, 1:cix.

for shared authorship are now refuted. He or she may indeed even have recognized the potential of the Nine Worthies passage in "The Avowis" for independent circulation and accordingly excerpted and adapted it for this purpose. I therefore follow Craigie in proposing that the *OA*'s author be considered the most likely author of the *Balletis*.

Taken as a whole, the *Balletis* has an intriguing textual history. This independent poem derives jointly from a passage within the French *Les Voeux* and Scots "Avowis," and was also influenced by Barbour's *Bruce* and Geoffrey of Monmouth's *Historia Regum Britanniae*. It first excerpts and abridges material from a much larger romance, and then comes to gloss another large text, this time Bower's *Scotichronicon*. This relationship of the *Balletis* is comparable to the inclusion of the mid-fifteenth-century *De Regimine Principum* and *Complaint for the death of Margaret, Princess of Scotland* (the latter edited elsewhere in this volume) within two manuscripts of another fifteenth-century Scottish chronicle (the *Liber Pluscardensis*), and to the preservation of verse within the *Scotichronicon* itself.[26] The relationship also rather interestingly parallels the manuscript context of short verse narratives on the Nine Worthies in Middle Dutch miscellanies. There, such verses are frequently found in manuscripts made in an urban context and alongside chronicles and, as Gerard Bouwmeester has noted, this juxtaposition produces an intriguing "two-way effect" since a "Nine Worthies text is a moralized synopsis in narrative form of the history described in the chronicles, summarized around nine heroes, and [. . .] the chronicles are factual, wider histories, (usually implicitly) putting the achievements of the Nine Worthies in a broad historical context."[27] As far as the *Balletis* is concerned, the histories of the Nine Worthies are placed quite deliberately within a specifically Scottish political context: one that endeavors to promote the reputation of Robert I and extol the continued independence of his realm.

THIS EDITION

The *Balletis* has been partially edited on several previous occasions. In 1895, David Laing included a copy of the poem (from MS E) in volume 1 of his *Early Popular Poetry of Scotland and the Northern Border*, and W. A. Craigie then produced an edition of the poem in the 1899 edition of the journal *Anglia* (also using MS E, but listing variants from John Law's text). A text derived jointly from Laing and Craigie's edition was subsequently printed in the appendix to volume 1 of Gollancz's *Select Early English Poems* (1913–33). R. L. Graeme Ritchie also printed an eclectic text in volume 1 of his *Buik of Alexander*.[28]

This edition is the first modern critical edition of the poem, complete with full textual and explanatory notes. As observed above, the copytext is MS C since all other manuscript witnesses are derived either directly or indirectly from this. Emendations are, however, on occasion made by selecting readings from other manuscripts, either where MS C is defective, or to restore sense at moments of apparent scribal error.

In MS C, every two lines of the *Balletis* are copied as one, but here the lineation of all other manuscripts is followed, such that each stanza comprises six lines. Stanzas in MS C are signaled through the use of paraphs and the first letter of each stanza is also copied as an

---

[26] Bower, *Scotichronicon*, ed. Watt, 9:245–46.

[27] Bouwmeester, "The Nine Worthies in Middle Dutch Miscellanies."

[28] *Buik of Alexander*, ed. Ritchie, 1:cxxxiv–cli.

enlarged majuscule in bold black ink; stanzas are here distinguished from one another by a double space.

Laing, Craigie, and Ritchie entitled the poem *Ane/The Ballet of the Nine Nobles*. The poem is un-titled in all manuscript witnesses, with the exception of **MS E** where the poem is prefaced by a Latin title, *De nouem nobilibus*. I here follow the poem's closing *demande* in entitling the poem the *Balletis of the Nine Nobles*.

Punctuation in **MS C** is limited to odd virgules at the end of certain lines (see textual note to line 5). Modern punctuation, capitalization, and word-division are introduced in this edition. Thorn and yogh are represented by their modern equivalents (*th* and *y/z*) (or as *s* where the yogh appears at the end of a word, e.g., "Achilles," line 5; "Charles," line 43), as are *i/j* and *u/v/w* spellings. Contractions and marks of abbreviation have been silently expanded.

THE BALLETIS OF THE NINE NOBLES

	Hector of Troy throu hard feichtingis	*through violent battles*
	In half thrid yeris slew xix kingis,	*half of three years (eighteen months); killed 19 kings*
	And ammirallis a hunder and mare,	*admirals; 100 more*
	With smal folk at unrekkynnit war;	*a small, insignificant army*
5	He slew so fele at was ferli,	*It was a wonder he killed so many*
	Quham Achiles slew tresnabili.	*[He] whom Achilles; treacherously*
	Alexander als nobil king,	*also [a]*
	In xii yere wan throu hard feichting	*In 12 years conquered*
	Al landis under the firmament.	*the heavens*
10	Equhethir a dai in til parlement	*Nevertheless one day in parliament*
	He said he had, but variance,	*without a doubt*
	Our litil til his governance.	*Too few [lands] under his command*
	Julius Cesar wan halili	*completely*
	The ilis of Grece and al Surry;	*isles; Syria*
15	Affrike, Arab, Bretan wan he,	*Africa; Arabia; Britain*
	And discumfit his mawche, Pompe:	*defeated his son-in-law, Pompey*
	Throu hard batel and stalwart stour	*strong conflict*
	He was the first emperour.	
	The geanntill Jew schir Josue	*well-born (kindly); sir*
20	Ane and xxx kingis throu weer wan he,	*Defeated thirty-one kings through war*
	And conquirit thair landis also.	
	The Flum Jordan partit in two,	*River Jordan [he] parted*
	Throu Goddis grace and strang power:	*God's grace*
	Men suld him loff on gret maner.	*should glorify him in high fashion*
25	David slew michti Golias,	*Goliath*
	And Philestens at felon was;	*Philistines that were savage*
	He was so wicht and wele fechtand	*physically strong and good at fighting*
	That he was never sene recriand;	*never seen admitting defeat*
	Tharfor men call him, loud and stil,	*loudly and quietly (i.e., in every way)*
30	A trew prophet of hardi will.	*valiant disposition*
	Michti Judas Machabeus	*Mighty*
	In batel slew Antiochus,	

Appollonius, and Nichanore,   *Nicanor*
At in his dais wald never for schore
35   No multitude be edrad of men,
Theroff he war ane egaynis ten.[1]

Arthur wan Dace, Spanye, and France   *Denmark (Dacia); Spain; France*
And hand for hand slew two geantis;   *at close quarters; giants*
Lucius the publik procuratour[2]
40   Of Rome, with milleonis in stalwart stour;   *with millions in fierce battle*
And in til Pariss schir Frollo,   *in Paris; sir*
In leystis slew withoutin mo.   *In the lists [he] killed single-handedly*

Charles of France slew Aygoland,   *Charlemagne; Agoulant*
And wan Spanye fra hethoun hand;   *conquered Spain from the heathens*
45   He slew the Sowdon of Pavy,   *Sultan of Pavia*
And wan the Saxonis halili;   *Saxons completely*
And quhar God deid for our safté,   *where God (Christ) died; preservation*
He put the hali Cristianté.   *installed; holy Christianity*

Godfrey Bolyon slew Solimant,
50   Befor Antioche, and Corborant;[3]
Quham he throu ful strak has ourtane,
Throu corps and harnes his glave his gane.[4]
Sere hethounis he slew throu hard feichtyng,   *So many heathens*
And of Jerusalem a yere was king.   *for a year*

55   Robert the Brois throu hard feichting   *the Bruce*
With few vencust the michti Kyng   *With a few [men] vanquished; mighty*
Of Ingland, Edward, twyse in ficht,   *twice in battle*
At occupide his realme but richt;   *[He, i.e., Edward] that; unjustly*
At sumtyme was set so hard[5]
60   At had nocht sex til him toward.   *That he did not have six on his side*

Yhe gude men at thir balletis redis,
Demis ye quha dochtiast was in dedis.[6]

---

[1] Lines 34–36: *[He] that in his days would never for sure / be in dread of a multitude of men, / even though he was one against ten*

[2] *[And] Lucius the public procurator*

[3] *Before [conquering] Antioch and Corborant*

[4] Lines 51–52: *His sword has gone through the body and defensive armor of him whom he overtook with a fulsome blow*

[5] *[He, i.e. Bruce] who was sometimes so hard-pressed*

[6] Lines 61–62: *You good men who read these verses, / judge who was the most valiant in deeds*

ABBREVIATIONS: ***Alexander***: *Buik of Alexander*, ed. Ritchie; ***Bruce***: Barbour, *The Bruce*, ed. McDiarmid and Stevenson; **C**: Cambridge, Corpus Christi College Library, MS 171, fol. 371r; **JL**: Edinburgh, University Library, MS Dc.7.63, fols. 155v–56r (John Law's abbreviation of Bower's *Scotichronicon*); ***Les Voeux***: *Les Voeux de Paon* (original French), in *Buik of Alexander*, ed. Ritchie; ***OA***: *Octosyllabic Alexander* (Older Scots translation of French *Les Voeux de Paon*) in *Buik of Alexander*, ed. Ritchie.

1   *Hector of Troy*. Hector was a prince of Troy, son of King Priam. Barbour compares his second hero, James Douglas, to "gud Ector of Troy" in the *Bruce* (1.395).

     throu hard feichtingis. This phrase recurs throughout the *Balletis*. Compare lines 8, 53, 55.

2   *In half thrid yeris slew xix kingis*. Medieval accounts of the Trojan War document Hector's killing of many kings and dukes; in Benoît de Saint-Maure's *Le Roman de Troie* (c. 1160–65), for instance, he is responsible for the death of 21 people, at least thirteen of whom were kings. The *Balletis* follows both *Les Voeux* (*Alexander*, 4:403, line 7492) and *OA* (*Alexander*, 4:403, line 9909) in listing nineteen kings. The time-scale ("half thrid yeris") is shared only with the latter text ("Into the half thrid ōeir all anerly," *Alexander*, 4:402, line 9907).

3   *ammirallis a hunder and mare*. Benoît notes that during one battle Hector killed the Greek warrior, Patroclus, *E bien mil chevaliers e plus* ("And also more than one hundred knights," translation mine); Hector's epitaph also recorded his killing of many *amirauz* ("admirals") (*Le Roman de Troie*, ed. Constans, 1:15, line 258; 3:108 line 16846). The killing of over a hundred admirals appears only in *Les Voeux* (*Alexander*, 4:403, line 7493), not in the *OA*.

4   *smal folk*. The motif of a few fighting against many recurs three times later in The *Balletis* (lines 34–36, 56, 59–60). It is also a running theme throughout Barbour's *Bruce* (e.g., 2.333 ff.).

5   *so fele at was ferli*. There is no equivalent to this comment in *Les Voeux* but it does appear in the *OA*. Of Hector's killings, the narrator comments, "That was sa fell it is ferly" (*Alexander*, 4:403, line 9911).

6   *Quham Achiles slew tresnabili*. In the medieval Trojan tradition, Hector is killed by Achilles shortly after himself killing a Greek king, Polyboetes. In an attempt to despoil Polyboetes' body of its armor, Hector set aside his own shield and therefore left himself vulnerable to Achilles' attack. The *Balletis*' author takes a

dim view of Achilles' decision to kill Hector when unarmed, but elsewhere in the medieval Trojan tradition (e.g., Lydgate's *Troy Book* and Christine de Pizan's *Épître d'Othéa la déesse à Hector*) Hector's death is attributed to his own covetousness. See Benson, "Prudence, Othea and Lydgate's Death of Hector."

7   *Alexander als nobil king*. Alexander is similarly described as a "nobill King" in the *OA* (*Alexander*, 4:403, line 9918). Alexander the Great (356–23 BCE) was King of the ancient Greek kingdom of Macedonia and famed for a career of conquests that led to the creation of an exceptionally large empire. Two separate fifteenth-century Older Scots romances about Alexander the Great survive: the *Buik of Alexander* or *Octosyllabic Alexander* (a translation of two French Alexander texts, *Le Fuerre de Gadres* and *Les Voeux du Paon* completed by an anonymous author c. 1438) and *The Buik of King Alexander the Conquerour* (an encyclopedic account of Alexander's career, conquests, and death produced by Sir Gilbert Hay c. 1460). Three Scottish monarchs were also named Alexander in the twelfth and thirteenth centuries. It has been suggested that the popularity of Alexander the Great in Older Scots culture was due in no small part to his being Greek, and thus of the same stock as Scotland's mythological founding father, Gaythelos. See Edington, "Paragons and Patriots," p. 71; Caughey and Wingfield, "Conquest and Imperialism," pp. 463–66.

8   *In xii yere*. *Les Voeux* (*Alexander*, 4:403, line 7500) similarly refers to a twelve year period of conquest, as does Barbour's *Bruce* (1.532). The *OA* refers just to seven years (*Alexander*, 4:403, line 9918) but this may be the result of an error in the sole surviving print witness or a prior exemplar ("xii" might have been mistakenly copied as "vii"). 1 Maccabees 1:8 records that Alexander reigned for twelve years before he died (*et regnavit Alexander annis duodecim et mortuus est*; "And Alexander reigned twelve years, and he died").

9   *under the firmament*. This phrase appears both in *Les Voeux* (*desous le firmament*, *Alexander*, 4:403, line 7501) and *OA* ("vnder the firmament," *Alexander*, 4:403, line 9919).

10–12   *Equhethir a dai . . . . til his governance*. Alexander the Great is here imagined as a medieval monarch addressing a contemporary parliament. In touching upon Alexander's insatiable desire to rule as many lands as possible, the *Balletis* narrator hints at (but does not condemn) something of the increasingly covetous nature for which Alexander was criticized in other treatments of his legend. In the Older Scots *Buik of King Alexander the Conquerour*, for instance, Alexander is criticized for his greed in the final stages of the romance by a succession of individuals, including Dindimus, king of the Brahmins, and the philosopher Diogenes, and in the *Talis of the Fyve Bestes* (edited elsewhere in this volume) Alexander again has to be steered away from his desire to conquer the town of Lapsat. See further Caughey and Wingfield, "Conquest and Imperialism." The more subtle account of Alexander's career in the *Balletis* bears comparison with that of Chaucer's Monk in *The Canterbury Tales*. For a comprehensive overview of attitudes towards Alexander in the Middle English tradition see Ashurst, "Alexander the Great."

13–18   *Julius Cesar wan . . . . the first emperour.* Certain elements of this stanza match
        details in *Les Voeux* and *OA*; the catalogue of countries conquered condenses the
        slightly more extensive list in the original French and Scots, and the comment
        that Caesar "discumfit his mawche, Pompe" (line 16) appears both in the French
        (*Pompeë son serorge . . . / Desconfist il en Gresce, Alexander,* 4:403, lines 7508–09)
        and Scots ("In Grece alsua discumfit he / Pompeyus, his mauch . . ." *Alexander,*
        4:403, lines 9927–28). However, the stanza as a whole is far closer to the lines on
        Julius Caesar in Barbour's *Bruce*:

> Iulius Cesar als, yat wan
> Bretane and Fraunce as dowchty man,
> Affryk Arrabe Egipt Surry
> And all Evrope halyly,
> And for his worschip & valour
> Off Rome wes fryst maid emperour . . . (1.537–42)

In the years immediately prior to the composition of the *Balletis*, Andrew of
Wyntoun wrote about Caesar at considerable length in his *Original Chronicle* (c.
1408–20x4) (MS Cotton: book 4, chapter 25).

13–15   *Julius Cesar wan . . . . Bretan wan he.* Julius Caesar, Roman statesman and general,
        achieved a series of notable victories in Africa and the Middle East in 47 and 46
        BCE. Rome's earlier Gallic Wars between 58 BCE and 50 BCE, led by Caesar,
        had resulted in the expansion of the Roman Empire over the whole of Gaul
        (modern day France and Belgium), and Caesar also led invasions of Britain, one
        in 55 BCE and one in 54 BCE.

16   *his mawche, Pompe.* Pompey married Caesar's daughter, Julia. A civil war between
        Caesar and Pompey (erstwhile political allies) broke out in 50 BCE. After a series
        of battles, Pompey fled to Egypt where he was assassinated.

18   *He was the first emperour.* Caesar's victory against Pompey placed him in a
        position of unrivalled power. He was appointed Dictator of Rome in 48 BCE,
        usually a temporary position, but in 44 BCE Caesar declared himself Dictator for
        life. Increasing political enmity led to Caesar's assassination on the Ides of
        March 44 BCE, and a subsequent series of civil wars. Caesar's adopted grandson,
        Gaius Julius Caesar Octavianus, later became the Emperor Augustus.

19   *The geanntill Jew schir Josue.* A central figure of the Old Testament, Joshua
        became the leader of the Israelite tribes after the death of Moses and led them
        in the conquest of Canaan. See the book of Joshua.

20   *Ane and xxx kingis.* As observed in the textual notes, MS C originally had Joshua
        defeat twelve kings, but a later hand emended this to 31. The latter number
        appears in all other manuscript witnesses and is the number also given in the
        Bible (Joshua 12:24) and in a section on the Nine Worthies in John Rolland's
        late sixteenth-century Scots *Court of Venus* (ed. Gregor, p. 54, line 217). In the
        OA, Joshua "wan" "tuelfe Kingis" (*Alexander,* 4:404, line 9954), whilst in
        manuscripts of the French *Voeux* the number of kings is either 12 or 41.

22   *The Flum Jordan partit in two.* The Jordan is a river of over 250km running through the Middle and Near East into the Dead Sea. In Joshua 3, the River Jordan miraculously divides into two to allow Joshua and the Israelites to pass over. The event parallels Moses' earlier crossing of the Red Sea (Exodus 14). In the Declaration of Arbroath (the famous 1320 letter of Scottish barons to Pope John XXII), the Scots are paralleled with the Israelites and their leaders with Moses, Joshua, and Judas Maccabeus; Scottish ancestors are said to have journeyed from Egypt "twelve hundred years after the people of Israel crossed the Red Sea" and Robert Bruce is described as "like another Maccabaeus or Joshua." See *Declaration*, ed. and trans. Fergusson and Borthwick.

25   *David slew michti Golias.* Depicted variously as a warrior, poet, and musician, King David was the second King of Israel and reported ancestor of Christ. Although not without fault (he committed adultery with Bathsheba and brought about the death of her husband, Uriah), he was generally held throughout the medieval world as a righteous and effective king. David's triumph over the Philistine giant, Goliath, is documented in 1 Kings 17:4–51. Although designed to demonstrate David's identity as a true king of Israel, the story is also about the triumph of a small, weak force against a larger and stronger opponent. A similar motif of a few against many runs throughout the *Balletis* and Barbour's *Bruce*. See the note to line 4 above.

26   *And Philestens at felon was.* The Biblical Book of Samuel contains several accounts of battles between the Israelites and their enemies, the Philistines (a non-Semitic people occupying the southern coast of Palestine in biblical times). David's battle against Goliath represented the defeat of the Philistines. Subsequently, Saul is praised for his slaying of thousands of Philistines, but David for slaying tens of thousands (1 Kings 18:7). The French *Les Voeux* and Scots *OA* have David instead kill many *felon payen* (*Alexander*, 4:404, line 7532) or "mony ane fell pagan" (*Alexander*, 4:404, line 9961). Although the name given to those killed differs in the *Balletis*, it echoes the French adjective *felon*.

28   *was never sene recriand.* The *OA* similarly notes that David "was neuer recryand" (4:404, line 9964); *Les Voeux* that he was *ne recrëant* (*Alexander*, 4:404, line 7534).

31   *Michti Judas Machabeus.* Judas Maccabeus, the son of a Jewish priest, led a revolt against the Seleucid (Hellenic state) ruler, Antiochus IV Epiphanes, around 166 BCE. The Seleucids had forbidden certain Jewish practices. Events are related in two Old Testament books: 1 Maccabees and 2 Maccabees. As discussed in the note to line 22 above, Robert Bruce was compared to Judas Maccabeus in the 1320 Declaration of Arbroath. Comparisons are also made to the Maccabees throughout Barbour's *Bruce*. See 1.465; 14.312–16.

32   *In batel slew Antiochus.* The death of Antiochus is reported three times in the two books of Maccabees: 1 Maccabees 6:1–16; 2 Maccabees 1:14–17; and 2 Maccabees 9.

33   *Appollonius, and Nichanore.* Apollonius, governor of Samaria, was killed by Maccabeus on the battlefield (1 Maccabees 3:10–12); two Biblical accounts of the

death of Nicanor, leader of a Seleucid force, survive (1 Maccabees 7:39–47; 2 Maccabees 15:20–36).

37–42   *Arthur wan Dace . . . . slew withoutin mo.* As observed in the textual note to line 37, attitudes towards Arthur in medieval and early modern Scotland were mixed. During the Anglo-Scots Wars of Independence, the Arthurian legend (and Arthur's rule over the whole of Britain) was used by the English to bolster their claims to lordship and ownership of Scotland (Wingfield, *Trojan Legend*, pp. 10–15). As a consequence, it used to be thought that the Scots adopted a persistently hostile attitude towards Arthur, but this view has been revised over recent years. Whilst it is indeed true that a number of Scottish chronicles (both Latin and English) stress Arthur's illegitimacy and consequent lack of right to the British throne, the Arthurian legend nevertheless remained popular, as evidenced by the Older Scots romances *Lancelot of the Laik* and *Golagros and Gawane*, and Arthur himself was increasingly presented with what Nicola Royan has termed "a curious mixture of praise and condemnation" ("Fine Art," p. 44). See also Göller, "King Arthur in the Scottish Chronicles"; Alexander, "Late Medieval Scottish Attitudes"; Royan, "'Na les vailyeant.'"

This stanza is notably different from both the French *Voeux* and *OA*. It appears to stem either directly or indirectly from Geoffrey of Monmouth's account of Arthur's enemy, Lucius, in his *Historia Regum Britanniae* (c. 1136). Geoffrey and the *Balletis* author both describe Lucius as a "procuratour," whereas he appears elsewhere, for instance in the *Alliterative Morte Arthure* (ed. Benson, lines 554, 1293) or Barbour's *Bruce* (1.555) as an "emperour." The *Balletis* description of Arthur may also owe something to Andrew of Wyntoun's *Original Chronicle* (c. 1408–20x4), book 5, chapter 13 (MS Cotton). In a well known passage where Wyntoun discusses the enigmatic poet "Huchon of þe Aule Reale" (4:21–27, lines 4279–360, quotation on line 4279), he spends some time discussing whether Lucius should be called "emperoure." He clarifies that Huchown in fact states that "Lucyus Hyberius in his dayis / Was of þe hee state procuratoure" (4:23, lines 4302–03).

37   *Dace.* In book 9 of Geoffrey of Monmouth's *Historia* (ed. Reeve, pp. 206–07), Arthur subdues Norway, Dacia, Aquitaine and Gaul. Throughout Reeve's edition, wherever the Latin word *Dacia* appears, it is translated as Denmark, and this is the country given in the JL witness of the *Balletis*. It is, however, also possible that "Dace" referred to the ancient kingdom of Dacia, which included the present-day countries of Romania and Moldova, as well as parts of Ukraine, Eastern Serbia, Northern Bulgaria, Slovakia, Hungary, and Southern Poland.

38   *hand for hand slew two geantis.* Like David, Arthur is here presented as a conqueror of giants as well as humans. In book 10 of Geoffrey of Monmouth's *Historia* (ed. Reeve, pp. 224–27), Arthur kills a Spanish giant (Rithio) on St. Michael's Mount. In *Les Voeux* and *OA*, this giant (there named Ruiston/Rostrik) is presented as separate from the giant of St. Michael's Mount, and Arthur is also said to have killed "ma gyantis in vther places" (*Alexander*, 4:405, line 9991); giants *[e]n plusours autres lieus* (*Alexander*, 4:405, line 7556).

39   *Lucius the publik procuratour.* A public procurator was an officer in charge of
         finance and taxation in a province of the Roman Empire. In book 9 of Geoffrey
         of Monmouth's *Historia* (ed. Reeve, pp. 214–17), Lucius writes to Arthur
         demanding tribute. After taking the advice of his council, Arthur agrees to a war
         with the Romans and refuses to pay tribute. A series of European battles follow,
         culminating in a personal battle between Arthur and Lucius, during which the
         latter is killed. See also the notes to lines 37–42 and 37 above.

41   *And in til Pariss schir Frollo.* Frollo was a Roman tribune who held the province
         of Gaul. Arthur agrees to a dual with Frollo in Paris and is eventually victorious
         after a fierce round of fighting. The episode is described in book 9 of Geoffrey
         of Monmouth's *Historia* (ed. Reeve, pp. 206–09).

43–48   *Charles of France . . . . the hali Cristianté.* This stanza is particularly close to lines
         in the *OA*:

> Charles of France slew Agoment,
> And wan Spane to his commandement,
> And slew the duke of Pauy,
> And wan the Saxones halely,
> [. . . .]
> And quhair God deit for our sauetie,
> He put the haill christintie (*Alexander*, 4:405, lines 9993–10,000)

Charlemagne, King of the Franks from 768 to 814 and later Holy Roman
Emperor, enjoyed widespread literary popularity throughout the Middle Ages
and he and his knights were repeatedly depicted as defenders of the Christian
faith. Only one Older Scots Charlemagne romance survives (*Rauf Coilyear*), but
other texts in the tradition appear to have been known in fifteenth- and
sixteenth-century Scotland. The mid-fifteenth-century *Complaynt of Scotland*, for
instance, collocates *Rauf Coilyear* alongside "the siege of millan" (ed. Stewart,
Complaynt, p. 50); in Barbour's *Bruce*, King Robert reads from the "Romanys of
worthi Ferumbrace" to comfort his men as they attempt to cross the shores of
Loch Lomond (3.435–62, quotation from line 437); and accounts of
Charlemagne are found in the chronicles of Wyntoun, Bower, Boece, and
Bellenden, and in Sir Gilbert Hay's *Buke of the Law of Armys* and John Ireland's
Meroure of Wyssdome. Several English Charlemagne romances survive from the
fourteenth through to sixteenth centuries. See Lupack, *Three Middle English
Charlemagne Romances*; Smyser, "Charlemagne Legends"; and Hardman and
Ailes, *The Legend of Charlemagne*.

43   *Aygoland.* Ago[u]lant or Aigolandus was a Saracen king of Africa. Charlemagne's
         battle against him is recounted in the twelfth-century Latin chronicle known
         variously as the *Historia Karoli Magni et Rotholandi* or *Pseudo-Turpin Chronicle*. See
         The Pseudo-Turpin, ed. Smyser, pp. 22–31 (especially pp. 22–23n4).

45   *Sowdon of Pavy.* In *Les Voeux* this figure is described as *Desÿer de Pavie* (*Alexander*,
         4:405, line 7560) and in the *OA* as "duke of Pauy" (*Alexander*, 4:405, line 9995).
         The individual intended is Didier de Pavia, king of the Lombards (757–74).

Charlemagne conquered the Lombard kingdom in 773–74. See McKitterick, *Charlemagne*, pp. 28, 107–14.

46   *wan the Saxonis halili*. Charlemagne's war against the Saxons (and Franks) lasted from the beginning of his reign until c. 803/04. See McKitterick, *Charlemagne*, pp. 103–06.

47–48   *And quhar God . . . . the hali Cristianté*. Although Charlemagne is thought to have not in fact visited Jerusalem personally, legendary accounts, including the *Pseudo-Turpin*, see him journey to Jerusalem to restore the Christian faith.

49–54   *Godfrey Bolyon slew . . . . yere was king*. Godfrey of Bouillon (1060–1100), a medieval Frankish knight and Lord of Bouillon, was one of the leaders of the First Crusade. After the Siege of Jerusalem in 1099 he became the first ruler of the Kingdom of Jerusalem. See Lock, *The Routledge Companion to the Crusades*, p. 237. And, for Scotland's relationship to the Crusades, see Macquarrie, *Scotland and the Crusades*. Given the appearance of Robert Bruce immediately below and Charlemagne above this stanza it is interesting to observe that during the Wars of Independence the Bishops of Glasgow and St Andrews reportedly preached that "it was no less meritorious to fight for Robert Bruce against the English than to go to the Holy Land to fight against pagans and saracens" (Macquarrie, *Scotland and the Crusades*, p. 71); as already noted, Bruce was also compared to Charlemagne by Barbour (*Bruce*, 3.435–62). He is again implicitly presented as a crusading hero within this poem.

49–50   *Godfrey Bolyon slew . . . . Antioche, and Corborant*. These lines are close to the *OA*: here, Godfrey "Wincust the michty Salamant, / And, before Anthioche, Corborant" (*Alexander*, 4:406, lines 10005–06).

49   *Solimant*. Kilij Arslan I, ibn Suleiman, Sultan of Nicea (1079–1107). See Lock, *Routledge Companion to the Crusades*, p. 244; Runciman, *A History of the Crusades*, p. 77n1.

50   *Antioche*. Antioch, a Muslim city near to the modern city of Antakya in Turkey, was conquered in the Crusaders' Siege of 1098. See Lock, *Routledge Companion to the Crusades*, p. 23; Runciman, *A History of the Crusades*, pp. 236–50.

       Corborant. Corborant or Corboran was a prince of Mosul and sultan of Aleppo, who commanded the army of the sultan of Persia and was involved in the Siege of Antioch. See Runciman, *A History of the Crusades*, pp. 236–49, 62; Cropp, "Les Vers Sur Les Neuf Preux," p. 479n7569.

54   *of Jerusalem a yere was king*. Contrary to the opinion of the *Balletis* author (and the authors of *Les Voeux* and *OA*), Godfrey in fact refused the title of King. See Lock, *Routledge Companion to the Crusades*, p. 237.

55–60   *Robert the Brois . . . . til him toward*. This stanza positions the Scottish king Robert I (Robert the Bruce) (1274–1329) as a tenth Worthy.

56–57   *With few vencust . . . . twyse in ficht*. It is likely that one of the battles referred to here is the Battle of Bannockburn (24 June 1314) during which Robert Bruce's army triumphed against the much larger English host, led by Edward II. The battle is depicted visually on fol. 265r of MS C.

61–62   *Yhe gude men . . . . was in dedis*. The closing *demande* echoes a moment in Barbour's *Bruce* where the narrator compares Bruce, after he has fought single-handedly against a large number of men from Galloway, to Tydeus, who (in the French *Roman de Thèbes*, ed. Petit) single-handedly killed fifty men (6.181–286). The narrator asks firstly "Ōe yat yis redys, cheys yhe / Quheyer yat mar suld prysit be / Ye king . . . / Or Thedeus," and secondly, "Now demys quheyer mar lowing / Suld Thedeus haiff or ye king" (6.271–77, 285–86).

TEXTUAL NOTES TO THE *BALLETIS OF THE NINE NOBLES*

ABBREVIATIONS: **B**: National Records of Scotland, MS GD 45/26/48, fol. 420v; **C**: Cambridge, Corpus Christi College Library, MS 171, fol. 371r (base manuscript); **D**: Darnaway Castle, Forres, Donibristle MS, fol. 433v; **E**: Edinburgh, University Library, MS 186, fol. 434r; **JL**: Edinburgh, University Library, MS Dc.7.63, fols. 155v–56r (John Law's abbreviation of Bower's *Scotichronicon*).

\ / indicates words inserted by the scribe; words/phrases deleted by the scribe are struck-through; [ ] indicates letters supplied where the MS is defective or difficult to read.

1 *Hector.* The first letter of this stanza in C (like all other stanzas) is copied as an enlarged majuscule in bold black ink. In D the initial letters of each line are touched in red and in E the initial letter of the first stanza is in red, with subsequent initial letters of stanzas alternating in red and blue.

2 *In half thrid yeris slew xix kingis.* C: the word "throu" is erased between "yeris" and "slew" and the final three letters of "kingis" are now lost. JL: *In xiii yeris.*

4 *smal folk at unrekkynnit war.* So C. JL: *small folk that not reknit war.*

5 In C, virgules appear at the end of this line, as well as lines 9, 11, 13, 15, 17, 19, 21, 29, 33, 43, 47, 49, and 55.

7 *Alexander als nobil king.* So C. D: *Alexander als nobil a kyng.* E: *Alexander als nobil a king.* JL: *Alexander of macedo[n] the nobil kyng.*

10 *Equhethir a dai in til parlement.* So C. B: *Quhil a day in til parliament.* JL: *Quhil a day ~~he said~~ in plain parliament.*

11 *He said he had, but variance.* So C. JL: *He said for owthyn wariance.*

12 *Our litil til his governance.* So C. D: *Our litill til his guidu[n?]ance.* JL: *He had ouer litill to his gowarnance.*

13 *wan halili.* So C. JL: *wan ~~halely~~ all halely.*

14 *The ilis of Grece and al Surry.* So C. JL: *The landis of grece and of surry.*

15 *Affrike, Arab, Bretan wan he.* So C. D: *Affrik \and/ arabi ~~heathen~~ wan he.*

18 *He was the first emperour.* C: *He was the first was emperour.* JL: *In rome the first he was emperour.*

20 *Ane and xxx kingis.* In C a later hand has erased the original number of kings (12) and replaced this with what appears to be the number 31 (the hand is now hard to read): \ane and thr — / ~~twelff~~ kingis. This latter number appears in all other manuscript witnesses.

24 *Men suld him loff on gret maner.* So C. JL: *we suld him loif in gret maner.*

25 *michti.* At this point in C the word is abbreviated. In expanding it, I adopt the form found at line 31.

26   *Philestens.* So C. B: *filestes.* D: *Filestens.* E: *philisteus.* JL: *philistanis.*

29   *Tharfor.* So C. JL: *Heir for.*

34   *for schore.* Only C prefaces "schore" with "for," but its reading is here retained
        on grounds of sense.

36   *Theroff.* So C. JL: *Thot.*

        ten. In MS C this word is now lost where the MS is defective. It is here supplied
        following all other witnesses.

37   *Arthur wan Dace, Spanye, and France.* So C. D: *Arthur* ~~wan dace~~ \saw neuer/ *spanye*
        ~~and~~ \nor/ *france.* JL: *Arthur van denmark span and france.* A later hand has
        emended D to deny or downplay Arthur's achievements. Attitudes towards
        Arthur in medieval and early modern Scotland were notably mixed. See the
        explanatory note for lines 37–42.

38   *And hand for hand slew two geantis.* The final three letters of the line in C are
        missing. These have been supplied following the reading of all MSS except
        JL. D: ~~And~~ \Bot/ *hand for hand slew two giantis.* E: *And hand for hand slew giantis*
        \tua/ (the number is supplied by a later hand). JL: *And hand for hand slew tua*
        gyance. JL's spelling best preserves the rhyme with the previous line but the
        reading of all other witnesses is here preferred on grounds of sense.

40   *Of Rome, with milleonis in stalwart stour.* B: *In Rome.* JL: *In Rome slew in stalwart*
        stour. With the exception of JL, this line contains a notably lengthy number
        of syllables in all other witnesses, as does line 39. I have, however, decided
        not to emend as the poem as a whole is metrically irregular. The final four
        letters are lost in C but supplied from other witnesses.

41   *And in til Pariss schir Frollo.* So C. D: *And* ~~in till~~ \not in/ *Pariss sir Frollo.*

44   *And wan Spanye fra hethoun hand.* So C. E: *And wan spanye fra hethon land.*

48   *He put the hali Cristianté.* So C. JL: *He put hail it in cristinite.*

51   *Quham he throu ful strak has ourtane.* So C. JL: *Quhan he wyt[h] strak hais ouer tain.*

52   *Throu corps and harnes his glave his gane.* C lacks the final three words of this line,
        and begins *throu corps and harmes his.* Although "harmes" is a valid form of the
        word "arms," "harnes" ("defensive armor") is the reading of all other
        manuscript witnesses and is preferred here. The second half of the line is
        taken from D. B: *cops and hernies.* E: *cops and harnieō.* JL: *Throw cors and harnes*
        hais glawe his gain.

54   *And of Jerusalem a yere was king.* The final two letters of this line are missing in
        C and are here supplied from other witnesses; the first three words are also
        unnecessarily repeated in C on the following line (by the same scribe). JL:
        And of Jerusalem twa yere was kyng.

57   *Of Ingland, Edward, twyse in ficht.* So C. B: *Of Inglonde Edward ii in fycht.* JL: *Off*
        Ingland Edward the secund in ~~feitl~~ *feyt.* The reading of C is here retained, but
        the readings of B and JL have much to recommend them since Robert's
        opponent was Edward II of England.

59   *At sum tyme.* So C. B: *Ande sum thym.* JL: *And sum tym.*

60   *At had nocht sex til him toward.* So C. JL: *That he had not sex to hym toward.*

61–62 *Yhe gude men . . . . was in dedis.* Only C has "ye" after "Demis." JL: *Gud men at thir*
        ballatis reddis / Deim quha ~~hard~~ *dowchtyast was in deide.*

INTRODUCTION TO THE
 COMPLAINT FOR THE DEATH OF MARGARET, PRINCESS OF SCOTLAND

The literary significance of Margaret, daughter of James I of Scotland, was first brought to scholarly attention by Priscilla Bawcutt in a series of articles: one about three daughters of James I, co-authored with Bridget Henisch; a second on women and their books in medieval and renaissance Scotland; and a third in which she identified for the first time the French source of the Older Scots *Complaint for the Death of Margaret, Princess of Scotland* (*NIMEV* 3430) edited here.[1] This poem deserves greater critical attention, not least because of the way in which it introduces, parallels, and anticipates literary traditions better known from late fifteenth- and early sixteenth-century Scottish literature. From a formal perspective, it anticipates Henryson's use of the ten-line stanza form in *Orpheus and Eurydice*; in terms of subject matter it anticipates William Dunbar's elegy for the Scottish French ambassador, Lord Bernard Stewart ("Illuster Lodouick, of France most cristin king"),[2] and David Lyndsay's poem on the death of the French princess, Magdalene (first wife of James V) (*The Deploration of the Deith of Quene Magdalene*);[3] and thematically it accords with the far broader Scottish tradition of advice on personal and public governance.

BIOGRAPHY OF PRINCESS MARGARET

James I's eldest daughter, Margaret (1425–45), was married at the age of eleven to the French dauphin Louis (later Louis XI) (1423–83), following a protracted set of negotiations that began in 1428.[4] Margaret arrived at La Rochelle on 15 April 1436 and traveled from there, via Poitiers, to Tours, which she reached on 24 June.[5] She and Louis were married in a ceremony the following day, at which Louis apparently wore a sword that had previously belonged to the Scottish king, Robert Bruce (1274–1329). Most of Margaret's Scottish entourage departed soon after, and she was placed in the care of her mother-in-law, Queen

---

[1] "Scots Abroad," "'My bright buke,'" and "A Medieval Scottish Elegy."

[2] *Poems of William Dunbar*, ed. Bawcutt, 1:100, line 1. See also Bawcutt, "Medieval Scottish Elegy," p. 11.

[3] *Selected Poems*, ed. Hadley Williams, pp. 101–08.

[4] For fuller biographies of Margaret see: Barbé, *Margaret of Scotland*; Champion, *La Dauphine Mélancolique*; Champion, *Louis XI*, 1:99–105, 175–82; ODNB, "Margaret [Margaret of Scotland] (1424–1445)." Also see the following earlier accounts: Duclos, *Histoire de Louis XI*, 3:20–50; Le Roux de Lincy, *Les Femmes Célèbres*, 1:447–53; Villet de Viriville, *Histoire de Charles VII*, 3:83–90; du Fresne de Beaucourt, *Histoire de Charles VII*, pp. 89–111.

[5] Margaret's entry to Tours is depicted in Paris, Bibliothèque Nationale, MS fr. 2691, fol. 93r (a manuscript copy of a chronicle of Charles VII by Jean Chartier).

Marie d'Anjou (1404–63). Little is known of her subsequent public role, beyond her attendance at the marriage of Margaret of Anjou (1430–82) and Henry VI (1421–71) in 1444–45, and her accompaniment of Isabelle, duchess of Burgundy (1397–1471), during the latter's residence at the French court. Evidence also survives of Margaret's role in a court dance, found on the flyleaf of a manuscript (Paris, Bibliothèque Nationale, MS fr. 5699) that belonged to Jean d'Orléans, Comte d'Angoulême (1399–1467), who had just returned to France after 33 years' captivity in England.[6]

Despite the very good relationship she apparently had with her father- and mother-in-law, Charles VII (1403–61) and Marie d'Anjou, Margaret's relationship with her husband appears to have been less than cordial, and her short life in France came to a sad conclusion when she died aged only twenty on 16 August 1445. Margaret had accompanied Charles on a pilgrimage to the church and shrine of Notre-Dame de l'Epine near to Châlons, and she caught a chill from which she failed to recover. At the subsequent inquest held into her death, extremely interesting information was revealed about her wider literary activities.

The dauphin's chamberlain, Jamet de Tillay, suggested that Margaret had fallen ill through lack of sleep, caused by the long hours she spent each night writing rondeaux and ballades:

> ledit Nicole lui demanda ce qu'elle avoit, & d'où procédoit cette maladie, & il qui parle lui répondit que les Médecins disoient qu'elle avoit un courroux sur le cœur, qui lui faisoit grand dommage, & aussi que faute de repos lui nuisoit beaucoup, & lors ledit Nicole dit que lesdits Médecins lui en avoient autant dit, & aussi dit plût à Dieu qu'elle n'eût jamais eu telle femme à elle! & quelle, dit-il qui parle? & lors ledit Nicole lui répondit Marguerite de Salignac; & il qui parle, lui dit, plût à Dieu, ne aussi Prégente, ne Jeanne Filloque! requis pouquoi il dit lesdites paroles, dit pour ce qu'il avoit oüi dire, que c'étoient celles qui la faisoient trop veiller à faire rondeaux & balades.

> the said Nicole asked him what was wrong with her and what caused her illness, and he [Jamet] replied that the doctors said she had such anger in her heart, which did her great harm, and also that it was made worse through lack of sleep; and then the said Nicole said that the doctors had said the same thing to him, and also said, 'Would to God that she never had such a woman with her!' 'Which one', he [Jamet] replied, and the said Nicole answered 'Marguerite de Salignac'; and he [Jamet] added 'Would to God, nor also Prégente, nor Jeanne Filleul!' Asked why he said these words, he [Jamet] said that he had heard that they were the ones who made her stay up late writing rondeaux and ballades.[7]

Questioned further about what he had said to Charles VII concerning Margaret's death, Jamet reported:

> le Roi lui demanda, d'où procéde cette maladie? & il qui parle, lui dit qu'il venoit de faute de repos, comme disoient les Médicins, & qu'elle veilloit tant, aucunefois

---

[6] For more on the manuscripts owned and copied by Jean and his brother, Charles d'Orléans, see Ouy, "Charles d'Orléans and his Brother Jean d'Angoulême"; Ouy, *La librairie des Frères Captifs*. It is possible that Margaret's father, James I, shared periods of his captivity with Charles d'Orléans.

[7] Duclos, *Histoire de Louis XI*, 3:42–43. Translation mine. The three women named were Margaret's female attendants, discussed in further detail below.

plus, aucunefois moins, que aucunes fois il étoit presque soleil levant avant qu'elle s'allât coucher, & que aucunefois Monseigneur le Dauphin avoit dormi un somme ou deux avant qu'elle s'allât coucher, & aucunefois s'occupoit à faire rondeaux, tellement qu'elle en faisoit aucunefois douze pour un jour, qui lui étoit chose bien contraire.

the King asked him what caused this illness and he replied that it came from a lack of sleep, as the doctors had said, and that she frequently stayed up, sometimes more, sometimes less, and that it was sometimes almost dawn before she went to bed, and sometimes the dauphin had been sleeping for an hour or two before she came to bed, and often she was busy writing rondeaux, such that she sometimes made twelve in a day, which was not good for her.[8]

To date, no poetic compositions by Margaret are known to survive, and it is possible that those poems reportedly written by Margaret were lost when Louis XI ordered the destruction of his wife's papers shortly after her death. However, it is also possible, as Paula Higgins has suggested, that Margaret's work survives without attribution alongside the known work of her female attendants and others in her literary circle. Poetry by two of the women named in the inquest as Margaret's fellow writers (Jeanne Filleul and Marguerite de Salignac) survives alongside verse by other contemporary royal and aristocratic French women and their attendants in a series of fifteenth-century French manuscript anthologies and one early sixteenth-century printed collection,[9] where some poems appear in named form and others anonymously.[10] That the work of these women survives both in named and anonymous form lends hope to the idea that verse by Margaret might also survive in anonymous form, perhaps in the same manuscript and printed anthologies.

As well as writing verse, Princess Margaret also owned a number of books. I have written elsewhere about the likelihood of Margaret's having read the recently composed French romance *Cleriadus et Meliadice* (c. 1440–44), which her lady-in-waiting, Prégente de Mélun, borrowed from Marie de Clèves (1426–87), the wife of Charles d'Orléans (1394–1465),[11] and she is also known to have had a chest (kept by another lady-in-waiting, Annette de Cuise) which contained *un livre qui parle d'amours, et de chansons et ballades, et aucunes lettres d'estat* ("a book about love, with songs and ballads, and other letters of estate").[12] In addition, she owned a verse paraphrase of the Book of Job, known as *Les Vigiles des Morts*, written by Pierre de Nesson, the uncle of another poet and female attendant in Margaret's circle

---

[8] Duclos, *Histoire de Louis XI*, 3:44. Translation mine.

[9] The manuscripts are: Paris, Bibliothèque Nationale, MSS f. fr. 9223, nouv. acq. fr. 15771, and fr. 1719, and Berlin, Staatliche Museen, Kupferstichkabinett MS 78.B.17. The printed collection is *Le Jardin de Plaisance*, an anthology of mid-fifteenth-century verse first published by the Parisian printer Antoine Vérard c. 1502.

[10] Higgins, "Parisian Nobles," p. 171. See also Higgins, "The 'Other Minervas,'" and Müller, "Autour de Marguerite d'Écosse."

[11] Wingfield, "'And He, That Did it Out of French Translait'." See also *Clariodus*, ed. Irving.

[12] Paris, Bibliothèque Nationale, MS Dupuy 762, fol. 53. Quotation in Higgins, "Parisian Nobles," pp. 165 and 165n65. Translation mine.

(Jamette de Nesson),[13] and we know too that she gave a richly decorated book of hours to one Abbot Nicolas Godard as security for the debt she had accrued in commissioning the founding of a chapel at Saint-Laon in Thouars, where she had hoped to be buried.[14]

FRENCH POETRY ON THE OCCASION OF MARGARET'S DEATH

Margaret's death appears to have inspired an outpouring of literary grief and five complaints about Margaret — four in French and one in Scots (edited here) — are extant.

1. The first poem about her death was written by the French court poet, Blosseville,[15] and appears in a manuscript anthology (Paris, Bibliothèque Nationale, 9223, fols. 65v–66) alongside verse by other members of Margaret's courtly circle.[16] Beginning *Vous qui parlés de la beauté d'Elaine*, this poem of three eight-line stanzas and a concluding quatrain, refers to Margaret by the letter 'M' and lauds her as superior to worthy women from the Bible and classical legend such as Helen, Judith, Polyxena, Lucrece, and Hester; at the end of each stanza, Blosseville requests: *Je requier Dieu qu'il en vueille avoir l'ame* ("I pray to God that he guards her soul").

2. The next set of memorial verses concerning Margaret (beginning *La très-doulce Vierge Marie*) survive at the end of a parchment books of hours dated after 1455 and commissioned by Margaret's sister, Isabella (Paris, Bibliothèque Nationale, MS lat. 1369 [p. 446]).[17] Four stanzas in the voice of the deceased dauphine are framed by two initial stanzas addressing the Virgin Mary and describing Margaret's consciousness of her impending death, and a concluding stanza in which the writer prays for the redemption of his or her own soul. In the intervening stanzas the dauphine is imagined as bidding farewell to those she knew including *Le Daulphin, son loial mary* ("the Dauphin, her very loyal husband"), the *très-noble roy de France* ("very noble king of France"), her *père, roy d'Escosse* ("father, king of Scotland"),

---

[13] *Les Vigiles des Morts* is a 1674-line octosyllabic poem in stanzas of six lines offering a vivid and didactic paraphrase of nine lessons from the Book of Job used in the Office of the Dead. In it, de Nesson places himself very closely at the level of Job and meditates, following his Biblical and liturgical models, on the transience of earthly life and death, suffering and riches, divine providence, predestination and free will, citing along the way various authorities such as Plato, Aristotle, Ovid, Boethius, and St. Augustine and drawing graphic descriptions of death itself. See de Nesson, *Les Vigiles*, ed. Collet. Margaret's copy of the poem was described as extant in the late nineteenth and early twentieth century but its present whereabouts are unknown. See Delisle, *Le Cabinet des Manuscrits*, 1:91; Bryce, *The Scottish Grey Friars*, 1:51–52, and 52n1. In the latter reference Bryce refers to a book of Job by Pierre de Nesson containing an image of Margaret. Private correspondence with the most recent editor of *Les Vigiles*, Alain Collet, reveals that none of the surviving 25 witnesses of the poem match Deslisle or Bryce's descriptions of Margaret's copy.

[14] Barbé, *Margaret of Scotland*, pp. 168–70.

[15] For the most recent identification of the poet Blosseville, see the introduction to *Une nouvelle collection de poésies lyriques*, ed. Inglis.

[16] *Rondeaux et Autres Poésies*, ed. Raynaud, pp. 108–09. See also p. 72 for another poem about Margaret by Blosseville.

[17] The poem is printed in Barbé, *Margaret of Scotland*, pp. 173–74.

Dame Isabeau, noble duchesse de Bourgoigne ("Dame Isabelle, noble duchess of Burgundy"), and her sister, *duchesse de Bretaigne* ("the duchess of Brittany").

3. The next anonymous French text, known as *La Complainte pour la mort de Madame Marguerite d'Escosse, daulphine de Viennoys* ("Lament on the death of Madame Margaret of Scotland, dauphine of Vienne"), has up until now been thought to survive just in one manuscript, Paris, Bibliothèque de l'Arsenal 3523 (pp. 461–73), but I have discovered its presence in two further manuscripts: The Hague, Koninklijke Bibliotheek, MS 71.E.49 (fols. 335r–40v) and Paris, Bibliothèque Nationale, MS fr. 1952 (fols. 52r–61r).[18] The only modern edition of the poem (from the Arsenal manuscript) forms part of an unpublished doctoral thesis by Claude Thiry.[19] It comprises 36 stanzas, each of ten octosyllabic lines, and the poem is, furthermore, formally divided into two halves. The first half of the poem represents the complaint proper. In it the speaker requests that God make the natural world weep with him (e.g., *Faictes aux nues espuiser / Toutes les mers pour plourer lermes / Avecques mes yeulx*; "Make the clouds empty / All the seas so as to cry tears / Alongside my eyes," lines 2–4) and asks the same of his nation's princes and princesses, and the Scottish royal house:

> Escosse, maison triumphant,
> Venez lamenter vostre enffant,
> En gemissant et nuyt et jour.
> Vers France, qui de dueil a tant,
> Par mer venez, vous embatant,
> Amener des larmes secours.

> Scotland, triumphant house,
> Come to mourn your child
> By groaning both night and day.
> Come by sea to France, which has
> So much grief, hasten in
> To bring the aid of tears.
> (lines 61–66)

He then proceeds to document Margaret's virtues, such as her *Bonté, doulceur, grace et humblesse* ("Goodness, sweetness, grace and humility," line 71) before, in a manner somewhat reminiscent of Pierre de Nesson's *Les Vigiles*, crying out against Nature and Death itself. The first half of the poem then concludes and is followed by a rubric: *Cy après s'ensuit la responce et consolacion de la complainte cy dessus escripte* ("Hereafter follows the response and consolation to the lament written above"). In the second half of the poem the voice of reason counsels the previous speaker to accept the inevitability of death rather than rail against it, and reminds him that God did not spare even his own son from death: *Dieu son propre filz*

---

[18] Further discussion will appear in my forthcoming monograph, *Reading and Writing Scotland's Queens c. 1424–1587*, on the texts associated with the female members of Scotland's royal family from Princess Margaret to Mary Queen of Scots.

[19] Thiry, "Recherches sur la déploration funèbre française," 2:9–23. I am grateful to Dr. Thiry for sending me a copy of his edition and for allowing me to quote from it. My thanks also to Erika Graham-Goering of the University of York for supplying me with a translation of the French.

n'espargna ("God did not spare his own son," line 251). The second section of the poem ends with a final prayer for Margaret's soul:

> Si lui prions à peu de plait
> Que à celle dont cy l'en recorde
> Face grace et misericorde
>
> Thus to Him we pray with few words
> That to her, of whom we have remembrance,
> He give grace and mercy.
> (lines 358–60)

4. In its third (and latest) manuscript witness, Paris, Bibliothèque Nationale, MS fr. 1952, the *Complainte pour la mort de Madame Marguerite d'Escosse, daulphine de Vennoys* is prefaced by another, hitherto unknown and therefore unpublished, *Complaincte de feue ma dame Marguerite Descosse, daulphine de viennoys, faicte a Chaalon en Champaigne pour son piteux trespassement* ("Lament for my late lady Marguerite of Scotland, dauphine of Vienne, written at Châlons in Champagne for her sad passing," fols. 40r–52r).[20] Comprising 45 mainly ten-line stanzas, and written in the elaborate rhyming style favored by the Grands Rhétoriqueurs, such as Jean Marot and Jehan d'Auton (e.g., *Hee, Dieu! quel perte / Nous est ouverte / Et descouverte, / Durement verte*, "Ah, God! What a loss / is presented to us / and revealed / cruelly unripe," fol. 41v),[21] the poem anticipates the sentiments of the better-known *Complainte* in its call for universal mourning,[22] outcry against Death, and its extended praise for and cataloguing of the princess' virtues and physical beauty.

This second complaint's similarities with Blosseville's verse, the seemingly genuine expressions of grief articulated in its concluding stanzas, (*Toute ma joye cest destraincte*, "All my joy has vanished," fol. 52r), and the poem's title would suggest that it was composed in Châlons, very soon after Margaret's death, perhaps by a member of her courtly and literary circle, and the same might well be true of the first *Complainte*. We know that Margaret was associated throughout her life with court administrators and servants who combined their day-to-day activities with the production of verse. As such, it is not too much of a stretch to imagine that those same courtiers were prompted to express their grief for Margaret's death in a medium they shared with her on an apparently daily basis. In her analysis of medieval French complaints for figures such as the English kings Edward I and II, Diana Tyson

---

[20] I am again grateful to Erika Graham-Goering for providing me with a transcription and translation of the second French compaint.

[21] Even though no direct parallels have been established, correspondences have been detected between the Scottish poet William Dunbar and the Grands Rhétoriqueurs. See Norman, "William Dunbar: Grand Rhetoriqueur" and Bawcutt, "French Connections?" The rich internal and external rhyme of the Rhétoriqueurs is also later exhibited by the sixteenth-century Scottish poet Alexander Scott (c. 1520–82/3).

[22] For example, the poet writes: *Chacun en soy dung tresbien humble vueil / Morne maintien de noir, portant le dueil, / Allant venant tousjours la lerme a loeil, / Et de joye ne fair nul recueil* ("it is necessary for us each to make, / with a most humble will inside them, / sad display of black, wearing mourning, / coming and going always with a tear in the eye, / and make no gathering of joy," fol. 41r).

concluded that these "laments were emotional effusions written soon after the subjects' deaths, without much literary pretension but with sincere feelings of sorrow and loss," and one suspects the same is true of the complaints about Margaret of Scotland.[23] Some support for this proposal is found when one analyzes the Scots language adaptation of the *Complainte pour la morte de Madame Marguerite d'Escosse*, edited here.

THE OLDER SCOTS *COMPLAINT:* DATE, AUTHORSHIP, STYLE, AND LITERARY CONTEXT

Full versions of the Older Scots *Complaint for the Death of Margaret, Princess of Scotland*, survive in two manuscripts of a mid-fifteenth-century chronicle, known as the *Liber Pluscardensis* (*LP*).[24] This Latin prose chronicle of the history of Scotland, based on Walter Bower's earlier chronicle (*The Scotichronicon*),[25] was composed by an unknown author for the abbot of Dunfermline during the 1450s and completed by 1461.[26] The two manuscripts are: Oxford, Bodleian Library, MS Fairfax 8 (SC 3888), fols. 188ra–89va (F)[27] and Brussels, Bibliothèque Royale, MS 7397 (Van de Gheyn 4628), fols. 229ra–30va (B).[28] The first two lines of the poem are also found in another manuscript of the *Liber Pluscardensis*: Glasgow, Mitchell Library, MS 308876, fol. 248v (c. 1489–1500) (G). This manuscript is written in the same hand as the latter part of MS B, and material evidence suggests that it once contained a full copy of the *Complaint*.[29] Although the *Complaint* does not appear in all six surviving manuscripts of the *LP*, its appearance in three suggests that it formed part of the chronicle at an early stage of its history. As such, we can narrow down its date of composition to the period after Margaret's death and the composition of the French *Complainte* (c. 1445) and before the completion of the *LP* (sometime between the mid-1450s and 1461). Accordingly, the *Complaint* was written in a fifteen-year interval between 1445 and 1460.

The *Complaint* is the first of two vernacular poems included within book 11 of the *LP*. The embassy arranging Margaret's marriage to the dauphin is first recorded in Chapter 3, after an account of James I's execution of political enemy, Murdoch Stewart, duke of Albany; the marriage itself is narrated in Chapter 4, followed by an account of James I's vexed relationship with the Lord of the Isles, his children (Chapter 5), English attempts to break the old alliance between France and Scotland (Chapter 6), and James I's Siege of Roxburgh (Chapter 7). Margaret's death is lamented in the same chapter, and then marked by the

---

[23] Tyson, "Lament for a Dead King," p. 374.

[24] *Liber Pluscardensis*, ed. Skene. All Latin quotations and translations will be from this edition. The *Complaint* is given in 1:382–88.

[25] *Scotichronicon*, ed. Watt.

[26] Mapstone, "*Scotichronicon*'s First Readers," pp. 34–35, 48n24. Mapstone's dating, which I here follow, is slightly later than that of R. J. Lyall who instead positions the chronicle between 1449 and 1452. See Lyall, "Politics and Poetry," pp. 18–20 and "The Court as a Cultural Centre," p. 29.

[27] *Summary Catalogue*, ed. Hunt, 2:775–76. This manuscript is internally dated to 1489.

[28] Van de Gheyn, *Catalogue des Manuscrits de la Bibliothèque royale*, 7:38.

[29] Ker, *Medieval Manuscripts in British Libraries*, pp. 862–63. This manuscript comprises quires of mainly twenty leaves, lettered at the beginning and end and foliated (anew for each individual book of the chronicle) in a late fifteenth- / early sixteenth-century hand. The quire containing the initial two lines of the Scots complaint contains only fourteen leaves but a gap in the early foliation reveals that the manuscript did once contain a complete copy of the poem.

vernacular *Complaint* that forms Chapter 8. The murder of James I is lamented (in Latin prose) in Chapter 9, before the gruesome punishment of his murderers is detailed in Chapter 10. At the end of this chapter the chronicler regrets that Scotland has been left in the hands of a minor (the young James II). He observes, however, that *Sed quia in defectu justiciae multi periunt fame, quidam siciens et esuriens justiciam quandam instruccionem ignaris judicibus in vulgari nosto compilavit* ("As, however, for want of justice many perish with hunger, a certain hungerer and thirster after justice has compiled in our vernacular a lesson for ignorant judges.")[30] A Scots poem, known variously as *De Regimine Principum Bonum Consilium* [*DRP*] or "The Harp," then concludes the chronicle. Beginning with a metaphor of a good king ruling his kingdom as a harpist successfully maintains the harmony of his harp, this poem (written during the reign of James II, and perhaps especially between 1455 and 1460) calls for reformation of the contemporary justice system and relationship of king and counsel.[31]

The identity of the *LP*'s author and authorship of the *Complaint* and *DRP* remains unknown, nor is it certain that the three texts were written by the same individual.[32] The chronicler states that he spent several years in France and that he knew Joan of Arc and Margaret. Of the latter he writes: "I, who write this, saw her every day alive, playing with the king and queen of France, and going on thus for nine years" (*Nam ego qui scribo haec vidi eam omni die vivam, cum rege Franciae et regina ludentem, et per novem annos sic continuantem, LP,* 1:381; 2:288). The *LP*'s nineteenth-century editor, F. J. H. Skene, suggested that the chronicler was Maurice Buchanan, treasurer to Princess Margaret who accompanied her on her journey to France, but this theory can be discounted since Buchanan was dead by 1438.[33] It is nevertheless likely that the author of the chronicle was another member of Margaret's entourage, and the same may well be true of the *Complaint* and *DRP*'s author(s).

Rather tantalizingly, Sally Mapstone has drawn a set of parallels between the *LP*, *DRP*, and the c. 1460 Scots romance, *The Buik of King Alexander the Conquerour* (*BKA*), written by Sir Gilbert Hay. Hay was in France and associated with the royal court between 1421 and 1445, and, in addition to composing the *BKA* from a variety of French sources, he also

---

[30] *Liber Pluscardensis*, ed. Skene, 1:391; 2:291.

[31] *Liber Pluscardensis*, ed. Skene, 1:392–400. *DRP* survives in two manuscripts of the *LP* (the aforementioned MSS F and G) but breaks off in both witnesses at line 291, suggesting that the exempla for both manuscripts were faulty. The poem also survives as one of the texts printed by Scotland's first printers, Chepman and Myllar, and as part of Maitland Folio Manuscript (Cambridge, Magdalen College, Pepys Library, MS 2553, pp. 96–105). One stanza from the poem was also commonly excerpted and appears in other Older Scots manuscripts. See Bawcutt, "A First-Line Index of Early Scottish Verse," pp. 259–60; "The Contents of the Bannatyne Manuscript," p. 109. It is perhaps worth noting that John Gower, following in the tradition that King David played the harp, designates harp playing as a requirement of good kingship (*Mirour de L'Omme*, ed. Macaulay, lines 22873–920).

[32] In his edition of the Maitland Folio Manuscript, Craigie suggested that the chronicler and author of the *DRP* were the same, *The Maitland Folio Manuscript*, 2:72–73. In her 1986 Oxford D. Phil. thesis ("The Advice to Princes Tradition in Scottish Literature"), Sally Mapstone inclined towards the same opinion (pp. 15–16, 28, 30), but she subsequently modified her opinions, as outlined below.

[33] *Liber Pluscardensis*, ed. Skene, 1:xviii–xxiii; Barbé, *Margaret of Scotland*, p. 81; Mapstone, "*Scotichronicon*'s First Readers," p. 48n25; *Calendar of Scottish Supplications to Rome*, ed. Dunlop et al. 4:110, no. 456.

translated (again from predominantly French sources) the *Buke of the Law of Armys*, *Buke of the Ordre of Knychthede*, and *Buke of the Gouernaunce of Princis* for William Sinclair, third Earl of Orkney and first Earl of Caithness (b. after 1407, d. 1480) who himself escorted Margaret on her journey to Scotland in 1436.[34] Mapstone has written that "Hay should be given serious consideration as the author of the *DRP*" and that "if the author of the *Liber Pluscardensis* was not Hay himself, he was yet someone Hay knew pretty well, since both of them would have been at the French court together."[35] Similar comments might be made about the relationship between Hay and the *Complaint*. Although I would not go so far as to propose Hay as the latter poem's author, Hay's later literary career certainly demonstrates his prowess for adapting French material into Scots, and he was also capable of adapting octosyllabic verse into decasyllabic verse.[36] This is significant since, as I discuss in further detail below, the French *Complainte* is octosyllabic, but the Scots *Complaint* is broadly decasyllabic. Hay's *BKA* moreover contains several episodes of complaint both in the run up to and following Alexander's death that combine, in a manner akin to the Scots *Complaint*, praise and lament for the loss of a royal figure with sober reflection on the transience of earthly life and need to make a good end. After Alexander's *douzepers* have each lamented his passing, for instance, Aristotle concludes:

> Sen it is sua that he is tane away,
> And him for duile recover we no may,
> I can not sie quhat is best to do þairfoir,
> Bot hald him in perpetuall memoir,
> And pray to Him quhilk well is of guidnes
> To tak him in His mercie and His grace. Amen.
> (lines 18808–13)

This juxtaposition of complaint and counsel mirrors the dialogue of complaint and reason first found in the original French *Complainte* and continued in the Scots *Complaint*. Further such verbal and thematic correspondences between the latter *Complaint* and works of Sir Gilbert Hay (listed in the explanatory notes) are intriguing; whilst not enough to prove shared authorship, they nevertheless suggest that the author of the *Complaint* was someone perhaps not far removed from Hay, and quite possibly known to him.

The *LP* chronicler writes specifically about Margaret in Chapters 4 and 7. In the first chapter he recalls Margaret's marriage to the dauphin and emphasizes both the splendor of the entourage which accompanied her to France (which was in reality considerably scaled back) and her own beauty: "she was a girl of ten, clad in splendid apparel, most costly and gorgeous, and with a fine figure and very lovely face" (*LP*, 2:282). In Chapter 7 he highlights the affection in which she was held by the king and queen of France, and (less accurately) by the dauphin, and suggests that "while in the bloom of youth, [she] almost ruled the king and kingdom at will by her advice, with consummate tact and wisdom;

---

[34] Hay, *The Buik of King Alexander the Conquerour*, ed. Cartwright; Brown, "'The Stock that I am a Branch of'."

[35] Mapstone, "The *Liber Pluscardensis* and *De Regimine Principum*," p. 18.

[36] He adapted the octosyllabic mid-fifteenth-century Scots advisory poem *The Thewis off Gudwomen* into decasyllabic verse and included it within *The Buik of King Alexander the Conquerour*. See Saldanha, "*The Thewis of Gudwomen*."

whereby she was most thoroughly beloved and trusted by the king and queen of France, and her words were listened to" (*LP*, 2:288). As we have seen, there is no evidence to support the assertion that Margaret played an important role in contemporary political affairs but the *LP* author nevertheless follows chronicle and romance narrative tradition in suggesting that Margaret fulfilled the advisory role expected of a princess or queen.[37]

At the end of Chapter 7, the chronicler laments that "Death, who snatches all living things equally, without distinction of persons, snatched away that lady after a short illness" (*mors, quæ cuncta rapit vivencia condicione pari, absque personarum differencia, eandem dominam . . . brevi langore eripuit, LP*, 2:288, 1:381) and he recalls seeing Margaret "dead and embowelled and laid in a tomb at the corner of the high altar, on the north side, in the cathedral church of the said city of Chalons, in a leaden coffin" (*mortuam ac evisceratam, et in casula plumbea in ecclesia cathedrali dictæ civitatis Calonensis, ad cornu magni altaris ex parte boriali, in quadam tumba posita, LP*, 2:288, 1:381). He then introduces the Scots adaptation of the French *Complainte* which follows in Chapter 8:

> Cujus epithapium sequitur consequenter hic, quod super ejus tumbam positum fuit post mortem in lingua Gallicana; modo hic in lingua Scoticana translata, ad præceptum inclitæ memoriæ regis Jacobi secundi, fratris ejusdem dominæ. (*LP*, 1:382)

> Here follows her epitaph, which was placed upon her tomb after her death, in the French tongue; only it is here translated into the Scottish tongue, by command of that lady's brother, King James II. of famous memory. (*LP*, 2:288)

Two features of this introduction are worthy of note. Of interest first of all is the description of the poem as an "epitaph" "placed upon [Margaret's] tomb after her death." Such texts did exist, a prominent example being a lament on the death of Richard duke of York, father of Edward IV, who died at the battle of Wakefield in 1460. Headed in one of its three surviving manuscript witnesses, "Epitaphium Ricardi ducis Eboracensis patris Ed. 4" (London, British Library, MS Stower 1047, fol. 217r), this poem is thought to have originally been "written to be displayed on the tomb itself" or "actually hung on the hearse" where it "stayed there long enough for people to admire and copy,"[38] and the same is true of surviving Latin eulogies for Anne of Bohemia (1366–94), wife of Richard II, which were originally composed in England either for or very soon after Anne's funeral, and later brought to Prague (the place of Anne's birth) by a Bohemian ambassador.[39] The heading in the *Liber Pluscardensis* manuscripts would indicate that the French *Complainte* on Margaret of Scotland might also have been displayed near her tomb.

A second point of interest is the *sequitur*'s suggestion that the Scots translation of the French *Complainte* was the product of a royal commission from James II — if true, this would

---

[37] For a discussion of the role played by queens and princesses as advisors in Older Scots romance see Wingfield, "The Thewis off Gudwomen."

[38] Green, "An Epitaph for Richard, Duke of York," p. 219; Hammond et al., "The Reburial of Richard, Duke of York," p. 130.

[39] van Dussen, "Three Verse Eulogies of Anne of Bohemia."

be the only concrete example of such a literary commission being made by this king.[40] A rubric at the head of the poem then follows: *Incipit Lamentacio domini Dalphini Francie pro morte uxoris sue, dictae Margaretae* ("Here begins the Complaint of the lord Dauphin of France for the death of his wife, the said Margaret"). Here the complaint is once again positioned as being authored by a royal figure, this time Margaret's husband, Louis, but, as Bawcutt has written, it is unlikely "that the dauphin himself composed a funeral lament for his wife," given what we know of their strained marital relations.[41] Furthermore, none of the surviving French witnesses link the original *Complainte* to the dauphin. It is the Scots author alone, therefore, who associates the *Complaint* with not one but two royal figures, thereby hinting for the first time that this poem might not function solely as a lament for Margaret's death, but also as a more advisory piece related to broader notions of good princely governance.

The *Complaint* is an adaptation rather than a direct and close translation of the original French *Complainte*. First of all, although there are a number of instances of almost direct translation (examples listed in the explanatory notes include lines 57, 58, 63–67, 71, 207 and 212), the vast majority of the poem translates the original French text much more loosely and there are a number of unique passages, including Scotticization of the natural landscape (lines 6, 11–12). The Scots *Complaint* is also written in irregularly decasyllabic lines rather than the octosyllabic lines of the original French, and comprises 23 ten-line stanzas rhyming *aabaabbcbc*, in contrast to the 36 ten-line stanzas of the French rhyming *aabaabbbcc*. This same stanza form was used later in fifteenth-century Scotland by Robert Henryson for Orpheus' "songis lamentable" upon the death of Eurydice (*Orpheus and Eurydice*, lines 134–81, quotation from line 184). Notable, too, is the Scottish poet's frequent use of alliteration (e.g., lines 1–2: "Thee myti Makar of the major monde, / Quhilk reuly rollis thir hevinly regions round"), and clearly conscious verbal patterning. Examples of the latter include lines 21–23 and 24–26 with each beginning with "Ger," "And," and "Turn," the similar and refrain-like concluding line(s) of the first five stanzas, the strong mid-line *caesura* and *anaphora* of line 58: "Sic is thi det, sic is thi dwyte," directly echoing (both in sense and structure) line 236 of the original French *Complainte* (*C'est son devoir, c'est sa nature*; "It is its duty, it is its nature"), and the chiastic construction of line 93: "Fra lyff to deed, fra deed to lyff agan." Finally, as Bawcutt first noted,[42] the Scottish poet introduces a number of quasi-proverbial statements into the second half of the poem. Examples include lines 113 ("We draw to deed and deis everilk day"), 161–62 ("warldis welth is al bot vayn glory, / And warldis wysdome all bot fyne foly"), 171 ("Quhat proffyt is it with fortoun for to flyt?"), and line 200 ("Sum ar heire crouss that thaire will syt full dum").

From a broader perspective, the Scottish poem does maintain the two-part structure of the original French but the two parts are no longer equal in length. Rather, after an initial five stanzas of complaint in which the Scots poet follows the French in calling upon a notably Scotticized natural world to weep with him ("Fill burnis, wellis, reveris and fontayns, / Baith stankis and louchis and valeis of montayns, / Of cloudis of sorow, of angger and distres," lines 11–13), a narratorial intervention declares (rubric):

---

[40] Mapstone, "Was there a Court Literature in Fifteenth-Century Scotland?," p. 413. See also work by Lyall, who suggests that the *DRP* was another royal commission: "Politics and Poetry," pp. 19–20; Lyall, "The Court as a Cultural Centre," pp. 29–30.

[41] Bawcutt, "Medieval Scottish Elegy," p. 6.

[42] Bawcutt, "Medieval Scottish Elegy," p. 10.

> Bot nocht withstandyng thaire is mare of this lamentacioun xviii coupill, and in the ansuere of Resoune als mekill, this ma suffyce for the complant is bot fenyeit thing. Bot becaus the tother part, quhilk is the ansuere of Resoun, is verray suth-fastnes, me think it gud to put mare of it quhilk folowis thus efterwarte.[43]

The Scots poet therefore omits much of the first half of the French *Complainte* including its stanzas addressing *Princes* ("Princes," line 41), *Princesses* ("Princesses," line 51), and *Escosse, maison triumphant* ("Scotland, triumphant house," line 61), and its six-stanza apostrophe to Death (lines 121–28). As Bawcutt has furthermore observed, the intervening comment suggests that the translator saw "'fenyeit thing', or poetic fiction, [as] inferior to moral and religious truth, 'verray suthfastnes.'"[44] Such an opinion notably anticipates the assessment of "feinõeit fables" (line 1) in Henryson's *Fables* and *Orpheus and Eurydice* and, although Henryson's narrator ultimately champions the educational (as well as entertainment) value of fictional tales, there are indeed a number of other notable parallels (verbal, thematic, and formal) between the *Complaint* and Henryson's works (listed in the textual notes). We know that the *LP* itself was commissioned by an abbot of Dunfermline and that two of its manuscript witnesses (including MS F) were themselves associated with Dunfermline: MS F may have been copied in Dunfermline Abbey and was certainly there by the early sixteenth century since documents relating to the abbey are copied onto its end-leaves; another manuscript, Glasgow, University Library, MS Gen. 333, was definitely copied at Dunfermline for William Scheves, Archbishop of St Andrews. As such, it is entirely possible that Henryson — schoolmaster and notary public in Dunfermline — knew both the *LP* and *Complaint for the Death of Margaret, Princess of Scotland.*[45]

Whereas the first half of the Scots *Complaint* contains fewer stanzas than the original French, the second half contains the same number of stanzas, but it nevertheless remains a rather loose adaptation. There are, as already noted, a number of instances of direct translation, and several more instances of paraphrasing or broad correspondence (e.g., 63–67, 91–93, 94–98, 138–40, 171–73, 194–95), but these lines more often than not are introduced in a different position or context (e.g. lines 53–55, 63–67). The increased relative length of the "Ansuere of Resoun" in the Scots version also has the effect, as Rebecca Marsland has observed, of privileging "the consolatory response over the original statement of grief"; "The foreshortening of the 'Playnt', so that the 'Ansuere' and its instructional theme comprise the majority of the lament, turns the poem into an actively exemplary piece. Not only are the virtues of Princess Margaret recounted in detail, but the occasion of her death is turned into an opportunity for moral reflection and teaching."[46] Thus a notable

---

[43] But notwithstanding there are eighteen more stanzas of this complaint and as many of Reason's answer, this may suffice for the complaint is but a fictional (or deceitful) thing. But because the other part, which is Reason's answer, is the very truthfulness, it is good to put more of it, which follows hereafter.

[44] Bawcutt, "Medieval Scottish Elegy," p. 7.

[45] John MacQueen similarly suggested that the "style, versification and subject matter [of the *DRP*] come very close to the *moralitates* of the *Morall Fabillis*" of Henryson and suggested "there must . . . be a reasonable possibility that it is Henryson's work." Although the earlier date of the *DRP* precludes this suggestion, it remains possible that Henryson knew the *DRP*, along with the *LP* and *Complaint*. See MacQueen, "The Literature of Fifteenth-Century Scotland," pp. 202–03.

[46] Marsland, "Complaint in Scotland," pp. 168–69.

emphasis of the second half of the poem — and one again shared by the Older Scots poet, Robert Henryson — is the comparison of rational man to beasts and contrasting of reason and sensuality (e.g., lines 63–67). The second half of the Scots poem corresponds more generally to the French original in stressing the notion of life as a pilgrimage, ineluctable nature of Death, and need to prepare for it by virtuous living, but the sentiment of certain passages (e.g., lines 171–73) is notably more Boethian than the original French, bringing to mind the notably Boethian nature of Margaret's father's famous poem, *The Kingis Quair*.

Striking too is the *Complaint*'s use of legal and parliamentary language: Nature is thus described as God's "lufftenand" (line 94) and Nature and Death as God's "diligatis" (line 99); the soul is depicted "haldyn in us as it war in presoun, / Ordant for to purvay for the parliament" (lines 143–44); earthly "lordschip['s]" are compared to the six feet of clay each of us is allotted in death (line 156); God is said to work like a monarch through "soverayn ordinance" (line 173); the acts of Death are "alowyt . . . at the parliament" (line 196); and Margaret has "assythit Deed of all his rentis" (line 207). Such language both Scotticizes the poem by echoing the wider legal and parliamentary discourse of fifteenth-century Scotland, and also looks forward to the much denser legal and parliamentary lexis found in the vernacular poem that appears shortly after the *Complaint* in MSS F and M: the aforementioned *De Regimine Principum*. The king addressed here, but never explicitly named, is James II and, although the poem does not correspond directly to contemporary political events, it nevertheless echoes throughout parliamentary discourse from the second half of James II's mature rule (1455–60) as it advises the young king on the need to accept wise counsel and exercise a fair system of justice. Comparable advice on good (private and public) governance is woven throughout the Scots *Complaint*. Thus, in the first half of the poem Death is figured (lines 30 and 61) as a tyrannical ruler offering neither mercy nor legal redress and God is depicted (as already noted) as working through lieutenants and delegates (lines 94, 99); in the *DRP* the king is depicted as a divinely-appointed "gouernoure" of his subjects (line 26) and counseled to ensure that those he appoints as "deputis" (line 29) are virtuous and well-qualified in the law.

The Scots *Complaint* also contains a notably political stanza (lines 121–30) that functions both as a complaint against the times and warning about the fall of (even just) princes:

Thair is nocht heire bot vayn and vanité,	*worthlessness and futility*
Baith pompe and pryd, with passand poverté,	*Both; pride; exceeding*
Weire and invy, with cankirryt cuvatis,	*War; envy; malignant covetousness*
And every man a lord desyris to be,	
Quhilk has na lest; rycht now away is he	*which [position] has no durability*
And efter hym another soun will rys.	*soon after him another will rise up*
Wyykkyt are welth and wourthy men perys.	*Wicked people are wealthy; perish*
A man weill syt thocht he be kyng with crowun,	*well set even though*
And he inclinde be for to do justis,	*is keen to practice justice*
Thai sall never ceiss quhill at thai bryng hym doun.	*cease until they*

This stanza — and a similar complaint against the times at lines 153–55 — both anticipates the broad thematic focus on kings as proponents of justice in the *DRP* and parallels the stinging attack on the ever-imminent fall of arrogant social climbers in the *moralitas* to Henryson's "Wolf and the Wether." Within the wider context of the *Liber Pluscardensis*, its warning about the fall of even a just monarch anticipates the death of James I that is narrated in the very next chapter of the chronicle. Here, James is presented as a paragon of virtue who nevertheless suffers a *proditoriæ tradicionis*, ("treacherous betrayal," *LP*, 1:389; 2:289).

As already noted, it is not clear whether the author of the *Complaint* is the same as the author of the *LP*, nor is there any evidence to suggest that the *Complaint* and *DRP* share an author (despite their shared frequent use of alliteration and the fact that in a later witness the *DRP* appears in two symmetrical halves in a manner akin to the *Complaint*).[47] The juxtaposition of the two vernacular poems in MSS F and G is nevertheless appropriate; in its material context, both within the *LP* and alongside the *DRP*, the *Complaint* functions rather more didactically than might first appear to be the case as a statement that ostensibly articulates and "synthesizes the losses of two princes" for the person of Princess Margaret whilst simultaneously pronouncing on correct self- and public governance.[48]

THIS EDITION

In this edition, MS F (fols. 188ra–89va) is the chosen copy-text, but on several occasions variants have been adopted from MS B, chiefly on grounds of sense. Elsewhere, there are a few instances of conjectural emendation. Line 43 provides an instance of the latter. Where I here print "Owresyle the sone with myst and with merknes," MS F has "Owre fyle" and B "Our fil." The "f" of both manuscripts no doubt represents scribal confusion in earlier manuscript witnesses of *f* and long *s*.

The poem here appears divided into its ten-line stanzas, as in MSS B and F;[49] in those two original manuscript witnesses, horizontal lines appear after the last line of one stanza and before the first line of another, and on fol. 229v of MS B the letters "cc" for *capitulum* are additionally written next to each stanza in the margin. I preserve the lineation of the intervening rubric in MS F.

Punctuation in MS F is limited to a *virgule* at the end of the first clause in the intermediary rubric ("Bot nocht withstandyng thaire is mare of this lamentacioun xviii coupill, and in the ansuere of Resoune als mekill /") and hair-line *virgules* to indicate that a space should be inserted between words or phrases miscopied by the scribe (e.g., "na/day," line 151 and "Quha/maist" (line 158). Punctuation in MS B is also limited, but more extensive. *Punctus* marks and *virgules* appear on several occasions throughout the poem, particularly in the intermediary rubric to separate subclauses, and elsewhere to mark mid-

---

[47] In the Maitland Folio MS (Cambridge, Pepys Library, MS 2553, pp. 96–105) *DRP* is divided into two halves, separated by a rubric. Each half contains 22 stanzas (*The Maitland Folio Manuscript*, ed. Craigie, 1:115–25). Mapstone ("The *Liber Pluscardensis* and *De Regimine Principum*") nevertheless cautions against seeing this arrangement as authorial since the "balance is achieved at the expense of the exclusion of four stanzas present in *DRP*'s earliest witnesses."

[48] For the quotation see Martin, *Kingship and Love in Scottish Poetry*, p. 93.

[49] It seems to have taken the scribe of all three manuscripts some time to get used to the transition from Latin prose (for the chronicle) to ten-line vernacular stanzas. The poem's first two lines appear in MS G as "He michti ma- / kar of the major munde / quhilk reuly rollis thir hevinly regiounis rownd" and in MS B as "The michti makar of the / major mond. Quhilk reu- / li reullis thir hevynli regiouns round." The handwriting of lines 77–80 on fols. 188ra and 167–70 on 189ra of MS F also becomes noticeably smaller as the scribe attempts to accommodate one whole stanza at the bottom of the column.

line *caesurae* (e.g., lines 63, 90, 93, 146, 151, 183, 200, 202, 208). Following METS policy, modern punctuation, capitalization, and word-division are introduced in this edition. Religious words and personal pronouns referring to Christ and God are also capitalized, as is Death where it appears personified or as an abstract noun. A final *e* has been added to *the* when it is a pronoun, to distinguish it from the article (i.e., *thee* rather than *the*, as in lines 67 and 69). Thorn and yogh are represented by their modern equivalents (*th* and *y/z*), as are *i/j* and *u/v* spellings. Contractions and marks of abbreviation have been silently expanded, as have strokes appearing at the end of words (particularly those with a penultimate *r*) which one would normally expect to end in final *e*. In many fifteenth-century manuscripts such strokes are considered otiose but they here appear so distinctive as to warrant expansion. I follow Skene and MS B in inserting an *i* before words ending *-oun* where it is lacking in MS F, but do not follow Skene in transcribing the rhyming words at lines 166–69 as "detestabile," "veriabile," and "lamentabile"; a tilde does appear over the final letters of the latter two words but not over all three, and as such I do not supply the additional *i*.

COMPLAINT FOR THE DEATH OF MARGARET, PRINCESS OF SCOTLAND

Incipit lamentacio domini dalphini
Francie pro morte uxoris sue dicte margarete[1]

Thee myti Makar of the major monde,   *mighty Creator of the greater world*
Quhilk reuly rollis thir hevinly regions round[2]
About this erd, be mocioune circuler,   *earth, in a circular motion*
Ger all the cloudis of the hevin habound,   *Make; heaven overflow*
5   And souk up all thir watteris hal and sounde,   *draw up; waters whole and sound*
Baith of salt sey, of burne, well and revere;   *Both; sea; brook; spring; river*
Syn to discende in tygglande teris tere,   *in trickling [and] distressing tears*
To weip with me this wofull waymentyng,   *weep; lamentation*
This petwys playnt of a princes but peire,   *piteous complaint; peerless princess*
10   Quhilk dulfull Deed has tane till his duellyng.[3]

Fill burnis, wellis, reveris and fontayns,   *Fill up brooks, springs, rivers*
Baith stankis and louchis and valeis of montayns,   *Both ditches; lochs; valleys*
Of cloudis of sorow, of angger and distres,   *With*
And baith my hart in endles wo that payns,
15   For derfnes and dyspyt of Deed nocht fayns,[4]
Quhilk as us reft so ryal a riches.   *Who has stolen from us such royal riches*
Wes never yit more gret peté of a princes,   *pity for*
In quhome regnyt floure of nobilité;   *whom reigned [the] flower of nobility*
Helpe me to murn and murn hir mare and les,   *mourn and mourn her completely*
20   Quhilk for diseis dayly but dreid I dee.[5]

Ger all the ayre that in the hycht above is,   *Make; air; sky*
And all the wyndis that under the hevyn amovis,   *are in motion*
Turn all in sobbyng and in sichyng soore;   *everything into; sighing sore*

---

[1] *Here begins the complaint of the lord Dauphin of France for the death of his wife, the said Margaret*

[2] *Who regularly rotates the spherical heavenly realms*

[3] *Whom distressing Death has taken to his dwelling*

[4] Lines 14–15: *And bathe my heart that suffers in endless woe, / [one] that does not shrink back before the severity and contempt of Death*

[5] *I who, without a doubt, daily die on account of distress*

	Ger all thir foulis that melody contruvis,	*the birds that make melody*
25	And all thir birdis that syngand heir for luveis,	*the birds; here for [their] loves*
	Turn all thair joy in soro and in coore,	*sorrow; care*
	And help to murn this dul my lady foore,	
	And wary Weird, quhilk banyst as of France[1]	
	The mirroure of vertu and warldis glore,	*world's glory*
30	Quhilk Deed has reft, but reuth or rapentance.[2]	

	God of nature, quhilk all this erd honouris	*who all this earth honors*
	With fruyt and fulye, with herbe, fluris and flouris,	*fruit; leaves; blossoms and flowers*
	Fair flurisand and freche in thair verdoure,	*Flourishing fair and fresh; greenness*
	Of quhilk the fleuvir to the hevyn retouris,	*which; smell returns to heaven*
35	And all the frechnes of thaire faire figouris[3]	
	Yeildis thaim and wourschip to thair Creatoure:	*They render [homage]; give worship*
	Defaid thaire freschnes for thi gret valoure	*Make their freshness fade; your; honor*
	And turn in blakynnyng all thaire lustines;	*into paleness all their loveliness*
	Heil never this erde more with plesand coloure	*Cover no more; earth; pleasant*
40	Quhill we have murnyt the dull of our mastres.	*Until; mourned; sorrow; mistress*

	Turn all in blak that aire was fresche of hew,	*previously; bright of color*
	And in murnyng all myrth, musik and glew;	*into mourning; mirth; game*
	Owresyle the sone with myst and with merknes;	*Obscure; mist; darkness*
	Ger every wy that are of luffe wes trew[4]	
45	Haif mynd of my regret and on me rew,	*Be mindful of my sorrow; pity me*
	And stanche in erde all solace and blythnes.	*extinguish; comfort and joy*
	Turn all atis blyth in breith and bitternes,	*pleasant oats; anger*
	And in murnyng all myrth and melody;	*into mourning; mirth*
	Quhill we have murnyt the dule of our mastres	*Until; mourned; sorrow; mistress*
50	Lat Nature thole na kyng leife heire gladly.	*permit no king to live here with joy*

[Rubric] Bot nocht withstandyng thaire is mare of this lamentacioun xviii coupill, and in the ansuere of Resoune als mekill, this ma suffyce for the complant is bot fenyeit thing. Bot becaus the tother part, quhilk is the ansuere of Resoun, is verray suth-fastnes, me think it gud to put mare of it quhilk folowis thus efterwarte.[5]

51	Thou man that is of poure and smal valoure,	*sorry and small worth*
	Leifful to joy, sone movyt to doloure,	*Quick to joy, soon moved to sorrow*

---

[1] Lines 27–28: *And help to mourn this sorrow on behalf of my lady, / And [for the] sorrowful Fate, which has banished from France*

[2] *Which Death has stolen, without pity or repentance*

[3] *And [which with] all the freshness of their fair forms*

[4] *Make all the people that formerly were true in love*

[5] [Rubric]: *But notwithstanding there are eighteen more stanzas of this complaint and as many of Reason's answer, this may suffice for the complaint is but a fictional (or deceitful) thing. But because the other part, which is Reason's answer, is the very truthfulness, it is good to put more of it, which follows hereafter. (see note)*

And thow knew weill thin auvyn creacioun, — *Since; aware of; own*
Thou makis gret falt in fors of thi furoure, — *commit; through the strength of*
55 All thus but caus to crab thi Creatoure. — *make your Creator angry*
And thou wald have consideracioun, — *If only you would remember that*
Thou art subject till all humain passioun: — *to; human pain*
Sic is thi det, sic is thi dwyté. — *Such is your debt; duty*
And thou will seik to thi salvatioun, — *If; look for*
60 Have mynd of miserabile humanité. — *Bear in mind*

Lat be thi dull, thir ar bot dualinys of Deed; — *Give over; mere deceptions of Death*
Quhare na reuth is quhy sekis thou remed? — *compassion; cure*
Quhy ravys thou, and thou man resonabile,
Finare of forge as gold is be the leid,
65 Off wyt and wysdome, of consale and of reed,
Fra nature bestiall? This is na fabill.[1]
Discrecioune schawys thee deferans veritable — *[the] true difference*
Betueix resoune and sensualité.
Sen God has gevyn thee wyt and knawlige abille,
70 Than suld thou schaw quhether man or best thou be.

Thou sais that this regratit he princes, — *says; high lamented princess*
Quhilk our the laif of vertu was peirles, — *above the rest*
Was tan owre soune in floure of hire fairheid;
And countand of hir bewteis mare and les, — *considering her full beauties*
75 And how with all men luffit and lovyt scho wes, — *beloved and praised*
Quhilk was gret worschip till all womanheid:
Thocht all this warld suld well in wo and weid — *be plunged into sorrow and mourning*
No wonder war, bot quhat ma this availye?
It mendis hir nocht to meryt na to meid, — *does not help her; reward*
80 Bot til hir frendis payn, tynsale and travailye. — *[brings] pain, harm, and suffering*

Thou suld weill knaw that He that all as made — *has made*
As langand governance of His Godhed — *pertaining to [the]*
Nathyng mysfaris bot all dois for the best; — *Nothing does amiss; does all*
And all this warld that is baith lang and braid — *long and wide*
85 He ordand for refeccioun of manhaid, — *recreation; mankind*
Bot nocht forthy that it suld allwais lest. — *not so that*
In heritage, bot as pilgryme or gest,
Of lawest lyme of erd al maid ar we,

---

[1] Lines 63–66: *Why do you rave, reasonable man, / [you who are] superior in form as gold is to lead, / of wit and wisdom, counsel and reason, / [compared to] bestial nature? This is no fictitious statement*

	And to wyn perdoun to bryng the saul to rest	
90	Eftir this lyff, for neydlings we mon dee.[1]	
	He maid this warld nocht to be ay lestand,	*everlasting*
	Bot to renew and ay be renewand,	*become new and always renew again*
	Fra lyff to deed, fra deed to lyff agan;	*From life to death*
	He maid Nature to be His lufftenand,	*regent*
95	To forge the werkis He has tan on hand;	*forge the works; taken*
	For He lest nocht Hymselfe to tak the payn.	*would not rather; take the effort*
	Syn ordand He that Deed suld be ay bayn	*Then decreed; always ready*
	To tak His werkis in thaire best sesoun.	*seize*
	His diligatis dois nathyng heire in vayn:	*deputies do nothing*
100	Oure thame He ordand Wisdome and Resoun.	*Over them; appointed*
	Quhat mycht God mare do till His creatoure	*for his creation (i.e., Margaret)*
	Bot dow hir with the gyftis of nature,	*Than endow her; gifts*
	With al bewteis of fresche feminité,	*beauties; womanhood*
	First giffand hir the fairnes of figoure	*giving her; shape*
105	With plesand propirnes of portratoure,	*pleasing good looks*
	Enforst with Fortoun in the heast gre,	*Strengthened; highest degree*
	Syn passand utheris of gudnes and beuté?	*Also excelling others*
	Thir thre gyftis cumys ay fra the Fader doun.	
	Suppos the twa may nocht ay lestand be,	*Even though; ever-lasting*
110	Thare is na ryches peire to gud ranoun.	*treasure equal to good renown*
	Fra we cum first in this warld mortelle,	*Ever since*
	Cled with this corruptible corps carnelle,	*Clothed; fleshly body*
	We draw to deed and deis everilk day;	*make our way towards*
	Syn mon we pas to lyffyng eternelle,	*Then must*
115	To lestand joy or payn perpetuelle.	
	We ma never wyt will we be went oure way	
	This warld is maid for that warld to purvay,	*as advance preparation for*
	Nocht heire to leif in lustis at all oure eis.	*Not [for us]; sensual pleasure*
	Men wynnis nocht hevin to dance and syng and play,[2]	
120	Bot payn and penitence oure Lord mon ples.	*But [instead]*
	Thair is nocht heire bot vayn and vanité,	*worthlessness and futility*
	Baith pompe and pryd, with passand poverté,	*Both; pride; exceeding*
	Weire and invy, with cankirryt cuvatis,	*War; envy; malignant covetousness*
	And every man a lord desyris to be,	
125	Quhilk has na lest; rycht now away is he	*which [position] has no durability*

---

[1] Lines 87–90: *As to [our] inheritance, [we are] only pilgrims or guests; / we are made altogether of the lowest slime of the earth, / and in order to achieve pardon [and] bring the soul to rest / after this life, of necessity we must die*

[2] *Mankind does not gain heaven by dancing, singing, and playing*

	And efter hym another soun will rys.	*soon after him another will rise up*
	Wyykkyt are welth and wourthy men perys.	*Wicked people are wealthy; perish*
	A man weill syt thocht he be kyng with crowun,	*well set even though*
	And he inclinde be for to do justis,	*is keen to practice justice*
130	Thai sall never ceiss quhill at thai bryng hym doun.	*cease until they*
	The lang lyff is nocht profitable heire,	
	Quhill we be went oure will is ever in weire;	*Until we are departed; spirit; in danger*
	And syn the passage is rycht peralus	*journey is very hazardous*
	We have bot bale til we be brocht on beire.	*bier*
135	Bot syn we ordande ar till have gud cheire,	*commanded to rejoice*
	And we do weill, traist weill it sall be thus.	*If we do well, trust*
	Cryst scheu quhen He rasyt Lazarus:	*showed [this] when; raised Lazarus*
	He grat oure hym, for He kneu weil the payn	*wept for him*
	He suld have in this lyffyng langarus,	*should; distressing life*
140	Never till have joy till he war deide agayn.	*to; until; dead*
	Sen we have heire na ceté permanent,	*Since; city*
	Oure saule, quhilk is in oure body lent,	*which dwells in our body*
	Is haldyn in us as it war in presoun,	*prison*
	Ordant for to purvay for the parliament,	*Commanded to prepare*
145	Till ansuere at the dreidful Jugement.	*reply [to a charge]*
	Thaire is oure rest, thaire is oure rycht sesoun.	*Then comes; time of ripeness*
	This warld is bot a permutacioun;	*an exchange (of one thing for another)*
	We suld it hayt and all that it ma feire;	*hate; may belong to it*
	Oure Lorde refusit the dominatioun,	*refused; authority [of this world]*
150	Sayand the prince of it was Lucifere.	
	The lust is schort, joy has na day till ende;[1]	
	Welth is oure bland, mysdeide has nan attende;	*too flattering, sin; no heed*
	The wykkyt win, and with wraik pass away;	
	Gud men ar lorn, the wykkyt weill ar kend;[2]	
155	Mychtty man counpt for all the gude thai spend,	*account for all the money*
	And, quhen thai pass, quhat lordschip mare have thai,	*more territory*
	Bot as the pure, that has his lenth of clay?	*poor [man]; length*
	Quha maist gud has, nocht heire has bot the name,	
	And blyndis thame that thai ma nocht heire purvay	
160	To graith thaire gait on to thaire langest hame.[3]	

---

[1] *(Earthly) pleasure is fleeting, (heavenly) joy is everlasting*

[2] Lines 153–54: *Wicked people are victorious, [and then] with utter ruin pass away; / Good men are brought to destruction, wicked people are well known*

[3] Lines 158–60: *Those who have the most goods have here simply a name [i.e. reputation] / and deceive themselves so that they do not prepare / to make a way for themselves towards their longest home [i.e. heaven]*

	Sen warldis welth is al bot vayn glory,	
	And warldis wysdome all bot fyne foly,	*only exceptional folly*
	And God as gevyn us wyt and knalage abille	*given us; sound knowledge*
	To depart resoun fra his contrary,	*separate; its*
165	And keip us that we eir not opinly,	*protect; do not go astray publically*
	To mak us till oure Makare detestable,	*[In a manner that] makes us*
	Be nocht in to thi vertu veriable,	*inconstant in your virtue*
	Bot soberly in paciens tak and gre:	*calmly [and] in patience be satisfied*
	For hire, scho thankis nan to be lamentable,	*her [part]*
170	Scho is in joy, as be oure fayth trast we.	*so we trust by faith*

	Quhat proffyt is it with Fortoun for to flyt?	
	Deed, Weird na Fortoun ar nocht for to wyt.	*Death; Fate nor; not to blame*
	Thai do nocht bot throu soverayn ordinance.	*work only by divine command*
	In that scho was of bowté mare parfyte,	*Given that; of more perfect beauty*
175	Of princis cummyng and in to peirles plyte,	*descended; matchless state*
	Hire deed dois al men gret cair and displesance.	*Her death; causes; distress*
	Hir vertu and hir gudly guvernance,	*noble governance*
	Quhilkis garris hir have sa mekil honor heire,	*Which makes; so great; here*
	Suld be till all youre paynis allegiance,	
180	To slok youre syt and gare you mak gud cheire.	*extinguish; grief*

	Thow suld traist that scho was virgyn pure and cleyn,	*trust*
	Born and upbrocht with vertu, ever has beyn	*raised*
	In hous ryalle in till hir tender age,	*in her youth*
	Leyffand but syn and mekyl gud, as seyn;	*as is evident*
185	Dyd never of plycth the pointyr of a preyn,	*Did never a pin-prick of sin*
	Tynt nocht hir madenheid for hir maritage.	*in spite of her marriage*
	Scho schew weill that scho was nocht of parage:[1]	
	Scho mad gud end and deit with all gud devys.	*died; intentions*
	Thus als fer as man may have knalage,	*as far as man may know*
190	We traist hir saule restis in paradis.	*trust; soul rests*

	It grevys God in His he magesté,	*distresses; high*
	Wenand that man is mair of micht than He;	*(see t-note)*
	Quhilk is contrare till his commandment.	*Which is contrary to*
	Deed makis na differens of na dignité,	
195	Of bonté, bewté, na of ryches he.	*goodness; beauty; high*
	His deed alowyt is at the parliament.	*Man's death is allowed*
	Sobris your wyt and stabill your entent,	*Calm; clarify your thoughts*
	For ye wait nocht how son your cas ma cum	*time*
	And have mynd of the dreidfull Jugment.	*keep in mind the Last Judgment*
200	Sum ar heire crous that thaire will syt full dum.	*here bold; unable to speak*

---

[1] *She showed well that she was [like (i.e., superior to)] no [lady] of high nobility*

Lat be thi mane and murne for hir no mare,	*Leave aside*
Thou suld mak joy quhare now thou makis care,	*pain*
Sen scho decest with all the sacramentis.	*Since she died*
Quhen scho was born men wyst scho suld cum thaire.	*there [i.e., heaven]*
205 Thaire is na thyng that ma lest ever mare	
That compunde is of brukyll alymentis.	*made up; brittle elements*
Scho has assythit Deed of all his rentis;	*She; paid Death all his rents*
Hir dule is done, scho as na more a do	*sorrow; she has no more to do*
Bot double hir joy eftir the Jugimentis.	
210 Weill war the wy that weil ma cum tharto.¹	
In this mater it feris no mare to pleid,	*is no longer appropriate to contend*
God sparyt nocht His awyn son fra the deid;	
Gart Hym manheid of the may Mary,	*Gave; maiden*
Syn offerit Hym for oure synnys remeid.	*as reparation for*
215 Quhare synful man mycht na thyng stand in steid,	*stand as a substitute*
He was ful worthy for that legasy.	*worthy enough to act as delegate*
Quha wald mak dule for deed in this party?	*in this (i.e., Margaret's) case*
Sen mony thousand martir and virgin cleyn	*Since; martyrs and pure virgins*
Was put to deed with tyrannis cruely	*put cruelly to death by tyrants*
220 Quhy suld we than for faire deed murn or meyn?	*moan*
Tak gud confurte and leife in hop of grace,	*live in hope of grace*
And think how scho throu vertu and gudnasse	
Baith luffit and lovit with God and man has beyn;	
And think how that X M yeiris that wasse,	*(see t-note)*
225 Quhen it is gane semys bot an houre of spasse,	
Lik till a dreme that we had dremyt yestreyn.	*last night*
Gar haly kirk have mynd on hir and meyn.	*Ensure that*
Thinke on thiselfe and all thi mys amend,	*make amends for your wrong-doing*
And pray to Mary, moder virgyn cleyn,	*the pure virgin mother*
230 That for hir grace scho bryng us to gud end. Amen.	*through her grace she may bring*

Explicit consolacio racionis ad lamentantem.²

---

¹ *Happy would be the man that could come to the same good fortune*

² *Here ends the consolation of reason to the complainer*

ABBREVIATIONS: *B*: Brussels, Bibliothèque Royale, MS 7397, fols. 229ra–30va; *BKA*: Hay, *Buik of King Alexander the Conqueror*, ed. Cartwright; *Complainte*: "Complainte pour la Mort de Madame Marguerite d'Escosse, Daulphine de Viennoys," ed. Thiry, trans. Graham-Goering; *DOST*: *Dictionary of the Older Scottish Tongue*; *F*: Oxford, Bodleian Library, MS Fairfax 8, fols. 188ra–89va; **Henryson**: Henryson, *Poems of Robert Henryson*, ed. Fox; *LP*: *Liber Pluscardensis*, ed. Skene; *MED*: *Middle English Dictionary*; *OED*: *Oxford English Dictionary*; *Poems*: Dunbar, *Poems of William Dunbar*, ed. Bawcutt.

Incipit.   In chapter 7 of the *Liber Pluscardensis*, the Scottish chronicler reports Margaret's death. He then introduces the Scots adaptation of the French *Complainte* which follows in chapter 8: *Cujus epithapium sequitur consequenter hic, quod super ejus tumbam positum fuit post mortem in lingua Gallicana; modo hic in lingua Scoticana translata, ad præceptum inclitæ memoriæ regis Jacobi secundi, fratris ejusdem dominæ* ("Here follows her epitaph, which was placed upon her tomb after her death, in the French tongue; only it is here translated into the Scottish tongue, by command of that lady's brother, King James II, of famous memory," *LP*, 1:382; 2:288). The *incipit* comes immediately after.

1–3   *Thee myti Makar . . . . be mocioune circuler.* The Scots poet here expands upon the opening line of the original French: *Dieu qui tant estes à priser* ("God, you who are to be so esteemed," *Complainte*, line 1).

2   *hevinly regions round.* Compare Henryson's *Orpheus* which refers similarly to the "rollyng of the speris [spheres] round" (Henryson, p. 139, line 222).

6   *Baith of salt sey, of burne, well and revere.* The French poet states, *Faictes aux nues espuiser / Toutes les mers pour plourer lermes / Avecques mes yeulx* ("Make the clouds empty / all the seas so as to cry tears / alongside my eyes," *Complainte*, lines 2–4). The Scots poet expands to include additional features of a notably Scottish landscape.

10   *dulfull Deed.* The adjective *dulfull* frequently appears with the alliterating noun *deed* in Older Scots literature. Compare, for instance, 20.256 of Barbour's *Bruce* (ed. McDiarmid and Stevenson): "dulfull dede approchit fast" and line 17 of Dunbar's poem on the death of Bernard Stewart ("Illuster Lodouick, of France most cristin king"): "O duilfull death" (*Poems*, 1:100). The French *Complainte* has a more expansive description of Death and its actions: *Quant la mort par ses crueulx termes, / Plus murtris que coups de gisermes, / A esvanouy de noz yeulx / La plus du monde soubz les cieulx* ("When by its cruel dictates Death / more grievous than

the blow of guisarmes [pole weapons], / made vanish from our eyes / the greatest woman of the earth under heaven," *Complainte*, lines 7–10).

11–12   *Fill burnis, wellis . . . . valeis of montayns.* The second stanza of the French *Complainte* refers to the weeping of *Lacz* (lakes), *Fleuves* (rivers), *montaignes* (mountains), *plains* (plains), a *Deluge* (flood), *Riviere* (river) and *Fontaine* (fountain) (lines 12–14, 17–19). As in stanza 1, the Scots poet here Scotticizes the natural landscape.

13   *cloudis of sorow, of angger and distres.* Compare *The Lufaris Complaynt* in which the poet — complaining against Love — states that "The blak, cloudy thochtis of dispaire / Ar enterit In myn hert, cald and wod" (lines 22–23).

14   *payns.* This verb, meaning "to suffer pain or grief," describes the action of the poet's heart. In the original French, the poet requests *Baignés mon cueur* ("Bathe my heart," *Complainte*, line 15).

18–20   *In quhome regnyt . . . . dreid I dee.* Margaret is not described as the flower of nobility at this point in the original French, nor does the speaker of the *Complainte* refer to his own figurative death. The concluding comment ("for diseis dayly but dreid I dee") might be compared to the grief of Alexander the Great's people upon his death in Sir Gilbert Hay's *Buik of King Alexander the Conqueror.* They cry out: "Our lyfe salbe bot deing evirie day" (*BKA*, 3.18595).

21–30   *Ger all the . . . . reuth or rapentance.* Although relatively close to the original French *Complainte* the Scots poet doubles the reference to the winds and birds in this stanza and makes unique reference to their singing on account of love. Birds similarly sing of love in James I's *Kingis Quair* (ed. Norton-Smith, lines 225–38).

28   *wary Weird.* This is simply *mort* in the original French (line 27). "Weird" or Fate is referred to again at line 172.

30   *Quhilk Deed has reft, but reuth or rapentance.* This final line is a loose adaptation of the French: *Encontre la mort ne peut rien* ("Nothing can be done against Death," *Complainte*, line 30).

31–50   *God of nature . . . . leife heire gladly.* As Priscilla Bawcutt ("Medieval Scottish Elegy," p. 9) has noted, these two stanzas, addressed to Nature, "are a free rendering of the *Complainte*, 91–120." Here the French poet also addresses Nature and asks it to exchange its colorful garments for mourning garb: *Je vous pry qu'effaciez à l'ueil / Sur terre toute couleur verte / Et porter en lieu de couverte / Couleur noire en signe de dueil* ("I beseech you to wipe from the eye / every green color on earth / and to bring in as a covering / the color black, in sign of mourning," *Complainte*, lines 113–116). As Bawcutt ("Medieval Scottish Elegy," p. 9) further notes, there is no equivalent in the Scots to stanzas 4 to 7 of the original French which address *Noblesse royale excellante* ("Excellent royal nobility," lines 31–40), *Princes* ("Princes," lines 41–50), *Princessse[s] de l'ostel de France* ("Princesses of the house of France," lines 51–60), and *Escosse, maison triumphant* ("Scotland, triumphant house," lines 61–70), and call for them to mourn, and no equivalent to stanza 8 (lines 71–80) which catalogues Margaret's virtues such as her *Bonté, doulceur, grace et humblesse* ("Goodness, sweetness, grace and humility," *Complainte*, line 71).

31–36 *God of nature . . . . to thair Creatoure.* The emphasis on flora here is an expansion of the original French which refers to *[s]ur terre toute couleur verte* ("every green color on earth," *Complainte*, line 114).

41 *Turn all in blak.* The poet here imagines the natural world turning black and therefore adopting the color of mourning. Compare *The Lay of Sorrow* (line 54), where the female complainer describes her spirit as "All clede in sable and In non othir hewe." As noted above, in the original French the poet requests that God *porter en lieu de couverte / Couleur noire en signe de dueil* ("bring in as a covering / the color black, in sign of mourning," *Complainte*, lines 115–16).

42 *And in murnyng all myrth, musik and glew.* The poet's wish that all music, mirth and game be turned into mourning parallels the command of Henryson's Orpheus to his harp: "Turne all thi mirth and musik in murnyng" (Henryson, p. 136, line 135). Compare also Job 30:31 ("My harp is turned to mourning").

43 *Owresyle the sone.* The French *Complainte* also asks the sun to adopt mourning garb: *O soleil, avec moy te dueil / . . . / L'air soit de tenebres noircy, / Puisqu'en mort n'a point de mercy!* ("O Sun, grieve with me / . . . / May the air be darkened with shadows / because there is no mercy in death!" lines 117–20). In a similar context of complaint, but with a different purpose, Henryson's Orpheus asks Phebus for help and begs "Lat nocht thi face with clowdis be oursyld" (Henryson, p. 137, line 170). In Hay's *Buik of King Alexander*, when Alexander died the sun "wes ouersyillit with ane selcouth hew" (*BKA*, 3.18581).

47 *atis.* Oats are most probably used here in a figurative sense as a symbol of health and prosperity. Compare their use as such in Wyntoun's encomium on Alexander III in his *Original Chronicle* (MS Wemyss, book 7, chapter 135, 5.3539–42: "Be his vertu all his land / Off corne he gert be haboundand [made abundant]. / A boll of aitis for pennyis foure / Off his payment and nocht attour [over]").

47–48 *Turn . . . . in murnyng all myrth and melody.* Compare lines 41–42. The complaint of Henryson's Orpheus contains a direct parallel to both lines: "Turne all thi mirth and musik in murnyng" (line 135).

49 *Quhill we have murnyt the dule of our mastres.* Compare line 40. The repeated phrase acts as a quasi-refrain. The echo of line 40 in line 49 might account for the reversal of lines 49–50 in MS B. See the corresponding textual note.

50 *Lat Nature thole na kyng leife heire gladly.* After this point the Scots poet omits six stanzas of outcry in the original French. This may be a deliberate omission, or possibly the result of a defective exemplar. One manuscript of the original French (Paris, Bibliothèque Nationale, MS fr. 1952) lacks lines 95–140, for instance.

[Rubric] *Bot nocht withstandyng . . . . folowis thus efterwarte.* The French rubric reads, *Cy après s'ensuit la responce et consolacion de la complainte cy dessus escripte* ("Hereafter follows the response and consolation to the lament written above"), *Complainte,* after line 180. As noted in the *Complaint* Introduction, the original French *Complainte* is symmetrical in structure: eighteen stanzas of complaint are followed by eighteen stanzas of consolation.

fenyeit. This word in Older Scots could mean variously feigned, pretended, falsely assumed or displayed; invented to deceive or entertain; imaginary; fictitious [frequently with the word *fabill*]; and characterized by deceit; deceitful. When referring to documents it meant "forged or spurious" and of things, "counterfeit, imitation." I here follow Bawcutt ("Medieval Scottish Elegy," p. 7) in considering "fenyeit thing" as "poetic fiction" but I note connotations too of deceit. Parallels might be drawn with the reference to "feinõeit fabils of ald poetre" in the opening line of Henryson's *Fables* (Henryson, pp. 3, 188, line 1), or attempts made to prove that the preaching of St. James was but "fenõet thinge" in the late fourteenth-century Scottish *Legends of the Saints* (ed. Metcalfe, 1:98, line 46). Compare also the reference to fictional statements at line 66.

51–52   *Thou man that . . . . movyt to doloure.* These lines are a close translation of the original *Complainte* (lines 181–82): *Homme de trespouvre valeur, / Ligier à joye et à douleur* ("Man of the poorest worth, / vassal bound to joy and grief").

53–55   *And thow knew . . . . crab thi Creatoure.* Reason's statement that man's excessive grief offends God corresponds to similar statements at a slightly later point in the original French that such grief is displeasing to God (*moult à Dieu desplaisans*; "very displeasing to God," line 217) and against His law (*à sa loy contredisans*; "contrary to His law," line 218).

57   *Thou art subject till all humain passioun.* This line corresponds to line 183 of the original French where man is described as *Serf à humaine passioun* ("slave to human passions").

58   *Sic is thi det, sic is thi dwyté.* This line — in sense and structure — echoes line 236 of the original French. Here, speaking of the ineluctability and commonality of death, the French poet writes: *C'est son devoir, c'est sa nature* ("It is its duty, it is its nature").

61   *dualinys of Deed.* Compare *OED*, *dwale*, (n.1): "Error, delusion, deceit, fraud." Alasdair Macdonald has suggested to me in private correspondence that this word, which does not appear in *DOST*, may have been a loan word from Dutch where *dwaling* is still a current word for "error." Loan words from Middle Dutch into Older Scots were by no means rare.

62   *Quhare na reuth is quhy sekis thou remed.* Compare line 30. Death is portrayed as a tyrannical ruler offering neither mercy or legal redress. Elsewhere in the Older Scots advice to princes tradition, rulers are exhorted to temper justice with mercy. See, for instance, line 1468 of Henryson's "Lion and the Mouse" ("In euerie iuge mercy and reuth suld be," Henryson, p. 59) and line 106 of Dunbar's *Thrissil and the Rose* ("Quhen Merche wes with variand windis past"): "Exerce iustice with mercy and conscience" (*Poems,* 1:166). Right royal justice is also a key theme in the poem which follows shortly after the *Complaint* in MS F, the *De Regimine Principum*. Here, the king is advised "in justice set al thi besy cure" (*LP,* 1:396) and provided with extensive practical and theoretical examples of how he might do so.

63–66   *Quhy ravys thou . . . . Fra nature bestiall.* The Scots poet here develops a simile already present slightly earlier in the original French (lines 184–86) where man is described as *Purgié de divine chaleur / Comme l'or, pour estre meilleur / Que bestiale condicïon* ("Refined from divine heat / like gold, to be better / than the condition of beasts").

63–70   *Quhy ravys thou . . . . best thou be.* The extended comparison of rational man to beasts and contrasting of reason and sensuality corresponds closely to sentiments expressed throughout Henryson's *Fables*. See for instance lines 50–56 and 397.

71   *this regratit he princes.* This phrase corresponds to the French *regrectée princesse* ("late-lamented princess," *Complainte*, line 191). The remainder of the stanza only corresponds very loosely to the original French.

77   *well in wo and weid.* Compare Holland's *Buke of the Howlat*: "The wyis quhar þe wicht went war in wa wellit" (*Howlat*, ed. Hanna, p. 72, line 499).

86–88   *Bot nocht forthy . . . . maid ar we.* People are here figured solely as temporary tenants of the world which must be left as inheritance for subsequent generations. There is no equivalent to this in the original French.

87   *pilgryme.* The notion of life as a pilgrimage also appears in the original French at line 323: *Ce monde est ung pellerinaige* ("This world is a pilgrimage"). Compare the description of life in the Scots *Dicta Salomonis* (*Ratis Raving*, ed. Girvan, p. 185, lines 310–12): "it is spedful to gouerne hyme wysly in this present pilgremage quhilk pasis as a schadow daily"; or *The Contemplacioun of Synnaris* (*Devotional Pieces*, ed. Bennett, p. 81, line 256): "we are pilgromes passing to and fro"; or Chaucer's Knight's Tale: "we been pilgrymes, passynge to and fro" (*CT* I[A] 2848).

91–93   *He maid this . . . . to lyff agan.* These lines correspond to the notion of Nature's *Renovacïon successive* ("successive renewal," line 312) in the original French.

94   *lufftenand.* In the *Meroure of Wyssdome* by John Ireland, Man is described as God's "louetennand jn his / realme" (ed. Macpherson, Quinn, and McDonald, 1:59, lines 24–25), whilst the late-fifteenth / early sixteenth-century advisory *Buke of the Chess* (ed. van Buuren, p. 38, lines 1108–10) notes: "And for ane king may nocht be aye present / In euery place to schaw thaim his entent, / Neidfull it is to haf his luftennend." God is therefore depicted here as a ruler who delegates the completion of tasks to officers throughout his realm (compare "diligatis," line 99). Contemporary readers might have been mindful of periods in Scotland's recent history when the country was ruled not directly by the king but instead by a regent or governor, either when the king was incapacitated (Robert III), imprisoned (James I), or a minor (James II). The *De Regimine Principum*, which appears shortly after the *Complaint* in MS F, is particularly concerned with the good governance of royal officers, especially in the exercise of justice. See *LP*, 1:392–400.

94–98   *He maid Nature . . . . thaire best sesoun.* Nature and Death are similarly depicted as working together in the original French, the former forging life, the latter bringing it to an end: *Nature n'est rien obligée / De soustenir la vie au corps; / Quant elle a son euvre forgée, / C'est affin que soit desforgée / Par la mort: ce sont leurs accors* ("Nature isn't at all obliged / to keep life in the body / when she has forged her work, / it is in order that it be unforged / by Death: this is their agreement," *Complainte*, lines 292–96).

101–10 *Quhat mycht God . . . . to gud ranoun.* This stanza on Margaret's physical beauty is not matched in the original French. Instead, the *Complainte* touches more briefly on her *grace et doulce manïere, / Sa façon, ses diz et ses faiz* ("grace and sweet manner, / her bearing, her speech, and her acts," lines 203–04), observing also that *elle estoit plus parfaicte / Et de haulte maison extraicte* ("she was more perfect, / and descended of a high house," lines 211–12). The Scots poet praises God for endowing Margaret with three superlative physical attributes but reminds his readers firstly that such gifts are not designed to last and secondly that a good reputation is far more valuable than physical beauty. One might compare the advice Aristotle gives to Alexander in Hay's *Buik of King Alexander* (c. 1460): "of all riches, gude name is þe sunne — / To gud name may be na comparisoun" (*BKA*, 3.10054–55). Contemporary accounts parallel the Scots poet in describing Margaret as *belle et bien formée, pourvue et ornée de toutes bonnes conditions que noble et haute dame pouvoit avoir* and as an *excellement belle et prudente dame* ("beautiful, well-formed, and gifted with all of the good attributes that such a noble and high-born lady could wish for" and as an "extremely beautiful and wise woman"). However, the sixteenth-century English chronicler, Richard Grafton, by contrast recorded that "The lady Margaret, maryed to the Dolphin, was of such nasty complexion and evill savored breath, that he abhorred her company as a cleane creature doth a caryon." See du Fresne de Beaucourt, *Histoire de Charles VII*, pp. 89–90 (quotation on p. 90n1; he also cites Mathieu d'Escouchy, *La Chronique Antonine* and Grafton's *Chronicle at large and meere history of the affayres of Englande*).

111–20 *Fra we cum . . . . Lord mon ples.* There is no equivalent in the original French to this stanza on the stark realities of the transience of earthly life and mankind's inability to prepare for the next world.

121–30 *Thair is nocht . . . . bryng hym doun.* Whilst the original *Complainte* touches three times on the commonality of death to rich and poor (*Puissance royal par droicture, / Par coustume et par escripture / E[s]t subgecte à mort necessaire*; "Royal power, by right, / by custom, and by scripture / is subject to inevitable death," lines 237–39; *La mort monstre à tous sa fureur, / A ung roy comme ung laboureur*; "Death shows its fury to all, / to a king as to a labourer," lines 249–50; *Drap de fin or et gros burel, / Hault prince et pouvre pasturel / Seront d'un poix à la despence*; "Fine cloth-of-gold and coarse woollens, / high prince and poor shepherd / will be of the same weight for spending," lines 287–89), only the Scots poem has a notably political stanza that functions both as a complaint against the times and warning about the fall of princes. See *Complaint* Introduction for further discussion.

133 *the passage is rycht peralus.* The theme of life as a journey or pilgrimage is continued here. Compare line 87 and note and also John Ireland's *Meroure of Wyssdome*: "þe way of paradice js / wnknawin to us. And þus þe entre and passage to paradice / js precludit to us" (ed. Macpherson, Quinn, and McDonald, 1:79, lines 19–21).

135–36   *we ordande ar . . . . sall be thus.* There are numerous instances in the Bible of injunctions to be joyful and assurances that all will be well for the righteous. See, for instance: Psalms 31:11 ("Be glad in the Lord, and rejoice, ye just, and glory, all ye right of heart"); Psalms 66:5 ("Let the nations be glad and rejoice: for thou judgest the people with justice, and directest the nations upon earth"); Psalms 67:4 ("And let the just feast, and rejoice before God: and be delighted with gladness"); Philippians 4:4 ("Rejoice in the Lord always; again, I say, rejoice"); 1 Thessalonians 5:16 ("Always rejoice").

137   *Cryst scheu quhen He rasyt Lazarus.* For Jesus' raising of Lazarus see John 11. In this miracle account, Jesus brings his friend Lazarus (brother of Martha and Mary) back to life four days after death. It is the final 'sign' or revelation of God's glory in John's Gospel, and anticipates Jesus' own death and resurrection. Reference to the miracle occurs in the Scots *Legends of the Saints* (ed. Metcalfe, 1:288, lines 125–30).

138–40   *He grat oure . . . . war deide agayn.* When Jesus witnesses the grief of those around Him He asks where Lazarus has been laid and, when invited to go and see, John reports: "And Jesus wept" (John 11:35). Much significance has been attached to this short verse. It has been interpreted as showing Christ's humanity (his ability to feel human grief), His compassion for mankind, anger at death, and sorrow at others' failure to understand that He was "the resurrection and the life" (John 11:25). The Scots poet here attributes Jesus' grief to an awareness that Lazarus' earthly life will never be as joyful as eternal life in heaven. The same sentiment is expressed in the original French, where Lazarus appears as *ladre*, defined variously as "leper" or "pauper" (line 265): Jesus weeps *Non pas pour sa mort regreter / Mais pour ce, car ressuciter / Devoit de rechief habiter / En ceste misere mondaine* ("Not to bemoan his death / but because he who came back to life / had to live again / in this worldly misery," *Complainte*, lines 266–69).

141   *na ceté permanent.* The Scots poet is here continuing to privilege the joys of heaven over those of earthly life and emphasizes the transitory nature of the latter. For the idea of earth as only a temporary dwelling place compared to heaven, see also line 160. Compare, too, St. Augustine who in his *City of God* distinguished between the Earthly City (the City of Man) and the eternal, Heavenly City of God.

142–43   *Oure saule . . . . war in presoun.* The idea of the human body as a prison of the soul was commonplace in medieval thought, originating with the church fathers, although no reference to the concept is made in the original French. See *MED prisoun* (n.), sense 3. In Older Scots, ready examples appear in the poetry of Robert Henryson. See, for example, the "Preaching of the Swallow" — "Thairfoir our saull with sensualitie / So fetterit is in presoun corporall, / We may not cleirlie vnderstand nor se / God as he is, nor thingis celestiall; / Our mirk and deidlie corps materiale / Blindis the spirituall operatioun, / Lyke as ane man wer bundin in presoun" (Henryson, pp. 64–65, lines 1629–35) — and the *Moralitas* to "The Paddock and the Mouse": "The lytill mous, heir knit thus be the schyn, / The saull of man betakin may in deid / Bundin, and fra the bodie may not twyn, / Quhill cruell deith cum brek of lyfe the threid" (Henryson, p. 109, lines 2948–51).

144–45   *Ordant for to . . . . the dreidful Jugement.* The Last Judgment is here figured uniquely as a parliament at which mankind will answer to a series of charges. For other such parliamentary or legal lexis see lines 94, 99, 156, 173, 196, and 207. Compare also (referring to the taking of prisoners in war) Sir Gilbert Hay, *Buke of the Law of Armys* (*Prose Works*, ed. Glenn, 2:152, lines 70–71): "gif thai do the contraire / thai ar behaldin till ansuere before god and the warld"; and also a stanza that appears in two later witnesses of the *De Regimine Principum* (but not in MS F): "Think on þat þow sall gif ane trew compt / and ansuer for thy iuges and thy sell / And wait nocht quhen thow salbe summont / ffor to compeir quhair þow sall langest duell" (*Maitland Folio Manuscript*, ed. Craigie, 1:117, lines 64–67).

145   *dreidful Jugement.* Sir Gilbert Hay also refers to the Last Judgment as the "dredefull jugement" in his *Ordre of Knychthede* (*Prose Works*, ed. Glenn, 3:3, line 39).

146   *Thaire is oure rest, thaire is oure rycht sesoun.* The structure of this line parallels that of line 58. Compare also line 98 for the figurative sense of mankind reaching its "rycht sesoun" (time of ripeness, maturity or fulfillment).

147   *This warld is bot a permutacioun.* In describing the world as a "permutacioun" — a place of constant change — the Scots poet echoes the original French: *Pour nostre constitussïon / C'est belle permutacïon, / Repos pour tribulacïon* ("For our ordination / it's a beautiful transformation, / rest for trial," *Complainte*, lines 336–38). Chaucer also uses the word to refer to the transitoriness of earthly life. See, for instance, "The world hath mad a permutacioun / Fro right to wrong, fro trouthe to fikelnesse, / That al is lost for lak of stedfastnesse" (*Lack of Stedfastnesse*, ed. Benson, lines 19–21) and his description of Fortune, "which that permutacioun / Of thynges hath," in *Troilus and Criseyde* (ed. Benson, 5.1541–42).

149–50   *Oure Lorde refusit . . . . it was Lucifere.* Matthew 4 tells of how Satan tempted Jesus during his time in the wilderness. The Scots poet here refers uniquely to the third temptation (Matthew 4:8–10): "Again the devil took him up into a very high mountain, and shewed him all the kingdoms of the world, and the glory of them, And said to him: All these will I give thee, if falling down thou wilt adore me. Then Jesus saith to him: Begone, Satan: for it is written: The Lord thy God shalt thou adore, and him only shalt thou serve." Satan/Lucifer is elsewhere described as the prince of earth in 2 Corinthians 4:4 ("the god of this world") and Ephesians 2:2 ("the prince of the power of this air").

154   *Gud men ar lorn, the wykkyt weill ar kend.* Compare line 127.

155–57   *Mychtty man counpt . . . . lenth of clay.* The message here is that rich and poor alike will receive just six feet of earth when buried (even if the rich own extensive territory in life). A similar message is delivered to Alexander the Great just prior to his death in Hay's *Buik of King Alexander*:

> Then said þe wise man, 'Richt thus sal it be,
> For all this warld mycht neuer suffice þe —
> The mare þow had, mare was þi covatese;
> Bot sen þi lenth of erde sall þe suffice —

> Quhen þow art dede, þe erde þat cover sall þe,
> Sall be no more bot of thai quantetie.' (*BKA*, 3.17866–71)

160   *To graith thaire gait.* For *To graith* [one's] *gate* or to make a way for oneself; compare *The Contemplacioun of Synnaris* (*Devotional Pieces*, ed. Bennett, p. 123, lines 859–60): "Eftir ōour ordour, gree, and conditioun / Õe graith ōour gaitys for iugement generall."

171–73   *Quhat proffyt is . . . . throu soverayn ordinance.* The sentiment of these lines — in which death, fate, and fortune are seen to operate as part of a larger providential plan — is notably Boethian. Although there is no precise equivalent to these lines and the remainder of the stanza in the original French, they nevertheless broadly correspond to lines 271–80:

> Harer la mort et accuser
> Ne pout n[ost]re vie excuser:
> Vie tollier est son office.
> Point n'y vanlt de [soy] refuser:
> La mort peut de son droit user
> Sans faire à nully prejudice.
> Ce n'est que divine justice
> Mise à naturelle police:
> A toute heure — ainsi m'ait Dieux —
> Aussi tost mourt jeune que vieux.

> Harrying and accusing Death
> cannot spare our life:
> to take away life is its office.
> There is no point at all in refusing it:
> Death can exercise its right
> without prejudice to anyone.
> It is only divine justice
> put to good natural order:
> at any hour — so may God help me —
> as soon may a youth die as an old man.

171   *to flyt.* Compare Walter Kennedy's *Passioun of Christ* (*Poems*, ed. Meier, line 1009): "O Cruell ded, with þe I think to flite"; the Scots poet here imagines mankind "flyting" with Fortune. Although common to Middle English as well as Older Scots, the verb (meaning "to quarrel, wrangle, or contend in abuse, with another or others," *DOST flyt(e)* (v.), sense 2) came to be particularly associated with the Scots literary tradition of *flyting* — a quarrel in verse. See for example Dunbar and Kennedy's *The Flyting of Dumbar and Kennedie* ("Shir Iohine the Ros, ane thing thair is compild," *Poems*, 1:200).

173   *soverayn ordinance.* The adjective "soverane" usually pertains to royalty or to things royal. God's divine providence is therefore here figured as a kind of royal or kingly command.

181–90   *Thow suld traist . . . . restis in paradis.* The original French *Complainte* does not contain as many details of Margaret's virtuous life or any mention of her virginity.

186   *Tynt nocht hir madenheid for hir maritage*. It is here suggested that Margaret retained her virginity despite her marriage to the dauphin. However, in the preceding chapter of the *LP*, the Scots chronicler reports that the marriage was in fact consummated "two and a half" years after the wedding ceremony: "though they were married and joined in matrimony, yet they did not seek the nuptial bed until two and a half years after, after the lapse of which they were of full marriageable age and were put to bed at Gien sur Loire; and thus the marriage was completely consummated in the name of Jesus Christ" (*LP*, 2:283); *non tamen in thoro nupciali intraverunt usque post duos annos vel cum dimedio; quibus transactis, completi sunt in eis anni nubiles, et in lecto positi apud villam de Gien Surlaare; et sic matrimonium perfecte consummatum est, in nomine Jhesu Christi* (*LP*, 1:375). In suggesting that Margaret retained her virginity through marriage, the author of the Scots complaint aligns her with the tradition of female saints and holy martyrs. Examples in the Scots *Legends of the Saints* include Margaret (of Antioch), Agnes, Agatha, Euphemia, Juliana, Tecla, and Catherine.

188   *Scho mad gud end and deit with all gud devys*. Despite the assertion here that Margaret made a good ending, she was in fact repeatedly pressed on her death-bed to forgive her caluminator, Jamet de Tillay (discussed further in the *Complaint* Introduction). Her final words are said to have been *Fy de la vie de ce monde! Ne m'en parlez plus* ("Out upon the life of this world! Let me hear no more about it," Champion, *La Daulphine*, pp. 109–111; Barbé, *Margaret of Scotland*, pp. 162–65, quoted on p. 165 and p. 165n1). Alexander the Great's wife, Roxanne, reminds him of the importance of making a good ending in Hay's *The Buik of King Alexander*: "Now think on God, and dispone weill ōour thing, / That all men say ōe mak ane guide ending, / And pray that þai ane guide conclusioune send. / All thing is guide þat makis ane guidlie end — / Quhen end is guide, na man can find ane lak" (*BKA*, 3.18293–97).

194–95 *Deed makis na . . . . of ryches he*. That death makes no distinction of rank, beauty, or wealth is expressed at greater length at lines 241–50 of the original French: Death is here described as affecting even those of *Plaisant jeunesse* and *bel atour* ("Pleasing youth" and "fair disposition," line 242), those in *Fors chasteaulx* and *haultes torelles* ("strong castles" and "high towers," line 248); *La mort monstre à tous sa fureur, / A ung roy comme ung laboureur* ("Death shows its fury to all, / to a king as to a laborer," lines 249–50).

201   *Lat be thi mane*. Compare line 61, "Lat be thi dull," and also lines 351–52 of the original French: *Je te pris, homme raisonnable, / Laisse ton dueil desraisonnable* ("I pray you, reasonable man, / leave your unreasoned grief").

206   *brukyll alymentis*. Although the poet most probably refers here to the four elements (earth, air, fire, and water), there is a sense too in which mankind is envisaged as made up of weak or base elements, developing the imagery of metal deployed earlier in the poem. For instance, compare line 64.

207   *Scho has assythit Deed of all his rentis*. The image of Margaret paying her dues to Death occurs also in the original French: *La bonne, debonnaire et gente / A paié la mort de sa rente* ("The good woman, benevolent and gracious, / has paid Death

its dues," *Complainte*, lines 341–42). Death is also depicted slightly earlier in the original French as exacting a toll or *peage* (line 326).

211–16   *In this mater . . . . for that legasy*. In observing that "God sparyt nocht His awyn son fra the deid," the Scots poet echoes the original French, *Dieu son propre filz n'espargna* ("God did not spare His own Son," *Complainte*, line 251), but comments uniquely on the incarnation, Mary, and Christ's unique ability to atone for the sins of mankind.

218–19   *Sen mony thousand . . . . with tyrannis cruely*. The reference to — and implicit comparison of Margaret with — virgin martyrs is unique to the Scots poem. Compare line 186 and note where is it suggested that Margaret maintained her virginity in marriage.

221–30   *Tak gud confurte . . . . to gud end*. There is no equivalent in the original French to the comparison here of ten thousand (see textual note) years to the space of an hour or dream (lines 224–26); instead the original French *Complainte* advises its audience to trust in God's benevolence. As Bawcutt observes ("Medieval Scottish Elegy," p. 11) the Scots poet also ends by transforming "the French poet's final prayer to God for Margaret's soul . . . into a more general prayer."

223   *luffit and lovit*. Compare line 75.

ABBREVIATIONS: *B*: Brussels, Bibliothèque Royale, MS 7397, fols. 229ra–30va; ***DOST***: *Dictionary of the Older Scottish Tongue*; ***F***: Oxford, Bodleian Library, MS Fairfax 8 (base manuscript), fols. 188ra–89va; ***G***: Glasgow, Mitchell Library, MS 308876, fol. 248v; ***LP***: *Liber Pluscardensis*, ed. Skene.

1	*Thee.* So F. B: *The.* G: *He. LP* (1.382) adopts the reading of G, but I retain the reading of F and B since the opening address to God is clearly designed to be a direct prayer.
2	*reuly rollis.* So F. B: *reuli reullis.* G: *reuli rollis.*
12	*stankis.* So F. B: *stagnis.*
13	*cloudis.* So B. F: *glowdis*; this is a *hapax legomenon* of unknown meaning. I therefore here adopt the more likely reading of B's *cloudis*, which corresponds to the "clouds" (*nues*) of line 2 of the original French *Complainte*.
	angger. So F. B: *angiris.*
14	*And baith.* In F three letters are initially erroneously copied and then erased at the beginning of the line.
	payns. So F. B: *paynis.*
15	*fayns.* So F. B: *faynis.*
16	*as.* B reads *has* but F's *as* (retained here) is a known variant of the verb *to have* and appears throughout the witness.
19	*Helpe me to murn.* So B. F: *Helpe to murn.* Although the reading of B is here preferred on metrical grounds, F is closer to the original French: *Aidés à plourer ma maistresse* ("Help [me] to weep [for] my mistress," *Complainte*, line 20).
22	*amovis.* So F. B: *mufis.*
28	*as.* So F. B: *has.* See note to line 16 above.
36	*Yeildis.* So F. B: *Yeirldis.*
37	*Defaid.* In F the word *gyf* is erased before *defaid.*
41	*blak that.* In F the word *was* is erased between *blak* and *that.*
43	*Owresyle.* B reads *our fil* and F *owre fyle*, but the *f* is in both cases most probably a mis-copying of long *s*.
44	*Ger.* So F. B: *For.*
45	*Haif mynd.* So B. F: *Of mynd.* B's reading is preferred on grounds of sense.
47	*all atis.* So F. B: *al latis.* See the corresponding explanatory note.
49–50	*Quhill we have . . . . leife heire gladly.* So F. This couplet is mistakenly reversed in B; the order in F follows the regular rhyme scheme of other stanzas.
[Rubric]	*lamentacioun.* F: *lamentacoun.* B: *lamenacioune.*

56	*consideracioun*. F: *consideracoun*. B: *consideracion*.
58	*dwyté*. B has *vince* before *dewte* and the same or a similar word appears to have been copied and then erased in F. It is likely that prior exempla of both manuscripts contained the word *duite*, which was at some stage mistakenly copied twice.
59	*salvatioun*. F: *salvatoun*. B: *salvacioune*.
61	*ar*. So B. F: *as*.
64	*be the leid*. So F. B: *in the lede*.
72	*Quhilk our the laif*. B's reading is here preferred to F's *Quhill owre the laue*.
78	*availye*. So F. B: *avale*.
80	*travailye*. So F. B: *travale*.
81	*as*. So F. B: *has*. Compare the notes to lines 16 and 28 above.
83	*Nathyng*. B: *Na thing*. F: *Na thyng*.
85–90	*He ordand for . . . . we mon dee*. The sense of these difficult lines is largely dependent on punctuation. I offer the readings given here after consultation with colleagues, but accept that alternative readings or ways of punctuating are possible.
86	*allwais*. F: *all wais*. B: *ayway*.
87	*bot as pilgryme or gest*. F: *bot pilgryme or gest*. I have here inserted "as" on grounds of meter and to aid sense.
88	*Of lawest lyme of erd al maid ar we*. So B. F begins *Of lauwast lym to . . .* but the second half of the line is deleted.
89	*And to wyn*. F: *And wyn*. B: *To wyn*. A combination of "And to" makes the best sense.
	the. So B. F: *hir*. B's reading is preferred on grounds of sense.
90	*neydlings*. B's *neydlings* fits the sense better than F's *neydles*.
96	*Hymselfe*. F: *Hym selfe*. B: *Him self*.
97	*bayn*. So B. F: *vayn*.
99	*nathyng heire in vayn*. F: *na thyng ħ heire in bayn*. B: *na thing bayn*. As with line 97 above, scribes seem to have confused the apperance of "vayn" and "bayn" within the stanza.
107	*uterhis* is deleted in F after *passand* and before the correctly copied *utheris*.
113	*everilk*. F. *ever ilk*. B: *ilke*.
116	*ma never wyt*. So F. B: *may not wyt*.
119	*hevin*. So B. F: *evyn*. B's spelling, more familiar to modern readers, is here preferred.
126	*efter hym another*. F: *eftir hym a nother*. B: *eftir this ane uther*.
127	*Wyykkyt are welth*. F: *wyykkytare welth*. B: *wekkitar in welth*. *Welth* is a known variant of the Older Scots adjective *welthy* (meaning "happy" or "wealthy").
130	*never ceiss*. *Se* deleted before *ceiss* in F.
134	*til we be brocht on beire*. So B. F: *will we be brocht on beire*. B's *til* is here preferred.
135	*ordande*. So F. B: *ordanit*.
136	*we do weill, traist weill it sall be thus*. So F. B: *we do weil traste it sal be thus*.
	thus. F: *thuss*. The final *s* of lines 136, 137, and 139 is written as a double *s*, but I here follow B in printing only a single *s*.

140   *agayn*. So B. F: *a gayn*.

153   *wraik*. So B. F: *braak*. I follow *DOST* in preferring the reading of B. F's *braak*
           is perhaps a scribal error for *vraak*.

154   *Gud men*. F: *gudmen*. B: *gude men*.

           lorn. So B. F: *loune*.

155   *counpt*. F's reading is a variant form of the Older Scots noun *compt(e*
           meaning "a monetary account" (*DOST compt* (n.1)). B: *cownt*.

158   *Quha maist gud has, nocht heire has bot the name*. So F. B: *Quha maist gude has*
           has not heir bot the name.

160   *gait*. So F. B: *gate*.

162   *fyne*. So B. F: *syn*. B's reading is here adopted on grounds of sense; F's
           reading is no doubt due to a miscopying of *f* for long *s* in the exemplar.

163   *knalage*. So F. B: *knawlage*.

166–69   *detestable . . . . veriable . . . . lamentable*. *LP* (1.387) transcribes the rhyming
           words as "detestabile," "veriabile" and "lamentabile." A tilde or otiose
           stroke does appear over the latter two words, but since it does not appear
           over all three (or necessarily suggest the need to supply an *i*) I do not
           here supply an additional *i* in any of the three words.

167   *thi vertu*. F: *mak* is deleted before *vertu*.

171   *Quhat proffyt is it*. So F. B: *Quhat fo profit is*.

172   *nocht for to wyt*. So F. B: *not to wyte*.

173   *throu soverayn ordinance*. So F. B: *throu thar soverane ordinance*.

174   *bowté*. So F. B: *beuty*.

176   *al men gret cair and displesance*. F: *al men gret cair displesance*. B. *almen cair and*
           displesance.

178   *garris hir have sa*. So F. B: *gerris hir sa*.

184   *as seyn*. So F. B: *hes seyn*.

186   *maritage*. So F. B: *mariage*.

187   *nocht of parage*. F: *nocht parage*. "of" has been inserted here to regularize
           meter and aid sense.

188   *with all gud devys*. So F. B: *with al gudnes*.

189   *knalage*. So F. B: *knawlage*.

192   *Wenand that man is mair of micht than He*. F: a word is interlined between *of*
           and *than* but it is now illegible. B: *Weynand that man is mair of than He*.
           Possibilities for the missing word might include "worth," "heicht,"
           "micht," or "richt." I here suggest "micht."

193   *commandment*. F and B both read *commandmentis*, but I have emended to the
           singular form to maintain the stanza's rhyme scheme.

202   *quhare now thou makis care*. F: *quhare now makis care*; B: *quhair now thou makis*
           car.

211   *feris no mare to pleid*. F: *feris no mare to ~~conclud~~ pleid*.

212   *God sparyt*. It took the scribe of F two attempts to write *sparyt*; the first
           erroneous version is crossed out.

218   *mony thousand*. So B. F: *mony a thousand*. I follow B's reading to prevent
           the line becoming excessively hypermetric.

224   *X M*. So F and B. The reading *X M* is shared by both manuscripts. It most
           likely represents a ten and a thousand (M), as in the hymn *Ten Thousand*

times Ten Thousand, where it is an abbreviated means of enumerating the saints. Compare Apocalypse 5:11 ("thousands of thousands") and Daniel 7:10 ("ten thousand times a hundred thousand"). The comparison to one hour of a significant internal of time is unique to the Scots translation and so cannot be compared to the original French. A gloss of 10,000 is suggested to best represent the interval of time intended. However, the form of Roman numeral given in both manuscripts is not quite correct — the *X* should have a bar or tilde over it.

yeiris that wasse. So F. B: *yeir that was*.

225   *Quhen it is gane*. So F. B: *Quhen that is gane*.

227   *have mynd on hir*. So F. B: *have mynde of hir*.

228   *thiselfe*. F: *thi selfe*. B: *thi self*.

230   *Amen*. So F. Only F concludes with this word.

INTRODUCTION TO *THE TALIS OF THE FYVE BESTES*

Despite the growth of Older Scots literary studies over the last thirty years, the *Talis of the Fyve Bestes* (*FB*) remains a little-studied and underappreciated poem. It is, however, worthy of far greater attention and scrutiny. Although on the surface a collection of disparate tales, each with a different subject matter, the tales are united by a set of common themes, most notably good governance (both of the self and others), and independence and sovereignty, effected by the subtle and deliberate changes made to source material. Across the collection we find a self-conscious concern with the notion of tale-telling and importance of good judgment (or "entent"), and this is in turn reflected for readers by the challenges posed by often surprising morals. As a collection of tales told by animals it has affinities with better-known story-collections such as Henryson's *Fables*. The *Fyve Bestes* is, however, distinctive in having animals tell stories about humans.

The poem survives uniquely in the sixteenth-century Asloan Manuscript (Edinburgh, National Library of Scotland, MS 16500 olim Acc. 4243), but this copy is defective, and we therefore lack its beginning. It nevertheless appears to have begun with a Prologue (perhaps in the form of a dream vision) in which a lion-king holds court at a beast-parliament; four royal counselors (a horse, hart, unicorn, and boar) come to offer advice, which they give in the form of a tale. Their tales are followed by the speech of a fifth beast, a wolf. Each tale is given a *moralitas*, and a final *moralitas* allegorizes the work as a whole.

Douglas Gray has written of the widespread interest in animals in the medieval period:

> A delight in the plentitude and variety of natural species [in the medieval world] is reflected in the thousands of insects, birds and animals which are scattered over the margins of medieval illuminated manuscripts, in the menagerie of creatures which inhabit the capitals, bosses, misericords and bench-ends of churches, in the crowds of birds who surround the goddess Nature in Chaucer's *Parlement of Foules* and the animals who fill the forest in his *Book of the Duchess*.[1]

Late-medieval Scottish literary culture proves no exception to this rule. Alongside the aforementioned *Fables* of Henryson, animals also appear in such works as Richard Holland's *Buke of the Howlat*, William Dunbar's *Thrissil and the Rose*, and David Lyndsay's *Testament of the Papyngo*. Animal fables were widely used as vehicles of instruction, both on the pulpit and in schools, and whilst almost always short and sweet they often end with deceptively simple but in fact enigmatic morals that require readers (both medieval and modern) to work hard in interpreting them. This is certainly the case with the *Fyve Bestes*.

---

[1] Gray, *Robert Henryson*, p. 47. See also Mann, *From Aesop to Reynard*.

TELLERS, TALES, AND SOURCES: AN OVERVIEW

(1) "The Horsis Tale"

The horse recounts a version of a popular exemplum in which two travelers, here (but not always) brothers, have to choose between two paths — the one fair, the other appearing to be perilous. The wise man does not wish to take the fair way but follows the fool in doing so. The pair subsequently fall in with thieves, are apprehended, and sentenced to death. In the *moralitas*, the exemplum of the two brothers is allegorized to illustrate the dangers the body poses to the soul and readers are urged, as they are in the concluding *moralitas*, and the *moralitas* to "The Unicornis Tale" and "Baris Tale," to repent of and refrain from sin and instead follow a virtuous path to heaven. As Gregory Kratzmann and Sally Mapstone note,[2] the exemplum of the two travelers appears in various collections, including the late thirteenth-century Latin *Gesta Romanorum* (later translated on more than one occasion into English) and an earlier collection by Etienne de Bourbon, as well as Vincent of Beauvais' *Speculum Morale*, John Bromard's *Summa Predicantium*, the *Alphabetum Narratioun* (or in English, *Alphabet of Tales*), and John Ireland's c. 1490 Scottish *Meroure of Wyssdome* (2:141–43). As outlined in the explanatory notes, "The Horsis Tale" bears similarities with each of these versions, but differs to such an extent that none of the above texts can be claimed as an immediate source. It is nevertheless interesting to note that the *Alphabet* also contains the story of Alexander and the philosopher told in "The Baris Tale." Although again not a direct source, the sharing of two tales across both collections is striking.

(2) "The Hartis Tale"

Although defective at its start, this tale begins with praise for William Wallace and his defense of Scotland, justifying the subsequent place he apparently gained in heaven. The remainder of the tale documents the ascent of Wallace's soul to heaven, as revealed by an angel to a hermit in a vision. As Kratzmann,[3] McDiarmid,[4] and Mapstone[5] have each noted, "The Hartis Tale" bears similarities with Blind Hary's *Wallace* (c. 1476–78) (book 10, lines 1238–1301) and Walter Bower's earlier *Scotichronicon* (book 12, chapter 8), but it also contains material not found in either of these sources, including the accompanying angel. Mapstone has found analogues for the angel in a Spanish account of a vision of the soul of Richard I the Lionheart (the *Libro de Patronio* of Don Juan Manuel) and in earlier accounts of the ascensions to heaven of the souls of St. Bernard and St. Thomas Becket, and she suggests how — even though none of these works were a direct source — their "various elements could [nevertheless have been] mixed into the Scottish tradition of Wallace's heavenly ascent."[6]

---

[2] *Fyve Bestes*, ed. Kratzmann, pp. 27–28, 125; Mapstone, "Advice to Princes Tradition," pp. 217–19; Mapstone, "*The Talis of the Fyve Bestes*," pp. 243–44.

[3] *Fyve Bestes*, ed. Kratzmann, pp. 28–29, 127–28.

[4] *Hary's Wallace*, ed. McDiarmid, 2:277–79.

[5] Mapstone, "*The Talis of the Fyve Bestes*," p. 244.

[6] Mapstone, "*The Talis of the Fyve Bestes*," p. 244.

The *moralitas* is rather mixed. The first six lines assert the moral worth of fighting in a just cause, but the final two lines assert the value of peace. As Mapstone again observes, the message is thus "two-fold, but rather blurred: a just cause, and presumably particularly Scottish independence, is worth fighting for, but peace is of infinite value too, no matter what the popular feeling may be."[7] This tale's key theme of independence and sovereignty is repeated in "The Baris Tale."

(3) "The Unicornis Tale"

"The Unicornis Tale" recounts how, in his youth, a boy named Gundulfus threw a stone and broke a cockerel's thigh bone. He leaves home to study and returns on the night before he is due to travel to Kent to receive a benefice. His family and friends convince him to stay rather than travel that night, promising that the cock's crows will wake him in the morning. The cock refuses to crow as an act of revenge and Gundulfus loses his position.

The source of this tale is a twelfth-century Latin anti-clerical satire by Nigel Wireker, the *Speculum Stultorum* ("Mirror for Fools"). The work was widely known in the Middle Ages, and is alluded to by Chaucer in his Nun's Priest's Tale:

> I have wel rad in 'Daun Burnel the Asse,'
> Among his vers, how that ther was a cok,
> For that a preestes sone yaf hym a knok
> Upon his leg whil he was yong and nyce,
> He made hym for to lese his benefice.
> (*CT* VII[B^2] 3312–116)

In its mock-heroic depiction of the relationship between the cock and his wife, "The Unicornis Tale" draws on the latter text and other *Canterbury Tales*,[8] as well as upon on a number of Henryson's *Fables*, including "The Cock and the Fox," "The Lion and the Mouse," and "The Wolf and the Lamb."

The *moralitas* is surprising for a number of reasons. First of all it differs from that in the original *Speculum Stultorum* where the cock is blamed for the downfall of Gundulfus and ruin of his family. Secondly, the apportioning of blame in "The Unicornis Tale" to Gundulfus is at odds with the fact that he was apparently only protecting his father's goods — and livelihood — when, as a child, he wounded the cock.

(4) "The Baris Tale"

There has been some confusion over whether this title refers to a bear or boar, but boar is now generally accepted.[9] The Boar's story of Alexander the Great's attempt to conquer the town of Lapsat appeared first in Valerius Maximus' *Dictorum et Factorum Memorabilium*, a collection of exempla produced around 30 or 31 CE, and also in the *De Ludo Scaccorum* by Jacobus de Cessolis, a Latin treatise of c. 1300 which uses the game of chess as a starting

---

[7] Mapstone, "*The Talis of the Fyves Bestes*," p. 245.

[8] Kratzmann, *Anglo-Scottish Literary Relations*, pp. 94–99.

[9] Bawcutt, "Bear or Boar."

point for discussing social classes and the duties of noblemen. This latter work was translated and printed by Caxton (*The Game and Playe of the Chesse*, 1474), and a Scots version appears along with *The Fyve Bestes* in the Asloan manuscript (fols. 41r–76v), although the manuscript is defective just after the start of the relevant exemplum. English versions appear too in the *Alphabet of Tales* (an analogue for the earlier "Horsis Tale"), and in Hoccleve's *Regiment of Princes* (1410–11). Mapstone showed that neither the *Alphabet* nor Caxton's *Game* has much in common with the *Fyve Bestes*, but demonstrated that there are some similarities with the account in Hoccleve's *Regiment*, including the shared use of "Lapsat" (*Regiment*, line 2304) for the town's name (in Caxton it is "Lapsare" and "Lampsascus" in Valerius), lack of name for the philosopher, similar use of direct dialogue, and some resemblances in phrasing (*Regiment*, line 2305, *FB*, line 315; *Regiment*, line 2306, *FB*, line 325; *Regiment*, line 2309; *FB*, line 321).[10] There is, however, no evidence for a direct relationship between the two texts and "The Baris Tale" contains a number of unique features that focus on themes of independence and sovereignty in a manner reminiscent of the 1320 Declaration of Arbroath, Barbour's *Bruce* and the late fifteenth-century Scots romance, *Golagros and Gawane*. In the *moralitas* the importance of a king sticking to his word — a point first made by the clerk within the tale — is repeated.

Additional Scottish analogues include Sir Gilbert Hay's c. 1460 *Buik of the King Alexander the Conquerour* and the anonymous (c. 1460s) *Lancelot of the Laik*. The same exemplum appears in Hay's romance (lines 4892–5228). Here, however, the town Alexander attempts to conquer is Athens, and the philosopher is Aristotle; the exemplum is also much longer and related in far more detail. The explanatory notes detail how the anonymous clerk's advice to Alexander is matched in *Lancelot of the Laik* by the advice given to Arthur by his wise clerk Amytans.

(5) "The Wolfis Tale"

Unlike the other four tales, this is not so much an exemplum as an instance of tale-telling for false ends. In an attempt to replace the lion-king's current royal counselors with his own factional alliance, the wolf suggests that the king should consume *venysoun*, *wyld meit*, and *gret bestis* (i.e., the other four beasts who advise the king). After recognizing his true purpose, the king exiles the wolf from the court. A concluding moral is then offered for the poem as a whole. The four beasts are here again allegorized as the four Cardinal Virtues (Prudence, Justice, Magnanimity, and Temperance) which should inhere in a monarch.

Before exploring the key concerns of these tales in further detail, it is worth pausing to consider the choice of tellers and the way each beast is described. Before each tale begins the narrator takes time to describe, in a notably stylized manner, the physical appearance of each animal and the courteous manner in which they approach the lion-king. First of all, each portrait focuses on the animal's head, and emphasis is placed either upon their rank or inherent good nature. The hart is thus described as "ryall" (line 58) and "gentill" (lines 127–28). The narrator also pays particular attention to colors and materials — the hart's antlers are "[o]f polist gold and silver birnist bricht" (line 60), for instance, whilst the boar's bristles and hair were "[o]f reid gold" (lines 282, 283). Such descriptions might well remind

---

[10] Mapstone, "Advice to Princes Tradition," pp. 235, 237.

us both of the illustrations and miniatures of animals found in richly decorated medieval bestiaries and also of the use of animals in heraldic art. It is likely that the poet was recalling something of these visual images in his descriptions. The emphasis on the redness of the boar might, for instance, recall boars' heads *gules* (heraldic red) found on arms such as those of the Elphinstone family, whilst the different colored horns (or *tynes*) of the hart might recall those arms where the deer also displays different colored horns (described as *attired*).[11] It is, however, much harder to match up the appearance and description of animals in *FB* with known bestiary or heraldic traditions. As Sally Mapstone has discussed, the horse, hart, unicorn, boar, and lion all appear on fifteenth-century Scottish arms and seals, including (in the case of the horse, lion, and unicorn) on royal seals, and sometimes two or three of the animals in *FB* appear together, but we are yet to find an instance where all five — or even six beasts (if we include the wolf) — appear together.[12] It nevertheless remains possible that some veiled allusion to particular Scottish families or events lies behind the choice of animals. A central heraldic excursus celebrating the service of the Douglas family to Robert Bruce and the cause of Scottish Independence appears in Robert Holland's mid-fifteenth-century *Buke of the Howlat*,[13] for instance. This suggests that a similar story might lie behind the choice of animals in the *FB*, but it is of course equally possible (as Mapstone has suggested) that "the poet is using heraldic images that had widespread distribution not to disguise specific nobles or families but to invoke the idea of innate nobility and importance of these counselors to the king."[14] At the very least, the descriptions demonstrate the poet's interest both in self-conscious artifice and in notions of nobility and governance, themes developed throughout each of the tales.

KEY THEMES: POETRY, SOVEREIGNTY, AND GOOD GOVERNANCE

Much Older Scots and Middle English literature is characterized by a notable level of self-consciousness and thematic interest in poetry and fiction per se, and *FB* is no exception. Of particular note first of all is the poem's prominent first-person narrator who offers himself both as an eye-witness to and interpreter of each individual tale. As observed above, it is likely that the poem began with some sort of dream-vision prologue in which the narrator first encountered the lion-king's beast-parliament, and throughout the rest of the poem this narrator comments on the action as it unfolds. In each *moralitas* he is keen to stress his own allegorical interpretation of the preceding tale (lines 43–44, 119, 269, 353, 405). He also depicts himself as a witness of the unfolding action and offers his initial impressions of it. The unicorn is thus described as "so sweit unto my sicht" (line 129) and "it did me sic delyte" (line 133), the boar is "ane blyth sicht" (line 281), and the narrator "thocht" the wolf's "habit" was "of cottoun gray" (line 370). In addition, the narrator occasionally interrupts each individual tale to offer a comment on the action. And so, he begins "The Hartis Tale" by stating "I hald in bretta[ne] . . . / That ever was . . . / William Wallace worth

---

[11] McAndrew, *Scotland's Historic Heraldry*, pp. 19, 350.

[12] Mapstone, "Advice to Princes Tradition," p. 214, citing Stevenson and Wood, *Scottish Heraldic Seals*, 1:1–36; 2:223, 262–65, 270–75, 365–66, 373–78; 3:501–02, 545–47, 576, 610–20.

[13] Riddy, "Dating *The Book of the Howlat*," Stewart, "Holland's 'Howlat'"; *Buke of the Howlat*, ed. Hanna, pp. 31–45.

[14] Mapstone, "Advice to Princes Tradition," p. 215; compare *Fyve Bestes*, ed. Kratzmann, p. 32.

. . . / And that I trowe be rich[t resoun]" (lines 63–65, 70), and, in keeping with the mock-heroic tone of the rest of the tale, the narrator steps into "The Unicornis Tale" after the cock has been wounded to ask "Quhat will ye mar? He was bot slane or schent" (line 149). Elsewhere the narrator is keen to assert the authoritative nature of the tales that he reports. In writing of the hermit who witnesses Wallace's heavenly ascent, for instance, he refers to the "autentik writ we reid" (line 76), and he ends "The Unicornis Tale" by stating "This was the tale that he tald thar, / I coppyt it with all my cure" (lines 287–88). In this final comment, the narrator most definitively shores up the authority of his narrative by suggesting that he is drawing not just on oral narratives but also on a written source.

A concern with authority, meaning, and intentions runs throughout the tales themselves, and this is emphasized via the repetition across several tales of the word "entent." In defending himself the fool thus asks "quha wald trow a wysman wald assent / And I a fule so sone to myne entent?" (lines 29–30), and proves that his wiser brother "left his awne entent" (line 35); the cock is described as "Clerast of voce and wyest in his entent" (line 161); the shamed Gundulfus as "[a]ne hevy man forsuth in his entent" (line 256); Alexander as "in entent to cast the cite [of Lapsat] doun" (line 315); and a king is urged to consider his speech lest it "suld him grief or muf in his entent" (line 359). Elizabeth Archibald has drawn attention to the significance of the word "entent" in Chaucer's *Troilus and Criseyde* where it is used by Pandarus and of Criseyde "to invite interpretation as an indication either of insincerity or of sexual desire and intrigue," in turn raising questions about Chaucer's own aims in telling the story.[15] Although not used in quite the same way in *FB*, the repeated use of the term does nevertheless draw attention to the way in which the poem is self-conscious about its own fictional status and concerned with the ethics of story-telling.[16]

The imitation of Chaucer's Nun's Priests's Tale and several of Chaucer's other *Canterbury Tales* in "The Unicornis Tale" is part of the poem's self-consciousness, and readers are furthermore forced to pay greater attention to the unfolding tales by careful verbal patterning that unites the different tales, in particular the repetition of key words and phrases such as "entent" (30, 35, 161, 256, 315, and 359), God's "grace" (lines 37, 78), "bocht and sauld" / "sauld and bocht" (lines 116, 416), "sely saull" (lines 46, 123), a "fair" or "farest way" (lines 1, 209), and an injunction that "A kingis word in more effect suld be / Than ony of lawar degre" or "More precious in worschipe of his crowne / Than gud or gold or ony wallit toune" (lines 333–34, 355–56). The royal judgment of the two brothers and thieves at the beginning of the poem is also mirrored by the royal judgement of the wolf at the end, and the king's taking of advice from his counselors here further parallels Alexander's eventual concilliar approach in "The Baris Tale." This lends a certain circularity to the poem that would, no doubt, have been further apparent had the original dream-prologue survived.

---

[15] Archibald, "Declarations of 'Entente,'" p. 210.

[16] Given the discussion of heraldry above, it is worth noting that in one late fifteenth-century Scots heraldic manual (Adam Loutfut's translation known as the *Deidis of Armorie*), the word "entent" makes a striking appearance in the description of the unicorn: "The wnicorn is a strenthy best / . . . / he þat first bur þaim in / armes wes stark in mony maneris, /. . . and þat he had wit in / his entent and in his hed attour [above] all vtheris to cum till / his entent" (lines 1096–11). See *The Deidis of Armorie*, ed. Houwen, 1:27–28.

Notable also is the formal shift in "The Hartis Tale" from broadly decasyllabic couplets elsewhere in the poem to eight-line largely octosyllabic stanzas here rhyming *ababbaab* for lines 63 to 118, that then change again in the *moralitas* to two eight-line stanzas of rough decasyllabic couplets. Reminiscent, perhaps, of the formal changes in works by Henryson such as *Orpheus and Eurydice*, where the seven-line stanzas of the tale (rhyming *ababbcc)* are swapped in the *moralitas* for couplets, this *moralitas* has a notably mixed message. As noted above, the first six lines assert the moral worth of fighting in a just cause, but the final two lines assert the value of peace. This parallels the unexpected nature of other morals throughout the poem, such as that to "The Unicornis Tale." In the original *Speculum Stultorum* the cock is blamed for the downfall of Gundulfus and ruin of his family, whilst the apportioning of blame to Gundulfus in "The Unicornis Tale" is at odds with the fact that he was apparently only protecting his father's goods — and livelihood — when, as a child, he wounded the cock. The concluding *moralitas* also throws up challenges. Here, after the preceding individual series of allegorizations, the wolf and four other beasts are allegorized as the vice of covetousness and four cardinal virtues, respectively, the latter of which must inhere in a monarch. It is, however, not easy to match the four virtues with the four tales. The boar, for instance, usually associated with ferocity in battle, does not easily sit as an emblem of "continence" (temperance, line 410), even if within the tale Alexander comes to demonstrate such moderation, and "The Unicornis Tale" of the cock's revenge on Gundulfus seems to represent the opposite of "magnanimite" (line 409). Thus, as Mapstone observes, "we should not look for a close match between the representation of the four beasts and the virtues to which they are ultimately assigned," nor should we search for an always clear-cut relationship between tale and moral.[17] Instead, the *FB* author should be seen as challenging us in the manner of Henryson, who repeatedly provides his *Fables* and *Orpheus and Eurydice* with surprising morals that encourage us to take responsibility for discovering the tale's true "entent."

Another notable part of the poem's self-consciousness is the thematization of tale-telling at notably significant points in the narrative. The central lines of the *FB* thus document precisely the point where the cock refuses to tell the time of day: "Sone come the tyme that he suld say his voce, / The hour yeid our, the cok he held him clos" (lines 221–22). The cock's silence here, and attempt in turn to silence his wife, contrast with his earlier proud crowing and the singing of Gundulfus, and look ahead to the message delivered to Alexander in "The Baris Tale" and to readers in its concluding moral (lines 354–60). Finally, in "The Wolfis Tale," the wolf begins addressing the lion-king by disparaging and turning away from fiction by saying, "Soverane lord, I can nocht fabillis fene" (line 377) and himself claiming to tell the truth by complaining on behalf of the poor. The wolf's truth is, however, revealed as a falsehood, and in his exile we see what Kratzmann has neatly termed "a vindication of poetry, and of the allegorical mode in particular."[18] This in turn encourages us to think more carefully about the moral and ethical import of the poem's two other main themes: independence and sovereignty, and good governance (both of the self and others).

Themes of independence and sovereignty appear in "The Hartis Tale" and "The Baris Tale." The former's account of Wallace's career and posthumous ascent to heaven draws

---

[17] Mapstone, "Advice to Princes Tradition," p. 209.

[18] *Fyve Bestes*, ed. Kratzmann, p. 45.

upon Bower's *Scotichronicon* and Hary's *Wallace*, as well as upon a now-lost exempla tradition (originally concerned with the death of the English king, Richard the Lionheart) for details such as the accompanying angel.[19] The tale proposes that Wallace fought in a just cause and was rewarded for this after death. In comparing his death to that of the English martyrs, Saints Edmund and Thomas, the *FB* author (following Hary) furthermore similarly transforms the Scottish hero into a political and saintly martyr and ends the tale with a strong assertion of how hard Wallace worked to maintain Scottish independence (lines 113–16). Sally Mapstone has suggested that, like Hary's *Wallace*, this tale might in part have been designed to counteract an English literary tradition, represented by such works as Caxton's *Chronicles of England* (first printed in 1480 and again in 1482), in which Wallace was fiercely reviled. She argues, furthermore, that the tale's appropriation of sources "originally told about an English monarch to the cause of a Scottish hero may quite possibly have been originally a deliberately aggressive and slighting borrowing."[20] It is nevertheless difficult to ascertain whether or not "The Hartis Tale" is of topical significance. Hary's *Wallace* (c. 1476–78), from which "The Hartis Tale" draws quite significantly, has been interpreted as a piece of literary propaganda directed against James III's recent rapprochements towards the English.[21] It is possible that "The Hartis Tale" speaks to similar concerns, but it might equally, as Mapstone and Kratzmann have suggested, speak either to "the period around 1488 and the new monarchy of James IV when quite a body of advice literature was composed or recopied," or stand "as an oblique warning to James IV's policy of rapprochement with England, symbolized by the royal marriage [of James IV to Margaret Tudor, daughter of Henry VII] of 1503."[22] The poem's uncertain dating makes firm conclusions impossible and unwise, but the poet's interest in themes of independence and sovereignty remains undeniable, as we see again in "The Baris Tale."

"The Baris Tale" of Alexander's failed attempt to conquer the city of Lapsat stems from the exempla tradition, but also contains a number of unique elements that focus on themes of independence and sovereignty in a manner reminiscent of other Older Scots literary texts. When faced with Alexander's demands, the citizens of Lapsat respond with the following message:

That quhill we leif we will this toune defend	*while we live*
In sic fredome as our antecessouris	*ancestors*
Has left till us and till this toune of ouris.	*to; ours*
Erar we cheis with worschipe for to de	*We would rather choose; to die*
Than for to leif in subjectioun to be."	
And in this querell maid thaim ilkone boune	*they each made ready*
With ane assent to defend this toune.	*common consent*
(lines 302–08)	

[19] For further discussion of the latter tradition, see Mapstone, "Advice to Princes Tradition," pp. 223–25.

[20] Mapstone, "Advice to Princes Tradition," pp. 226–29 (quote appears on p. 226); "*The Talis of the Fyve Bestes*," p. 245.

[21] *Hary's Wallace*, ed. McDiarmid, 1:xiv–xxvi.

[22] Mapstone, "Advice to Princes Tradition," p. 230; *Fyve Bestes*, ed. Kratzmann, p. 39.

In its use of terms such as "fredome," "subjectioun," and "querell" this response recalls the nationalistic focus of "The Hartis Tale," and the latter two words directly echo lines 114 and 120 of that tale. The rhetoric of freedom and appeal to the town's lengthy sovereignty also strongly parallel Golagros' refusal to accept Arthur's demands of homage and overlordship in the Older Scots romance *Golagros and Gawane* (c. 1475–1508), which originally appeared in the Asloan Manuscript with *FB*:[23]

> Sen hail our doughty elderis has bene endurand
> Thriuandly in this thede, vnchargit as thril,[24]
> If I for obeisance or boist to bondage me bynde,
> I was worthy to be
> Hingit heigh on ane tre
> That ilk creature might se
> To waif with þe wynd.
>
> [. . . .]
>
> I will nogth bow me ane-bak for berne [any person] that is borne,
> Quhill I may my wit wald [wit possess].
> I think my fredome to hald
> As my eldaris of ald
> Hes done me beforne.
> (lines 436–42, 451–55)

As Rhiannon Purdie notes,[25] for a Scottish audience such language is likely to have recalled the sentiments and phrasing of two key Older Scots texts: the 1320 Declaration of Arbroath and freedom rhetoric of Barbour's *Bruce* (1.225–32) written c. 1375–76. The former text asserts the intention of Scots to fight to the death to maintain their freedom, and the same determination is expressed repeatedly throughout *The Bruce*:

> ...for, as long as a hundred of us remain alive, never will we on any conditions be subjected to the lordship of the English. It is in truth not for glory, nor riches, nor honours that we are fighting, but for freedom alone, which no honest man gives up but with life itself.[26]
>
> A, fredome is a noble thing,
> Fredome mays [lets] man to haiff liking,
> Fredome all solace to man giffis,
> He levys at es yat frely levys.

---

[23] The manuscript's original contents page (discussed below) reveals that *Golagros and Gawane* was once included in the Asloan Manuscript, but now only survives in a print of c. 1508 by Scotland's first printers, Walter Chepman and Andro Myllar. See *The Knightly Tale of Golagros and Gawane*, ed. Hahn, pp. 234–77.

[24] *Since as free men our noble ancestors have always lived in prosperity among this people, not bound as vassals*

[25] Purdie, "The Search for Scottishness in *Golagros and Gawane*," pp. 104–06.

[26] "The Declaration of Arbroath," ed. Ferguson and Borthwick.

> A noble hart may haiff nane es
> Na ellys nocht yat may him ples
> Gyff fredome failōhe, for fre liking
> Is ōharnyt [desired] our all oyer thing.
> . . . .
> And thryldome [thralldom] is weill wer [worse] yan deid,
> For quhill a thryll his lyff may leid
> It merrys [afflicts] him body and banys,
> And dede anoyis him bot anys (Barbour's *Bruce*, 1.225–32, 269–72).

In its engagement with themes of sovereignty and national identity — and use of a lexis common to many late fourteenth and fifteenth-century Scottish texts — FB should be seen very much as a part of a distinct strand of Scotland's literary tradition that emerges out of and reflects upon the issues inherent in prior and continuing periods of Anglo-Scots conflict.

In the next episode, Alexander is forced to abandon his conquest of the town after making a rash vow to his former tutor in front of his royal peers. Knowing that the anonymous clerk will ask him to spare the town, Alexander commands him:

> Desyre na thing at me this daye for quhy   *Ask nothing of me today since*
> Quhat evir ye ask that thing I will deny
> And in the contrar wirk at all my micht.   *And work with all my power to do the opposite*
> (lines 329–31)

In response, the clerk both takes Alexander at his word and turns those words back around, using them to his own advantage:

> I thank your hienes and I ask no more
> Bot hold the purpos that ye ar cummyn for,   *Stick to the purpose you came for*
> To sla yone folk and to distroye yone toune,   *kill*
> To do no grace to cast yone wallis doune.   *To offer no mercy in razing down the walls*
> No may ye cheis to lat your wordis stand   *choose to let you words stand*
> And tyne the cost or tak this toune on hand   *lose the expense; capture*
> And brek your word before this riall rowte.
> (lines 337–43)

Faced with the choice of sticking to his word and the cost of losing the conquest, or reneging upon his word and being shamed in front of his peers, Alexander decides to spare the citizens of Lapsat after all.

In the tale's *moralitas*, the same lesson about the importance of a king adhering to his word is repeated:

> Nowe be this taile it may richt wele be sene
> Ane kyngis word in till effect suld bene   *should be of value*
> More precious in worschipe of his crowne   *honor*
> Than gud or gold or ony wallit toune.   *goods; walled town*
> Richt sad of langage suld he be ane kyng   *sober of speech*
> And weile avysit or he said the thing   *well-advised before saying anything*
> That suld him greif or muf in his entent: *make him change his mind*
> Erar speike nocht than speike and syne repent. *Better to not speak than speak and then repent*
> (lines 353–60)

Although proverbial, the message is nevertheless strikingly similar to the lesson given to Arthur by Amytans in the Older Scots romance *Lancelot of the Laik* (c. 1460–70):

> And of thi wordis beis trew and stable,
> Spek not to mych, nore be not vareable.
> O kingis word shuld be o kingis bonde
> And said it is, a kingis word shuld stond.
> O kingis word, among our faderis old,
> Al-out more precious and more sur was hold
> Than was the oth or seel of any wight.
> (lines 1671–78)[27]

It is also very similar to the opening of the same exemplum in the Asloan Manuscript's *Buke of the Chess*:

> A king*is* word in-till effect suld stand
> Mor than the aith of ony fre m*er*chand.
> Alexander he tynt the tovne of Lapsat,
> For rekleslye he swor in his estait.
> (lines 357–60)[28]

That the moral is repeated twice within the one tale demonstrates how keen the *FB* poet was to stress this piece of princely advice, but he immediately follows it with a caveat:

> Or gif a kyng has said or done amys   *if; wrong*
> That to justice oucht grevand is,   *Anything that; at all grievous*
> It is more worschipe till his hie estait
> For to revoke than to be obstinat.   *rescind [his speech]*
> (lines 361–64)

Sally Mapstone's interpretation of these lines is worth quoting in full:

> The implication is that a monarch and justice are separate entities, that a king can be judged against an absolute of justice as much as anyone. In Scottish advice literature it is of course common to find remonstrances being made to the king as the chief representative of justice that he should keep his house in order; yet the inclusion of a similar argument here is intriguing, particularly since it in practice contradicts the events of the tale, where the king does have to keep his word. Clearly the poet felt it necessary to establish, however gently, the potential fallibility of the monarch; but having done so, we should observe that he also shows that the power of correction is seen to reside within the king himself, rather than being imposed from the outside.[29]

We might note, too, that repeated minorities throughout fifteenth- (and indeed sixteenth-) century Scotland led to a concern that the king should be able to revoke decisions made

---

[27] *Lancelot of the Laik and Sir Tristem*, ed. Lupack.

[28] *Buke of the Chess*, ed. van Buuren, p. 14.

[29] Mapstone, "*The Talis of the Fyve Bestes*," p. 248.

during his youth once he assumed adult power. This again need not imply that the *moralitas* to "The Baris Tale" held any particular topical significance, but it may be that the poem had renewed significance for its scribe, John Asloan, when copied sometime between c. 1513 and 1530 — either during the minority of James V, or very early in his adult rule.

The advice to princes elements of "The Baris Tale" are just one instance of a concern with good governance — both private and public. With regard to the former — rule of the self — we find several instances of characters seemingly unable to govern themselves, including the two brothers in "The Horsis Tale," the fool "[t]hat with no ressoun rewlit wald . . . be" (line 25) and the wiseman who "left the wit that God gaf him of grace" for "affectioun naturale of his blud" (brotherly love) (lines 37, 22); Gundulfus and his friends who mistakenly place their trust in the cock being able to wake them up and fill themselves with so much "michti ale and wyne" that they "slepis as ony swyne" (lines 213–14); and Alexander who, as we have already seen, makes a rash vow and is quick to anger in response to the citizens of Lapsat ("he was amovit so," line 309). This latter example reminds us of the close relationship between self and public governance — an ability to govern the former often being indicative of an inability to govern others — and it is therefore no surprise to find a complementary concern across the poem with good public governance. Small scale examples of public governance include the "lord for his regioun" who died "[i]n his defence" (lines 107–08) and was seen ascending to heaven with Wallace in "The Hartis Tale," as well as the depiction of the cock as lord of his own particular domestic space in "The Unicornis Tale" (lines 172–74). The latter tale's rather surprising *moralitas* is also directly addressed to those who hold a position of power and responsibility for others. Here the *FB* author challenges his readers and offers the cock as a type of the poor who suffer under the oppression of tyrannous rulers. As Mapstone suggests, however, the fact that the story is set in Kent (line 135) ensures that it again bears no obvious direct relationship to contemporary Scottish politics.[30]

After "The Baris Tale," the poem ends on a strongly advisory note in "The Wolfis Tale" and concluding *moralitas*. In the former tale, Alexander was redeemed when he showed himself able to accept advice from his former tutor and royal peers, and in the final tale it appears as though the lion-king has similarly learned from the tales told by his royal peers. After listening carefully to the wolf's complaint, the king realizes that the wolf is urging him to replace ("ete," line 390) the members of his council (the four other beasts) with his own faction of wolves. After consulting them, and learning further that it is in fact the wolf and his allies who are ravaging the realm, the king exiles the wolf and the poem segues neatly into the concluding *moralitas* which impresses the importance of a king eschewing covetousness and espousing the four Cardinal Virtues. This time the neat juxtaposition of tale and moral suggests both that the king is receiving appropriate advice from his counselors, and also that he contains within himself the capacity for self-governance and regulation. As such, the poem concludes on a strikingly positive note with an image of good self and public governance.

As with the other elements of advice to princes in the *FB*, it is possible that this final episode bears some kind of topical importance. The factional challenge posed to the king by the wolf and his allies could speak to several episodes in fifteenth-century Scottish history when the monarch was challenged by powerful members of the nobility — one thinks, for

---

[30] Mapstone, *"The Talis of the Fyve Bestes,"* p. 246.

instance, of the magnate rebellion against James III in 1482, known as the Lauder Bridge crisis, or even that of 1488, leading to James III's death, where the rebels attracted support of the future James IV,[31] and it is also possible that the wolf's disaffection with the lion-king's counselors — described as his "cosingis" or kin (line 390) — might refer to some specific anxieties about the members of a king's council, but such topicality (if intended) is certainly never pursued and the poem ends, as do the previous *moralitates*, on a largely universal note, by urging the need to prepare well in this life for the next. As such, we might follow Sally Mapstone and "conclude that the poem is deliberately generalized in much of its advice, though distinguished by its nationalism, and not aimed at a particular monarch or a particular state of events."[32]

DATE AND AUTHORSHIP

The above discussion has made clear that whilst the poem may speak to particular events in late fifteenth-century Scottish politics, the generalized tone of its advice and enigmatic heraldic references suggest that it has no firm desire to do so. As such, there is very little internal evidence to help us date the poem, and just as little external evidence. A rough *terminus a quo* of 1476–78 might be established from the poem's use of Hary's *Wallace*, and it was certainly composed before its copying into the Asloan manuscript sometime between 1513 and 1530, but it is difficult to be much more precise that this. Parallels with other Older Scots works such as Henryson's *Fables* and *Orpheus and Eurydice* (c. 1470s–90s), *Lancelot of the Laik* (c. 1460–70), *Golagros and Gawane* (c. 1475–1508) and *The Buke of the Chess* (late fifteenth /early sixteenth century) are suggestive, but since none of these works can themselves be dated with any certainty, we can best position *FB* within a 40-year window of the last two decades of the fifteenth century and the first two decades of the sixteenth. A more specific dating must await further textual and linguistic study.

The poem's authorship is similarly unknown but a number of parallels have been detected between it and another poem in the Asloan manuscript, *The Buke of the Chess* (*BC*).[33] This late fifteenth- /early sixteenth-century text is a Scots verse translation of Jacobus de Cessolis' *De Ludo Scaccorum*, a Latin treatise of c. 1300 which uses the game of chess as a starting point for discussing social classes and the duties of noblemen. In addition to sharing a concern with advice to princes, both works also contain the exemplum (albeit defective in *BC*) of Alexander's failed attempt to conquer the town of Lapsat, as well as a penchant for parataxis, and use of similar phrasing:

- Takin thai war . . . . (*FB*, line 10)
  Takyne he was (*BC*, line 121)[34]

- Nowe be this tale ye sall wele understand (*FB*, line 269)
  Be thir thre ōe sall weile vnderstand (*BC*, line 1570)

---

[31] Macdougall, *James III*, pp. 162–63, 319–38.

[32] Mapstone, "*The Talis of the Fyve Bestes*," p. 247.

[33] *Fyve Bestes*, ed. Kratzmann, p. 27; Mapstone, "Advice to Princes Tradition," pp. 250–51.

[34] Quotations from *BC* in the list are taken from *Buke of the Chess*, ed. van Buuren, pp. 7, 54, 12, 6.

- Thir worthy folk war avysit sone (*FB*, lines 299–300)
  This worthy prince he was avysit sone (*BC*, line 282)[35]

- Erar we cheis with worschipe for to de
  Than for to leif in subjectioun to be (*FB*, lines 305–06)

  . . . erar for to de
  Than for to leif and to behald and se (*BC*, lines 111–12)

- Now be this wolf schortly be myne avys (*FB*, line 405)
  . . . be myne awys (*BC*, line 97)

Mapstone also observes that the only instances in the *Dictionary of the Older Scottish Tongue* of the phrase "in till / to effect" occur in the Lapsat exemplum in *FB* (line 354) and *BC* (line 357) and that the Prologue to *BC* "has a slightly neo-Chaucerian or neo-Lydgatian tone, which, though not the adept mimicry of the unicorn's tale, might again prompt the suggestion of common authorship with *The Talis of the Fyve Bestes*."[36] The influence of Chaucer is, however, commonly detected across much Older Scots literature, and short parallel phrases are a slippery basis on which to base common authorship. As such, the similarities between *FB* and *BC* can — for now — be taken no further, but they remain tantalizing examples of the correspondences one can detect between works that survive in the same manuscript witness.

MANUSCRIPT CONTEXT

FB appears on fols. 229r–35v of the Asloan Manuscript, after Richard Holland's *Buke of the Howlat* (fols. 213r–28v) and before Henryson's "The Two Mice" (fols. 236r–39v). There is a leaf missing after the *Howlat*, so we lack the prologue with which *FB* most probably began and the beginning of "The Horsis Tale." A good number of lines in "The Hartis Tale" are also lost or defective as a result of a tear and subsequent loss of most of the top half of fol. 230.

The manuscript's 307 surviving leaves are now individually mounted within a nineteenth-century gold-tooled leather binding (411 x 300mm), identified on the spine as 'SCOTTISH / TRACTS / IN PROSE & VERSE / MS. TEMP. JAC. V.' The original pages are 235 x 170mm wide, and text throughout is written in a single column of 29–34 lines, with no frame or guide-lines. The written space is 200–15 x 125–50mm (prose) / 95–100mm (verse). No catchwords or quire signatures survive but Cunningham successfully reconstructed the collation of the volume's surviving leaves from an analysis of its different watermarked papers: i^{16}, $ii–vi^{12}$, vii^{16}, $viii^{16(-16)}$, ix^{16}, $x^{16(-1, 5, 12, 16)}$, xi^{14}, $xiii–xiv^{16}$, $xv^{16(-6)}$, xvi^{16}, $xvii^{16\ (-1,\ 16)}$, $xviii–xix^{16}$, xix^{16}, $xx^{16\ (-1,\ 16)}$, xxi^{16}.[37] Soiled pages at the front and back of gatherings suggest that they were once unbound for quite some time.

The manuscript contains two series of contents pages, one (fol. i) in the hand of a later owner, Alexander Boswell (1775–1822), the other (fols. iii–v) in the hand of the manuscript's

---

[35] In these instances both texts share the same rhyming word, "done" in their previous lines.

[36] Mapstone, "Advice to Princes Tradition," pp. 236, 254.

[37] Cunningham, "The Asloan Manuscript," pp. 121–27.

scribe, John Asloan.[38] The latter contains 71 numbered items,[39] roughly divided into prose in the first half of the manuscript and verse in the second. 34 items are now lost, and seven are imperfect.

The scribe, John Asloan, signs fols. 40v, 76v, 92v, 166v, 209v, 228v, 235v, 290r, and 300v. The entire manuscript is in his hand, with the exception of fol. 53 which was replaced in the seventeenth century, and fols. 137r–50v containing *The Spectacle of Luf*, signed "per M G Myll." Asloan's career has been thoroughly researched by Catherine van Buuren.[40] He was active in Edinburgh in the first half of the sixteenth century and appears in legal documents between 1494/95 and 1532 as both a witness and notary public. His hand appears elsewhere on eleven folios of the First Edinburgh Manuscript of Andrew of Wyntoun's *Original Chronicle* (c. 1408–20) in the National Library of Scotland, MS Advocates' 19.2.3, and on some 80 folios of Oxford, Bodleian Library, MS Douce 148. This latter manuscript is one of two witnesses of the *Scottish Troy Book* (a now-defective late fourteenth-/ early fifteenth-century translation of Guido delle Colonne's *Historia Destructionis Troiae*), and a colophon in Asloan's hand on its final page reads: "Heir endis the sege of troye / writtin & mendit at the Instance of ane honourable chaplane sir Thomas / ewyn in Edinburgh."[41] Asloan's hand was also associated by van Buuren with London, British Library, Harley MS 4700 (a compendia of medieval Scottish law),[42] and with the Wemyss Castle manuscript of Wyntoun's *Chronicle*,[43] but Hanna has recently doubted the former attribution and remains uncertain about the second.[44]

Following his reconstruction of the manuscript's gatherings, Cunningham suggested that there "is a remarkably good correlation between the inferred gatherings . . . and the items of the manuscript"[45]; with the exception of the occasional "filler [items]," "only related material appears in the same gathering or group of gatherings."[46] He posited that "this correlation was maintained in the parts [of the manuscript] now lost" and concluded that Asloan's manuscript therefore "consisted of a series of more or less independent fascicles" which remained separate for some time before being bound together in an organized fashion.[47] Van Buuren by contrast suggested that "Asloan, or his exemplar, copied the items as they became available to him."[48] The reality is most probably somewhere in between. As Mapstone states, "[i]t *is* quite true that not all the materials in Asloan's MS follow a

---

[38] *Asloan Manuscript*, ed. Craigie, 1:xi–xv.

[39] Items i–xii are part of the same text, xii (bis) has to be added, and liiii removed.

[40] Van Buuren, "John Asloan, an Edinburgh Scribe"; *The Buke of the Sevyne Sagis*, ed. van Buuren, pp. 26–30; "John Asloan and his Manuscript"; *Buke of the Chess*, ed. van Buuren, pp. xiii–xvi.

[41] Wingfield, "Towards an Edition of the *Scottish Troy Book*."

[42] Van Buuren, "John Asloan, an Edinburgh Scribe," p. 371.

[43] Van Buuren, *The Buke of the Sevyne Sagis*, p. 27.

[44] Holland, *The Buke of the Howlat*, ed. Hanna, p. 8.

[45] Cunningham, "The Asloan Manuscript," p. 128.

[46] Cunningham, "The Asloan Manuscript," p. 129.

[47] Cunningham, "The Asloan Manuscript," p. 129.

[48] Van Buuren, "John Asloan and his Manuscript," pp. 49–50.

discernible patterning. It seems most probable, however, that the organization of his MS reflects a combination of the calculated and the contingent."[49]

A discernible pattern — or at least common grouping of material — is apparent in the gatherings surrounding *FB*. The poem appears in Cunningham's reconstructed quire 11, where it is followed in the same quire by Henryson's "Two Mice" and *The Crying of a Play*, and in the next quire by Henryson's *Orpheus and Eurydice* and the anonymous *Thre Prestis of Peblis*. *FB* was preceded in quire 10 by Holland's *Buke of the Howlat*, which, in the manuscript's original form, was itself preceded by a number of Henryson's other *Fables* (including "The Paddock and the Mouse," "The Preaching of the Swallow," "Lion and the Mouse," "Fox and the Wolf," and "Trial of the Fox"), *Colkelbie Sow* (a comic tale about a peasant Colkebie and his sow, and the three pennies that resulted from her sale), and unattributed and now-lost "Buke of þe þe otter and þe ele," plus a couple of filler lyrics, and Dunbar's *Flyting*. With the exception of the latter three items, and *Crying of a Play*, the other items cohere together very well. This section of the manuscript — which seems to have "formed a core to Asloan's book"[50] — comprises a sequence of fables, many of them, like *FB*, involving animals and tales-within-tales, and a number of these fables are further concerned, again like *FB*, with good governance, either self or public. Looking just at the works of Henryson, *Orpheus and Eurydice* contains a number of unique elements that present the young king Orpheus as a king unable to control his private emotions and therefore his public realm, whilst in the central stanza of the "Lion and the Mouse" a mouse advises the tyrannical lion that "In euerie iuge mercy and reuth suld be" (line 1468); the moral to the "Two Mice" counsels against greed and advises that one be content with "small possessioun" (lines 372, 380, 388, 396); and that to the "Fox and the Wolf" advises on the need to repent of one's sins and be ready for death. "The Trial of the Fox" furthermore contains a beast-parliament headed by a lion-king, akin to that in *FB*, whilst the "Preaching of the Swallow" and "Paddock and the Mouse" address the need for prudence and the tension between the body and soul, a theme also explored in "The Horsis Tale." Indeed, the explanatory notes to this edition make clear just how many parallels there are between *FB* and Henryson's works, both thematically and structurally, including a concern with social justice and what appears at first glance to be an apparent disconnect between tale and moral.

Good self- and public-governance are themes addressed too in *The Thre Prestis of Peblis*, in which, as part of a story-telling competition, three priests (Masters John, Archibald, and William) each tell "stories dealing with the subjects of good governance and royal amorousness";[51] Master John thus tells of a king who summons a parliament to discover the cause of the ills affecting his realm. The same themes appear as well in Holland's *Buke of the Howlat*, a darkly comic tale (c. 1447–52) of an owl's pride and fall. In this poem, we find too a bird-parliament and a central heraldic excursus celebrating (in a not entirely unambiguous fashion) the service of the Douglas family to Robert Bruce and the cause of

---

[49] Mapstone, "Introduction: Older Scots Literature and the Sixteenth Century," p. 177 (italics Mapstone's).

[50] Holland, *The Buke of the Howlat*, ed. Hanna, p. 4. I would note too that all of the surviving items in this section of the manuscript were copied on the same paperstock, and it is likely that those missing items were too.

[51] See Martin, *Kingship and Love*, pp. 103–29; quotation on p. 104).

Scottish Independence.[52] Even though the heraldic symbolism perhaps lying behind *FB* cannot be reconstructed it is, as Sally Mapstone has remarked, nevertheless "striking that two works so closely positioned in one manuscript should share such a number of features,"[53] and even more striking that *FB* should have so much in common with those other texts immediately surrounding it.

THIS EDITION

The *Fyve Bestes* has been edited on three previous occasions.[54] It was first printed in 1885 by J. Small in his edition of David Laing's *Select Remains of the Ancient Popular and Romance Poetry of Scotland*, and then as part of W. A. Craigie's two-volume edition of the Asloan Manuscript.[55] Gregory Kratzmann provided the first critical edition when he edited the poem alongside *Colkelbie Sow* (from the Bannatyne Manuscript: Edinburgh, National Library of Scotland, Advocates' MS 1.1.6).[56] This edition is much indebted to his astute critical commentary.

Following METS practice, modern punctuation, capitalization, and word-division are introduced in this edition. Thorn and yogh are represented by their modern equivalents (*th* and *y*), as are *i/j* and *u/v/w* spellings, and contractions and marks of abbreviation have been silently expanded.

Several features of Asloan's scribal practice are worthy of additional note:

- According to Hanna, "Craigie universally expanded *þ* to represent the modern words 'their' and 'there' as *þair*," but since the full form appears elsewhere as *þar* I follow Hanna in expanding to this form (here represented as *thar*).[57]

- As Hanna and van Buuren note,[58] a back-curving loop or curl connected with the previous letter stands customarily for *-er* at the end of a word, and also within. However, as Hanna also observes, there is ambiguity surrounding Asloan's practice, such that "this loop appears virtually universally and indicates almost any combination of vowel + *r*."[59] We find apparent inconsistency too between abbreviated and full forms. *Ever* and *never*, for instance, when abbreviated both alone and in compound forms appear to be spelled *ever* and *never* but the former

---

[52] For further discussion of this context, see Riddy, "Dating *The Book of the Howlat*"; Stewart, "Holland's 'Howlat'"; Holland, *The Buke of the Howlat*, ed. Hanna, pp. 31–45.

[53] Mapstone, "Advice to Princes Tradition," p. 213.

[54] "The Unicornis Tale" appears too in *The Oxford Book of Late Medieval Verse and Prose*, ed. Gray, pp. 156–59.

[55] *The Asloan Manuscript*, ed. Craigie, 2:127–40.

[56] *Fyve Bestes*, ed. Kratzmann, pp. 89–103.

[57] Holland, *The Buke of the Howlat*, ed. Hanna, p. 55.

[58] Holland, *The Buke of the Howlat*, ed. Hanna, p. 55; *Buke of the Chess*, ed. van Buuren, p. cxliii; *The Buke of the Sevyne Sagis*, ed. van Buuren, p. 203.

[59] Holland, *The Buke of the Howlat*, ed. Hanna, p. 55.

appears in unabbreviated form as *evir*. In this edition I follow Craigie and van Buuren in adopting *ever* and *never* for all abbreviated forms.[60]

- Asloan is fond of using a flourished *r*, often at the end of a line, but following the editorial practices of Hanna and van Buuren, this is treated as otiose and so not expanded to *re*.[61] On occasion horizontal or curved lines (usually used to indicate the absence of *n* or *m*) appear above *-ioun*; these are again treated as otiose.

- Long *s* has been printed as *s*; *ff* at the beginning of a line is rendered by *F*.

- ß, most often found in word-final position, is transcribed as *s*. However, on occasion it appears in combination with *s* to represent a plural form (*-is*) and is transcribed as such ("encresis," line 123; "decesis," line 124; "housis," line 171).

For further in-depth discussion of Asloan's hand see the introductions to the *Buke of the Howlat*, edited by Hanna, as well as *Buke of the Chess*, and *Buke of the Sevyne Sagis*, edited by van Buuren.

- In the defective portions of the text, I follow Kratzmann in supplying within square brackets words suggested by Craigie. Three-dot ellipses are used to indicate those portions of the text that cannot possibly be reconstructed.

- Throughout the poem, either at the start of new tales or the beginning of a *moralitas*, two-line gaps with guide-letters are left for the initial letter of the section and the start of following line is indented; for example, the initial flourished *I* of line 43 is present. Asloan uses headings sporadically to introduce individual tales (e.g., "The Unicornis Tale") or the moral (*moralitas fabule*). For the sake of consistency, headings are here used for each tale and moral. Those editorial headings are enclosed in square brackets.

---

[60] *The Buke of the Sevyne Sagis*, ed. van Buuren, p. 203; *Asloan Manuscript*, ed. Craigie, *passim*.

[61] Holland, *The Buke of the Howlat*, ed. Hanna, pp. 56–57; *The Buke of the Sevyne Sagis*, ed. van Buuren, p. 201.

THE TALIS OF THE FYVE BESTES

[Prologue]   *(see note)*

[. . . .]

[The Horsis Tale]

" . . . . And in this fair way persaif I wele a thing,		*pleasant; perceive*
To no gud rest this nycht it sall us bring.		*night; it will not bring us*
This plesant way, the way is of dissait,		*deceit*
And in this firth ar thevis in our gait."		*wood; thieves; way (path)*

5   But nevertheles, for ony argument,   *in spite of this argument*
       This plesand streit this verray fule furth went;   *path; utter fool; took*
       Richt so this wysman did and left the tother   *wise man; other (i.e., path)*
       For verray effectioun of his carnale brother.   *true love; fleshly (i.e., blood)*
       So has this waye tham to the brigantis brocht,   *brought them to the robbers*
10   Takin thai war and with thaim went and wrocht.   *and were ruined*
       So come the kingis justice of the land   *came; king's justice*
       And tuke thaim all and to law gart thaim stand.   *face the law*
       So quhen thir theifis all war justifyed   *tried*
       Than everilk brother for himself replyid.   *each*
15   This wysman said, "Of all this gret trespas   *fault*
       Herof the quhilk that I accusit was,   *of which I am accused*
       This verray fule my brother had the wyte,   *is at fault*
       That tuke the way of plesance and delyte   *[He] that; worldly pleasure*
       And left the way that suld us bring to rest,   *(eternal) rest*
20   And brocht us baith unto the thefis nest.   *both; thieves'*
       And with him furth the samyn way I yud   *same; went*
       Bot for affectioun naturale of his blud.[1]
       So sen this fule was causar of this scaith,   *since; perpetrator; harm*
       Richt so suld he be punist for us baith,   *should; both*
25   That with no ressoun rewlit wald he be."[2]
       "Nay," said this fule, "the falt was nocht in me   *does not reside with me*
       Bot all in you that God has gevin to wit   *to whom God has given wisdom*

---

[1] *Only because of innate fondness for his blood (i.e., because we are related)*

[2] *He that would not be ruled by reason*

91

	To rewle us baith and nocht disponit it.	*you did not use it*
	For quha wald trow a wysman wald assent,	*who would believe; agree*
30	And I a fule so sone to myne entent?	*a fool so quickly in my intentions?*
	Bot your effectioun, se I weile be this,	*[loving] inclination; I see well by*
	Has blyndit us and gart us boith go mys.	*blinded; made; go astray*
	Thus in this mater all the falt ye haf."	*you bear all the blame*
	And so furthwith this juge the sentens gaf,	*gave the sentence*
35	And sen this wysman left his awne entent	*That since; put aside; plan*
	And to this fulis deid gaf his assent,	*act; agreed*
	And left the wit that God gaf him of grace	*wisdom (or free will); by grace*
	For the effectioun naturale that he has,	*On account of brotherly affection*
	And for this fule he wald nocht rewlit be	*since; would not be ruled*
40	Be this sentence he jugit baith to de.	*sentenced both to death*
	And in remembrans evir of thar deidis	*perpetual; deeds (or deaths)*
	Gart thaim sit doune and straik of baith thar heidis.	*struck off; heads*

Moralitas fabule   *The moral of the tale*

	In more effect of this mater I mene,	
	Thir brethir two in every man thai bene.[1]	
45	The wantone flesche it is the foly brothir,	*wanton; foolish*
	The sely saull forsuth it is the tothir.	*blessed (or innocent); forswear; other*
	So quhen the saull affermes the delyte	*follows*
	Off the foule fleschis lust and appetit,	*foul flesh's*
	Alson with dedly synnis ar thai wrocht,	*At once; deadly sins; ruined*
50	Takin and slane and to confusioun brocht.	*killed*
	Forbere this way of lust that ye se heir,	*Abstain from; you see here*
	And take the way of buskis, thorne and brer.	*bushes, thorn; briar*
	That is the way of pennance and of grace	
	To bring our saulis to that joyfull place	*Which will bring*
55	Of paradis and of perfectioun richt.	*right*
	Now Jhesus bring us to that blisfull sicht.	*sight*

	So quhen this riall hors his tale had endit,	*royal horse*
	This ryall hart richt gentilly commendit,	*commended it in a courteous manner*
	His statly hed with tyndis set on hicht	*splendid head; horns (tines); on high*
60	Of polist gold and silver birnist bricht.	*polished; burnished bright*
	Befor this kyng he laid his tyndis law,	*low*
	And in this wys his tale began to schawe.	*way; reveal (tell)*

---

[1] Lines 43–44: *Speaking more specifically about this matter, I find that / These two brothers appear in every man*

The Hart[is Tale]

I hald in bretta[ne] . . .   *believe that in Britain*
That ever was . . .
65   William Wallace worth . . .
Saif reverence of the . . .   *With due respect to*
He tuke fro no man t . . .   *took from*
He wan all Scotland in . . .   *won all of*
Tharfor in hevin is his . . .
70   And that I trowe be rich[t resoun].   *is quite justified*

The samyn day the sutheren [seid]   *same; southern seed (i.e., men)*
Had wrocht thar will apon W[allace],   *wrought their will upon*
As thai had done befor in d[eid]
With Sanct Edmond and Sanct [Thomas].
75   Ane haly heremed quhar he [was],   *holy hermit where*
As in autentik writ we reid,   *[a] trustworthy account*
The staitis of this warld but dreid   *conditions; world without fear*
Desyrit to see throu Goddis grace.   *Desired; through God's*

Sa come ane angell fra the hicht   *So; from on high*
80   And schew him baith of hevin and hell,   *showed; heaven*
The joye amang thir angellis bricht,   *the*
The fyre amang thir fendis fell,   *foul fiends*
Of purgatory thus hard I tell;   *[And] of; heard*
And of thaim all he had a sicht   *sight*
85   That deit as that day and nicht,   *[Those] that died that*
And quhar thar saulis thaim schupe to duell.   *made themselves ready to dwell*

And so he saw in colour sabill   *black*
Of saulis doune to hell declyne,   *descend*
Ane multitud innomerable   *innumerable*
90   Perpetually to suffer pyne.   *pain*
To purgatory he saw pas syne   *then*
        . . . le
        . . . tin fable
        . . . fra hyne

95   . . . thre
        . . . ais in
        . . . degre
        . . . [d]edly syn
        . . . thai begyn
100   . . . may se
        . . . ace fulfillit be
        . . . of hevin thai wyn

	[The first that tha]re to hevyn up ran,	*first [person]*
	[Levit ane l]yf of religioun.	*Lived a religious life*
105	[Ane heremei]t was the tothir man,	*hermit; other*
	[Luvit h]aly mess and confessioun.	*[Who] loved holy mass*
	[The th]rid a lord for his regioun,	*third; in his region*
	In his defence deit as than	*died defending himself just as*
	Wallace with his woundis wan	*bloody wounds*
110	That day tholit deid at Londoun toune.	*suffered death*
	Thar was na force mycht gar him fald,	*make him lose courage*
	Na yit reward of warldly gud,	*Nor*
	Bot Scotland ay defend he wald	*he would always defend*
	Fra subjectioun of Saxonis blud.[1]	
115	Thus for his realme stedfast he stud	*[fighting] for;*
	And to his deid was bocht and sauld.	*purchased and sold*
	Therefor in hevin his saull I hald[2]	
	Or he was cald. Thus I conclude.	*before he (i.e., his body) was cold*

[*Moralitas fabule*]

	Now be this tale I wald ye understud,	*understand [how]*
120	Movand avert to haf ane querell gud,	*Proceeding prudently; just quarrel*
	Quhat corage in a mannis hart it bringis,	*What courage; man's heart*
	The fame of it how lovably it ryngis,	*honorably; reigns*
	And quhat of grace the sely saull encresis	
	Thro just batle, quho so tharin decesis.[3]	
125	Bot nevertheles, quhatever the pepill deme,	*whatever; people judge*
	The gud of pece thar can no man expreme.	*benefit of peace; express*
	On fut than gat this gentill unicorne,	*foot; goes*
	This gentill best this king he come beforne.	*beast; came before*
	So fair a best, so sweit unto my sicht,	*sweet*
130	Was never sene with ony erdly wicht.	*by any earthly person*
	The onely tynd that on his hed he bair	*one horn; bore*
	A kyngis ransoun it was worth and mair.	*king's ransom*
	To luke on him it did me sic delyte,	*such*
	And on this wys he tald his tale perfyte.	*in this way; perfect*

The Unicornis Tale

135	Befor this tyme in Kentschire it befell	
	A bonde thar was, his name I can nocht tell;	*peasant (i.e., bondsman)*

---

[1] *Against subjection by [those] of Saxon blood (i.e., the English)*

[2] *Therefore I maintain that his soul reached heaven*

[3] Lines 123–24: *And how much grace the blessed soul gains / though just battle, whoever dies in that way*

Gundulfus was his sonis name I ges, *guess*
Of tender age of nyne yeris ald he wes, *old*
And wele he usit for to rys at mornys *he was accustomed; in the morning*
140 To kepe the grange and his faderis cornis *granary; father's corn*
Fra cokis, crawis and uther foulis wyld. *cocks; crows; other wild birds*
So on a day this litill prety child *small comely child*
Seand thir birdis lukand our the wall, *Seeing the; watching over*
Toward the grange Gundulfus gois withall, *as well*
145 And with the casting of a litill stone *throwing*
Of ane litill bird the theis bone *thigh bone*
Brokin he has in sounder at a cast, *into two in one throw*
And sone the fowlis flokit about him fast. *quickly; birds flocked*
Quhat will ye mar? He was bot slane or schent. *only struck down or injured*
150 Sore for him wepit all the hennis of Kent. *hens*
Up was he takin and in a garding led *led into a garden*
Amang thir herbes thai haf maid him a bed, *herbs (or grasses)*
And quhat throu comfort and throu medecyne, *on account of*
Within the space of days viii or nyne *eight*
155 This bird was mendit hale and sound *healed completely*
Of all the panys of his bludy wound. *pains*
And Gundulfus with his frendis assent *friends' agreement*
To Oxinfurd to study is he went. *Oxford*
Sone efter this bird wox a cok, *became; cockerel*
160 The gudliest and farest of the floke, *most distinguished; flock*
Clerast of voce and wyest in his entent, *clearest; wisest in his intentions*
The cruellest of all the cokis of Kent. *fiercest*
And he had Copok to be his wyf,
And he had chosyn hir for terme of lyf, *for his entire lifetime*
165 And scho agane till him hir treuth plicht, *she had pledged her truth to him*
To luf him best of ony erdly wicht. *love; above all earthly men*
And so at evyne apon his perke he gat, *upon his perch he went*
On his richt hand dame Copok nixt him sat. *next*
And quhill he clapit durst thar no cok craw, *made a noise; crow*
170 Quhen he had clapit than craw thai all on raw. *in succession*
So weile he had the housis observance *respect of the house*
That of the flok he bair the governans. *was in charge*
Thus was he cheif cok of the bondis place, *peasant's*
And bair the rewle threttene yeris space. *ruled for thirteen years*
175 And all this tyme he had this child in thocht *thought about*
That brak his leg quhen he trespassit nocht. *when he had not sinned*
[. . . .] *(see note)*
He was na master in divinité *He (i.e., Gundulfus); divinity*
But he wald preche in to that science hie. *high science*
Weile couth he cast the bukis of decres. *consider; Gretian's Decretals*

180   Bot tharin no thing he had of his greis.[1]
       Prentis in court he had bene for a yer,   *An apprentice*
       He was a richt gud syngar in the quir.   *very good singer in the choir*
       He couth wele reid and sumpart write and dyte,   *read well; a little; indite*
       And in his gramer was he wele perfyte.   *perfect*
185   He was ane gret bachillar in sophistry,   *bachelor; fallacious reasoning*
       With part of pratik of nygramansy.   *some knowledge of sorcery*
       Of phesik he bair ane urynale   *medicine; carried a vessel for holding urine*
       To se thir folk gif thai war seike or hale,   *see if people*
       And in his clething was he wele besene,   *well dressed*
190   For goune and hude was all of Lyncome grene.[2]
       Gret was the joy that in the place was than
       To se the meting of that noble man.   *encounter with (i.e., return)*
       In come his frendis till him fast anone,
       And nochtwithstanding that the day was gone,
195   "Fader," he said, "I can nocht byde this nycht;   *stay tonight*
       To Rochister I mon thir wayis richt,   *Rochester I must make my way*
       To-morne is the day of my promotioun   *Tomorrow*
       Of holy ordour to resaif the croune,   *receive the tonsure*
       And tharin standis myne avansing hale   *advancement*
200   Unto ane benefice perpetuale.   *permanent benefice*
       And, falye this, the kirk gais to ane nother."[3]
       Than spak our dame that was the childis modir,   *child's mother*
       "Son, for my blissing, this nycht with us abyde   *stay*
       And all at eis to-morne son sall ye ryd.   *at ease; soon*
205   Our hous cok sall the houris of the nycht
       Alswele devyde as ony orlage richt,   *separate; clock*
       And at the first cok walkinnit sall ye be   *cock-[crow] wakened shall*
       And at your hors sone by the hour of thre.   *(i.e., 3am)*
       Ye have bot nyne myle of the farest way,[4]
210   At Rochister ye sall be sone be day   *by the start of day*
       And haf your tonsour be the hour of nyne."   *receive*
       And so he baid and drank with thaim the wyne.   *stayed*
       Quhen thai war full of michti ale and wyne   *strong*
       Thai gat to rest and slepis as ony swyne.   *went; slept like swine*
215   The nycht yeid our, the freindis thocht nocht lang,[5]
       For all thar trast was on the cokis sang.   *their trust*
       And all this sawe the cok apon the balk   *[sitting] on the wooden beam*
       And quhen he hard the mater of thar talk   *heard; subject*

---

[1] *But of that he has had no training in his degree*

[2] *For [his] gown and hood were all of a green cloth made at Lincoln*

[3] *And, failing this (i.e., if I am absent), the benefice goes to another*

[4] *You have only nine miles by the best road [to travel]*

[5] *The night passed by, [but] the friends thought it was not long*

	And on the breking of his theis bone,	*about; thigh bone*
220	This cok had mynd; Gundulfus he had none.	*thought about*
	Sone come the tyme that he suld say his voce,	*try out his voice*
	The hour yeid our, the cok he held him clos.	*passed by; kept quiet*
	With that dame Coppok putis on hir maike,	*pushes her mate*
	Said, "Slepe ye schir? Get up for Cristis saik!	*sir; Christ's sake*
225	Your hour is gone. Quhy syng ye nocht, for schame?	*Why; not; shame*
	Wait ye nocht weile yone clerk suld ryde fra hame,[1]	
	And all thar trast apon your sang thai lay?	*their trust*
	Schir, syng ye nocht, yone clerk sall slepe quhill day	*[if] you don't sing; until*
	And so in vane is all thing that thai wirk.[2]	
230	It war gret pete he suld tyne his kirk	*great pity; lose his benefice*
	And of the tynsall ye sall haf the blame."	*loss; will be to blame*
	Syng wald he nocht bot schrewitly said, "Madame,	*maliciously*
	Wysest ye ar quhen that ye hald you still,	*keep quiet*
	And yit ye wyfis evir speike ye will.	*you wives will always speak*
235	Dame, intromet you in your wyfis deid,	*occupy yourself with wifely deeds*
	Lytill ye wist quhen that my leg couth bleid,[3]	
	And yone is he that brak my leg in sounder.	*in two*
	Gif I suld crawe, madame, it war gret wounder	
	For thocht my leg be verray haile outwart,[4]	
240	Quhen I him se it bledis at my hart."	*When; my heart bleeds*
	As thai war talkand this fer thaim amang,	*speaking among themselves*
	Lang efter that the cok tuke up a sang,	*Long after*
	And all the birdis with ane voce thai cry,	
	"Get up, get up, we se the dayis sky!"	
245	And up he gat and saw that it was day,	*he (i.e., Gundulfus)*
	Said kirk and worschip fastly war away.[5]	
	On hors he gat, fast throw the toune he raid,	*mounted; rode*
	And all the doggis in till his tale he had,	*at his tail*
	Quhill at ane stone he styntit with sic fors	*Until; halted; such force*
250	That to the erd yeid baith man and hors.	*earth; were thrown*
	This hors gat up and ran our to the hill,	*over*
	And in the myr this worthy clerk lay still.	*swampy ground*
	And still he lay quhill it was tyme of none,	*until; midday*
	The kirk disponit and all the service done.	*disposed of; complete*
255	Than up he gat and hame agane is went,	*went home again*
	Ane hevy man forsuth in his entent.	*dejected; indeed in his spirits*
	His garment grene that was of colour gud	

---

[1] *Don't you know very well that this clerk should ride from home*

[2] *And so everything they work for is in vain*

[3] *You know little about when my leg was bleeding*

[4] Lines 238–39: *It would be a wonder, madam, if I were to crow / for although my leg appears healed from the outside*

[5] *And saw that the aforementioned church and its dignity would quickly be gone*

	Was so mismaide in the myre and mude,	*disordered; muck; mud*
	And quhat for schame he was so pale of hewe,	*indeed; shame; in color*
260	Quhen he come hame thar was no man him knewe.	*no one knew him*
	So quhen this clerk with schame come hame agane,	
	Than was this cok quyt of his legis pane,	*revenged for his leg injury*
	And said, "Madame Coppok, mak gud cheir,	*be cheerful*
	Now wepis he that leuch this hender yeir	*laughed; past year*
265	Quhen with ane stone my thees bone he brak	*thigh bone*
	Bot for I lukit till his faderis stak,	*Just because; looked over his father's fence*
	And quhen I bled he said the feild was his.	*he owned the field*
	Now God I loif this day has send us this."	*I glorify God who has; sent us*

[Moralitas fabule]

	Nowe be this tale ye sall wele understand,	
270	Gif ye be lord and rewlar of this land,	*If; ruler*
	Ye schape you nocht for till oppres the pure,	*Do not plan to; poor*
	For, and ye do, forsuth I you assure	*if you do, indeed; promise*
	The tyme may cum that your aventour standis	*fate*
	Paraventur in to sic mennis handis.	*Perhaps; men's*
275	Quha schapis him the pure for to oppres	
	At Goddis hand the mater has to addres.	*face the matter in front of God*
	Quhil that ye haf space tharfor ye suld amend,	*While; time; amend (or repent)*
	Byde nocht the straik of vengeans at your end,	*Do not wait for the stroke*
	For till amend als oft as ye do mys,	*But repent as often as you sin*
280	And we beseke Jhesu of His blis. Amen.	*ask Jesus for his bliss*

	It was ane blyth sicht of this bair,	*a pleasant sight [to see] this boar*
	Of reid gold was the birsis he bur,	*his bristles were of red gold*
	Of reid gold schynand was his hair,	*shining*
	His scheldis war richt sad and sure,	*shields [of skin]; steadfast; strong*
285	His tuskis scharpe that he with schur,	*cut with*
	Of stele thai war baith stark and stur.	*steel; powerful; fierce*
	This was the tale that he tald thar,	*told*
	I coppyt it with all my cure.	*copied it carefully*

The Baris Taile

	Gret Alexander, king of Massedoun,	*Macedonia*
290	The quhilk of the nyne nobillis was one,	*one of the nine worthies*
	Of his conquest tyme ner by the end,	*near the end of his conquests*
	To the cite of Lapsat in Araby he send	*Arabia; sent*
	And of the folk desyrit sic a thing	*such*
	To knaw him for thar soverane lord and king,	*[That they] recognize him as*
295	And to be subject to his hie empyr,	*great empire*
	And tak example at the toune of Tyr,	*look to the example of; Tyre*
	That was so strang and for rebellioun	*rebellious*

	Was utterly distroyit and castyn doun.[1]	
	To this desyr and quhat thai wald haf done	
300	Thir worthy folk war avysit sone,[2]	
	And in thir termes answer have thai send:	*in these words*
	"That quhill we leif we will this toune defend	*while we live*
	In sic fredome as our antecessouris	*ancestors*
	Has left till us and till this toune of ouris.	*to; ours*
305	Erar we cheis with worschipe for to de	*We would rather choose to die with honor*
	Than for to leif in subjectioun to be."	*Than to live in subjection*
	And in this querell maid thaim ilkone boune	*they each made ready*
	With ane assent to defend this toune.	*common consent*
	This riall prince he was amovit so	*royal; angered*
310	Quhen he this herd he micht no forder go,	*could not go any further*
	Bot to this toune this king agane is gone,	*to the town; returns*
	And with ane ost the riallest of one,	*the most royal of hosts (armies)*
	Of kyngis and princis and worthy men of weir	*[Made up] of; war*
	And with the cost nane uther man mycht beir,[3]	
315	And in entent to cast the cité doun	*intending to raze the city to the ground*
	And put yone pepill to confusioun	*bring the people down*
	Bot hope of grace for trety and debait,	*Without any hope; treaty*
	Into remembering of his hie estait.[4]	
	In to this toune thar was a noble man,	*In this town*
320	Ane worthy clerke the best of ane was than,[5]	
	And had bene master to this riall kyng	*tutor*
	In his scoling quhen at this prince was ying.	*education; young*
	And our all thing this toune he lufit best,	*above all else; loved*
	And of this prince he trastit grace of rest.	*expected the favor of peace*
325	So or this ost was cummyn to this toune	*before; arrived at*
	This clerk on kneis before this king fell doune.	*knees*
	The king was war and wele this clerk he saw,	*cautious; looked closely at*
	Said, "Master, ces, your erand weile I knawe.[6]	
	Desyre na thing at me this daye for quhy	*Ask nothing of me today since*
330	Quhat evir ye ask that thing I will deny	*Whatever you ask*
	And in the contrar wirk at all my micht."[7]	
	Than spak this clerk and set his word on hicht,	*loudly*
	"A kingis word in more effect suld be	*should be of more worth*

---

[1] *[But which] was utterly destroyed and razed to the ground*

[2] Lines 299–30: *[In response] to this request, and what they would do, / the worthy folk [of Lapsat] were soon advised*

[3] *And with such a cost that no one else could bear*

[4] *To ensure that they recognize his exalted estate*

[5] *He was at that time the best of all worthy clerks*

[6] *Said, "Master, stop, I know why you are here*

[7] *And work with all my power to do the opposite*

Than ony of lawar degré.   *Than any of lower degree*

335 Excellent, hie and mychti prince but peir,   *peerless prince*
     Now of this grace that ye haf grantit heir   *favor; you have granted here*
     I thank your hienes and I ask no more   *your highness*
     Bot hold the purpos that ye ar cummyn for,[1]
     To sla yone folk and to distroye yone toune,   *kill*
340 To do no grace to cast yone wallis doune.[2]
     Now may ye cheis to lat your wordis stand   *choose to let you words stand*
     And tyne the cost or tak this toune on hand   *lose the expense; capture*
     And brek your word before this riall rowte."   *in front of this royal army*
     The king was wo and to remuf that dowt   *dispel the difficulty of deciding*
345 To counsall yeid and quhen he was degest   *went; settled*
     To tyne this cost erar he thocht it best,   *Better to lose the expense*
     Than for to breke the wordis that he spak,
     And left this towne and wald nocht tak the lak.   *not be blamed*
     So throw the wit of his philosophouris   *through; its*
350 And the gret worschipe of his conquerouris   *honor; its*
     In rest and pece with fredome yit thai ryng,[3]
     And boith ar deid, this gret clerk and this king.   *And [now] both are dead*

                    [Moralitas fabule]

     Nowe be this taile it may richt wele be sene
     Ane kyngis word in till effect suld bene   *should be of value*
355 More precious in worschipe of his crowne   *honor*
     Than gud or gold or ony wallit toune.   *goods; walled town*
     Richt sad of langage suld he be ane kyng   *sober of speech*
     And weile avysit or he said the thing   *well-advised before saying anything*
     That suld him greif or muf in his entent: *he would regret; make him change his mind*
360 Erar speike nocht than speike and syne repent.[4]
     Or gif a kyng has said or done amys   *if; wrong*
     That to justice oucht grevand is,   *Anything that; at all grievous*
     It is more worschipe till his hie estait
     For to revoke than to be obstinat.   *rescind [his speech]; stubborn*
365 And to forbeir sic lust and sic delyte   *refrain from such*
     And tak tharfor everlestand lyf perfyte,   *thereby receive*
     Unto the quhilk the Lord of lyf but end   *Unto which; without end*
     Quhen we depart mot all our sawlis send.   *may convey all our souls*

---

[1] *But to stick to the purpose you came for*

[2] *To offer no mercy in razing down the walls*

[3] *In tranquility and peace with freedom still they [the people of Lapsat] maintain sovereignty*

[4] *Better not to speak than speak and then repent*

The Wolfis Tale

	This wretchit wolf neir by this lyoun lay,	*wretched; lay near*
370	His habit was, me thocht, of cottoun gray,	*clothing; grey cotton*
	And so evill favorit was his face on far[1]	
	That laif semed far farer than thai war.	*[the] rest; fairer*
	Thinkand to put this counsall fra that king,[2]	
	And his allya to the court inbring,	*allies; bring in*
375	He umbethocht him gretly of his wylis,	*carefully considered his tricks*
	And to thir staitis gaif he weile thar stylis.[3]	
	Said, "Soverane lord, I can nocht fabillis fene,	*tell lies*
	Bot for the commoun proffet I complene:	*public good; complain*
	In all this land thar is no schepe to get	
380	Within ten myle a mutone to your meit,[4]	
	Bot schepe and nolt distroyit ar and deid	*sheep; cattle; slaughtered*
	And for the quhilk, schir, this is the remeid,	*cure*
	To lat tham stand still that thai may store	*remain; breed*
	And multiply as thai war of before,	
385	Of venysoun and wyld meit mak gud cheir,	*feast on venison and game*
	And of gret bestis feid yow for a yeir.	*on large beasts feed*
	Schir, tak gud heid and understand me wele."	
	Than said the king, "Be your complant I feile	*apprehend*
	That for I haf na mutoun to my mete	*because; to eat*
390	My cosingis of my counsall I suld ete.	*my cousins in my council*
	Na, never more, thocht in defalt I de,	
	Than quha wald byde and of my counsall be?[5]	
	Bot with my counsall will I seike remeid,	*a remedy*
	Fynd how my schepe and how my nolt ar deid.	*[And] discover how*
395	So quhill this wolf was in this court thai fand	*discovered*
	That his allya forrayd all the land.	*ravaged*
	And so this lyoun sentence gaf he plane:	*clearly*
	No beist of reif suld in his court remane,	*animal of prey; remain*
	Nor of invy nor yit of covatis.	*envy; covetousness*
400	So was this wolf with all thar hale avys	*based on their sound advice*
	Exild the court and fled with all his micht.	*Exiled [from]; might*

---

[1] *His face was in such a bad condition even from a distance*

[2] *Planning to remove this council (i.e., the four other beasts) from the king*

[3] *To these estates of the realm he properly bestowed their titles*

[4] Lines 379–80: *It is impossible to find a sheep for your dinner within ten miles in this country*

[5] Lines 391–92: *No, never at all, even if by doing so I die, / then (i.e., if I did) who would remain and be in my council*

[Moralitas fabule]

	So sodanely this court went out of sicht	*sight*
	That all was gone in twynkling of an E,	*eye*
	And so gois all this warldis rialté.	*thus passes; world's royalty*
405	Now be this wolf schortly be myne avys	*in short in my opinion*
	Is understand the syn of covatis,	*covetousness*
	And be thir four of counsall to the king	*these four counselors*
	The vertuis four that in a king suld ryng,	*[Are understood] the four virtues; reign*
	Prudence, justice and magnanimité	*generosity of spirit*
410	And continence that is content to be.	*temperance; satisfied*
	The vertew no tyme suthly lestis	*virtue in truth does not last*
	In no persone that covatis in restis.	*any person who is covetous*
	Quha ma be prudent with that desyre	
	Or yit content had he the hale empyr?	*even if he had a whole empire*
415	Curage throw covatis is set at nocht	*courage because of; valued at nought*
	And be that mayn is justice sauld and bocht.[1]	
	Now mak this vyce exild for to be;	*exile this vice*
	Tak lawe and luf and leif in cherité	*Furnish oneself with law; love; live*
	And think quhat suld this warldis fals vanglor.	*what should [mean]; vainglory*
420	And for the joye that lestis evermore	*everlasting*
	Beseike we Him that bocht us with His blud,	*Beseech; blood*
	Eternale God the ground of every gud.	

Amen.

Heir endis The Talis of the Fyve Bestes Per M. Io. Asloan.   *By M[aister] Jo[hn]*

---

[1] *And through these means is justice bought and sold*

EXPLANATORY NOTES TO *THE TALIS OF THE FYVE BESTES*

ABBREVIATIONS: *A*: Edinburgh, National Library of Scotland MS 16500 olim Acc. 4243, fols. 229r–35v (the Asloan Manuscript); ***BKA***: Hay, *The Buik of King Alexander the Conquerour*, ed. Cartwright; ***CT***: Chaucer, *The Canterbury Tales,* ed. Benson; ***DOST***: *Dictionary of the Older Scottish Tongue*; **Gesta Romanorum**: *Gesta Romanorum*, ed. Herrtage; **Henryson**: Henryson, *The Poems of Robert Henryson,* ed. Fox; **Kratzmann**: *Colkelbie Sow and The Talis of the Fyve Bestes,* ed. Kratzmann; ***Poems***: Dunbar, *Poems of William Dunbar,* ed. Bawcutt; ***Speculum Stultorum***: *Speculum Stultorum,* ed. Mozley and Raymo; ***Hary's Wallace***: Hary, *The Wallace,* ed. McDiarmid; **Whiting**: Whiting, *Proverbs, Sentences, and Proverbial Phrases.*

[Prologue]	A, the sole surviving manuscript witness is defective, and we therefore lack the poem's beginning. It is likely that the poem opened with a prologue (perhaps in the form of a dream vision) in which a lion-king holds court at some kind of beast-parliament; four royal counselors (a horse, heart, unicorn, and boar) come to offer advice, which they give in the form of a tale. Their tales are followed by the speech of a fifth beast, a wolf. The now acephalous poem begins so far through "The Horsis Tale" — a version of a popular exemplum of two traveling brothers, a wise man and fool, who are deciding between them which of two paths to take to reach their destination. We begin with the words of the wise brother.
The Horsis Tale	See *Fyve Bestes* Introduction for summary.
1–6	*And in this . . . . fule furth went.* In the *Alphabet of Tales* (ed. Banks, 2:483–44), the choice between the roads is reversed; the wise man wishes to take the pleasant way, the fool a stony and thorny way.
8	*verray effectioun; carnale.* Such words and phrases, and others below, including "affectioun naturale" (line 22), "your effectioun . . . Has blyndit us" (lines 31–32), and "effectioun naturale" (line 38) are repeatedly set in opposition to others such as "ressoun" (line 25) and "wit" (line 37). Strikingly similar lexical sets are found in Henryson's poetry, particularly in the *moralitas* to *Orpheus and Eurydice*, where "affection," linked to "wardly lust" and offered (as here) as an allegory of the body, is repeatedly set against "reson" (*passim*), or man's soul (Henryson, p. 153, lines 623–27).
	brother. The two travelers are not always brothers. In the *Gesta Romanorum* they are unrelated knights; in the *Meroure of Wyssdome* pilgrims.

11 *the kingis justice*. How the brothers are brought to justice differs across each analogue. In the *Gesta Romanorum*, for instance, a "domys-man" (p. 21) comes to sit in judgment, whereas no judge is mentioned at all in the *Speculum Morale*; in some other versions the brothers/travelers are brought before a justice system, including a king in the *Alphabet of Tales*, and in others still the brothers/travelers are harmed instead by their captors (See Kratzmann, pp. 125–26n11; Mapstone, "*Talis of the Fyve Bestes*," p. 243). As Mapstone notes ("Advice to Princes Tradition," pp. 218–19): "In the horse's tale it is specifically the 'kingis Iustice' who deals with them, and they are not brought before him — he comes, apprehends, and brings them to justice . . . Thus, whereas in most versions where justice is pronounced, it is carried out either by the king or a justice figure, in the horse's tale judge and king are both included . . . , and there is a strong sense of the justice figure actively bringing criminals to law."

 Although we must be cautious about drawing direct connections to contemporary events, the presentation here of a king actively effecting justice throughout his realm might reflect something of the justice-ayre system in fifteenth-century Scotland (the circuit court of the sovereign's Justice), and particularly the repeated parliamentary calls for James III to engage in this practice. In 1473, for instance, Parliament exhorted James III to "travel throw his realme and put sic justice and polycy in his awne realme, that the brute and the fame of him mycht pas in uthiris contreis and that he mycht optene the name of sa just a prince and sa vertewsis and sa wele reuland his awne realm in justice, policy and peax, that uthiris princis mycht tak exemple of him and gif him credence" (*Records of the Parliaments of Scotland*, 1473/7/9) whilst in 1485 "the lordis forsaid that for the encres of justice and tranquilité in the realme, that oure souveran lord cause his justice airis to be haldin universaly in al partis of his realme" (*Records of the Parliaments of Scotland*, 1485/5/10).

27 *wit*. Although here glossed as wisdom — or reason — this word might also bear connotations of the free will bestowed on mankind by God's grace (compare line 37). In the subsequent judgment, the wise man is punished for allowing instinct and emotion to triumph over his reason and free will.

31–32 *your effectioun . . . Has blyndit us*. The metaphorical description of reason (or the soul, in the subsequent *moralitas*) being "blinded" by the will (or body or appetite) appears commonly throughout Middle English and Older Scots poetry. Compare, for instance, Henryson's *Fables* (Henryson, pp. 53, 64, 65, 74, lines 1305, 1606, 1634, 1906) and *Orpheus and Eurydice* (Henryson, pp. 145, 147, lines 388, 454) and Dunbar's *Goldyn Targe* (*Poems*, 1:190, line 214).

41 *deidis*. As Kratzmann observes (p. 126n41), this word can mean both "deaths" and "deeds." Whereas Kratzmann prefers the latter, I here allow both meanings to remain in play in my suggested glosses.

42 *straik of baith thar heidis*. Mapstone notes ("Advice to Princes Tradition," p. 219; "*Talis of the Fyve Bestes*," p. 243, citing Irvine Smith, "Criminal Procedure," p. 20) that the beheading is a specifically Scottish detail. In all other accounts the

travelers are put to death by hanging, but in medieval Scotland beheading was a set punishment for habitual thieves.

43–56   *Moralitas fabule.* The exemplum of the two brothers is here allegorized, as elsewhere, to illustrate the dangers the body poses to the soul. This allegory is also represented, as already noted, in Henryson's *Orpheus and Eurydice,* and in his "The Paddock and the Mouse." The ultimate Biblical source of this and other medieval body/soul debates is Galatians 5:17 ("For the flesh lusteth against the spirit: and the spirit against the flesh; for these are contrary one to another: so that you do not the things that you would"). As Kratzmann notes (p. 127n49, citing Owst, *Literature and Pulpit,* p. 106), the figure of thieves as sins occurs frequently in medieval sermons, whilst the allegorization of the difficult way as penance occurs also in the *Gesta Romanorum* and the *Speculum Morale.*

58   *gentilly commendit.* Throughout Chaucer's *CT* the pilgrims similarly commend (or criticize) each other's tales. The same is true of the tale tellers in the Scots *The Thre Prestis of Peblis,* which also appears in MS A. See *The Thre Prestis of Peblis,* lines 445–46, 1005–06.

60   *polist gold and silver birnist bricht.* All of the four beasts are described in this highly visual, stylized manner. As discussed in the *Fyve Bestes* Introduction, such descriptions are reminiscent of medieval heraldry and may have held some symbolic value now lost to us, rather like the heraldic imagery found in *The Buke of the Howlat* (lines 334–631), which precedes *The Fyve Bestes* in MS A.

The Hartis Tale   See *Fyve Bestes* Introduction for summary.

65   *William Wallace.* William Wallace (d. 1305) was a famous patriot and guardian of Scotland who repeatedly led the Scots to victory against the English during the Wars of Independence. His exploits are recounted in Blind Hary's *The Wallace* (c. 1476–78), as well as in Bower's earlier *Scotichronicon.* See further *ODNB,* "Wallace, Sir William (d. 1305)."

66   *Saif reverence of the.* Compare *Hary's Wallace* (12.1208): "sauff reuerence off the croun."

68–70   *He wan all . . . . be rich[t resoun].* Compare *Hary's Wallace* (12.1235–37):

> Scotland he fred and brocht it off thrillage;
> And now in hewin he has his heretage,
> As It prewyt be gud experians.

In his *Scotichronicon,* Bower also depicts Wallace as *pro fidelitate et patria sua usque ad mortem legitime decertantis, qui numqaum Anglis se submisit vel homagium prestitit* ("rightly striving until his death for faithfulness and his native land, a man who never submitted to the English or offered homage"), book 12, chapter 8.

69   *Tharfor in hevin is his . . .* Compare *Hary's Wallace* (12.1288): "Tharfor in hewyn he sall that honour hawe."

71   *sutheren [seid].* Compare "Saxonis blud" (line 114). As Kratzmann notes, "This is more moderate than Hary's 'fals Sotherun' (*Wallace* XII, 1305)" (p. 127n71).

74 *Sanct Edmond and Sanct [Thomas].* Wallace is similarly aligned with Saints Edmund and Thomas (and presented as a martyr) by Hary in *Hary's Wallace* (12.1308). St. Edmund (d. 869), king of the Angles, was venerated soon after his death at the hands of the Vikings; St. Thomas is Thomas Becket (?1120–70), archbishop of Canterbury, murdered in his cathedral church by several of Henry II's knights. In the centuries after his death in 1170, the martyr Thomas Becket was increasingly associated with miracles and prophecies, and venerated on both sides of the Border. For Scottish devotion to Becket see: Wilson, "Scottish Canterbury Pilgrims" and Penman, "The Bruce Dynasty."

75 *haly heremed.* The vision in *Hary's Wallace* involves two monks rather than a hermit; there a "monk of Bery" (intriguingly reminiscent of the label used for the poet, John Lydgate, 12.1239) makes a pact with a younger monk to return after death and tell of his experiences of the afterlife. The *sanctus heremita* of Bower's *Scotichronicon* (6:316, book 12, chapter 8) is closer.

76 *in autentik writ.* It is not clear what source the author has in mind here, and it is possible that the allusion functions as an authorizing device, rather like Chaucer's use of "Lollius" in *Troilus and Criseyde* (1:394), Henryson's "vther quair" in *The Testament of Cresseid* (Henryson, p. 113, line 61) or Hary's allusion to his (most probably fictional source) — a "Latyne buk" by one Maister John Blair, written with the assistance of Thomas Gray, "persone off Libertoune" (*Hary's Wallace*, 5.540–42); Hary also begins his account of Wallace's ascent by referring to "Wys clerkys ōeit It kepis in Remembrans" (12.1238). Nevertheless, as Kratzmann (p. 29) points out, by the beginning of the sixteenth century the story of Wallace's ascent to heaven was well known. He cites the following example from John Major's *History of Greater Britain*:

> Our chroniclers here tell a story of how an English hermit was witness of several souls taking their flight from purgatory to heaven, and how one of these was Wallace; and as he marvelled much how this could be, seeing that Wallace had shed man's blood, he got for answer that it was in a just cause, and when fighting for his country's freedom, that he had slain others. And indeed I do not forget that it may be lawful to fight when the cause is just . . . (Major, *A History of Greater Britain*, p. 204).

78 *Goddis grace.* Compare this reference to God's grace to that in line 37.

79 *ane angell.* As noted above, the angel does not appear in Hary's *Wallace*, although Bower does refer to the removal of souls (along with Wallace's) *per ministerium Angelorum*, ("with the help of angels," 6:316–17, book 12, chapter 8). As McDiarmid (*Hary's Wallace*, 2:277n1238–1301) and Mapstone ("Advice to Princes Tradition," pp. 224–25) further observe, an angel and hermit both appear in the aforementioned fourteenth-century Spanish *Libro de Patronio*, by Don Juan Manuel. Here a dying hermit is told by an angel that he will be accompanied on his journey to heaven by the soul of Richard I, and — as in the moralization to this tale — the hermit is told by the angel that Richard's place in heaven is justified, despite his having killed so many, since those he killed were infidels. Mapstone cites too ("Advice to Princes Tradition," p. 225) an exemplum (in British Library, Arundel MS 506, fol. 57r) in which a hermit is

visited by an angel who explains that he has been accompanying the soul of Thomas Becket (mentioned at line 74) to heaven. Although it is unlikely that the author of *The Fyve Bestes* had direct recourse to either tale, especially the Spanish, he may have come across the angel, hermit, and 'justified war' argument in other collections of exempla and supplied these features to the story of Wallace found in Bower and Hary.

79–102   *Sa come ane . . . . hevin thai wyn.* Literary visions of heaven, hell, and purgatory abound in medieval literature. See Easting, *Visions of the Other World in Middle English*, and Patch, *The Other World*. Gavin Douglas aligns the third part of his *Palis of Honoure* with this literary tradition but his dreamer is only afforded a brief glimpse of Honor (described as "a god armypotent," line 1921) and then again denied a vision of the judgment or punishment of sinning souls. See *Shorter Poems of Gavin Douglas*, ed. Bawcutt, p. 119.

89   *multitud innomerable.* McDiarmid (*Hary's Wallace*, 2:277–78n1238–1301) and Kratzmann (p. 127n89) both compare this phrase to Bower's *innumeras animas* ("countless souls," 6:316–17, book 12, chapter 8). However, as Mapstone notes ("Advice to Princes Tradition," p. 221), the state of the souls in Bower's account is more favorable than in "The Hart's Tale": the hermit *vidit quasi innumeras animas de penis purgatorii liberatas, quasi prestolantes aditum regni celestis* ("saw practically countless souls freed from the pains of purgatory, who seemed to be awaiting entrance into the kingdom of Heaven," 6:316–17, book 12, chapter 8).

103–07   *[The first that] . . . . for his regioun.* Drawing on Craigie, ed. *The Asloan Manuscript: A Miscellany in Prose and Verse* and *The Wallace*, McDiarmid (*Hary's Wallace*, 2:277–78) reconstructs these lines as follows:

> [A haly fad]re to hevyn wp ran,
> [Had led a l]yf of religioun.
> [A pres]t was the tothir man,
> [For d]aly mes and confessioun;
> [The t]hrid a lord for his regioun . . .

In *Hary's Wallace* the three souls seen are Wallace, "a pure preist" (12.1289), and the monk himself.

106   *mess and confessioun.* Compare *Hary's Wallace* (12.1291): "For dayly mes and heryng off *con*fessioun."

109–10   *Wallace with his . . . . at Londoun toune.* Wallace's gruesome (but there pain-free death) is described in *Hary's Wallace*, 12.1310–1409.

114   *Saxonis.* Hary similarly refers to the English as Saxons throughout *Hary's Wallace*.

116   *to his deid was bocht and sauld.* In *Hary's Wallace*, Wallace is betrayed by Sir John Menteith for "Thre thowsand pundys off fyn gold" (12.822) and Hary also uses the word "sauld" at 12.1076. Compare also lines 415–16 of Kratzmann where justice is described as "sauld and bocht" by "covatis."

119–26   *Moralitas fabule.* Although we still have an eight-line stanza here, the rhyme scheme changes to irregularly decasyllabic couplets. The value of fighting for a just cause is similarly asserted by Douglas in *The Palis of Honoure*, where the dreamer sees those who "in iust battell wer fundyn maist of name" (line 1968, London text). See also quotation by Major in note to line 76 above.

123   *sely saull*. Compare line 46 above.

126   *gud of pece*. Compare line 351 below.

The Unicornis Tale   See *Fyve Bestes* Introduction for summary.

129   *so sweit unto my sicht*. The narrator says he is present at the court or parliament of beasts, witnessing the tales as they are told.

135   *Kentschire*. The original story in the *Speculum Stultorum*, titled "Narratio Arnoldi de filio presbyteri et pullo gallinae," is set in Apulia. That the setting here is England rather than Scotland ensures that any potential political messages remain non-specific. See Mapstone, "*Talis of the Fyve Bestes*," p. 245. Kratzmann (*Anglo-Scottish Literary Relations*, pp. 95–96) also compares these opening lines to those beginning Chaucer's The Summoner's Tale (*CT* III[D] 1709–12). Both authors lead their audience into the narrative "by a mixture of precision and indefiniteness" (p. 96).

136   *A bonde*. In the *Speculum Stultorum* (lines 1257–64) the boy is the son of a priest rather than a peasant or serf.

142   *litill*. As Kratzmann (p. 129n142) notes: "The repetition of *litill* in lines 145 and 146 and the associated bathos are reminiscent of The Prioress' Tale (*CT* VII, 503, 509, 516, etc.), and have no counterpart in [*Speculum Stultorum*]." *DOST* also records a relevant definition for the adjective: "Used pregnantly to imply modest depreciation, affection, affectionate or amused disparagement, or the like" (sense 4).

145   *litill stone*. In the *Speculum Stultorum* the cock is hurt with a rod (virga) and the boy is mad with anger (line 1281). The change of instrument makes it ironic that Gundulfus later (line 249) meets his downfall after his horse trips on a stone.

149   *slane*. For gloss as "struck down," compare the note to line 776 of the *Historie of Squyer Meldrum* elsewhere in this volume.

150   *wepit all the hennis*. The weeping of the hens is mock-heroic, recalling the grief of the hens at the capture of Chauntecleer in Chaucer's Nuns's Priest's Tale (*CT* VII[B^2] 3355–73) and also Pertok's lamentation in Henryson's "Cock and the Fox" (Henryson, p. 23, lines 495–508).

151–52   *in a garding led / Amang thir herbes*. The herb garden might be designed to recall in mock-heroic fashion the traditional *locus amoenus* of medieval love poetry.

157   *And Gundulfus with his frendis assent*. Kratzmann (p. 130n157) suggests that this line implies Gundulfus received financial support from friends so that he could attend Oxford, adding that this was not uncommon. In the General Prologue of *CT*, Chaucer's Clerk (*CT* I[A]299–300) and Nicholas in The Miller's Tale (*CT* I[A]3220) are given such assistance.

158   *Oxinfurd*. Kratzmann (*Anglo-Scottish Literary Relations*, pp. 94–99) suggests that the English setting of the poem — and additional Chaucerian allusions — are designed to advertise "The Unicornis Tale" as an alternative *CT*.

162   *cruellest of all the cokis*. Chaucer similarly describes Chauntecleer in the Nun's Priest's Tale as a bird who "looketh as it were a grym leoun" (*CT* VII[B^2] 3179).

163   *Copok*. The hen is named Coppa in the *Speculum Stultorum* (line 1378). Hens named Coppok appear in Henryson's "Cock and the Fox" and in the Older Scots *Colkelbie Sow* (in Kratzmann, line 925).

163–66   *he had Copok . . . . ony erdly wicht*. The vows exchanged here between the cock and Copok may be a parody of medieval marriage vows.

167–68   *apon his perke . . . . nixt him sat*. Chauntecleer and Pertelote similarly sit side-by-side in Chaucer's Nun's Priest's Tale (*CT* VII[B^2] 2883–85).

171–74   *So weile he . . . . threttene yeris space*. That the cock is here depicted as a kind of ruler fits in with the wider concern of *The Fyve Bestes* with good governance (both self- and public).

174   *threttene yeris*. The space of time in the *Speculum Stultorum* is six years (line 1311).

176–77   Craigie (ed., *The Asloan Manuscript: A Miscellany in Prose and Verse*, 2:280) and Kratzmann (p. 130n176) both observe that several lines must be missing here, perhaps focusing on Gundulfus' time at Oxford and announcing his return home.

177   *was na master in divinité*. The first of many ironic statements about Gundulfus' skills (or lack thereof). Given that he has been away for thirteen years, Kratzmann (p. 131n177–90) explains that Gundulfus can only have obtained the degree of Master of Arts and not the subsequent Bachelor of Decrees where he would have acquired such theological knowledge. Gundulfus nevertheless pretends (line 178) to be more skilled than he in fact is.

179–80   *Weile couth he . . . . of his greis*. Gundulfus claims to have knowledge of canon law (the "bukis of decres" are Gratian's *Decretals*, a collection on canon law compiled in the twelfth century), but he actually does not have any training in this area. As Kratzmann (*Anglo-Scottish Literary Relations*, p. 99) notes, the phrase "Weile couth he cast" is another Chaucerian echo of the description of the Physician in the General Prologue (*CT* I[A]417–18).

182   *He was a richt gud syngar in the quir*. Gundulfus' singing may recall that of Nicholas in The Miller's Tale (*CT* I[A]3216–18). His singing might also form an ironic counterpart to the crowing of the cock, described at line 161 as "Clerast of voce."

183   *sumpart write and dyte*. That Gundulfus can only write "a little" calls his education and literacy into serious question.

184   *in his gramer was he wele perfyte*. As Kratzmann notes (p. 131n177–90, citing Durkan, "Education in the Century of the Reformation," p. 151) "perfect grammar" meant only mastery of spoken Latin, a requirement for University entrance.

186   *nygramansy*. This was a synonym for sorcery, which Helen Cooper *(English Romance in Time*, p. 161) defines as "magic on the edge of acceptability" deriving from "sources other than God."

187–88   *Of phesik he . . . . seike or hale*. Gundulfus' knowledge of and ability to practice medicine is likely to be as limited as his knowledge of theology and law. Despite such lack of skills we might remember, as Kratzmann observes (p. 131n177–90, citing H. Rashdall, *Universities of Europe in the Middle Ages*, 3:329, 353) that "only about a third of matriculants ever actually took out a degree" and "that benefices were frequently held by young men who had no university training at all."

192   *that noble man*. The ironic description of Gundulfus as "noble" recalls Chaucer's mock praise of his flawed pilgrims in the General Prologue in *CT*. The narrator says of the monk, for instance, "Now certeinly he was a fair prelaat" (*CT* I[A]204) and the Friar is described as a "worthy lymytour" (*CT* I[A]269).

206   *ony orlage richt*. Of Chauntecleer's crowing, Chaucer's Nun's Priest states: "Wel sikerer was his crowyng in his logge / Than is a clokke or an abbey orlogge" (*CT* VII[B^2] 2853–54). The Cock in Henryson's "Cock and Fox" is also described as "our orlege bell" (Henryson, p. 23, line 498).

209   *the farest way*. Within the wider context of the poem as a whole this recalls the "fair" and "plesant way" of "The Horsis Tale" (lines 1, 3).

210   *Rochister*. Rochester is a town in Kent, England and it is in the latter country that the "Unicornis Tale" as a whole is set. Gundulfus' mother indicates (line 209) that their home is just nine miles away from Rochester. In the Prologue to Chaucer's Monk's Tale, the host Harry Bailey exclaims, "Loo, Rouchestre stant heer faste by!" (*CT* VII[B^2] 1926). Interestingly, this tale occurs in Fragment VII/B2 which also contains the Nun's Priest's Tale. This adds further support to our sense that the *FB* author was more widely familiar with the *Canterbury Tales* as a whole.

214–15   *Thai gat to rest . . . . nycht yeid our*. The *Fyve Bestes* author omits the dream of the *Speculum Stultorum* where Gundulfus has a vision of the Mass celebrated after his ordination in which the cock plays the role of cantor (lines 1385–98).

219–20   *And on the . . . . he had none*. As Kratzmann (p. 133n219–20) observes, the "And" at the beginning of this line is awkward; the "sense is that the Cock *had mynd* of his own injury rather than of the clerk's aspirations."

222   *the cok he held him clos*. The cock's silence in the original *Speculum Stultorum* has been discussed by Jill Mann *(From Aesop to Reynard*, pp. 116–21). The cock's silence, and attempt to silence his wife, contrast with his earlier proud singing and the singing of Gundulfus. It also forms part of the poem's wider metatextual exploration of the values and ethics of speech and tale-telling, discussed more fully in the *Fyve Bestes* Introduction.

223   *Coppok putis on hir maike*. In the *Speculum Stultorum*, Coppok attempts to wake up the human sleepers herself. See lines 1361–84 for this and the subsequent exchange between the birds.

224–40   *Slepe ye schir . . . . at my hart.* The rapid and often ill-tempered nature of the exchange between the cock and Coppok recalls that between Chauntecleer and Pertelote in Chaucer's Nun's Priest's Tale. There, the cock and hen also address each other as "Madame" and "Schir" and Pertelote similarly scolds her husband (*CT* VII[B^2] 2908–21, 2970, 3122, 3158). Furthermore, in Henryson's "Tale of the Cock and the Fox," Coppok is the most sanctimonious of the three hens, believing that Chantecleir is damned for his sins.

231   *of the tynsall ye sall haf the blame.* Coppok suggests that the cock will bear the blame for Gundulfus' losing his benefice. Her logic is reminiscent of the wise man's attempt to blame his foolish brother in "The Horsis Tale." Like the wise man, even though the cock did fail to wake up Gundulfus, the latter is himself to blame for the error of his ways since, in drinking heavily the night before his promotion, he displayed a signal lack of self-governance.

243–44   *birdis with ane voce . . . . the dayis sky.* Dunbar's dreaming narrator is similarly awoken by loud birdsong at the end of his *Thrissil and the Rose* (*Poems*, 1:168, lines 183–84).

246   *Said kirk and worschip fastly war away.* My gloss comes from Kratzmann, p. 133. He there suggests that it is also possible "that the line should be direct speech; viz., *Said, 'Kirk and worschipe fastly war away!'* [. . .] If this reading is adopted, *war* must be an unorthodox spelling of *weir*, 'to waste,' 'go.'"

246–47   *Said kirk and . . . . toune he raid.* The *Speculum Stultorum* contains an account, omitted here, of Gundulfus' rapid attempt to find his clothes (lines 1425–30).

249   *at ane stone.* See the note to line 145 above.

251   *This hors gat up.* The horse is another member of the animal kingdom deserting Gundulfus in his hour of need.

252–62   *worthy clerk lay . . . . his legis pane.* In the *Speculum Stultorum* Gundulfus' parents die and he is subsequently reduced to abject poverty (lines 1495–98). This detail is omitted from *Fyve Bestes*.

262   *quyt.* This term runs throughout the fabliaux of Chaucer's *CT*, especially in the Miller's and Reeve's Tales where the pilgrim-narrators and characters within the tales attempt to better or get revenge on each other.

269–80   *Moralitas fabule.* The *moralitas* is surprising for a number of reasons. It differs from its source and the apportioning of blame is somewhat troubling. See *Fyve Bestes* Introduction for further discussion.

273–74   *The tyme may . . . . sic mennis handis.* This warning parallels the situation in Henryson's "Lion and Mouse" where the lion finds himself in need of the assistance of a troop of mice he earlier tyrannized.

284   *scheldis. DOST, s(c)held, s(c)heild(e)*, (n.), sense 7 defines this word as "The thick, tough skin on the sides and flanks of the boar."

288   *I coppyt it.* The narrator here presents himself as working with a written source. Compare line 76 and note above.

The Baris Tale   See *Fyve Bestes* Introduction for summary.

289   *Gret Alexander, king of Massedoun.* Alexander the Great (356–23 BCE) was king of the ancient Greek kingdom of Macedonia and famed for a career of conquests that led to the creation of an exceptionally large empire. Legends of Alexander were particularly common in the medieval period and two separate fifteenth-century Older Scots romances about him survive: the *Buik of Alexander* or *Octosyllabic Alexander* (a translation of two French Alexander texts, *Le Fuerre de Gadres* and *Les Voeux du Paon*, completed by an anonymous Scottish author c. 1438) and Sir Gilbert Hay's *BKA*. Three Scottish monarchs were also named Alexander in the twelfth and thirteenth centuries. It has been suggested that the popularity of Alexander the Great in Older Scots culture was due in no small part to his being Greek, and thus of the same stock as Scotland's mythological founding father, Gaythelos. See Edington, "Paragons and Patriots," and also Caughey and Wingfield, "Conquest and Imperialism." For discussion of the wider Alexander tradition see Cary, *The Medieval Alexander*, and Stone, *From Tyrant to Philosopher-King.*

290   *nyne nobillis.* This detail is unique to "The Baris Tale." The Nine Worthies comprised of three pagans (Hector of Troy, Alexander the Great, and Julius Caesar); three Jews (Joshua, David, and Judas Maccabeus); and three Christians (King Arthur, Charlemagne, and Godfrey of Bouillon). First formulated in *Les Voeux du Paon*, an originally independent poem composed c. 1310–12 by Jacques de Longuyon, the Nine Worthies tradition subsequently became increasingly popular across medieval art, drama, and literature, and was used either to represent a chivalric or monarchical ideal, or alternatively as an exemplum of the vanity of all earthly things. For more discussion of the Nine Worthies tradition, see the *Fyve Bestes* Introduction.

292   *Lapsat.* The town appears as "Lapsare" and in Caxton and "Lampsascus" in Valerius' *Dictorum et Factorum Memorabilium*, but as Lapsat here and also in MS A's *Buke of the Chess* (ed. van Buuren, p. 14, line 359) and Hoccleve's *Regiment of Princes* (line 2304). The spelling in Valerius suggests that the town intended was indeed Lampsacus, an ancient Greek city located on the eastern side of the Hellespont. The former city's name is echoed in the nearby modern town of Lapseki, Turkey. See further *Fyve Bestes* Introduction.

294–95   *To knaw him . . . . his hie empyr.* Alexander demands that the people of Lapsat recognize him as overlord.

296   *Tyr.* Alexander's conquest of Tyre is related in several medieval Alexander texts, including the *BKA* (2.2869–3298), but it is not referred to in any other version of the Lapsat exemplum.

299–308   *To this desyr . . . . defend this toune.* The response of the citizens is a further unique feature of "The Baris Tale." In its use of terms such as "fredome," "subjectioun," and "querell" it recalls the nationalistic focus of "The Hartis Tale" (with the latter two words recalling lines 114 and 120 of that tale). See further *Fyve Bestes* Introduction.

309–11   *This riall prince . . . . agane is gone*. Alexander's anger and sudden return to the town after it has denied him sovereignty are signs of his tyrannical, intractable behavior, reminiscent of Arthur's insatiable desire to besiege Golagros' castle in *Golagros and Gawane* (ed. Hanna, lines 267–73), such that he hastily completes the pilgrimage he had previously planned to undertake.

312   *riallest*. Alexander's host appears to be made up of fellow kings and princes. The horse is similarly described as "riall" (line 57).

320   *Ane worthy clerke*. Within the context of Older Scots romance, the anonymous clerk who appears to advise Alexander recalls Aristotle in Hay's *BKA* and Amytans in *Lancelot of the Laik*. See further *Fyve Bestes* Introduction.

325–27   *So or this . . . . clerk he saw*. The clerk's approach and Alexander's cautious recognition of him recalls the approach of Amytans in *Lancelot of the Laik* (although Arthur's reception of Amytans is far warmer):

> So was he [Arthur] ware thar cummyne to the ost
> O clerk, with whome he was aqwynt befor —
> [. . . .]
> The King befor his palyoune one the gren,
> That knew hyme well and haith his cummyn senn
> Uelcummyt hyme and maid hyme rycht gud chere.
> (ed. Lupack, lines 1294–95, 1305–07).

333–34   *A kingis word . . . . of lawar degré*. The importance of a king's word was proverbial. See Whiting K48. The clerk's moral is repeated using almost exactly the same words in the subsequent *moralitas* (line 354).

342   *tyne the cost*. The option of losing money rather than 'face' does not appear in other versions of the tale.

345   *To counsall yeid*. Contemporary advice to princes literature recommended that monarchs regularly seek counsel. That Alexander here does so is a redeeming feature and the same is true of the lion in "The Wolfis Tale." For further discussion of the poem's alignment with the advice to princes tradition, see *Fyve Bestes* Introduction.

348   *wald nocht tak the lak*. Several characters throughout *The Fyve Bestes* are keen to avoid taking blame, including the wise man and the cock.

354–56   *Ane kyngis word . . . . ony wallit toune*. This moral echoes the lesson given to Alexander in the main body of the tale (lines 333–34). It is strikingly similar to the lesson given to Arthur by Amytans in *Lancelot of the Laik*. See further *Fyve Bestes* Introduction.

357–59   *Richt sad of . . . . in his entent*. For the value of remaining silent compare Proverbs 17:28: "Even a fool, if he will hold his peace shall be counted wise: and if he close his lips, a man of understanding."

359   *entent*. This is a key term, repeated on several occasions throughout the poem. Compare lines 30, 35, 161, 256, and 315. See further *Fyve Bestes* Introduction.

361–64   *gif a kyng . . . . to be obstinat.* These lines — in which the poet places a caveat on the importance of a king sticking to his word — are unique to *The Fyve Bestes*. See further *Fyve Bestes* Introduction.

The Wolfis Tale   Unlike the other four tales, this is not so much an exemplum as an example of tale-telling for false ends.

369   *This wretchit wolf neir by this lyoun lay.* Whereas the other beasts approach the lion-king in a respectful manner, the wolf is already lurking nearby in a decidedly threatening manner.

370   *habit.* This word may — but not necessarily — refer to a clerical garment. Grey habits were worn by Franciscan friars (compare, for instance, "Freir Volff Waitskaith" who wears a "russet coull off gray" in Henryson's "Fox and the Wolf," pp. 29–30, lines 667, 679).

371–72   *And so evill . . . . than thai war.* The wolf's loathsome appearance makes the other beasts look even fairer by comparison. In the medieval period the practice of physiognomy held that a person's character or personality could be judged by his or her outer appearance, especially the face. The wolf's "evill favorit" face is therefore a hint of his inner moral corruption. Compare Henryson's "Fox and the Wolf" (p. 30, line 680) where the wolf is described as having a "lene cheik" and "paill and pietious face."

373–74   *Thinkand to put . . . . the court inbring.* The wolf and his allies represent an alternative faction, a rival to the king's current body of counselors.

376   *staitis.* The wolf is here deliberately obsequious. The word "staitis" may refer simply to "ranks" or "conditions of men" or to "estates of the realm" in parliament. I follow Kratzmann (p. 137n376) in adopting the latter reading.

377   *fabillis fene.* The wolf claims that he will speak truthfully, but his choice of phrase is notably metatextual, disparaging the literal tale-telling of the other beasts.

378   *commoun proffet.* The wolf claims to be speaking on behalf of the public good, no doubt the commons. Throughout the medieval period, in England and in Scotland, those appealing to, and even rebelling against, the king would frequently claim that they had in mind the "commoun proffet." As Mapstone ("Talis of the Fyve Bestes," p. 248) notes, "The protection of the people and the nation has of course featured as a theme in the other tales."

379–86   *In all this . . . . for a yeir.* There is the potential for contradiction here. As Kratzmann (p. 137n379–81) observes: "The *schepe and nolt* are presumably the commons, but the king is hardly to be imagined as eating them: rather, the image expresses the traditional medieval view of the commons as the providers of food for the other orders of society . . . The literal sense of the wolf's advice would seem to be that the king is to turn his attention away from the commons so that they will be more vulnerable to his own assaults."

383   *store.* See *DOST store(e, stoir* (v.), sense 2a.

385–86   *Of venysoun and . . . . for a yeir.* The wolf advises in effect that the king should not 'consume' his own counselors: the hart and boar are the "venysoun" and "wyld meit," the horse and unicorn the "gret bestis."

393–94   *Bot with my . . . . nolt ar deid.* As with Alexander in the previous tale, it should be seen as a sign of good governance that the lion-king seeks the advice of his counselors.

394–96   *Fynd how my . . . . all the land.* The king and his counselors here discover that the wolf and his allies are responsible for the destruction of the sheep and cattle. Wolves are depicted as bringing similar destruction in David Lyndsay's *Dreme* (*Selected Poems*, ed. Hadley Williams, pp. 32–33, lines 890–96).

403   *That all was gone in twynkling of an E.* This phrase appears in Dunbar's *Goldyn Targe* (*Poems*, 1:191, line 235) and *Thrissil and the Rose* (*Poems*, 1:165, line 85), suggesting that *The Fyve Bestes* might itself have been a dream vision.

404   *And so gois all this warldis rialté.* This reminder of earthly mortality, even for royalty, is reminiscent of the closing lines of the previous *moralitas* from the "The Baris Tale."

406   *covatis.* Given the appearance in "The Hartis Tale" of William Wallace it is interesting to note that Menteith's betrayal of Wallace in Hary's poem is blamed on this vice (*Hary's Wallace*, 12.835–48).

408–10   *The vertuis four . . . . content to be.* After the individual *moralitates* of each tale, the four beasts are here again allegorized as the four Cardinal Virtues which should inhere in a monarch. As Mapstone ("*Talis of the Fyve Bestes*," p. 241) observes, "the final rather clever effect is that the beasts who have told the tales and given counsel are allegorized into aspects of the monarch's wisdom. Thus while the necessity for giving advice has been well established, the image of the monarch as containing all virtue within himself has also been preserved. This is a delicate sleight of hand, and a distinctly diplomatic way of giving advice." Kratzmann (pp. 33–34) suggests that the individual morals of the "Horsis," "Hartis," and "Baris" tales prepare us for their allegorization but he has to work harder (and perhaps less convincingly) to explain the link between the moral of "The Unicornis Tale" and allegorization of the unicorn as magnanimity: "the tale of the cock's victory over the negligent clerk may be seen as an ingenious definition of magnanimity in terms of its opposite" (p. 34). In Lyndsay's aforementioned *Dreme* (*Selected Poems*, ed. Hadley Williams, p. 38, lines 1065–67), James V is encouraged to follow the Four Virtues.

411–16   *The vertew no . . . . sauld and bocht.* On the dangers of covetousness compare 1 Timothy 6:10: "For the desire of money is the root of all evils; which some coveting have erred from the faith, and have entangled themselves in many sorrows." The sheep also refers to the "cursit syn of couetice" at line 1300 of Henryson's "Sheep and the Dog" (Henryson, p. 53).

414   *Or yit content had he the hale empyr.* The reference to a covetous man's inability to be satisfied even with a large empire recalls Alexander's greed in the first half of the "Baris Tale."

416   *sauld and bocht*. Compare line 116 and note.

420–22   *And for the joye . . . . of every gud*. The poem concludes with an appeal to God, as
             did the *moralitas* to "The Horsis Tale," "The Unicornis Tale," and "The Baris
             Tale."

TEXTUAL NOTES TO *THE TALIS OF THE FYVE BESTES*

ABBREVIATIONS: *A*: Edinburgh, National Library of Scotland MS 16500 olim Acc. 4243, fols. 229r–35v (the Asloan Manuscript; base manuscript); **Craigie**: *The Asloan Manuscript: A Miscellany in Prose and Verse*, ed. Craigie; **Kratzmann**: *Colkelbie Sow and The Talis of the Fyve Bestes*, ed. Kratzmann.

[Prologue]	A's beginning of *Fyve Bestes* is defective. See the corresponding explanatory note.
7	*Richt so*. A: *Richtso*.
14	*himself*. A: *him self*.
43–44	*In . . . . Thir*. The initial *I* of line 43 is flourished and extends for two lines; the start of line 44 is indented.
48	*fleschis*. So K. A: *flesche*. I follow Kratzmann in amending here on grounds of sense and meter.
63–102	*I hald in . . . . hevin thai wyn*. A number of lines are here missing due to a significant tear that resulted in the loss of much of the top half of fol. 230. I follow Kratzmann in supplying within square brackets words suggested by Craigie to reconstruct the lost text.
63–64	*I . . . . That*. A two-line gap, with guide letter, is left for the initial *I* of line 63; line 64 is indented.
112	*warldly*. A: *wardly*.
118–19	*[Moralitas fabule]*. The start of the moral is not signaled in A as it is for the first tale. I have inserted it.
125	*quhatever*. A: *quhat ever*.
135–36	*Befor . . . . . A*. A two-line gap, with guide letter, is left for the initial *B* at the start of line 135; line 136 is indented.
144	*grange*. A: *grangis*. The singular form agrees better with "grange" in line 140 above and works better metrically.
163	*Copok*. A: *copyng*. "Copok" is the form used for the remainder of the tale and so that is adopted here too.
170	*craw*. A: *crav*.
176–77	Craigie and Kratzmann both observe that, based on sense, several lines must be missing here, but neither attempt to reconstruct them. Laing supplies two lines from the *Speculum Stultorum* (lines 1313–14) as his text's lines 178–79 (*Select Remains*, ed. Laing, p. 286n1), but given the changes the Scots poet made to this source it is difficult to be sure how closely he might have followed it at this point. I do not attempt to reconstruct

missing material but do discuss what information the missing lines may have contained in the corresponding explanatory note.

185   *ane*. A: *na*. I follow Craigie in suggesting that Asloan's "na" be emended to "ane" since being able to practice sophistry well is in fact a criticism; Gundulfus is by contrast able to practice virtuous pursuits and admirable skills less well.

206   *Alswele*. A: *Als wele*.

235   *deid*. Asloan originally wrote "deidis" (perhaps mistakenly echoing the *-is* ending of the previous word, "wyfis") but crossed out the final *-is* abbreviation upon realizing it did not fit the poem's rhyme scheme. The plural form, however, interestingly makes better sense.

268–69   *[Moralitas fabule]*. The start of the moral is not signaled in A. I have inserted it.

269–70   *Nowe . . . . Gif*. A two-line gap, with guide letter, is left for the initial *N* of line 269; line 270 is indented.

273   *tyme may*. A: *tymemay*.

281–82   *It . . . . Of*. A two-line gap, with guide letter, is left for the initial *I* of line 281; line 282 is indented.

282   *bur*. Asloan miscopies and then deletes the word "bair" before "bur."

330   *I*. Asloan miscopies and then deletes "ye" before "I."

352–53   *[Moralitas fabule]*. The start of the moral is not signaled by a heading, nor separated spatially from the preceding tale.

353–54   *Nowe . . . . Ane*. A two-line gap, with guide letter, is left for the initial *N* at the start of line 353; line 354 is indented.

362   *That*. Asloan miscopies and then deletes "In" before "That" at the start of the line.

369–70   *This . . . . His*. A two-line gap, with guide-letter, is left for the intial *T* of line 369; line 370 is indented.

371   *evill*. A: *weile*. This is likely to be an instance of metathesis, a miscopying of "evill" where the scribe has accidentally reversed the letters *ew* and *we*.

401–02   *[Moralitas fabule]*. The concluding *moralitas* is not distinguished in any way from "The Wolfis Tale" in A.

BIOGRAPHY OF SIR DAVID LYNDSAY

The sixteenth-century Scottish poet Sir David Lyndsay[1] is relatively little known to modern audiences, overshadowed as he is in histories of Scottish literature by his more famous predecessors and near-contemporaries Robert Henryson, William Dunbar, and Gavin Douglas. But from his own lifetime until the eighteenth century, Lyndsay was the most famous Scottish poet of all, having an iconic status similar to that which Robert Burns would later enjoy, whereas Henryson, Dunbar, and Douglas faded into relative obscurity, their works out of print, until they were rediscovered by antiquarian scholars of the eighteenth and nineteenth centuries. Sir Walter Scott, in his novel *Rob Roy*, has his gruffly nationalist character Andrew Fairservice pour scorn on the literary pretensions of the English narrator Frank Osbaldistone with "Gude help him! twa lines o' Davie Lindsay wad ding a' he ever clerkit."[2] By 1817, when Scott was writing *Rob Roy*, Burns had already replaced Lyndsay as the nation's favorite poet, but Fairservice's reverence for Lyndsay is part of Scott's romantic recreation of Jacobite Scotland in 1715. In his 1808 work *Marmion*, Scott's similarly nostalgic homage to medieval metrical romance, he paints an affectionate portrait of Lyndsay as Lyon King of Arms and poet, dubbing him "the Herald-bard" (4.14.5):

> He was a man of middle age;
> In aspect manly, grave, and sage,
>   As on King's errand come;
> But in the glances of his eye,
> A penetrating, keen, and sly
>   Expression found its home;
> . . . .
> Still is thy name in high account,
>   And still thy verse has charms,
> Sir David Lindesay of the Mount,
>   Lord Lion King-at-arms!
> (*Marmion*, ed. Masterman, Canto 4.7.1–6, 28–31)

As for the real David Lyndsay of the Mount, Kinsley quipped memorably that he "steps vividly into history wearing a coat of blue and yellow taffeta for a play at Holyrood in

---

[1] His surname can also be spelled "Lyndesay," "Lindesay" or "Lindsay." The spelling adopted here, Lyndsay, is that preferred in recent scholarship. It corresponds to his only known signature and distinguishes him from the modern science fiction writer David Lindsay.

[2] *Rob Roy*, ed. Duncan, p. 252. Elsewhere, Fairservice muses "What wad Sir William Wallace, or auld Davie Lindsay, hae said to the Union, or them that made it?" (p. 313).

October 1511."[3] This is not strictly true, for Douglas Hamer's painstakingly assembled catalogue of over 100 historical records relating to Lyndsay includes several important earlier references,[4] but it is the first record in which the national figure that he would become — chief herald (Lord Lyon, King of Arms), poet, playwright — is clearly recognizable.

Lyndsay seems likely to have been born in 1486. Hamer points to a charter of 19 October 1507, in which he is confirmed by his distant kinsman, Patrick, Lord Lindsay of the Byres, in the lands of "Garmylton-Alexander" (Garleton, East Lothian) as the eldest son and heir of "David Lindesay de Month," suggesting (though not absolutely proving) that he had reached 21, the age of majority.[5] The title "de Month" is taken from their lands at the Mount, near Cupar in Fife. Lyndsay and his four younger brothers may have grown up in Fife or in East Lothian, although Lyndsay eventually retired to Fife. Nothing is known of his youth. There is a "Da. Lindesay" in a list of students incorporated in St Salvator's College, University of St Andrews (in Fife) for 1508 or 1509 which was once assumed to refer to our poet,[6] but Lyndsays proliferated in Scotland and an inconvenient number of them were named David. Hamer points instead to a record in the *Exchequer Rolls*, also for 1508, of "one called Lyndesay in the stable of the late prince" (the "prince" was the short-lived first Prince James, 21 February 1507 – 17 February 1508).[7] The fact that in later records Lyndsay is not referred to as "maister" argues against identifying him as the St Andrews student,[8] whereas his career-long involvement with the pageantry and chivalric display of court — with its inevitable requirement for well-trained horses — suggests he may well have started off managing the prince's stables.

---

[3] Kinsley (*Squyer Meldrum*, p. 2) thus brings to life the dry record of the payment for this outfit and its purpose in *TA* 4:313, although he mistakenly cites it as *TA* 4:269 (which is a less glamorous record from the same year of pensions of £40 paid to various men, including a "David Lindesay" who is probably our poet).

[4] Hamer, *Works*, Appendix 1, 4:241–77. There are excellent discussions of Lyndsay's career and works in Hamer (4:ix–xl); Edington, *Court and Culture*, pp. 11–66; Hadley Williams, *Selected Poems*, pp. vii–xiii.

[5] In one of his maddeningly casual asides, David Laing writes that he found the charter after being "kindly favoured by Thomas Graham Murray, Esq., with a sight of the MS. Inventories, and also with the use of some of the original deeds specially connected with Garmylton," and he quotes it only in part: "*dilecto nostro consanguineo David Lindesay filio et heredi apparenti David Lindesay de Montht* nostri eciam consanguinei . . . quas terras de Garmiltoun cum pertinem. quondam David Lindesay consanguineus noster AVUS DICTI DAVID habuit hereditarie et de nobis tenuit, &c. It is dated 19th October 1507; and the Sasine on the 6th April following." (Laing, *Poetical Works*, 1:ix, italics his). The charter has not been traced, although its authenticity has not been seriously questioned; see Edington, *Court and Culture*, p. 231n8. See also p. 228 for a family tree illustrating the kinship between the Lyndsays of the Mount and the Lords Lindsay of the Byres.

[6] Laing, *Poetical Works*, 1:x–xi. See Anderson, *Early Records*, pp. 203–04.

[7] *ER* 13:127: "uno vocato Lyndesay in averia quondam domini principis." The fact that full names are recorded for everyone else in this entry may indicate that the "one called Lyndesay" was new to them.

[8] Lyndsay is styled "maister" in a record of parliamentary judicial proceedings from December 1543 (RPS Mary I, 1543/12/10), but Edington notes that "such references are so scarce as to suggest clerical error" (*Court and Culture*, p. 231n14).

In 1512 Lyndsay is recorded as an "ischar to the Prince," this now referring to the second Prince James, born 10 April 1512. Lyndsay continued in this role after his charge was crowned James V following the disastrous battle of Flodden (9 September 1513) at which his father James IV died. Records refer to Lyndsay variously as *hostiario domini regis* or "the Kingis uschare," "kepar of the Kingis grace," *hostiarii camere regis* ("usher of the king's chamber").[9] An usher was not a tutor — that role was filled by others — but a companion, and Lyndsay would reminisce about these days in later poems to James, with whom he evidently remained on close terms for the whole of the king's life:

Quhen thow wes young, I bure the in myne arme	*carried*
Full tenderlie, tyll thow begouth to gang	*began to walk*
And in thy bed oft happit the full warme,	*wrapped*
With lute in hand syne sweitlie to the sang.	
Sumtyme in dansing, feiralie I flang,	*vigorously; leapt about*
And sumtyme playand fairsis on the flure,	*short dramas; floor*
And sumtyme on myne office takkand cure.	*looking after*
[. . . .]	
So, sen thy birth, I have continewalye	
Bene occupyit, and aye to thy plesoure,	
And sumtyme seware, coppare, and carvoure,	*table attendant, cup-bearer; carver*
Thy purs maister and secreit thesurare,	*privy treasurer*
Thy ischare, aye sen thy natyvitie,	*usher; birth*
And of thy chalmer cheiffe cubiculare,	*chamber; groom*
Quhilk, to this houre, hes keipit my lawtie.	*loyalty*
(*The Dreme*, lines 8–14, 19–25)[10]	

In the *Complaynt*, he reminds the king

Quhow, as ane chapman beris his pak,	*pedlar*
I bure thy grace upon my bak	
And sumtimes strydlingis on my nek,	*astride*
Dansand with mony bend and bek.	*leaps and bows*
The first sillabis that thow did mute	*syllables; speak*
Was, "Pa, Da Lyn". . . [perhaps "Play, Da(vid) Lyn(dsay)!"]	
(lines 87–92)	

The *Treasurer's Accounts* are missing from September 1518 to June 1522. When they recommence, they record a "Jenet Dowglas, spous to David Lindsay maister Ischare to the King" who was a seamstress at court.[11] But things would soon become awkward at court for

---

[9] See *TA* 4:441 for the 1512 reference; Hamer collects this and the other citations (*Works*, 4:247–50).

[10] All quotations from Lyndsay's other works are from Hadley Williams' *Selected Poems*.

[11] *TA* 5:196. The latest record Hamer found for her was a charter of 5 May 1542 as witnessed by William Meldrum (see Introduction to the *Squyer Meldrum* Poems, "Squire of Cleish and Binns," elsewhere in this volume) which confirmed her and Lyndsay in the lands of Garmilton-Alexander, and he assumed she had died not long after this (Hamer, *Works*, 4:xiii). In fact, she resurfaces in a letter

Lyndsay. Archibald Douglas, sixth Earl of Angus and estranged husband of the Queen Mother, Margaret Tudor, returned from exile in 1524. By 1525 he had gained control of both government and adolescent king, clearing away Margaret's supporters and those — presumably like Lyndsay — who might have influenced the young king in ways inconvenient to Angus. Lyndsay was not left entirely out in the cold, however. Although not at court, he still drew a pension: the *Exchequer Rolls* for 1525 describe him as being *quondam hostiario domini regis* — "formerly usher to the king" — and award him the forty-pound annuity that he *solebat percipere* "was accustomed to receive."[12] Hamer speculated that he was working as a pursuivant (a junior herald), but there is no evidence for this.[13] His wife, Janet Douglas, continued to work at court throughout this period, possibly thanks to Douglas family connections.[14] In 1528, the sixteen-year-old king broke free of Angus' control and embarked on his personal rule, dismissing many Douglas followers from office and installing his own supporters.[15] Hamer had dated Lyndsay's earliest known poem, *The Dreme*, to this year since it seems to be a plea for a return to the king's personal favor, but Carol Edington has since placed it more convincingly c. 1526 on the grounds of references in it to an on-going civil war and the fact that John the Commonweal is waiting until the country should be "gydit / Be wysedome of ane gude auld prudent kyng," which he thinks will happen soon (lines 992, 1004–05 and 1002).[16] Lyndsay did return to both court and favor (if he had ever really fallen out of the latter): the *Exchequer Rolls* for 1528 describe him once again as *familiari domini regis* (i.e., a member of the king's household, but also perhaps a familiar friend), and they record a payment of eighty pounds to cover the current and previous years' annuities.[17]

By 1530, Lyndsay appears in records as "herald," and by 1531 he is Snowdon Herald:[18] his only known holograph signature appears in a diplomatic letter sent from Antwerp in this year.[19] Over the next several years Lyndsay would spend a lot of time on the continent on the king's business: diplomatic missions were an important part of the herald's job alongside the management of court ceremony, tournaments, and matters of heraldry and arms.[20] Lyndsay was a member of embassies to France in 1532, 1534, and 1535–37 to negotiate on

---

of reversion to Walter Lundyn (or Lundy) by "Sir David Lyndesay of the Mounth, kt. and Lyon herald, and Jonet Dowglas, his spouse," dated 28 August 1552 (NRS GD160/281, item 8).

[12] *ER* 15:116.

[13] Edington, *Court and Culture*, p. 26; Hamer, IV:xviii–xix.

[14] See, for example, *Reg. Sec. Sig.* 1:541, no. 3570, a letter of December 1526 granting Janet livery and an annual pension of £10, associated payments in 1526 and 1527 (*TA* 5:314 and 329), and a payment in April 1527 for "David Lindesayis wife to sew the Kingis sarkis" (*TA* 5:301). Further discussion in Hamer, *Works*, 4:xii–xiv.

[15] See Emond, "Minority of King James V," pp. 552–59.

[16] Hamer, *Works*, 4:xiv-xv; Edington, *Court and Culture*, pp. 24–25.

[17] *ER* 15:395.

[18] "David Lyndesaye, Snawdon herald" in *LP Henry VIII*, 5:116, no. 254.

[19] He signs himself "Dauid Lyndsay harauld to our sowerain Lord": Antwerp, 23 August 1531 (London, British Library, MS Cotton Caligula B.1, fol. 313); see Hadley Williams, "'Of officiaris serving thy senyeorie.'"

[20] On the various roles of Scottish officers of arms, see Stevenson, "Jurisdiction, Authority and Professionalisation," pp. 62–66.

James' behalf for a wife, latterly for the hand of Madeleine, daughter of the French king Francis I; James and Madeleine married in Paris on 1 January 1537. The third Lyndsay poem in the present collection, *The Answer to the Kingis Flyting*, seems to date from the period of marriage negotiations in 1535–36 (see the Introduction to that poem). They became particularly tricky thanks to the reluctance of Francis I to let the sixteen-year-old Madeleine go out of fear for her frail health, and his fears were well founded: Madeleine would die within two months of her arrival in Scotland (7 July 1537). Lyndsay found himself canceling the festivities planned for her State entry to Edinburgh in order to arrange her funeral instead. The following year, Lyndsay directed the elaborate pageantry welcoming the second royal bride, Mary of Guise, to St Andrews, and probably also her entry to Edinburgh.[21]

Hamer argues that Lyndsay had been acting as the chief herald of the realm, Lyon King of Arms since about 1535 — certainly he is cited as "David Lindesay, Lyoun herald" in the *Treasury Accounts* for 1538 — but he would not be formally invested in the role until 1542, the same year he completed a still-authoritative Armorial Roll (an illustrated collection of recognized coats of arms).[22] This was the year in which James V himself died of illness at Falkland Palace in Fife, on 14 December, aged just 30. As Lyon King of Arms, Lyndsay had to organize James's state funeral. He continued to serve as Lyon King of Arms under the second duke of Arran, acting Regent for the infant Queen Mary, and he evidently impressed the English court in 1543 on his visit there to return James' Order of the Garter. Henry VIII wrote to Arran to say that the Lord Lyon had fulfilled himself "right discreetly."[23]

The Arran administration proved a fickle master, however. Regular pension payments to Lyndsay stop in 1543. He attended parliaments in Edinburgh in 1544 and Linlithgow in 1545 as a burgh commissioner for Cupar, but he appears to have spent the majority of his time in Fife.[24] He seems likely to have socialized with his distant cousin John, Lord Lindsay of the Byres, whose family seat, the Struthers, was within five miles of Lyndsay's own estates and who had in his employ the William Meldrum who is the subject of the *Historie* and *Testament* edited here. But Lyndsay cannot really be said to have retired: when a group of Fife lairds with strong Protestant sympathies broke into St Andrews castle on 29 May 1546 to assassinate Cardinal David Beaton, holding the castle thereafter with Arran's own son as hostage, it was Lyndsay who was sent to negotiate with them — a shrewd move given that Lyndsay would have known them personally and was likely to have commanded their

---

[21] Hamer, *Works*, 4:xxiii–iv. The pageant at St Andrews, and Lyndsay's participation in it, are described enthusiastically by Pitscottie, *Historie and Cronicles* 1:379.

[22] On his responsibilities in the late 1530s, see Hamer, *Works* 4:xx–xxi; Edington, *Court and Culture*, pp. 26–41; and *TA* 6:423. His formal appointment as Lyon King of Arms is recorded in *Reg. Sec. Sig.* 2:742, no. 4910. Lyndsay's Armorial is Edinburgh, NLS MS Advocates 31.4.3. See *Fac-Simile of an ancient heraldic manuscript: emblazoned by Sir David Lyndsay of the Mount. Lyon king of armes 1542*, ed. Laing.

[23] *LP Henry VIII*, 18.i:342, item 591.

[24] Hamer (*Works*, 4:270–73) lists a series of records including Lyndsay's witnessing of a proclamation in Cupar in 1543 (now RPS Mary I, 1543/12/10), or payments for letters sent "to the Mont for Lyoun herold" in 1544, 1547, and February 1549–50 (*TA* 8:275, *TA* 9:96 and 381). Lyndsay's attendance at parliament as a burgh commissioner for Cupar in 1544 and 1545 is confirmed in RPS 1544/11/3 (7 November 1544) and 1545/9/28/10 (1 October 1545); see also *LP Henry VIII*, 19:2, p. 375, no. 626 (Nov. 1544).

respect.[25] His bitterly satirical *Tragedie of the Cardinall* (a dramatic monologue by the murdered Beaton) was published swiftly after this experience, and it demonstrates how much sympathy he had with the rebels' hatred of Beaton, whatever he may have thought of their actions.[26] After a last diplomatic mission to Denmark in 1548–49,[27] Lyndsay returned to Fife and turned his attention more fully to writing. The vast play for which he is now most famous — *Ane Satyre of the Thrie Estaitis* — was first performed in Cupar in June 1552. Evidently successful, it would be performed again in Edinburgh in August 1555 before the regent Mary of Guise. The year 1554, meanwhile, saw the first printing of his long contemplative work *Ane Dialogue betuix Experience and Ane Courteour* (or *The Monarche*). Lyndsay seems to have retained the title of Lyon King of Arms until his death, even if younger heralds were by then performing most of the associated duties. He is recorded as presiding over a trial on 16 January 1555 as Lyon King,[28] but the next record to name Lyndsay is a charter of 13 March 1555 in which both he and his wife are listed as deceased.[29]

Despite Lyndsay's distinctly secular career, his soaring popularity as a poet after Scotland's Protestant Reformation of 1560 rested partly on his reputation as an apparent champion of the Protestant cause. John Knox noted approvingly that the rebels at St Andrews castle in 1546 invited him, Knox, to preach to them "having with thame in counsall Schir David Lyndesay of the Mont,"[30] and seventeenth-century historians of the Reformed Scottish Kirk praised Lyndsay alongside avowed Reformers as if he were one of their number.[31] This probably did much to keep his reputation buoyant while those of his fellow-poets Henryson, Dunbar, and Douglas languished in the seventeenth century. In fact, Lyndsay is not known to have converted to Protestantism, but he was certainly a sharp critic of Church corruption in poems such as the *Tragedie of the Cardinall* or *Ane Dialog betwix*

---

[25] Edington, *Court and Culture*, pp. 62–63.

[26] The earliest surviving print is by John Day and William Seres in London, probably from 1548 (STC 15683), but Hamer argues for a now-lost print of 1547, probably by John Scot at Dundee or St Andrews (Hamer, *Works*, 4:19–22). In terms of Lyndsay's reformist sympathies, Hadley Williams argues that Lyndsay's original poem manages to remain "astutely moderate," in contrast to its treatment in the overtly Protestant London print of 1548 ("The Earliest Surviving Text," p. 30).

[27] *TA* 9:259 (Dec 1548): "to Schir David Lindesay, King of Armes, send with certane writtinges and directiounes to the King of Denmark, to be his expensis , . . . vii^xx li. [i.e., 120 pounds]." See also *TA* 9:347 (July 1549).

[28] Messenger William Crawar was tried in the chapter of the abbey of Holyroodhouse before "Sir David Lindsay of the Mount knight lyon king of armes" for his "manyfold oppressions, extortions and complaints," for which Crawar was duly convicted and removed from office. Chalmers quotes this from "a MS. Col. in the Advocates' library, Ja. V.7.12 " (*Poetical Works*, 1:39). The modern shelfmark is Advocates 34.6.24, and the entry for the trial is on pp. 277–78 (fols. 139r–v in pencil numbering), in amongst various copies of documents relating to the Lindsay earls of Crawford. The record was extracted and signed by "Adam Makculloth [sic], bute persevant [i.e., Bute Pursuivant] Clerk of the office of armes with my hand."

[29] *Reg.Mag.Sig.* 4:225, no. 1006: "quondam Jonete Dowglas sponse quond. Davidis Lindesay de Month."

[30] Edington, *Court and Culture*, p. 63, quoting from John Knox, *Works*, 1:186.

[31] See for example the 1639 *History of the Church of Scotland* by John Spottiswoode, 1:144 and 192, quoted in Hamer, *Works*, 4:267–68.

Experience and ane Courteour, and he was explicit in his support of specific individual Protestant goals such as making the Bible available in the vernacular. Speaking of those who have "no Leid except thare toung maternall" (no language except their mother tongue), he protests: "Quhy suld of god the maruellous heuinly werk / Be hid frome thame? I thynk it not fraternall" (*Ane Dialog*, lines 554–55).

The basic meaning of *flyte* (v.) as given in the *Dictionary of the Older Scottish Tongue* is "to wrangle violently; to employ abusive language towards others; to scold." Flyting seems to have been a common phenomenon in early modern Scottish society, indulged in by both men and women: it is the subject of many disciplinary hearings in burgh and church session records, and the details of the insults exchanged appear to have been recorded with relish by the session scribes.[1] Margo Todd notes that the Aberdeen session records make a helpful distinction between mere "common skoldis" and "flyttaris":

> In general, flyting was mutual — with epithets exchanged on both sides; it was public, generally conducted in the street; and its language was formulaic and colourful — so much so that, unlike the scolding and defamation cases that dominated English church court agendas in the same period, it had excited the attention and imitation of the Scots makars (poets) from at least the fifteenth century.[2]

This "imitation" flyting by the Scots makars took the form of scurrilous yet highly formalized exchanges of insults in verse, in which each poet's aim was to display his (for they are all male) own poetic skill while destroying the reputation and artistic credibility of his opponent. The language of the street, or the gutter, is clearly heard in these poetic flytings, but it is not their sole inspiration. The Older Scots poetic flyting is a distinctive manifestation of a much broader literary tradition of competitive invective, which includes examples as diverse as the invectives traded by the heroes in Homer's *Iliad*;[3] Celtic and Icelandic satires, lampoons, cursings,[4] and learned exchanges such as the famously vicious and personal dispute between the fifteenth-century Italian humanists Poggio Bracciolini and Lorenzo Valla over (among other things) who was the best Latin scholar.[5] This was played

---

[1] See Todd, *Culture of Protestantism*, pp. 235–49, and Bawcutt, "Art of Flyting," pp. 6–7. Ewan makes a useful distinction between numbers of men and women actually accused of defamation in pre-Reformation church courts, and the portrayal of flyting in some legislative and literary sources as a primarily female activity. She gives a total from the surviving pre-1560 records of 82 women accused of defamation against 52 men — i.e., a less gendered activity than is sometimes assumed in modern literary scholarship ("'Many Injurious Words,'" pp. 176–78).

[2] Todd, *Culture of Protestantism*, p. 236n35, citing Aberdeen, St. Nicholas Kirk session minutes, 1562–78, p.7 (NRS CH2/448/1).

[3] Hesk, "Homeric Flyting."

[4] Touched on by Gray, "Rough Music," pp. 22–23. Bawcutt is more skeptical about the relevance of these more distant parallels to Older Scots flytings (see *Poems of William Dunbar*, ed. Bawcutt, 2:429).

[5] McLaughlin, "Dispute between Poggio and Valla."

out in 1452–53, but was still famous enough to be cited by Dunbar's contemporary Gavin Douglas in his 1501 *Palis of Honoure*:

| And Pogyus stude with mony gyrn and grone | *Poggio; sneer; groan* |
| On Laurence Valla spyttand and cryand "Fy!" | *spitting and crying* |

(ed. Parkinson, lines 1232–33)

The most famous Older Scots flyting is *The Flyting of Dunbar and Kennedy*, printed by Chepman and Myllar in 1508 but composed before 1505.[6] It established the pattern followed by later literary flytings such as Lyndsay's *Answer*, William Stewart's *Flytting betuix þe Sowtar and the Tailōour* (1530s) or the spectacular flyting of c. 1584 between Alexander Montgomery and Patrick Hume of Polwart, poets of King James VI's literary circle.[7] William Dunbar and Walter Kennedy were both well-educated, well-known figures at the court of James IV, and both had established reputations as poets. Their *Flyting* consists of two short challenges followed by a single long invective from each poet. There has been much speculation as to where and how such flytings circulated; Priscilla Bawcutt notes that *The Flyting of Dunbar and Kennedy*'s opening lines "imply the existence of an earlier attack mounted by Kennedy . . . and it is likely that the work originated in a series of separate invectives that first circulated in manuscript."[8] This corresponds to the situation described by Lyndsay, in which he has "red" the king's "ragment," been disparaged by his "prunyeand pen" (piercing pen), and had his reputation amongst the ladies ruined by James' "libellis" (letters; lines 1–8). Bawcutt and others have speculated that Dunbar and Kennedy's *Flyting* might also have been performed as a court entertainment, designed to whip up an audience to cheers: such performative aspects are explored further in Caitlin Flynn and Christy Mitchell's comparison between Older Scots poetic flytings and modern rap battles.[9]

As befits a poetic contest, Dunbar and Kennedy flyte in complex eight-line rhymed stanzas heavily studded with alliteration, and the diction is a dizzying combination of formality and salty colloquialism. Dunbar in particular works himself up into a frenzy of foul-mouthed alliterating invective for which a modern reader is helplessly reliant on a glossary: "Forflittin, countbittin, beschittin, barkit hyd, / Clym ledder, fyle tedder, foule edder, I defy thee!" (Out-flyted, cunt-bitten [i.e., either "poxed" or impotent], shit-covered, tanned-hide / Ladder-climber, noose-defiler, foul adder, I defy thee!, ed. Conlee, lines 239–40). This puts Lyndsay's single use of "fukkand . . . fornicatour" (line 49) in *The Answer* into perspective.

Some of Dunbar and Kennedy's favored categories of insult are off-limits for Lyndsay. The earlier poets make much of each other's hideous appearance, something that may not have gone down well with the young bachelor king no matter how jokingly presented.

---

[6] *Poems of William Dunbar*, ed. Bawcutt, 2:429.

[7] For the text of Stewart's *Flytting*, see *Bannatyne Manuscript*, ed. Ritchie, 3:22–26; for discussion see Fisher, "Contemporary Humour" (see p. 16 for suggested dating in the early 1530s). For Montgomery and Polwart, see Montgomerie, *Poems*, ed. Parkinson, no. 99 (1:139–75). James VI quotes from this as an example of flyting verse in his 1584 "Ane Schort Treatise Conteining Some Reulis and Cautelis to be Observit and Eschewit in Scottis Poesie" (*Mercat Anthology*, eds. Jack and Rozendaal, p. 470).

[8] *Poems of William Dunbar*, ed. Bawcutt, 2:428.

[9] Bawcutt, "Art of Flyting," pp. 11–12; Flynn and Mitchell, "'It may be verifyit.'"

Shameful lineage is another major theme for the earlier poets, but as Janet Hadley Williams observes, "a Dunbarian attack on the king's ancestry . . . could amount to treason."[10] Even the element of poetic competition is a potentially dangerous one for Lyndsay to introduce: he acknowledges the trope by offering praise (rather than criticism) of James' verse while writing in beautifully measured rhyme royal stanzas himself. Such inversion of the tropes established by Dunbar and Kennedy's *Flyting* is in fact one of Lyndsay's key techniques in *The Answer*. He wishes that "sum tygerris toung wer to me lent" (line 4) rather than demonstrating possession of one himself (though other satirical works show that he can exercise a "tygerris toung" perfectly well when he wants to). Where Kennedy promises that Dunbar will be made to beg for mercy and cry "*cor mundum*" (line 20) on his knees, Lyndsay claims that he will be reduced to this himself by James' invective.

It seems at first as if another major category of insult — accusations of sexual impotence — will likewise be handled by simple inversion: Lyndsay complains that James' insults have made him a laughing-stock amongst women and had him metaphorically "dejectit" from Venus' court (lines 7–13), and he notes in contrast how James is "in till Venus werkis maist vailyeand" (line 26). But this praise is the very thing that Lyndsay allows to sour over the next few stanzas. First he offers himself as an example of one who has grown wiser with age and now regrets that he ever pursued women for sex (lines 31–33); then he outlines the dire physical consequences of too much sex, hastening death by expending one's life-force too wastefully (see note to lines 40–42 for the contemporary medical beliefs underlying these claims). Not only does this neatly turn Lyndsay's supposed lack of sexual activity from a failing into a virtue, but it also turns James' promiscuity from a matter of pride to one of national concern. At this point Lyndsay, ever the diplomat, softens the blow by inverting another flyting trope: instead of cursing James, he curses the king's advisers — "I give your counsale to the feynd of hell" — for not providing him with an appropriate bride (see note to lines 43–44).

Continuing the theme of the king's sexual incontinence, Lyndsay turns to another flyting trope. This is the dramatized scene in which the opponent is comically humiliated. The most memorable example from Dunbar and Kennedy's *Flyting* is Kennedy's vivid account of Dunbar's alleged voyage on the Katryne (*Poems of William Dunbar*, ed. Bawcutt, lines 449–72), where his sea-sickness resulted in such spectacular bouts of vomiting and diarrhea that he "beschate the stere [helm], the compas and the glas [hourglass]" and "spewit and kest out many a lathly lomp / Fastar than all the marynaris coud pomp" (vomited and threw up many a disgusting chunk / faster than all the sailors could pump; lines 460 and 462–63) so that the captain had to order Dunbar off at the Bass Rock, and the ship's ropes were still encrusted with excrement twenty years later. In *The Answer*, Lyndsay describes a scene in which James pounces on an eager "quene" (wench, but with an undoubted pun on the royal title) in the brew-house, throwing her across a "stinking" trough (line 53) and copulating so energetically that they knock over a mashing-vat and empty its contents all over themselves, leaving them "swetterand lyke twa swyne" (wallowing like two pigs; line 58). This bit of slapstick may be less spectacular than Kennedy's tale of

---

[10] "'Thus euery man said for hym self,'" p. 264. Todd observes: "As in the works of the makars, street flyting abounds with demeaning references to physical appearance and to clan and ancestry, especially charges that one's forebears or kin were immoral, diseased or criminal" (*Culture of Protestantism*, pp. 237–38).

the beshitten ship, but it fulfills its purpose of appearing to laugh with James about his sexual adventures, while delicately suggesting that, if he is not more careful, some may start to laugh at him.

Many of the accusations hurled in Dunbar and Kennedy's *Flyting* are deliberate fantasy, but Lyndsay's accusations of sexual promiscuity would seem to have been not far from the truth. James is known to have fathered at least eight illegitimate children on various high-born mistresses (see note to line 57), and the eldest of these was born when James was just seventeen. One may surmise from this that there were more whose humbler circumstances kept them out of the historical record.[11] It was clearly a genuine worry for Lyndsay. In his *Complaynt*, when he writes of the period of the earl of Angus' ascendency during which he was unable to keep such a close watch over James, he imagines a series of sycophantic courtiers tempting the teenaged king with a girl at every royal palace: "ane maid in Fyfe, / Ane of the lusteast wantoun lassis" (presumably at Falkland Palace); another "lusty las" in Linlithgow; a "dayis derlyng" in Stirling, and finally an offer to visit the "hie boirdall" (i.e., "great brothel").[12] It is notable how careful Lyndsay is to lay the blame for James' promiscuity elsewhere, as he does at lines 43–44 of *The Answer*. Hadley Williams notes that *The Answer*'s deft portrait of James' lack of self-control may suggest a "momentary parallel" (albeit in a different sphere of action) to his father James IV, who died leading a rash charge at the battle of Flodden in 1513, "Distroyit . . . / Nocht be the vertew of Inglis ordinance, / Bot be his awin wylfull mysgovernance" (*Testament of the Papyngo*, ed. Hadley Williams, lines 512–13).[13] Lyndsay may also have been genuinely concerned for the king's health: the "grandgore" (line 63) that James has so far escaped only by the grace of God is syphilis, a serious sexually-transmitted disease (certainly in the days before antibiotics) which was only recorded in Scotland from the 1490s onwards (see note to line 63). On the other hand, he may introduce it here (in characteristically indirect form) because it is appropriate for a flyting: Dunbar calls Kennedy "countbittin" in line 239 (which may imply venereal disease), and Todd notes that to call someone "gangorie" or accuse them of having "the gangore" was a common insult recorded in the sixteenth-century church session accounts of flytings and slander.[14]

In sum, *The Answer to the Kingis Flyting* may retain enough genuine "flyting" features to justify its title, but Lyndsay has effectively commandeered the form in order to offer veiled advice to his wayward king.

DATE AND HISTORICAL CONTEXT

The Answer was clearly written before James V married, but Lyndsay's final coy reference to "ane bukler" [a shield] who will come forth, "sum sayis," from France to endure James' strokes (lines 68–69) suggests that negotiations for a French bride were reasonably well advanced. This would seem to date the poem to 1535–36. Although the Franco-Scottish Treaty of Rouen of 1517 had included a promise to provide a French royal bride for the

---

[11] See Thomas, *Princelie Majestie*, pp. 41–43, and the telling *ODNB* entry, "James V, mistresses and children of."

[12] "The Complaynt of Schir David Lindesay" (*Selected Poems*, ed. Hadley Williams, lines 238–52). She speculates that the "hie boirdall" (great brothel) might be a reference to Edinburgh.

[13] Hadley Williams, "Thus euery man said for hym self," p. 265.

[14] *Culture of Protestantism*, p. 239.

Scottish king, succeeding years had seen the consideration of candidates from Portugal, England, Denmark, the Netherlands, Lorraine, and Italy, as well as several from France itself. It was not until 6 March 1536 that a marriage contract was finally drawn up between James and Marie de Bourbon, daughter of the Duke of Vêndome.[15] The contemporary chronicler Adam Abell reports that James was rumored to have visited the court of the Duke of Vêndome in disguise in September 1536 to make a secret assessment of Marie, the apparent result of which was his determination to win the teenaged Madeleine de Valois, daughter of Francis I, instead.[16] Although the French king was reluctant to let Madeleine go, James was successful in his suit and they were married at Nôtre Dame on 1 January 1537. Alas, Francis' fears about Madeleine's fragile health were justified: Madeleine fell ill in March and died at Holyrood Palace on 7 July 1537.[17]

EARLY PRINTS AND THIS EDITION

The present text was edited from the earliest extant witness, the 1568 *Warkis* of Lyndsay published by Henrie Charteris.[18] This is the earliest surviving edition to contain what Hamer labels the second series of minor poems.[19] In the Table of Contents, *The Answer* is excitingly labeled "neuer befoir Imprentit," and Charteris would not drop this advertising tag until his 1592 edition. The poem occupies only three of the 1568 edition's 392 pages, and the text does not alter across the several editions Charteris brought out in the later sixteenth century; it thus does not seem necessary to offer detailed descriptions of all of these early prints of the *Warkis* here. The copy of *The Answer* in Bassandyne's 1574 *Warkis* (see below) was consulted but not collated, since textual differences are entirely trivial, consisting of spelling variants (e.g., line 1 "haif" for Charteris' "have," or line 54 "feind" for Charteris' "feynd") or differing practice with abbreviations, which Bassandyne tends to use more heavily — particularly the suspension for missing *n/m*. Otherwise, Bassandyne's text follows that of Charteris right down to the punctuation.

Lyndsay's works were also printed outside Scotland in the sixteenth century, but neither the anglicized London editions of Lyndsay's poems published by Thomas Purfoote (*A Dialogue betweene Experience and a Courtier and Other Poems*, 1566, 1575, and 1581)[20] nor the selection of Lyndsay's poems translated into Danish by Jacob Mattssøn and published by Hans Stockelmann the Younger (Copenhagen, 1591) include *The Answer*.[21]

---

[15] Cameron, *James V*, pp. 131–33.

[16] See Stewart, "Final Folios,'" p. 252. The story was later reported by Pitscottie, *Historie and Cronicles*, 1:358–59.

[17] Cameron, *James V*, p. 133.

[18] *The Answer* has previously been edited by Chalmers, Laing, Hamer, and Hadley Williams (see the list of editions at the end of the present volume's introductory Biography of Sir David Lyndsay).

[19] Hamer, *Works*, 4:45–46. These are: "The Deploratioun of the Deith of Quene Magdalene," "The Answer," "The Complaint and Publict Confessioun of the Kingis auld Hound, callit Bagsche," "Ane Supplicatioun . . . in Contemptioun of syde Taillis," "Kitteis Confessioun," and "The Iusting betuix Iames Watsoun and Ihone Barbour."

[20] STC 2nd ed. 15676–78. See Hamer, *Works*, 4:38, 52–53, and 57–59.

[21] See Swanson, "Scotia extranea" (pp. 139–40). Hamer traces an astonishing twenty surviving copies of this volume (*Works*, 4:60–62).

• Edinburgh: Johne Scot for Henrie Charteris, 1568 (STC 2nd ed. 15658)

The warkis of the famous and vorthie Knicht Schir Dauid Lyndesay of the Mont, Alias, Lyoun King of Armes. Newly correctit, and vindicate from the former errouris quhairwith thay war befoir corruptit: and augmentit with sindrie warkis quhilk was not befoir imprentit. The contentis of the buke, and quhat warkis ar augmentit, the nixt syde sall schaw.
Viuet etiam post funera virtus. IOB. VII.
Militia est vita hominis super terram.
Newlie Imprentit be IOHNE SCOT, at the expensis of Henrie Charteris: and ar to be sauld in his Buith, on the north syde of the gait, abone the Throne. CUM PRIUILEGIO REGALI, ANNO. DO. M.D.LXVIII.

Quarto volume; 392 pages (no page numbering); 28–29 lines per page. Printed in blackletter, but with Roman typeface for running headers (in this case "THE FLYTING") and italics for Latin phrases (e.g., "Cor mundum crea in me," line 20).
The Answer . . . to the Kingis Flyting occupies 2K4b–2K5b.

Extant Copies
1. San Marino, CA, Henry E. Huntington Library and Art Gallery. Shelfmark 17425. This copy was filmed for *EEBO*.

2. Washington, DC, Folger Shakespeare Library. Shelfmark STC 15658. Formerly in the library of Sir Leicester Harmsworth. Hamer measured this copy as 173 x 120mm.[22]

3. Winchester, England, Fellows' Library, Winchester College. Shelfmark Bk6065. Bound together with Robert Charteris' print of *Ane Satyre of the Thrie Estaits* (Edinburgh, 1602; STC 2nd ed. 15681.5). The binding is late seventeenth-century, and the volume was gifted to the library by Alexander Thistlethwayte in 1767. Pages measure 170 x 124mm.[23]

Charteris reissued the 1568 *Warkis* twice with new preliminaries, first in 1569[24] and then in 1571.[25] He then seems to have had a new edition printed in 1580 by John Ross (both extant copies are damaged and missing their date).[26] He reissued this himself with new

---

[22] Hamer, *Works*, 4:46.

[23] Private communication with Richard Foster, Fellows' Librarian.

[24] STC 2nd ed. 15658.5. See Hamer, *Works*, 4:48–49. Sole extant copy in St. John's College, Upper Library, shelfmark Aa.2.23, but missing its title-page, thus leading to occasional confusion with the original 1568 edition; see, for example, the *ESTC* database, which lists this item as one of the extant witnesses the 1568 edition (*ESTC* citation number S109439) as well as giving it its own entry (*ESTC* citation number S2191).

[25] STC 2nd ed. 15659. The sole extant copy (incomplete) is Oxford, Bodleian Library, Tanner 187. See Hamer, *Works*, 4:49–51.

[26] Hamer, *Works*, 4:54.

preliminaries in 1582 and 1592,[27] then brought out two further editions in 1597 alone.[28] At the time of his death on 29 August 1599, Charteris apparently had 788 "Dauid Lyndesayis" in stock, valued at eight shillings each.[29] His fellow printer Thomas Bassandyne, responsible for the edition of the *Warkis* described below, left 505 unbound "Lyndesayis" as well as five bound copies (at three and eight shillings each respectively) amidst the famously vast inventory recorded at his death on 18 October 1577.[30] Lyndsay seems to have been extremely good business for printers at the end of the sixteenth century.

- Edinburgh: Thomas Bassandyne, 1574 (STC 2nd ed. 15660)

The warkis of the famous and worthie Knicht Schir Dauid Lyndesay of the Mont Alias, Lyoun King of Armes. Newly correctit, and vindicate from the former Errouris quhairwith thay war befoir corruptit: And augmentit with sindry warkis quhilk was not befoir imprentit. The Contenttis of the Buik, and quhat warkis ar augmentit the nixt syde sall schaw.
Viuet etiam post funera virtus. IOB VII.
Militia est vita hominis super terram.
Imprentit at Edinburgh be Thomas Bassandyne, dwelland at the nether Bow. M.D.LXXIIII.
Cum Priuilegio Regis.

Quarto volume, 12+362 numbered pages; 30–32 lines per page. Blackletter, but with the printer's "Adhortation of all Estatis" and Lyndsay's "Epistil Nvncupatorie" in Roman typeface, as well as the running headers (in this case "The Answer / to the Kingis flyting") and Latin quotations such as "Cor mundum crea in me" at line 20. Thinner paper than used by the Charteris editions, with much show-through.
The Answer appears on pp. 338–40.

Extant copy: Edinburgh, NLS. Shelfmark F.5.b.40. Measures 176 x 120mm. Stamped "Lauriston Castle Library," and a pencil note reads "Bought Quaritch 26.11.30." Bound in red leather; spine stamped in gold with "The warkis of Lindesay. 1574."

In accordance with METS editorial policy, the letters þ (thorn, letter-form identical with printed *y*) and the rarer ӡ (yogh) have been transcribed with their modern equivalents *th* and *y* respectively (the latter is always the value intended in these texts for yogh). The distribution of *i/j* and *u/v/w* has been normalized according to modern spelling practice — e.g., "Venus" and "dejectit" for original "Uenus" and "deiectit," (both line 7) and "vennemous" for original "wennemous" (line 16). Abbreviations have been silently expanded. Punctuation, capitalization, and word division have also been modernized.

---

[27] Hamer, *Works*, 4:55, 63.

[28] Hamer, *Works*, 4:64–66.

[29] Laing, Scott, and Thomson, eds.,"Wills of Thomas Bassandyne and Other Printers," 2:225. Charteris' will was registered 16 September 1606. Margaret Wallace, widow of Henrie's son, the printer Robert Charteris, also left an impressive 600 "Dauid Lyndesayis buikis" (at the slightly lower price of seven shillings) upon her death on 1 February 1603 (2:236).

[30] See Laing, Scott, and Thomson, eds., "Wills of Thomas Bassandyne and Other Printers," 2:191, 197. Bassandyne's will was registered on 6 February 1579.

THE ANSWER QUHILK
SCHIR DAVID LINDESAY MAID TO THE KINGIS FLYTING

Redoutit roy, your ragment I have red,[1]
Quhilk dois perturb my dull intendement: *Which; understanding*
From your flyting, wald God that I wer fred,   *would God; rescued*
Or ellis sum tygerris toung wer to me lent.
5   Schir, pardone me thocht I be impacient,   *if (though)*
Quhilk bene so with your prunyeand pen detractit,   *Who; piercing; disparaged*
And rude report, from Venus court dejectit.   *harsh; cast out*

Lustie ladyis, that your libellis lukis   *Lovely; letters consult*
My cumpanie dois hald abhominable,
10   Commandand me beir cumpanie to the cukis;   *keep company with cooks*
Moist lyke ane devill, thay hald me detestable.   *Most*
Thay banis me, sayand I am nocht able   *banish*
Thame to compleis, or preis to thare presence.   *satisfy; advance*
Apon your pen I cry ane loud vengeance!

15   Wer I ane poeit, I suld preis with my pen   *strive*
To wreik me on your vennemous wryting.   *avenge myself; venomous*
Bot I man do as dog dois in his den —   *must*
Fald baith my feit, or fle fast frome your flyting.   *Fold both*
The mekle devil may nocht indure your dyting.[2]
20   Quharefor *cor mundum crea in me* I cry,   *(see note)*
Proclamand yow the prince of poetry.

Schir, with my prince pertenit me nocht to pley.   *it is not for me*
Bot sen your grace hes gevin me sic command   *since*
To mak answer, it must neidis me obey.   *I must*
25   Thocht ye be now strang lyke ane elephand,   *Although; strong*
And in till Venus werkis maist vailyeand,   *valiant*
The day wyll cum, and that within few yeiris,
That ye wyll draw at laiser with your feiris.

Quhat can ye say forther, bot I am failyeit   *except that; impaired [by age]*
30   In Venus werkis, I grant schir, that is trew;

---

[1] *Formidable king, I have read your lengthy discourse*

[2] *The powerful Devil may not withstand your composition*

135

The tyme hes bene, I wes better artailyeit   *armed*
Nor I am now, bot yit full sair I rew   *Than; I greatly regret*
That ever I did mouth thankles so persew.
Quharefor tak tent and your fyne powder spair,   *heed*
35   And waist it nocht bot gyf ye wit weill quhair.[1]

Thocht ye rin rudelie, lyke ane restles ram,   *Although you run about wildly*
Schutand your bolt at mony sindrie schellis,   *Shooting; various targets*
Beleif richt weill, it is ane bydand gam.   *Believe you me; waiting game*
Quharefore bewar with dowbling of the bellis,   *So beware*
40   For many ane dois haist thair awin saule knellis,[2]
And speciallie quhen that the well gois dry,   *spring dries up*
Syne can nocht get agane sic stufe to by.[3]

I give your counsale to the feynd of hell   *Council; fiend*
That wald nocht of ane princes yow provide,   *princess*
45   Tholand yow rin schutand frome schell to schell,
Waistand your corps, lettand the tyme overslyde.[4]
For lyke ane boisteous bull ye rin and ryde   *violent; run*
Royatouslie, lyke ane rude rubeatour,   *Wildly; rough scoundrel*
Ay fukkand lyke ane furious fornicatour.   *Perpetually*

50   On ladronis for to loip ye wyll nocht lat,   *common women; leap; cease*
Howbeit the caribaldis cry the corinoch.   *Although; (see note)*
Remember how, besyde the masking fat,   *mashing vat*
Ye caist ane quene overthort ane stinking troch?   *cast a wench across; trough*
That feynd, with fuffilling of hir roistit hoch,   *fiend; (see note)*
55   Caist doun the fat, quharthrow drink, draf and juggis   *vat, so that; grains; dregs*
Come rudely rinnand doun about your luggis.   *gushing; ears*

Wald God the lady that luffit yow best   *Would God; loved*
Had sene yow thair ly swetterand lyke twa swyne!   *wallowing; swine*
Bot to indyte how that duddroun wes drest —   *tell; slut*
60   Drowkit with dreggis, quhimperand with mony quhryne —[5]
That proces to report, it wer ane pyne.   *Those events; would be an effort*
On your behalf, I thank God tymes ten score
That yow preservit from gut and frome grandgore.   *gout; syphilis*

---

[1] *And do not waste it unless you are certain you know exactly where you are [i.e., whom you are with]*

[2] *For many a one hastens their own death knell*

[3] *Such substance (i.e., semen) cannot be bought again afterwards (see note)*

[4] Lines 45–46: *Suffering you to run shooting from target to target, / Wasting your body, letting time overrun*

[5] *Drenched with dregs, whimpering with many squeals*

Now schir, fairwell, because I can nocht flyte,
65 And thocht I could, I wer nocht tyll avance   *even if; to be praised*
Aganis your ornate meter to indyte.[1]   *verse; compose*

Bot yit, be war with lawbouring of your lance: *working your lance*
Sum sayis thar cummis ane bukler furth of France,   *shield out of*
Quhilk wyll indure your dintis, thocht thay be dour.   *Which; strokes; hard*
70 Fairweill, of flowand rethorik the flour!   *flowing eloquence; flower (i.e., the best)*

Quod Lindesay in his flyting
Aganis the Kingis dyting.

---

[1] Lines 65–66: *And even if I could, I would not be worthy of praise / if I were to compose [lines] against your ornate verse*

EXPLANATORY NOTES TO *ANSWER TO THE KINGIS FLYTING*

ABBREVIATIONS: *Acts of Council (Public Affairs)*: *Acts of the Lords of Council in Public Affairs*; *AND*: *Anglo-Norman Dictionary*; *Cal. State Papers (Venice)*: *Calendar of State Papers and Manuscripts relating to English Affairs*; *CT*: Chaucer, *Canterbury Tales*, ed. Benson; *DOST*: *Dictionary of the Older Scottish Tongue*; **EETS**: Early English Text Society; *ER*: *The Exchequer Rolls of Scotland*; **Hadley Williams**: Lyndsay, *Sir David Lyndsay: Selected Poems*, ed. Hadley Williams; **Hamer**: Lyndsay, *The Works of Sir David Lindsay*, ed. Hamer; *LP Henry VIII*: *Letters and Papers, Foreign and Domestic, of the Reign of Henry VIII*; **MdnE**: Modern English; **ME**: Middle English; *MED*: *Middle English Dictionary*; *NIMEV*: *New Index of Middle English Verse*; **NLS**: Edinburgh, National Library of Scotland; *ODNB*: *Oxford Dictionary of National Biography*; **OE**: Old English; *OED*: *Oxford English Dictionary*; *Poems*: Dunbar, *Poems of William Dunbar*, ed. Bawcutt; *Reg. Mag. Sig.*: *Registrum Magni Sigilii Regum Scotorum* (*Register of the Great Seal of Scotland*); *Reg. Sec. Sig.*: *Registrum Secreti Sigilli Regum Scotorum* (*Register of the Privy Seal of Scotland*); *SP Henry VIII*: *State Papers Published under the Authority of His Majesty's Commission: King Henry VIII*; **STC**: *A Short-Title Catalogue of Books Printed in England, Scotland and Ireland and English Books Printed Abroad 1473–1640*, ed. Pollard and Redgrave; **STS**: Scottish Text Society; *TA*: *Accounts of the Lord High Treasurer of Scotland*, ed. Dickson and Paul; **Whiting**: Whiting, *Proverbs, Sentences and Proverbial Sayings from English Writings Before 1500*; **Wing**: Wing, *Short-Title Catalogue of Books Printed in England, Scotland and Ireland, Wales and British America and of English Books Printed in Other Countries 1641–1700*.

3   *flyting*. See the *Answer* Introduction for a discussion of this term.

7   *Venus court*. In medieval and early modern writings Venus, the Roman goddess of love, was used metaphorically to represent human sexuality, sensuality, and love, while in astrological terms, the planet Venus was understood to govern heat and moisture, the qualities associated with sexual desire (see Tinkle, *Medieval Venuses and Cupids*, pp. 1–8 and 144–46). The court of Venus was thus, as the narrator of Gavin Douglas' *Palis of Honoure* describes it, "the court so variabill / Of erdly luf" ("the changeable court of earthly love"; ed. Parkinson, lines 484–85) and was peopled by those whose love was pure and noble as well as those consumed by lust. It is here that James I, as the imprisoned narrator of the earlier fifteenth-century *Kingis Quair*, imagines bringing his petition to Venus after he has fallen in love with the lady in the garden (ed. Mooney and Arn, lines 530 ff.) This honorable version of the court of Venus is what Lyndsay has in mind in a later poem when, after the tragic death of James V's first queen — the French princess Madeleine de Valois — only a few months into their marriage, he imagines the royal pair reunited there:

O Venus, with thy blynd sone, Cupido,
Fy on yow baith, that maid no resistance!
In to your court ye never had sic two,   *such*
So leill luffaris, without dissimulance,   *loyal lovers*
As James the Fift and Magdalene of France.
("The Deploratioun of the Deith of Quene Magdalene," ed. Hadley
Williams, lines 36–40)

Venus' court governed not only ennobling earthly love, however, but everything down to prosaic lust, and this latter end of the scale is clearly what Lyndsay intends in the present line: the phrase "Venus werkis," used at lines 26 and 30, was more often a euphemism for sexual activity (see *DOST Venus* (n.) sense 2). Lyndsay is here lamenting that his reputation has been so badly damaged by James' skillful insults that he has been utterly rejected by the court ladies.

8   *your libellis lukis*. Hamer and Hadley Williams emend to *on your libellis lukis*, or "look upon your letters" (Hadley Williams on metrical grounds), but none of the early modern prints emend this line (see for example Charteris' re-issued prints of 1569, 1582, and 1592, or Bassandyne of 1574), and *DOST* records a well-established transitive sense of the verb (with no preposition) meaning to "view, inspect, examine, consult" (see *luke* (v.), sense 6).

10   *beir cumpanie to the cukis*. Kitchens would normally be staffed entirely by men and boys, thus a good place to exile oneself from female company, and they were hot, dark, noisy, smelly, and messy, lending themselves to comparisons with hell (see Henisch, *Medieval Cook*, pp. 9–15). In the late-medieval *Chester Mystery Cycle*, the play of the Harrowing of Hell is given to the Cooks' guild (ed. Lumiansky and Mills, play 17 "The Cookes Playe," 1:325). The temptation to relate this association of Lyndsay with the cooks to the idea of "roasting" or ridiculing someone is quelled by the fact that the *OED* offers no instances of such a usage until 1710 (see *roast* (v.), sense 5b) and the sense is not recorded at all by *DOST* (*rost* (v.)), *MED* (*rosten* (v.)), nor by the *AND* for Anglo-Norman *rostir*.

20   *cor mundum crea in me*. From Psalm 50, in which David repents *quando intravit ad Bethsabee* ("after he had sinned with Bathsheba," 50:2): *Cor mundum crea in me, Deus, et spiritum rectum innova in visceribus meis* ("Create in me a clean heart, O God, and renew a right spirit within my bowels," 50:12). This penitential psalm was a central text in the devotional catechesis of the late Middle Ages, translated several times into Middle English. See Sutherland, *English Psalms in the Middle Ages*, pp. 35–43. Hadley Williams notes that the *cor mundum* formula also occurs in the famous *Flyting of Dunbar and Kennedie*, in which Kennedy sneers "I sall ger crop thy tong [I'll have the tip of your tongue cut off] / And thou sall cry *cor mundum* on thy kneis" (*Poems*, 1:213, lines 393–94). Confirming its place in literary flyting tradition, it appears again in Montgomerie's later sixteenth-century flyting with Polwart: "cor mundum þow cryd, / Condempnit to be dryd and hung vp fra hand" (*Invectives* 1, lines 11–12 [*Alexander Montgomerie: Poems*, 1:141]). See Bawcutt, "The Art of Flyting," p. 10. See the *Answer* Introduction on how Lyndsay inverts this trope.

21   *prince of poetry*. Hadley Williams notes that this epithet is more often associated with Virgil, as it is in Lyndsay's later *Dialog betwix Experience and ane Courteour*: "Famous Virgill, the prince of poetrie" (line 571). Gavin Douglas, in translating the *Aeneid*, worries (with slightly unconvincing modesty) that he "dyd perchance pervert / Thys maist renownyt prynce of poetry" (*Eneados*, ed. Coldwell, 3:171, Prol. 9, lines 74–75).

26, 30   *Venus werkis*. See note to line 7 above.

28   *draw at laiser with your feiris*. *DOST*'s sense II.10 for *draw* (v.) is "put in writing, compose," which conjures up a delightful — but probably mistaken — notion of Lyndsay imagining literary soirées presided over by a sober middle-aged James V. The general sense is certainly that James' wild days will soon be over, but the specific sense of "draw" may be one recorded by the *OED* from the sixteenth century onwards (*draw* (v.), sense 2b), a figurative sense of pulling together like draught beasts, thus "to be in like case with." Compare Shakespeare's *Othello* 4.1.66, "Think every bearded fellow that's but yok'd, / May draw with you." Lines 27–28 might thus be translated: "The day will come, and that within a few years, / that you will find yourself at leisure, in the same boat as your [less vigorous] peers." Compare also Chaucer's sketch of the rueful horse Bayard in *Troilus and Criseyde*: "Yet am I but an hors, and horses lawe / I moot endure, and with my feres drawe" (1.223–24).

31   *artailyeit*. This means "furnished with artillery" (see *DOST artailōeit*, ppl. adj.). The term "artillery" relates primarily to projectiles and the weapons that discharge them — spears, bows and arrows, guns, and siege-engines. In medieval and early modern allegories of love and seduction, imagery of hunting and battle is common, whether the bows and arrows of a predatory Cupid or Venus, a lover "jousting" (see note to line 67 below) or shooting at targets (see note to line 37 below), or a siege of the beloved's castle. In Dunbar's *Goldyn Targe* — a poem which Lyndsay certainly knew since he cites it by name in his *Testament of the Papyngo* (line 18) — Venus' female archers fire arrows at the narrator, himself cowering beneath the shield or "targe" of Reason, "quhill wastit was thair artilye" (until their artillery was exhausted, *Poems*, 1:189, line 179). Spearing has observed of this line that the word "artilye" "may also suggest the feminine artfulness allegorized by Venus' weapons" (*Medieval Poet as Voyeur*, p. 243): Lyndsay's assertion that he was once better "artailyeit" may exploit a similar pun on artillery and "art," i.e., the arts of love and poetry, since the latter art is explicitly addressed in literary flytings and often — as here — confounded with the former.

The most influential representation of love as a siege is in the thirteenth-century French *Romance of the Rose* by Guillaume de Lorris and Jean de Meun, where Jealousy imprisons the sought-after Rose in her castle along with Fair Welcoming, who had unwisely allowed the Lover to kiss the Rose. At first all seems lost, but Venus, enraged, fires a burning brand through a suggestively narrow aperture situated at the front of the castle, between two fair pillars, and sets the whole castle aflame, freeing Fair Welcoming who in turn allows the

Lover to "pluck" the Rose (*Romance of the Rose*, trans. Dahlberg, pp. 347–54 [lines 21251 ff.]). Lyndsay's double-entendres are subtle by comparison.

33   *mouth thankles*. The depiction of a woman's vagina as a greedy "mouth" was a well-established convention. See Whiting M763 and the entries for "mouth" in Whiting, "Proverbs . . . Scottish Writings Before 1600," and Williams, *Dictionary of Sexual Language*. In the fifteenth-century Older Scots fabliau *The Freiris of Berwik*, an unfaithful wife prepares herself for her lover's visit thus:

Scho pullit hir cunt and gaif hit buffetis tway	*gave; two slaps*
Upoun the cheikis, syne till it cowd scho say,	*cheeks; then to it she said*
"Ye sowld be blyth and glaid at my requeist:	
Thir mullis of youris ar callit to ane feist.	*These lips; feast*
(*Ten Bourdes*, ed. Furrow, lines 139–42)	

Lyndsay's use of the specific phrase "mouth thankles" (ungrateful mouth) may have been directly inspired by Walter Kennedy's brief poem from the first decade of the sixteenth century, "Ane aigit man twyss fourty ōeiris" (*Poems of Walter Kennedy*, ed. Meier, pp. 2–5; this poem is in fact the only citation for Whiting's M763). In it, a bitter and decrepit friar regrets "That evir I serwit mowth thankles!" since the ungrateful women will not even look at him now. Variations of this line form the refrain for all six stanzas. Kennedy is little known now but was one of the Scottish poets praised in Lyndsay's *Testament of the Papyngo*: "quho can, now, the workis cuntrafait / Of Kennedie, with termes aureait?" (lines 15–16). Kennedy was also, of course, Dunbar's opponent in the famous *Flyting* (see the *Answer* Introduction). The longevity of Kennedy's poem is demonstrated by the fact that it survives in two later sixteenth-century manuscripts, the Bannatyne MS of c. 1568 (NLS Advocates MS 1.1.6) and the Maitland Folio of c. 1570–86 (Cambridge, Magdalene College, MS Pepys 2553) — manuscripts which also contain copies of the *Freiris of Berwik*. Kennedy's poem is the earliest citation given by *DOST* for *mouth* (n.), sense 5: "*To serve, persew* or *mell with, mouth thankles*, to go whoring." On the *vagina dentata* trope more generally, see Miller, "Monstrous Sexuality."

34   *your fyne powder spair*. I.e., "don't waste your gunpowder." *DOST* records only this line for the figurative sense of (gun) powder as "semen" (*pouder* (n.), sense 4) and *MED* and *OED* do not record it at all. On martial imagery in relation to love and sex, see note to line 31 above.

37   *Schutand your bolt at mony sindrie schellis*. Literally, "shooting your bolt at many different targets," but the expression is used elsewhere as a euphemism for sex. See *DOST s(c)hell* (n.), sense 2. The *OED* indicates that both the figurative sense of a "target" (from its resemblance to a seashell) and the transferred sense of "vagina" are early Modern Scottish usages. The expression recurs at line 45. See the notes to line 31 above on martial imagery associated with love and sex, and to lines 40–42 below on the apparent physical consequences of this behavior. On James' numerous mistresses and illegitimate children, see the *Answer* Introduction and note to line 57 below.

In *The Complaynt*, when Lyndsay writes of the period during the earl of Angus' ascendency when he was effectively exiled from court (see the *Answer* Introduction) he imagines a series of sycophantic courtiers tempting the teenaged king with a girl at every royal palace: "ane of the lusteast wantoun lassis" (line 239) in Fife (presumably Falkland Palace), another "lusty las" in Linlithgow (line 244), a "dayis derlyng" (line 248) in Stirling, and finally an offer to visit the "hie boirdall" (line 250), i.e., "great brothel." Hadley Williams speculates the last might be a reference to Edinburgh (p. 233n250). The number of illegitimate children fathered by James in his youth — at least eight of high birth, with the eldest born when James was just seventeen — suggests this picture is not entirely inaccurate. See Thomas, *Princelie Majestie*, pp. 41–43, and *ODNB*, "James V, mistresses and children of."

39   *dowbling of the bellis*. Bells were rung to strike the hours and mark the passing of time, to summon people to worship, or to give other kinds of public notice, all of which are relevant here, although the primary sense must be that James' youth is nearly spent, and Lyndsay is pushing him to think of the serious matters of marriage and the royal succession.

40–42   *For many . . . . sic stufe to by*. These lines seem to imply that wild promiscuity could hasten a man's death ("haist thair awin saule knellis"), or cause him to run out of semen ("the well gois dry") so that, when he needs it — in this case, when James needs to father a legitimate heir — he may find there is no more to be had ("Syne can nocht get again sic stufe to by," i.e., such "stuff" cannot be got again, even for money). The sentiments and imagery are remarkably similar to those found in an obscure poem "My hart is quhyt" — i.e., "My heart is released" — in the Bannatyne manuscript of c. 1568 (the poem's actual date of composition is unknown). In it, the aged male narrator explains that he is finished with women and suggests that his addressee, "my Io" (Jo) would do well to heed his example. He says the man is "vnnaturall" who "hes but small / stufe corporall / Syne schutis at þat schell" (i.e., who has little bodily "stuff" but nevertheless engages in sex), because when he has expended everything — from his "principall" (i.e., main capital, presumably his ability to reproduce) and "materiall" to his very "natur" (desire, potency or actual semen — see below) — "Than be the wall / he lyis our thrall / gar bring him the hand bell." To "lie at the wall" is to succumb in conflict (see *DOST wal(l* (n.), sense 5d); the hand-bell was used in towns to announce deaths, among other things. He concludes: "the suth Is [s]o / quhen dry my Io / of natur growis the well / To seik our all na stufe thow sall / ffor no gold get to sell" (It's the truth: when the well runs dry of semen, my Jo, you won't find any such stuff for sale for any gold! [see *DOST natur(e* (n.), sense 3c and *sel(l* (v.), sense 5]). See *The Bannatyne Manuscript*, ed. Ritchie, 4:19, lines 29–31. The general notion that excess promiscuity can lead to impotence also underpins the complaint of one of Dunbar's married women in *Tua Mariit Wemen and the Wedo* that her husband "has bene lychour so lang quhill lost is his natur" ("has been a lecher for so long, his potency is lost"; *Poems*, 1:45, line 174).

43–44   *your counsale . . . . That wald nocht of ane princes yow provide*. On the lengthy
          process of finding a bride for James, see the *Answer* Introduction. It is not clear
          whether Lyndsay is serious in this criticism of James' advisers, or if it is a way of
          avoiding any direct criticism of a wayward king. If it is a genuine objection, it
          may be a general one to the drawn-out marriage negotiations on James' behalf,
          or a more particular concern that they had not yet succeeded in contracting
          marriage with a French princess. Matters were evidently not helped by James,
          who continued to father illegitimate children on the noblewomen of his own
          realm. See note to lines 37, 57, and 68–69.

45–46   *Tholand yow rin . . . . the tyme overslyde*. See note to lines 40–42 above.

49   *Ay fukkand lyke ane furious furnicatour*. "Forever fucking like a furious fornicator."
          It is worth observing that the earliest examples of *fuck* recorded by the *OED* are
          in Older Scots works — Dunbar's "In secreit place" ("he wald have fukkit,"
          Poems, 1:106, line 13) and this line from Lyndsay, to which may be added
          another example from Lyndsay's *Satyre of the Thrie Estaitis* supplied by *DOST*,
          and the splendid participial adjective *wanfukkit*, literally "misfucked" from
          Kennedy's part of the *Flyting* with Dunbar (*Poems*, 1:201, line 38). This is almost
          certainly because Older Scots writers were just more willing to write the word
          than their English counterparts. Conlee notes that there may be an earlier
          occurrence in a collection of proverbs and sayings contained in the English
          fifteenth-century manuscript National Library of Wales, Peniarth 356B, fol.
          149v, in which angry women swear "That thay owyles fuc ne men" ("that they
          fuck neither owls nor men"); owls were often used to represent extreme ugliness
          or evil (see *MED oule* (n.), sense 2b). See note to line 13 of "In a Secret Place"
          (*Dunbar: The Complete Works*, ed. Conlee, p. 367).

          Although Charteris' 1568 edition clearly reads *fukkand*, his 1582 edition reads
          sukkand, as does Bassandyne, while Charteris' 1592 print reads *tukkand*.
          Charteris reinstated *fukkand* only in his 1597 prints. Laing, similarly anxious to
          avoid the offending word on behalf of his Victorian readers, prints *lukkand*.
          Chalmers had printed the original *fukkand* without comment.

51   *caribaldis*. The term "car(r)ybald" occurs twice in Dunbar (in the *Flyting* with
          Kennedy [*Poems*, 1:206, line 184], and *The tua mariit wemen and the wedo*, [1:43,
          line 94]), in both cases describing men. Andrew Breeze suggests an origin in the
          Gaelic term *carbad* ("hard palate, jaw, gums"), and he points to Modern Irish
          derivatives *carbadán* ("toothless person") and *carbóg* ("woman with large gums
          and gap teeth"). See Breeze, "Dunbar's *Brylyoun, Carrybald, Cawanderis, Slawsy,
          Strekouris, and Traikit*," p. 126, with Irish terms taken from Dinneen, *Foclóir
          Gaedhilge agus Béarla*. Although Breeze does not mention Lyndsay's use of the
          term, the gap-toothed element is reminiscent of Chaucer's description of the
          Wife of Bath as "gat-tothed," carrying suggestions of boldness, receptiveness,
          and irreverence (*CT* I[A]468 and note): such a feature would be quite
          appropriate for James' casual lovers. Such a derivation remains speculative,
          however. Hamer had glossed "caribald" as "cannibal" without explanation, but
          MacKenzie, discussing the use of "carrybald" in Dunbar and Kennedy's *Flyting*,
          relates it to "'Caribal,' a native of the 'Carib' or Carribee Islands, a people

reputed by their discoverers — the Spaniards — to eat human flesh, hence=monster" (*Poems of William Dunbar*, ed. MacKenzie, p. 199). This connection to "cannibal" had appeared in the first edition of *DOST* and seems to be the root of this and other glosses such as "monster" (e.g., by Hadley Williams). However, the *OED* lists no citation for *caribal* (n.) earlier than the nineteenth century and the most recent edition of *DOST* now describes *caribald* as "an abusive term of doubtful origin and meaning," adding a little shamefacedly that "the suggestion that it is an early variant of cannibal is not clearly supported by the evidence."

corinoch. This term likewise has a Gaelic origin in *corranach*, "outcry" (see *DOST corenoch* (n.)).

52–56   *masking fat*. A *masking fat* or *mask-fat* is a vat in which the malt is mashed in the process of brewing ale and beer, one of the few businesses in which women played a significant role in medieval and early modern Scotland (see Spence, *Women, Credit and Debt in Early Modern Scotland*, pp. 102–27, and Ewan, "'For Whatever Ales Ye'"). The "draf" and "juggis" are the sodden grains of malt and the dregs left over from brewing. James is cavorting in the brew-house with the ale-wives and wenches. The vat itself might suggest a well-used vagina (or not); see John Heywood's play, *Johan Johan*, where the husband is stuck with filling a leaky pail while the priest enjoys the real thing.

54   *fuffilling of hir roistit hoch*. The "hoch" is the hough or the back of the thigh. The woman is either bending over, or on her back with her legs in the air. The general sense of what is being described is clear, but "fuffilling" and "roistit" are less so. Hadley Williams (and Hamer in his Glossary, 4:395) relate "roistit" to early modern English *roist* (compare *OED roist* (v.), meaning "delight or revel in") and *roister* ("to behave uproariously"). Although *roist* is not recorded as transitive verb and thus does not seem to lend itself to forming a participial adjective *roistit*, this derivation is plausibly supported by her suggestion that "fuffilling" may be an error for "ruffilling," because "ruffle" can be found paired with "roist" and its derivatives elsewhere, for example in Arthur Dent's 1601 *Plain Man's Pathway to Heaven*: "Many profane serving men also do falsely suppose that they were born only to game, riot, swear, whore, ruffle it, and roist it out, and to spend their time in mere idleness" (Dent, p. 138).

Without emendation, the *OED* offers only two citations for the verb *fuffle*, meaning "to jerk about, hustle" (this line, and another doubtful occurrence of 1635) although a related verb *curfuffle* occurs in Scots writer Robert Sempill's works of 1583, and the more widespread colloquial modern noun *kerfuffle* derives from this. If the present example is a copying error, this might at least explain how it came about. For *roistit*, *DOST* offers a figurative sense of *rostit* — i.e., modern "roasted" — as "Overheated (by sexual intercourse)," sense 2c) Given the medieval and early modern association of male sexual potency with heat, this notion of "roasting" the woman would make sense, but this line is the only citation. On the importance of heat and moisture for sexual performance and fertility, see for example the discussion in Constantine the African's brief treatise *De coitu* ("On Sexual Intercourse") in *Medieval Medicine*, ed. Wallis, pp. 511–23.

57   *the lady that luffit yow best*. This coy reference is probably to James' favorite
        mistress Margaret Erskine, daughter of John, fifth Lord Erskine and captain of
        Stirling Castle. She was already the wife of Sir Robert Douglas of Lochleven by
        the time of their liaison (she had married him in 1527. See Lee, *James Stewart,
        Earl of Moray*, p. 17). In 1531 Margaret bore James a son, James Stewart, his
        second illegitimate son to be so named (the first was by Elizabeth Shaw in 1529,
        when the king himself was only seventeen). Despite a number of different
        mistresses and further illegitimate children after the birth of the second James
        Stewart, Margaret apparently remained his favorite, and in 1536 James seems
        to have interrupted advanced marriage negotiations for the hand of Marie
        Bourbon of Vendôme (on which see the *Answer* Introduction) to try to arrange
        a divorce for Margaret so he could marry her instead. As Lord Howard wrote to
        King Henry VIII on 25 April 1536:

> Syr, I here, bothe by the Qwens Grace your susster, and dyvers other, that
> the maryage ys brokyn bytwyxt the Kynges Grace your nephewe and
> Monsr de Vaindom, and that He wyll marye a gentyllwoman in Scottland,
> the Lord of Arskynes douhter, who was with Your Grace the last somer at
> Thornbery; by whom He hath had a chyld, havyng a hosband; and Hys
> Grace hathe found the means to devorse them. And ther ys grett
> lamentation made for yt yn thys contre, as farr as men dare.
> ("Correspondence relative to Scotland and the Borders," *SP Henry VIII*,
> 5.4:41, no. 290).

63   *gut . . . grandgore*. Gout ("gut") was conflated with venereal disease ("grandgore")
        or used as a euphemism for it in the medieval and early modern periods: see
        "gout" in Williams, *Dictionary of Sexual Language*. "Grand gore" is syphilis: the
        term "grandgore" first appears in Scottish records from the 1490s and was
        clearly considered to be a new kind of epidemic at the time, although it is now
        thought to have been present in the population before this. By 1497, the burgh
        council of Aberdeen was vainly trying to halt its spread by banning prostitution,
        while Edinburgh's burgh council ordered all infected persons to present
        themselves to the harbor of Leith for shipment to the island of Inchkeith, there
        to remain unless they recovered (with what degree of compliance is unclear). See
        Oram, "Disease, Death and the Hereafter," p. 214.

        Hadley Williams suggests that the 1568 print reads *gtandgore* (corrected in later
        editions) but the cleaner Winchester College copy of the 1568 *Warkis* clearly
        reads *grandgore*. The 1592 *Warkis* spells it *grangoir*.

67   *lawbouring of your lance*. The scarcely veiled innuendo of "working your lance"
        was a long-lived euphemism for sex; in the twelfth-century Anglo-Norman
        romance of *Ipomédon* by Hue de Rotelande, the narrator remarks that love's
        main delight is *le juster enz el lit* "jousting in bed" (ed. Holden, line 4314). See
        note to line 31 above on martial imagery in relation to love and sex more
        generally.

68–69   *ane bukler furth of France*. The "shield out of France" who might withstand James'
        "dintis" (blows) is a reference to the expectation that James would take a French
        bride, and probably dates this poem to 1535–35; see the *Answer* Introduction.

The vagueness of Lyndsay's reference here, preceded with the circumspect "sum sayis," suggests that the poem was written when it was not certain which, if any, potential French bride James would win (and see note to line 57 above for another potential spanner in the marriage works).

INTRODUCTION TO THE *SQUYER MELDRUM* POEMS

THE *HISTORIE* AND *TESTAMENT OF SQUYER MELDRUM*

The Historie

C. S. Lewis enthused that "*Squire Meldrum* . . . ought to be in everyone's hands; a lightly modernized and heavily glossed text at a reasonable price is greatly to be desired . . . . We have greater stories in verse; perhaps none, even in Chaucer, more completely successful."[1] *The Historie of Squyer Meldrum* presents itself as a chivalric biography of Lyndsay's acquaintance and neighbor in northeast Fife, Squire William Meldrum. Its form (octosyllabic couplets), style, and choice of incident are modeled in part on medieval romance (see further below under "Romance and Irony in the *Meldrum*-poems"), a genre still eagerly read in Lyndsay's day and indeed still composed, as the sixteenth-century Scottish metrical romances of *Clariodus* and *Roswall and Lillian* testify.[2] Although presented as a biography, the bulk of the *Historie* focuses on a small selection of romantic and chivalric episodes from Meldrum's youth from 1513 to 1517, when a ferocious ambush ended his martial career. *The Historie of Squyer Meldrum* is accompanied by the shorter *Testament of Squyer Meldrum* in which Lyndsay has Meldrum himself — now an old man — issue detailed instructions for his own funeral ceremonies and the construction of his tomb. It is distinguished from the preceding *Historie* by the dramatic monologue format — the narrator is no longer Lyndsay but Meldrum himself — and by its stately rhyme-royal stanzas followed by a final eight-line stanza of mixed Scots and Latin. But readers' attention has always been captured by the fast-paced *Historie*.

As a dashing young squire, Meldrum sets out for France with the Scottish army to fight Henry VIII's troops at Calais (events which date this to 1513). In an initial detour via Ireland, the Scottish navy raids the English-held Carrickfergus. Meldrum rescues a grateful lady from rape by two pillagers, but refuses her offers to become his wife or, with increasing desperation, his camp-follower mistress. At Calais he defeats Talbart, a battle-hardened English champion whom no one else dares to fight and who is shocked to be bested by such a young squire. Making his leisurely way back to Scotland during the Anglo-French truce, Meldrum rescues a Scottish party besieged by Englishmen in the French town of Amiens, for which he is honored by the French king and sought vainly in marriage by another

---

[1] Lewis, *English Literature in the Sixteenth Century*, pp. 102–03. See also Kratzmann's more restrained comment that it "remains one of the most undeservedly neglected poems of the sixteenth century" ("Sixteenth-Century Secular Poetry," p. 109).

[2] *Clariodus* borrows demonstrably from William Dunbar's *The Thrissill and Rois* of 1503, while *Roswall and Lillian* must postdate *Clariodus*, since it cites *Clariodus*' protagonists twice. See Purdie, *Shorter Scottish Medieval Romances*, pp. 73–74.

nameless French lady. Sailing home, Meldrum leads his plucky band of Scots in the capture of a great warship captained by an English pirate. He returns at last to Scotland, where his glorious reputation precedes him and makes him welcome everywhere. He begins a passionate love affair with the widowed lady of Strathearn at her instigation, defending her lands from the depredations of her greedy neighbor MacFarland and fathering a daughter upon her. But the lovers are cruelly separated by a jealous neighboring knight, who arranges for a vicious roadside ambush that ends Meldrum's fighting career and very nearly his life. Meldrum and his lady never see each other again. The final 76 lines summarize Meldrum's subsequent decades of quiet but useful employment as a sheriff-depute of Fife, a medical practitioner, and a member of the household of the Lords Lindsay of the Byres at Struthers Castle, Fife.

Hamer's exhaustive trawl through the historical record confirmed many elements of Meldrum's story, and this seems to have persuaded him — and thence many modern critics — to take the whole work as a true record of Meldrum's life as well as of Lyndsay's unqualified admiration for him: "as we have seen from the records of William Meldrum, the Squire of Cleish and Bynnis was not a fictitious person. All that Lyndsay says about him in the poem is perfectly true."[3] James Kinsley evidently agreed:

> The *Historie* is a serious biography celebrating the virtues and deeds of a great man intimately known and lately dead, and there is no reason to doubt its essential truth. For all his witchery as a teller of tales in the royal nursery, Lindsay was (and by profession had to be) a reliable man."[4]

Squire of Cleish and Binns

The pleasure of reading the *Meldrum* poems is undoubtedly heightened by the knowledge that their subject was a real person known to Lyndsay. How accurate it is overall will be discussed further below, but the fundamental truth of Meldrum's existence is not in doubt.[5] The *Sheriff Court Book of Fife 1515–1522* contains several records of Meldrum's activities as sheriff-depute of Fife in 1522 (compare the *Historie*, line 1538), serving under the sheriff, Patrick, Lord Lindsay of the Byres (compare the *Historie*, lines 1519–23).[6] That Sir David Lyndsay knew Meldrum personally is confirmed by the fact that the latter is listed as a witness to charters confirming sales and grants of land to Lyndsay in 1541–42.[7] William

---

[3] Hamer, *Works*, 3:184.

[4] Kinsley, *Squyer Meldrum*, pp. 6–7. Hadley Williams also assumes that Lyndsay's aim was "to commemorate with affection the life of a much-admired friend," and that his claim that Meldrum himself was the source of many details (lines 31–34) "helps to establish the truth and reliability of his following account," though she also notes that this was a common rhetorical ploy (*Selected Poems*, pp. 284–85).

[5] See Hamer, *Works*, 3:177–81 for a catalogue of records relating to William Meldrum and his immediate forebears, including the majority of the documents discussed below.

[6] Dickinson, *Sheriff Court Book of Fife*, pp. 250, 255, 258, 259, 260, 261, 265, 266, 269, 270.

[7] 1) *Reg. Mag. Sig.* 3:580–81, no. 2529: charter confirming purchase of lands of "Ovir-Prates" in Fife from Walter Lundy, drawn up in Edinburgh, 30 December 1541, and confirmed 1 January 1541/2. Witnesses include "Wil. Meldrum de Bindis." 2) *Reg. Mag. Sig.* 3:636, no. 2748 gives confirmation of Lyndsay and his wife in lands of Garmyltoun-Alexander (Garleton) in East Lothian: charter drawn up at Struthers on 5 May 1542, witnesses include "Wil. Meldrum" (confirmed 8 August 1542).

Meldrum's last appearance in the historical record is as a witness to a charter drawn up at Struthers, 25 July 1550 (Struthers was the principal seat of the Lords Lindsay of the Byres), and he is assumed to have died not long after this.[8]

Meldrum's titles can likewise be corroborated by the historical record, although they have inspired some critical controversy not of Lyndsay's making. Lyndsay writes that Meldrum was "borne within the schyre of Fyfe; / To Cleische and Bynnis richt heritour" (lines 74–75). (Cleish was once part of the county of Fife, but later transferred to Kinross.)[9] In a document of 12 October 1506, one Archibald Meldrum, styled "de Bynnys," is recorded as selling lands within Cleish to a Robert Colvile, and one of the witnesses is "Wil. Meldrum filio suo et herede apparente" ("his son and heir apparent").[10] This is surely Lyndsay's Squire Meldrum, and suggests that he had reached the age of majority (21) by then. Cleish was in fact a collection of estates owned by different families. In a Fife tax roll from March 1517 (drawn up under the authority of the same sheriff Patrick, Lord Lindsay of the Byres, who would later employ Meldrum), there are returns for "Cliesh-Meldrum," "Cleish Allardice," "Winton's part of Cliesh," "Janet Kinloch's part of Cliesh" and "Lindsay's part of Cliesh and Carnbeath" (not our poet Lyndsay): clearly, there were several local lairds who could style themselves "of Cleish."[11] This might be enough in itself to explain why Lyndsay takes care to cite both of Meldrum's titles, "Cleische and Bynnis," and why the historical Meldrum signed himself "William Meldrum de Bynnis" or "de Binds" when he used a title at all (in the *Historie* Lyndsay has him exclaim "I wald gif all the Bynnis" if only he could get at the English attackers, lines 644–45). The earliest prints of the *Meldrum* poems also use only "The Squyer of the Bynnis" for their running headers.

While the name "Cleish" indisputably refers to an area southwest of Lochleven (confirmed by numerous contemporary records of taxes, land sales and inheritances), "Bynnis" is more problematic. The element "Bin" or "Ben" comes from the Gaelic for summit or peak; there are a lot of these in Scotland, and consequently a lot of place-names which are some variant of "Bin," including more than one in Fife.[12] Meldrum, too, is not an uncommon surname — even within Fife there is another well-established, armigerous family of Meldrums of Seggie.[13] The more the matter is investigated, the less clear it becomes how many different "Bynnis," or branches of Meldrums, we may be dealing with. Nevertheless, David Laing stated categorically that Squire Meldrum's Bynnis "is in the neighbourhood of

---

[8] *Reg. Mag. Sig.* 4:114, no. 490.

[9] For the administrative transfer of Cleish from Fife to the enlarged shire of Kinross, Hamer (*Works*, 3:186) cites a parliamentary act from 1685. See now RPS James VII, M1685/4/18, Parliamentary minutes from 11 June 1685.

[10] See *Reg. Mag. Sig.* 2:638, no. 2996. In the previous year, a charter had ratified the sale by "Arch. Meldrum de Bynnys" of other lands within Cleish; both sales were to Robert Colville, whose family name would remain associated with Cleish (*Reg. Mag. Sig.* 2:615, no. 2896, Edinburgh, 28 November 1505).

[11] Dickinson, *Sheriff Court Book of Fife*, p. 400.

[12] For example, a Walter Kynnard is described as the "lard of Bynnis" in a document of 11 March 1552–53, but his title derives from the estates of "Culbin and Byn" near Elgin, Morayshire (see *Reg. Sec. Sig.* 4:312, no. 1921, and *ER* 18:521).

[13] On the arms of Meldrum of Seggie, recorded from the fifteenth century, see McAndrew, *Scotland's Historic Heraldry*, p. 449.

Cleisch, and lies near the foot of Benarty, not far from Lochleven," and Hamer agreed, although neither provided contemporary evidence for identifying it as such.[14] There is documentary evidence for the existence of various estates called "Binns" in Fife; there is also documentary evidence for the use of the style "of Binns" by various Meldrums over the years, including William. But unlike with Cleish, there is no record of a Meldrum actually buying, selling, or otherwise dealing with lands called the Binns in Fife.

Records for sixteenth-century Fife offer at least three possible candidates for Squire Meldrum's estate, although two can probably be dismissed. A series of documents from 1540–42 detailing the resignation of the earldom of Morton by James, earl of Morton, in favor of Robert Douglas of Lochleven includes "Binis" or "Bynis" amongst the lands within his barony of Aberdour in the south of Fife; it lies by the distinctive geographic feature of Binn Hill which overlooks the town of Burntisland, between Aberdour and Kinghorn.[15] The register for Dunfermline abbey records an assize of perambulation (a formal marking-out of the borders) of the marshes between Wester and Easter Kinghorn on 6 October 1457, and one of the men involved is an "Archibaldus meldrum de Clesse."[16] Is this Meldrum involved because he owns neighboring property, or simply because he owns land somewhere within Dunfermline abbey's broader area of influence, which included Cleish? And what is the relationship between this Archibald Meldrum "de Clesse" and the Archibald Meldrum "de Bynnys," father of William, whose 1506 sale of some Cleish property was cited above? The Aberdour settlement of Binns is not listed separately in the 1517 Fife tax return, however, so it may have been of too little account at the time to furnish the squire with his preferred style.[17]

A second Fife estate can probably also be dismissed, although it *is* listed in this tax roll. "The half of Binn" (valued 1 pound) forms part of the barony of "Aringosk" (Arngosk) within the "Edin Quarter" of the county.[18] (The tax roll divides Fife into four quarters: Dunfermline, Inverkeithing, Leven, and Eden, the last being the area around the river Eden in the extreme northwest of Fife, some distance from Cleish). Apart from the place-name itself, however, there is no reason to connect this "Binn" to the Meldrums of Cleish.

More promising is the third Fife candidate. The 1517 tax roll lists "The Binnyes" within the regality of the Church for the same Dunfermline quarter as Cleish, and it is valued at 2 pounds — the same as "Cliesh-Meldrum."[19] The fact that these lands lie within the same quarter of Fife as Cleish would seem to argue in their favor, although proximity in itself proves nothing (Lyndsay's family owned estates in both Fife and East Lothian, for example).

---

[14] Laing, *Poetical Works*, 1:311; Hamer, *Works*, 3:187.

[15] *Registrum de Honoris de Morton* 2 (items 245 and 256): "terrarum et baronie de Abirdour terrarum de Tyrie terrarum de Wodfeild terrarum de Seyfeild terrarum de Binis Bawbartanis . . ." (p. 263) and "Terras de Tiry / Wodfeild / Seyfeild / Bynis / Babertanis" (p. 277); see the "Binn" and "Binn Hill" marked above "Brunt Illand" on Blaeu's 1654 map of East Fife: http://maps.nls.uk/view/00000450.

[16] *Registrum de Dunfermelyn*, no. 452, pp. 345–46.

[17] Dickinson, *Sheriff Court Book of Fife*, pp. 399–400 (Inverkeithing quarter).

[18] Dickinson, *Sheriff Court Book of Fife*, p. 396. On Blaeu's 1654 map of Fife it is labeled "Binnety" (see http://maps.nls.uk/view/00000444), but "Binn Farm" and "Binn Hill" are still marked on the modern Ordnance Survey map (accessed via https://canmore.org.uk/).

[19] Dickinson, *Sheriff Court Book of Fife*, pp. 401 and 400.

This "Binnyes" would seem to correspond to the estate described by Laing as lying at the foot of Benarty, just east of Cleish and south of Lochleven. The editor of the 1841 *Liber Conventus S. Katherine Senensis prope Edinburgum* had described this estate in more detail as "the lands, or 'Temple' lands of Binn or Binns, which are also now in the county of Kinross, though at that time in Fife, and are presently the property of Admiral Adam, of Blair-Adam" (this volume is not otherwise concerned with Lyndsay or his poem, so the passing attempt to locate the squire's estates indicates how famous and popular Lyndsay's poem once was in Scotland).[20]

Although neither the anonymous editor of the *Liber Conventus S. Katherine* nor Admiral Adam recorded their evidence for believing this to be the site of Meldrum's estate of the Binns, the fact that an estate named Bin did exist here in the sixteenth century can be verified elsewhere. In July 1576, the sacristan of Dunfermline and parson of Cleish issued letters of tack and assedation in favor of one James Lyndesay of Dowhill, Cleish, for a clutch of lands in and around Cleish including "templand of Bin." "Tempilland of Bin" is cited in two further letters of tack and assedation (from 4 May 1597 and 2 January 1617) preserved within the papers of the Lindsays of Dowhill.[21] A "Templand" or "tempilland" is one which belongs, or once belonged, to either the Knights Templars or the Hospitaller knights of St. John, which incidentally indicates that the name "templand of Bin" must predate the resignation of all remaining Hospitaller lands into royal hands in 1564 (the Templars had already been formally suppressed in the fourteenth century).[22] The Hospitallers owned hundreds of parcels of land across Scotland, many of which were leased out long-term to secular tenants. A great rental of all Hospitaller property in Scotland was drawn up by Sir Walter Lindsay, preceptor of the Order of St. John, in c. 1539–40 (this the same "Sir Walter" whom Meldrum would name as one of his executors in the *Testament* — see note to lines 26–27).[23] Within the sheriffdom of Fife, Walter records a "bynnis land ther . . . vj d." (i.e., worth 6 pennies rent). However, it is listed below "the temple of Inchemartyne of aberdor

---

[20] *Liber Conventus*, p. lxxix. Admiral Adam was a fan of Lyndsay's poem, for Laing reports that "having, in 1810, acquired this property, he placed the following inscription on the old house: — 'This house, in the reign of James V, belonged to Squire Meldrum of Cleish and Binns, celebrated in a Poem of Sir David Lyndsay of the Mount'" (*Poetical Works*, 1:311).

[21] NRS GD254/45 (1576), GD254/62 (1597) and GD254/80 (1617). The "templand of Bin" is listed immediately after "quarter of lands of Blaircrambeth" and "quarter of Kinnaird." On Blaeu's map of West Fife, Kinnard and Blair of Krammey are immediately adjacent to Bin Keltey, all near "Binn-Eartie mons" (on reading "Blair of Krammey" as Blaircrambeth, see *Place-Names of Fife*, entry for "Blair #"). Other later evidence for the existence of this estate can be found in Grant, *Commissariot Record of Edinburgh*: "Dewar, David, in Byn, par. of Cleisch in Fyfe 23 June 1597" (p. 74). See also Grant, *Commissariot Record of St Andrews*: "Barclay, Catherine, spouse to James Greve, in Bine, par. of Cleish 19 May 1626" and "Davidson, Christian, spouse to George Hoge, tenant in Binn, par. of Cleish 29 Nov. 1688" (pp. 26 and 94). The papers of the Erskine family of Cardross contain an instrument from 20 May 1585 relating to "lands of the Bin, in parish of Ballingrie" with an annual rent of 80 Scots merks: the parish of Ballingry includes the area proposed by Laing and Admiral Adam for Squire Meldrum's estate (NRS GD15/568).

[22] Cowan et al., *The Knights of St John*, p. liv (on date of resignation); pp. lvii–lxi on "temple lands" and leasing practices.

[23] See Cowan et al., *The Knights of St John*, Introduction, pp. lxxiv–xxxiii. The relevant part of the Fife list is on p. 26.

pertening to the erle of morton" (i.e., Inch Marton of Aberdour) together with other parcels of land belonging to named individuals ("robertsonis land," "David clerkis land ther"), which may indicate that it relates either to a man named Bynn or, more likely, to the settlement of Binn within the barony of Aberdour, as described above. Much later in the Fife list comes "the temple of the perrenwele perteni[n]g to the lard of Dowhill" followed by "the tempil land of newinstoun pertening to andro Howburn." These are modern Dowhill, Paranwell, and Nivingston in the parish of Cleish, settlements surrounding the Blair-Adam area identified by the *Liber* and Laing as the squire's "Bynnis." This is where one would expect Walter to list the "bynnis" if it referred to the estate identified by Laing and Admiral Adam.[24]

All the same, the assertion by Laing, Hamer and others that this was the location of Squire Meldrum's "Binnys" would probably stand unquestioned were it not for some compelling evidence for another "Binns" entirely. Kinsley revived a much earlier suggestion that the squire's title may derive instead from the more famous Binns within the barony of Abercorn, Linlithgowshire (now West Lothian), an identification which Hamer and Laing had firmly rejected.[25] A charter of 28 October 1363 granted one "David de Melgdrom" the lands of "Westbins" in the barony of Abercorn.[26] That there were also Meldrums in Cleish by the end of the fourteenth century is confirmed by another charter from the reign of Robert III granting an assortment of estates within the barony of "Cleis, Fyfe" to a "Willielmi de Melgdrum."[27] A charter of 30 April 1417 helpfully connects the Meldrums of Cleish in Fife to the barony of Abercorn: "William Melgdrum, laird of Clesch" granted lands in Philpston (an estate within Abercorn) to James of Dundas.[28] There is another significant connection to Abercorn via the Lords Lindsay of the Byres, who had held that barony for generations and would continue to do so throughout the period when they employed squire Meldrum.[29] A notarial instrument of 14 February 1440 recorded a resignation of lands by a "Dame Agnes of Erth" to "Sir John Lindissay . . . upon the ground of the lands of Bynnis, near the Castle of Manerstoun," and the witnesses included one "James of Meldrum, son and heir of the laird of Bynnis."[30] In 1478, an instrument of sasine dealing with lands within

---

[24] Early maps offer little help: although the modern Ordnance Survey map of West Fife and Kinross records a "Binn" and "Binn Wood" in the expected location at the western foot of Benarty hill (see https://canmore.org.uk/), and seventeenth-century maps of Fife reliably record the actual hill of "Binearty" or "Binn-Eartie mons," only Blaeu's 1654 map of West Fife (see http://maps.nls.uk/view/00000447) marks a settlement named "Bin Keltey" near it — then and now, this settlement is normally just known as Kelty (see *The Place-Names of Fife* entry for #Kelty).

[25] Hamer, *Works*, 3:187. Kinsley lists a few of the documents discussed here in a footnote, but without further comment (*Squyer Meldrum*, p. 5).

[26] *Squyer Meldrum*, p. 5; for this charter see *Reg. Mag. Sig.* 1:48 (no. 170).

[27] *Reg. Mag. Sig.* 1:630, no.1717 (Hamer cites this from a different source at *Works*, 3:177). The estates in question are "the 3d part lands of Cleis, 3d part of the milne of Cleis, third part of Wester Cleis, third part of Bordland, third part of Newistoun, third part of the town and miln of Newstoun."

[28] *Cal. Laing Charters*, pp. 25–26 (item 96).

[29] See for example a charter dated at Stirling, 2 January 1540–41, which reconfirmed John Lord Lindsay of Byres and his wife Helen Stewart in a long list of lands including "Bynnis" in the barony of Abercorn (*Reg. Mag. Sig.* 3:513, no. 2256).

[30] *Ninth Report of the Royal Commission on Historical Manuscripts*, Part 2:185, Muniments of the Lords Elphinstone, muniment 6.

Abercorn was witnessed by local landowners including "Archibald Meldrum, son and heir of the late James Meldrum of Bynnis."[31] A few years later, two documents from 1494 and 1498 record a dispute over lands within Cleish, Fife, between an "Archibald meldrum of the bynnis" and "James meldrum his brothir," who are described as the heirs to "Jonete meldrum of the Clesche."[32] A Jonete Meldrum is recorded as owning land in Cleish along with Annabelle and Margarete Meldrum in the 1470s (presumably sisters), but more importantly, Jonet Meldrum is identified as the "relict [i.e., widow] of James Meldrum of Bynnis" in a precept of sasine of 18 February 1485/86 in which she grants various Cleish properties to her "carnal son" James.[33] This inheritance seems to be the root of the acrimonious dispute between the brothers James and Archibald Meldrum over lands in Cleish. Given the fourteenth-century records of Meldrums in both Cleish and Abercorn, a mid-fifteenth century marriage between James and Jonete Meldrum might represent an effort to maintain ties between these two branches of an extended kinship, at least if Jonete's husband "James Meldrum of Bynnis" was the same man as the "James of Meldrum, son and heir of the laird of Bynnis" cited in those Abercorn documents of 1440 and 1478.

Some years later, an instrument of sasine dated 10 March 1516/17 and relating to the grant of lands within Abercorn by Patrick, Lord Lindsay (squire Meldrum's future employer) was witnessed by "Archibald Meldrum of Bynnis."[34] This seems likely to be the same Archibald Meldrum, "son and heir of the late James Meldrum of Bynnis," who, as a young man, had witnessed the 1478 document from Abercorn. The crucial question is whether he is also the "Archibald Meldrum of the bynnis," son of Jonete, who fought with his brother James over land-rights in Cleish in 1494–98, as well as the "Archibald Meldrum de Bynnis" whose son William — our protagonist — bore witness to a sale of lands in Cleish in 1506.[35] If William Meldrum, his father Archibald, and grandfather James *did* all hold Abercorn lands from the Lords Lindsay of the Byres, it might explain why Patrick, fourth Lord Lindsay was so ready to hire William Meldrum once he had recovered from the disastrous ambush of 1517, and to retain him permanently in the Lindsay's main seat at Struthers, in Fife.

---

[31] Dalyell, *Binns Papers*, pp. 5–6 (no. 16).

[32] *Acta Dom. Con.* 1 (1839), p. 369, 10 July 1494 (quoted in Hamer, *Works* 3:178n7). See also *Acta Dom. Con.* 2 (1918), p. 202, 10 May 1498 (in Hamer, *Works*, 3:178n9).

[33] There are instruments of sasine in the name of "Annabelle, Jonete et Margarete Meldrumis" for various lands within Cleish in 1473, and separate instruments for Margarete and Jonete in 1479 (*ER* 9:675, 680). The "[p]recept of sasine by Jonet Meldrum, relict of James Meldrum of Bynnis" from 1485/86 relates to "a sixth of the lands of Myddilcleische, a half of the lands of Doill a sixth of the lands of Bordland, and a sixth of the lands of Nevinstonis in the barony of Cleische" (NRS GD150/205). The fact that it calls James Meldrum her "carnal" son could indicate that he was illegitimate, since Meldrum was clearly her maiden as well as her married name (in early modern Scotland, women normally retained their maiden names in legal documents), but the term could also just be used to clarify that he was not merely a step-child (see Marshall, "Illegitimacy," p. 20).

[34] Dalyell, *Binns Papers*, p. 9, no. 30.

[35] "Arch. Meldrum de Bynnys" sold other Cleish estates to the same Robert Colvile in 1505; *Reg. Mag. Sig.* 2, p. 615, no. 2896 (28 November 1505). In Hamer's speculative family tree (*Works*, 3:181) he describes Squire Meldrum's father Archibald as "fl. 1478–1506." But the fact that the lady of Strathearn describes the squire as being an attractive marriage prospect because "ye ar your fatheris air" (*Historie*, line 972) may imply that his father was still living at that point (which was c. 1515).

Where might "Archibaldus meldrum de Clesse" — mentioned above as being involved in the perambulation of the marches in Kinghorn in 1457 — fit into all of this? The Dunfermline abbey register also lists an "Archibald Meldrum of Clesche" in an assize of perambulation of "the marches betwixt Gaytmilk & Admulti" (modern Goatmilk and Auchmuty, southeast of Lochleven) for 27 June 1466. This is surely the same man, and he is probably also the "Arch. de Meldrum de Cleesch" who appears in a list of witnesses to a royal charter of 30 October 1444.[36] It seems too early for him to be identified with the "Archibald Meldrum of the bynnis" who squabbled with his brother in the 1490s over their mother Jonete's Cleish estates, but it is possible that he was Jonete's father or other male relative.

So far, these scattered records allow us to construct the following conjectural family tree:

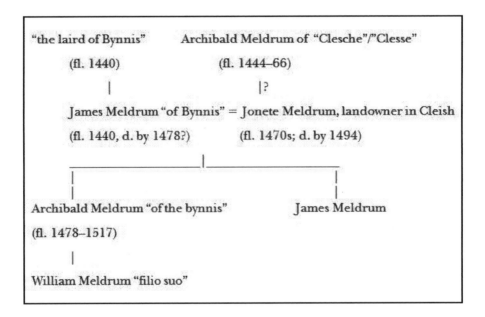

[36] *Registrum de Dunfermelyn*, pp. 354–56 (no. 458); *Reg. Mag. Sig.* 2:64, no. 279.

This differs substantially from the one proposed by Hamer, who denied all connection to the Abercorn Meldrums.[37] It is overwhelmingly tempting to leave it at this neat table, but significant difficulties remain. A charter issued by John, Lord Lindsay at Struthers on 4 June 1542, granted the lands of "Bynnis et Corslattis" in the barony of Abercorn to Robert Gib and his wife Elizabeth Schaw: the charter states that they were formerly held by James Hamilton of Kincavil (a neighboring estate within Abercorn) who was convicted of heresy.[38] Among the witnesses was "Wil. Meldrum," who did not sign himself "de Bynnis" on this occasion, although he would again in a document of 1550 so he clearly had not given this title up.[39] This identification of other men who, within Squire Meldrum's lifetime, claimed the style "of Binns" from the Abercorn estate must reopen the question of whether Meldrum could ever have derived his own style "of Binns" from Abercorn lands. Binns, like Cliesh, was divisible, but an earlier legal attempt in 1528 by James Hamilton's procurator to force Lord Lindsay to "infeft the said James Hammyltoun in *half the lands of Bynis* with Corsflat and half of Philipstoun, together with the superiority of *the other half of Bynis* (belonging to the said James Hammyltoun) [italics mine]" seems to leave little room for Squire Meldrum's involvement unless he were a tenant of the "the other half of Bynis" over which Hamilton claimed superiority.[40] (James Hamilton was unsuccessful: a charter issued by Lord Lindsay of the Byres in 1531 granted to Robert Gib "the lands of Bynnis, lying in the barony of Abircorne . . . which formerly belonged to James Hammyltoun of Kincavill, and were forfeited to the King for heresy.")[41]

There is an oddly suggestive link between the (or some) Meldrums and the Hamiltons of Kincavil; however, on 19 February 1518/19, an act of resignation to "Patrick Hammiltoune of Kyncawill, knight" was drawn up in Sir Patrick's Edinburgh chambers before witnesses including "William Meldrum fiar of Byning" (a fiar is usually a life-tenant); two years earlier, Sir Patrick had sat on an assize in Edinburgh with a group of men including "Archibald Meldrum of Bynnis."[42] Sir Patrick's elder son and heir was James

---

[37] *Works*, 3:181. I have omitted here all mention of another "Maister Williame Meldrum" who appears in records between c. 1525–54 as a notary public — often along with another notary James Meldrum — and who was vicar of Strabok. There is no suggestion either by Lyndsay or the historical record that his Meldrum was a university graduate ("Maister"), whereas this man is probably the William Meldrum who graduated from the University of St Andrews in 1523 (Anderson, *Early Records*, pp. 112). Hamer theorizes that William and James might have been the sons of James Meldrum of Cleish, and thus cousins to Squire William Meldrum (*Works*, 3:185–86).

[38] *Reg. Mag. Sig.* 3:629–30, no. 2725. Robert Gib was also addressed as "Robert Gib of the Bynnis" in a letter of 1 June 1542, issued from St Andrews (*Reg. Sec. Sig.* 2:706, no. 4678).

[39] Hamer, *Works*, 3:181, citing a precept of sasine dated "Ochterotherstruther" [i.e., Struthers Castle], 30 May 1550 and recorded in Fraser, *Memorials of the Earls of Haddington*, 2:261.

[40] Quoted from an instrument drawn up "[a]t the gates of Struthirs 18 October 1528," where "the said Lord sent out his servant John Baxster of Quhelt to intimate that he refused to see the procurator or to peruse the letters. Whereupon the said procurator took instruments" (Beveridge and Russell, *Protocol Books of Dominus Thomas Johnsoun*, p. 1, no. 2).

[41] Dalyell, *The Binns Papers*, no. 33, dated Edinburgh, 20 July 1531 (p. 10). James Hamilton of Kincavil was delated for heresy (i.e., formally accused) in 1532 and fled to England in 1534, although he would later return (Edington, *Court and Culture*, pp. 54–55).

[42] NRS GD86/80, dated 10 December 1516.

Hamilton of Kincavil, the same who would unsuccessfully attempt to assert his control over the "Bynis" in 1528. (Lord Lindsay's reluctance to hear James Hamilton's case in October 1528 may have been strengthened by the fact that James' younger brother, Patrick Hamilton, was burnt at the stake for heresy in St Andrews on 29 February 1528.) But the question that remains unanswered is whether either of these Meldrums — Archibald of Bynnis, or William fiar of Byning — has anything to do with Lyndsay's Squire Meldrum in the first place.

As so often happens in the study of early modern Scotland, we pick through the scattered debris of history for pieces which may or may not belong to the same puzzle. One such disappointing fragment is a couple of related entries in the *Treasurer's Accounts* from 1506–07 which record payments "de firmis terrarum [i.e., "from the fermes of the lands"] de Clesche et Bynning" in 1506, and again "de firmis terrarum de Cleisch et Bynning" in 1506–07.[43] Between the dates and the paired names, it is hard to believe this does not relate in some way to Meldrum's estates, but once again, this lead dissolves on closer inspection. Alongside the well-known Binns in Abercorn discussed above, there is another collection of Linlithgow estates called East, West, and Middle Binny or Binning (thus "the Binnys" or "Binnings" collectively), and it turns out that this is the "Binning" intended here. There are suggestive family connections between these Linlithgow "Binnys" or "Binnings" and Fife. The *Exchequer Rolls* list a sasine for one Margarete Prestoun for lands in "Wester Bynning," Linlithgow in 1478, as well as individual sasines for Margarete, Katerine, and Cristiane Prestoun for a collection of properties within Cleish, Fife in 1492.[44] That this is the same Margaret Preston is confirmed by two documents: a 1492 memorandum for one Robert Bruce "of the relese of Clesche, belangand to Margret Prestoun his spous," and a precept of 12 December 1500 instructing baillies to "infeft Robert Bruce of Bynning and Margaret Preston, his spouse, in conjunct-fee, in the lands of West Bynning called Abbotsland, lying in the town and territory of West Bynning, in the sheriffdom of Linlithgow."[45] On 15 February 1502/03 this Robert Bruce, described as "portionar of West Bynnyn," received a letter of tack of "the landis of Bynnyn and Clesch, with the pertinentis, liand within the schirefdomez of Linlithqw and Fiffe" through the death of "Christiane Preston, portionare of the said landis" before she reached the legal age of majority (i.e., 21; perhaps she was a younger sister of Margaret).[46] By 1506–07, Christiane's husband, Robert Levingstoun, was also dead, and it is to their deaths and the wardship of their properties in "Clesche et Bynning" that those *Treasurer's Accounts* in 1506–7 refer: the final record notes that the wardship of these Cleish holdings was sold to Robert Colville — the same man who also bought lands in Cleish from Archibald Meldrum in 1506.[47] In other words, we have

---

[43] *TA* 3:29 and 243; *TA* 4:8.

[44] *ER* 9:678 and *ER* 10:766

[45] *TA* 1:207 and Fraser, *Memorials of the Earls of Haddington*, 2:242–43 (no. 325).

[46] *Reg. Sec. Sig.* 1:134, no. 910.

[47] *TA* 3:29: "Item, idem onerat se de xviij ll., de firmis terrarum de Clesche et Bynning, de uno termino aute hoc compotum et de terminis compoti, existentium in manibus regis per mortem quondam uxoris Roberti Levingston, militis"; and 3:243: "Et de ix ll., de firmis terrarum de Cleisch et Bynning, in warda existentium per mortem quondam Roberti Levingstoun, militis, et Cristiane Prestoun sue sponse, de terminis compoti." *TA* 4:8: "Et de vi ll. xiij s. iiij d., pro warda certarum terrarum in Cleisch per mortem quondam Cristiane Prestoun, sponse Roberti Levingstoun, vendita Roberto Colvill."

uncovered yet more tangled connections between landowning families in Linlithgow and West Fife, but we are no closer to identifying Squire Meldrum's estate of "the Bynnis."

If Squire Meldrum did own land in the Binnys (rather than the Binns) of Linlithgowshire, it may indicate that he was, after all, that "William Meldrum fiar of Byning" who witnessed that 1519 document for Sir Patrick Hamilton of Kincavil.[48] But there are, in the end, too few pieces of too many puzzles for the matter to be settled. If the elegant family tree arrived at by combining the Linlithgow and Fife references to "Archibald Meldrum of Bynnis" is difficult to dismiss, so too is the persuasive simplicity of the assumption that the Meldrums owned adjacent estates of Cleisch and Binns in southwest Fife. This is by no means the only historical mystery attached to the squire and his biography.

ROMANCE AND IRONY IN THE *MELDRUM* POEMS

One of the great difficulties faced by readers of the *Meldrum* poems is the way in which tone and register sometimes shifts abruptly, with regular (if ambiguous) hints of irony, as well as odd discrepancies between the squire of the *Historie* and the narrator of the *Testament*.[49] Such features would normally make one suspect satirical intent, particularly in the work of a writer as famed for satire as Lyndsay, but this is difficult to square with a conviction that the *Meldrum* poems were intended as heartfelt praise of Meldrum. As David Irving put it back in 1804: "[t]hat Lindsay wished to render his deceased friend an object of ridicule can hardly be supposed: yet several passages of *Squyer Meldrum* have an appearance of intentional burlesque." Irving dismissed the puzzle with an urbane shrug: "in obsolete poetry, it must be recollected, the serious cannot always be readily distinguished from the ludicrous."[50] Hamer, with far more respect for Lyndsay as a poet, was determined to defend the *Meldrum* poems from charges of irony:

> The satire which we have come to look upon as characteristic of Lindsay is here completely wanting. Its place is occupied by kindliness, by deep appreciation of his old friend, and by a feeling of tender romance towards the ill-fated love affair. The narrative goes with a swing and an ardour like nothing else in Lindsay, and yet retains the simplicity of diction and outlook, and also subjective interest.[51]

---

[48] Between the Binnys and the Binns lies the Kincavil estate (modern Kingscavil) which supplied Sir Patrick Hamilton with his style. See the Blaeu 1654 map of Lothian and Linlithgow which shows "Binns" and, to the southwest, the cluster of "Bynny," "Wester Bynny," and "E. Bynny." These three are placed, slightly inaccurately, immediately next to "Kinkauil": http://maps.nls.uk/view/00000395.

[49] See notes to lines 13–22, 24–26, 30–34, 36, 120, 205–6, 781–88, and 875–80 (on misplaced allusions to Virgil's *Aeneid*), 900 ff. (the start of the love-affair), 1473, 1477–78, and much of the *Testament*.

[50] *Lives of the Scottish Poets* 2:114. See also Stauffer, who appended the description "boisterous and satirical" to his joint listing of the *Historie* and the (undoubtedly satirical) *Tragedie of the Cardinall* (*English Biography Before 1700*, p. 336). Hamer describes two more of his contemporaries as having "misunderstood Lindsay's intentions" (*Works*, 3: 226) although in fact one of the two, Kitchin, denied that the *Historie* was "naked burlesque," claiming only that "we seem to see a jocose element in the Last Will and Testament with which [it is] supplied" (*Survey of Burlesque*, p. 30). Smith had identified the *Testament* with Old French literary parodies (*French Background*, pp. 133–36).

[51] Hamer, *Works*, 4:xxxiii.

In his note to the passage in which Meldrum jousts with the English champion Talbart, Hamer again insisted that "there is no sense of burlesque."[52] Two decades later, Lewis continued to bat away suspicions of ironic intent:

> The strange idea that the poem is a burlesque, unless it is based on the first fifty lines or so, may come from the love scenes where much chivalry, good sense, and wholesome sensuality are mixed with much humour. But the humour is not burlesque; in English medieval romance homely realism thus often blends with courtly love . . ."[53]

A brilliant solution to the apparent contradictions between tone and authorial intent was offered in 1974 by Felicity Riddy. She argued that there was satire and criticism in the poem, but that it was literary rather than social, and Meldrum himself was not its target: "For Lindsay, Meldrum is an exemplar of noble conduct, and the central concerns of the poem are ethical, not historical nor psychological."[54] Rather, she argued that Lyndsay presented the life of his "old friend" in the form of a chivalric romance in order to show how outmoded and inappropriate the values and concerns of medieval romance had become for sixteenth-century society:

> As I see it, the variations of tone in the *Historie*, that have given rise to radically different views about its seriousness, are the necessary outcome of Lindsay's attempt to maintain an equilibrium between a poetic vision of life and life itself; during the course of the poem the vision is obliterated and something more prosaic but no less honourable offered in its place. [. . . .]
> The change that has taken place between Malory's day and Lindsay's seems to me a significant one. The way in which the *Historie* honours, laughs at, and in the end discards romance is an acknowledgement of the growth in the sixteenth century of new evaluations of the nature of the good life that render the old fictions obsolete.[55]

Riddy's reading of the *Historie* as illustrating a clash between old and new values was adopted by Edington:

> Although on one level *Squyer Meldrum* represents a sincere tribute to the memory of an old friend, admiration for the Squire was blended with an equally profound unease concerning the cultural values that inspired his adventures.[56]

Most recently, R. James Goldstein has modified this reading by arguing that Lyndsay did not consistently distance himself from romance; rather, he "was simultaneously *attached* to the traditional chivalric values embodied by his friend and *self-reproachful* for maintaining attachments to values he understood to be moribund."[57]

---

[52] Hamer, *Works,* 3:197.

[53] *English Literature in the Sixteenth Century*, p. 103.

[54] Riddy, "'Squyer Meldrum' and the Romance of Chivalry," p. 28.

[55] "'Squyer Meldrum' and the Romance of Chivalry," pp. 28 and 36.

[56] *Court and Culture*, pp. 122–23. This is also the line adopted by Calin in his comparison of the *Meldrum* poems to French chivalric biographies and literary testaments (*Lily and Thistle*, pp. 149–56).

[57] "*Squyer Meldrum* and the Work of Mourning," p. 148 (italics his).

The *Historie* is certainly suffused with the features of medieval romance, from conventions of vocabulary and phraseology to broader matters such as characterization, narrative pacing and the selection of scenes and incidents; this is part of what has contributed to the *Historie*'s great appeal. As Riddy notes:

> The actions that go to make up the poem all have to do with either war or love: there has been a drastic simplification therefore of Meldrum's real-life experiences [. . . .] it has not I think been sufficiently emphasized hitherto how far Meldrum's life is expressed in terms of established motifs.[58]

Among other well-loved motifs, Lyndsay offers his readers much spectacular single combat, usually against terrible odds and frequently on behalf of a lady; a prophetic dream (see note to lines 401–10 for the Arthurian allusions of Talbart's); a chivalric hero enjoying the gratitude of a nation; scenes of love-agony inspired more or less instantly by a lady's beauty on the one hand, and a hero's chivalric prowess on the other, all taking place in "the mirrie tyme of May" (line 927); rings exchanged as love-tokens (lines 195–96, 1002–06). The *Historie*'s promise that readers will be morally enriched by listening to tales of noble deeds signals its generic affiliation right from the start. Conventional romance diction and style is everywhere: ladies are invariably "bricht" (lines 486, 896, 1258); descriptions of battles are thick with alliteration; combatants are "brim as beiris" ("fierce as bears," line 1301) or "worthie and wicht" (lines 220, 1394); they are "vailyeand" and fight "vailyeandlie" (lines 14, 19, 217, 281, etc.), or like "wyld lyounis" (line 236, 629, 647) as they win the "pryse" (lines 241, 1047).

The world of romance is also evoked by the mysterious vagueness of some scenes and characters, a feature that sits rather awkwardly with the *Historie*'s self-presentation as a true story. Meldrum's beloved (whom we know from external evidence to be Marjorie Lawson, widowed lady of Gleneagles) is only ever called "the ladie" in the text, as indeed are all the other "ladies" who fall in love with Meldrum, turning them from individuals into a trope. Meldrum's "ladie" is from the vale of Strathearn, but instead of naming the famous estate, Lyndsay reports only that she lives in "ane castell . . . / Beside ane montane" (lines 858–59). The enemy from whom Meldrum rescues one of her other properties is named as "Makferland" (see note to line 1055 on why this mysterious character may have been so named), but the castle itself is again nameless (see notes to lines 1055 and 1057). The most deadly of Meldrum's foes is a "cruell knicht" who masterminds the 1517 ambush: his namelessness may be frustrating from a historian's point of view, but it does serve to align him much more readily with the traitorous villains of romance. Meldrum's first chivalric deed of rescuing the maiden of Carrickfergus takes place, not in the thick of the siege, but in a quiet, convenient "garding amiabill" (pleasant garden, line 105) in which the fascination with material luxury that characterizes romance is indulged through the detailed description of the maiden's rich clothing (lines 121–27).

Romances may also signal their generic affiliation by citing others of their kind. Thus, the battle prowess of the hero may be compared to — or claimed to excel — that of other famous heroes of romance and epic, as when Meldrum is compared to Gaudifer from the legend of Alexander (lines 1281–82), Tydeus from the siege of Thebes (lines 1310–12), Roland and Oliver from the legend of Charlemagne (lines 1313–14 and 1316), or Arthurian

---

[58] "*Squyer Meldrum* and the Romance of Chivalry," p. 28.

heroes such as Lancelot, Gawain, and the knights of the Round Table (lines 48–64, 1315, 1320). At one point Meldrum even compares himself to Lancelot (line 1079, in a scene of chivalric vow-making which itself is a stock motif of romance — see note to lines 1088–92). Apart from such explicit references to other romances, Lyndsay may have modeled aspects of the love-affair between Squire Meldrum and the lady Marjorie on a tremendously popular fifteenth-century English romance called *The Squire of Low Degree* (see notes to lines 907–26).

It is clear that Lyndsay's *Historie of Squyer Meldrum* is deliberately modeled on the medieval literary genre of romance, and reading this poem as a rueful criticism of that genre (as well as of the late-medieval chivalric values which romance celebrates) goes a long way towards explaining its shifting tone and occasional outright comedy. One aspect that it does not fully account for, however, is the discrepancy between the modest and charming protagonist of the *Historie* and the pompous, self-regarding narrator of the *Testament*.[59] (See further discussion of the *Testament* below) The claims and demands attributed to Meldrum in the latter poem make a sympathetic reading of his character difficult there, and this triggers a retrospective reinterpretation of the *Historie* and its adorable protagonist, one all the more effective for taking the reader by surprise. Within the *Testament*, Meldrum commands his audience to "reid the legend of my life" (line 72) and he specifies that at his funeral, "ane oratour" should declaim "at greit laser ['leisure'] the legend of my life, / How I have stand in monie stalwart strife" (*Testament*, lines 164, 167–68). Biographies celebrating the chivalric deeds of the deceased in a manner almost akin to saints' lives (as the term "legend" implies) were sometimes commissioned to be read at grand chivalric funerals,[60] and it is suddenly apparent that the *Historie* we have just read is the text so designated.

For Riddy, this revelation of the *Historie*'s status as funeral eulogy merely explains Lyndsay's choice of the idealizing mode of romance, but this is to ignore the status of the *Testament* as a dramatic monologue.[61] It would be one thing for Lyndsay to describe a magnificent funeral celebrating a friend; it is quite another for Lyndsay to depict this friend as demanding such magnificence for himself. This suddenly brings the *Testament*, and thence potentially the *Historie*, into line with Lyndsay's other satirical dramatic monologues such as *The Tragedie of the Cardinall* about the assassinated Cardinal Beaton, the unrepentant court dog in *The Complaint of Bagsche* (who only regrets his numerous past cruelties because they have led to his current poverty), the foolish parrot in the *The Testament of the Papyngo*, or any number of characters in his masterpiece, *An Satyre of the Thrie Estaitis*. As the uncomfortable disparity between the charming Meldrum of the *Historie* and the pompous elderly man of the *Testament* widens, Lyndsay's serene assertion at the opening of the *Historie* that Meldrum himself was the source for some of the incidents described ("secreitis

---

[59] Goldstein labels Meldrum's speech in the *Testament* as the "encrypted voice" of Lyndsay himself, grieving for his friend, but this does not explain why Lyndsay made his "friend" appear so comically vain ("*Squyer Meldrum* and the Work of Mourning," p. 159).

[60] Ariès, *The Hour of Our Death*, p. 223. At the 1524 funeral of Thomas Howard — earl of Surrey, second Duke of Norfolk and victor over the Scots at Flodden in 1513 — the Carlisle herald recited his noble deeds in much the same way that Meldrum seems to imagine "ane oratour" reading out the *Historie*; see Gittings, *Death, Burial and the Individual*, p. 37, and Daniell, *Death and Burial in Medieval England*, p. 45. On the 3,000-word essay detailing the civic and military triumphs of Howard's career that appears on an inscription fixed to his monument in the Priory of the Virgin Mary and St. Andrew, see Blomefield, *Topographical History*, 2:119–25.

[61] Riddy, "'Squyer Meldrum' and the Romance of Chivalry," p. 28.

that I did not knaw, / That nobill squyer did me schaw," lines 33–34) takes on a rather different meaning. Thus, although Lyndsay's brief *Historie* shares many characteristics with those great national chivalric biographies, Barbour's *Bruce* and Hary's *Wallace*, the difficulty in gauging its author's attitude towards his subject is a key difference. Although they, too, contain episodes of dubious historical accuracy, particularly the *Wallace*, their aim of glorifying their heroes is never in doubt.

THE *TESTAMENT*

Where the *Historie* takes the form of a romance or chivalric biography, the *Testament* is part of the equally well-established genre of literary testament.[62] Perhaps the most famous examples are the satirical *Testament* and the *Lais* (sometimes called *Le petit testament*) by the fifteenth-century French poet François Villon, although Villon was by no means the inventor of the genre and not all literary testaments are satirical, as Henryson's fifteenth-century Scots *Testament of Cresseid* demonstrates. In modern Scots legal terminology, a testament "is the collective term used to describe all the documents relating to the executry of a deceased person," whether a brief valuation of their goods, or one supplemented by a will indicating how the deceased wished to distribute them.[63] Wills might also specify the arrangements and expenditure for the deceased's funeral, as Meldrum's testament does here. The writing of a will sometimes coincided with the dying person's final confession, so literary testaments often have a confessional element to them and some, such as Lydgate's fifteenth-century *Testament*, are entirely confessional in nature.[64] All of these elements, including the satirical, can be seen in Lyndsay's other extended example of a literary testament, *The Testament and Complaynt of our Soverane Lordis Papyngo*.[65] The initial question which Meldrum's poetic Testament poses is thus whether or not it is to be understood as satirical. The contrast between the Meldrum who narrates it and the protagonist of the preceding *Historie* suggests that it is, and several internal features confirm this.

In the *Testament of the Papyngo*, the very first virtue Lyndsay lists among the glories of his sovereign's father, James IV, is that "he wes myrrour of humilitie" (line 491). It gradually becomes apparent that, whether or not this was true of James IV, it is not a virtue that the Meldrum of the *Testament* shares, although he opens innocently enough with remarks on the brevity of human life and his intention to take his leave of the world "with the help of God omnipotent" (line 11). Mimicking genuine legal convention, he names his executors as three

---

[62] See Rice, *The European Ancestry of Villon's Satirical Testaments*; Bach, *Das Testament als Literarische Form*. Literary testaments in English and Scots up to c. 1565 are catalogued in Wilson, "*The Testament of the Buck.*"

[63] *National Records of Scotland*, "Wills and Testaments," online at https://www.nrscotland.gov.uk/research/guides/wills-and-testaments.

[64] Boffey, "Lydgate, Henryson, and the Literary Testament." Wilson distinguishes between those literary testaments "which make bequests in the manner of a legal will" and more general confessional pieces ("*Testament of the Buck*," p. 159).

[65] See Clewett, "Rhetorical Strategy," p. 12, where he argues that Lyndsay's preferred method in *Papyngo* and other poems is one of "drawing successively, and not concurrently, on conventions from various genres"; the same might be said of the conjunction of chivalric biography and literary testament in the Meldrum diptych.

members of the Lindsay family whom he had served for the past three decades. His remark that their "surname failyeit never to the croun: / Na mair will thay to me, I am richt sure" (lines 19–20) may strike a slightly odd note with its implicit comparison of himself to James V, but he quickly returns to pious convention by commending his soul to God and his property to his next of kin (lines 29–37). His insistence that he never cared for "conquessing of riches nor of rent" and that he "never tuik cure of gold more than of glas — / Without honour, fy fy upon riches!" (lines 39, 41) implies a pleasing modesty, although an uncharitable reader might also wonder if this meant he had no wherewithal to pay for the elaborate funeral. The satirical potential of these two emerging motifs — an implicit comparison with James V, and the question of money — only really emerges when one compares the details of Meldrum's proposed funeral arrangements to contemporary wills and funerary practice.[66]

Meldrum asks that his body be disemboweled, embalmed with precious spices and enclosed in "ane coistlie carvit schryne / Of ceder treis, or of cyper fyne" (lines 53–54). His heart and tongue are to be enclosed separately in "twa caissis of gold and precious stanis" (line 57). His body should be presented to Mars while his embalmed tongue and heart are to go to Mercury and Venus respectively. Separate burial of heart and/or entrails was common for monarchs from the medieval period up to Meldrum's own day (see notes to lines 50–56 and 57–85), but the expense of the process involved — not to mention the "cases of gold and precious stones" to put them in — meant that this practice was necessarily restricted to the wealthiest and most important members of society, those whose funerals were to be so magnificent that the body would need some form of preservation to last through the weeks of planning.[67] Records for Scottish wills from this period are scant, but medieval and early modern wills from England record occasional requests for separate heart burial for the likes of Guichard, Earl of Huntingdon, in 1380 or Anthony Woodville, Earl Rivers, in 1483.[68] Lyndsay portrays Meldrum as having far greater social aspirations in death than he ever achieved in life.

Revealing in a different way are Meldrum's instructions regarding his tongue, which he wishes to be offered at the temple of Mercury, explaining that it is to give thanks for the way "My ornate toung my honour did avance" (line 84) before the kings of Scotland, England, and France. Mercury is an ambiguous figure: although revered as the god of rhetoric and eloquence, he was also the god of commerce, cheats, and thieves (see note to line 79). Meldrum's tongue certainly runs away with him as the *Testament* moves on: he imagines that his funeral will be commended "throw the warld" (line 46); muses smugly that Venus had made him so desirable that "Wes never ladie that luikit in my face / Bot honestlie I did obtene her grace" (lines 90–91); insists that "All creature . . . will me commend, / And pray to God for my salvatioun" when they hear his life-story (lines 171–72); demands a golden-lettered epitaph for his tomb that is grander than that on James V's tomb (see note

---

[66] Thomas, comparing the *Testament* to the historical funeral pageantry for James V in 1543 but not taking the *Historie* into account, simply assumed that the *Testament* was intended to be "sardonic," "sly," and "ironic" (*Princelie Majestie*, pp. 212–14).

[67] See Gittings, *Death, Burial and the Individual*, p. 166. John of Gaunt specifically forbade his executors to embalm his body despite decreeing a 40-day wait before burial (Nichols, *Wills of the Kings and Queens of England*, p. 146).

[68] Nicolas, *Testamenta Vetusta*, 1.109; 379–80.

to lines 199–203), and finally, describes the inconsolable grief of all the people he will leave behind, including particularly the "fair ladies of France" (who, several decades after last seeing Meldrum, will apparently still be overcome with "extreme dolour" and "weir the murning weid") along with similarly grief-stricken ladies in London and Scotland, his Carrickfergus maiden, and of course his beloved Lady of Strathearn (lines 211–30).

THE *HISTORIE* AND HISTORY

Meldrum's adventures as described by Lyndsay are carefully embedded in national historical events. This helps to give the *Historie* the feel of accurate biography, despite the romance mode of narrative. There is the Scottish raid on English-held Carrickfergus in 1513; there is the fighting against Henry VIII at Calais in 1513, during which Meldrum is supposed to have defeated an English champion. Key historical players are mentioned, such as James Hamilton, earl of Arran and commander of the Scottish fleet in 1513; Robert Stewart, lord d'Aubigny, captain of Louis XII's Scots guards; Antoine D'Arces (or Seigneur de la Bastie), acting regent of Scotland on behalf of the Duke of Albany in 1517 when the ambush of Meldrum took place. Meldrum's involvement in these international affairs is undocumented, of course, but the relative accuracy with which major historical events are cited appears to reinforce the truth of Meldrum's own adventures.

There *are* some historical records directly related to Meldrum's affair with the "lady of Strathearn" and the vicious ambush that ended it, however, and these shed very interesting light on Lyndsay's handling of Meldrum's biography. On the one hand, they reveal the identity of Meldrum's real-life love and confirm that both affair and ambush really happened, the latter in 1517 as Lyndsay says (see notes to lines 1389–90 and 1484–85). On the other hand, they also demonstrate that his version of events *cannot* be entirely true. For an audience who knows this — see below on Lyndsay's original audience and their knowledge of Meldrum's past — it offers a key to interpreting the squire's other adventures as well as Lyndsay's attitude towards his material.

The first record to consider is the *Historie and Cronicles of Scotland* by Robert Lindesay of Pitscottie. Pitscottie was probably a grandson of Meldrum's employer Patrick, fourth Lord Lindsay of the Byres. He lived c. 1532–78 and he cites Sir David Lyndsay himself among the sources for his history, so one might imagine that the version of Meldrum's story which he recounts would be accurate. J. G. Mackay notes, however, that in Pitscottie's account of the reign of James V, "there are more serious errors in the dates than in any part of his history," and he speculates this may be because Pitscottie was relying on hearsay rather than written accounts or his own memory.[69] Nevertheless, Pitscottie's social circle overlapped with that of Lyndsay, Meldrum, and the Lords Lindsay, so there is potential for input from eyewitnesses in his account (perhaps at second hand, since Pitscottie was only born fifteen years after the events in question) as well as from retellings of Lyndsay's version of events:[70]

---

[69] Pitscottie, *Historie and Cronicles*, 1:cliv. Hamer is inclined to treat discrepancies between Lyndsay's and Pitscottie's accounts as proof of the former's greater reliability: "The story which is unfolded in the poem is fully accepted as history, but the inconsistencies in the accounts of Lindsay and Pitscottie have been disregarded" (*Works*, 3:204).

[70] Pitscottie, *Historie and Cronicles*, 1:2 (Preface) and Mackay's discussion at 1:xxxv–vi.

In this meane tyme Dilabatie [De La Bastie] beand left regent as we haue schawin remanit in the abbay of Hallierudhous [Holyroodhouse] and ane gaird of frinchemen about him to the number of iiijxx [80] of hagbuttaris [carriers of a type of handgun] to be redy at his command quhene he chargit and so it hapnit at this tyme the monetht of [November] and in the zeir of God 1mvcand [xviii] zeiris.[71] At this tyme thair was ane gentillman in Edinburgh nameit Williame Meldrum laird of Binnis quho had in companie witht him ane fair lady callit the Lady Glennagieis [Gleneagles] quho was dochter to Mr Richart Lawsone provest of Edinburgh, the quhilk lady had borne to this laird tua bairnes [children] and intendit to marie hir gif he might haue had the popis lecence because hir husband befoir and hie was sibe [related]. Zeit nocht withstanding ane gentillman callit Luke Stirling inwyit [begrudged] this lufe and marieage betuix thir tuo persouns, thinkand to haue the gentill woman to himself in marieage, because he knew the laird micht nocht haue the popis licence be the lawis. Thairfor he solistit his brotheris sone the laird of Keir witht ane certane of [certain number of] airmitt men to sett wpoun the laird of Binnis to tak this lady frome him be way of deid [i.e., by killing him], and to that effect followit him betuix Leytht [Leith] and Edinburgh and sett on him beneth the Rude chapell witht fyftie airmett men and he againe defendit him witht fyue in number and faught cruellie witht thame and slew the laird of Keiris principall servandis befoir his face defendand himself, and hurt the laird of Keir that he was in perrell of his lyfe, and xxvj of his men; zeit throw multiplecatioun of his enemeis was oversett and drawin to the earth and left lyand for deid, hocht of his legis, strikin throw the body, the knappis of his elbokkis strikin fre him and also the liddis of his kneis[72] nathing of lyfe left in him zeit be the mightie powar of God he eskaipit the deid [death] and all his men that was witht him and leiffit fyftie zeir thairefter.

In the meane tyme come word to Monser Tillabatie [Monsieur De La Bastie] quhair he was at that tyme in the Abbay of Hallierudhous [Holyroodhouse] schawand to him that sic ane nobill man was slaine and murdreist at his hand and he incontenent [immediately] gart strike ane lairum [call to arms] and blaw his trumpatis and rang the common bell commanding all men to follow him baitht on fute or horse that he might revenge the said slaughter, and ruschit fercelie fordwart to the place quhair the battell was strikin and saw this nobill man lyand deidlie wondit and his men about him in the samin maner and passit fercelie efter the enemeis and committaris of the said cryme and ower hyit [overtook] thame at Lythgow [Linlithgow] quhair thay tuik the peill of Lythgow [the castle of Linlithgow] wpoun their heidis to be thair saifgaird and warand [guarantee], thinkand to defend them selffis thairin. Nochtwithtstanding this nobill regent lape manfullie about the house and seigit it continuallie quhill [until] thay randerit the samin and thame that was halderis thairof come into his will quho tuike thame and brocht thame to Edinburgh and gaif thame ane fair syse [judicial inquiry] quho was all convict and condamnitt of the said cryme, and thairefter was put in the castell of Edinburgh in suire keiping induring the Regent's will [for as long as the Regent wished].[73]

---

[71] As MacKay notes, "the true date is 1517" (Pitscottie, *Historie and Cronicles*, 1:299n2).

[72] That is, "cut in the backs of his legs (i.e., hamstrung), struck through the body, the caps of his elbows struck from him and also his kneecaps."

[73] Pitscottie, *Historie and Cronicles*, 1:298–300 (from James V, chapter 8). The spelling of this passage has not been normalized: in addition to the use of Scots *quh-* for modern English *wh-*, it uses *z* for yogh or modern English *y* (e.g., *zeir* "year," *zeit* "yet"); *u/v/w* are interchangeable (e.g., *wpoun* "upon"), and words ending in *-th* in modern English often take an extra *-t* (e.g., *monetht* "month," *witht* "with," *baitht* "both").

Much of this appears to confirm (and indeed supplement) the version of events given by Lyndsay, but given the circumstances, it is odd that there are any contradictions at all. Where Lyndsay says Meldrum and the lady had one daughter between them, Pitscottie cites two children;[74] Lyndsay describes Meldrum and eight followers as being ambushed by sixty armed men, against the five followers and fifty attackers in Pitscottie; in Lyndsay's *Historie* they ambush Meldrum while he is on his way from Edinburgh to the "ferrie" (i.e., Queensferry, a major crossing-point of the Firth of Forth), but in Pitscottie he is attacked on his way from the port of Leith back to Edinburgh; in Lyndsay's account, the lady is traveling with Meldrum and the ambush is in order to abduct her (although they appear to forget this and leave her behind) whereas Pitscottie merely says the ambush was to free the lady by killing Meldrum, and there is no suggestion that she was present. Finally, Lyndsay describes Antoine D'Arces as pursuing the lone "knicht" or "tyrane" (lines 1418, 1421) and imprisoning him in Dunbar Castle (see note to line 1422 on D'Arces' possession of this), whereas Pitscottie has him pursue a group of attackers to Linlithgow castle, then imprison them in Edinburgh castle.

Pitscottie proves correct in some details absent from Lyndsay's poem, most notably in the identification of Meldrum's lover, but the very external records that confirm Pitscottie's identification of Meldrum's paramour as Marjorie Lawson *also* confirm that neither Lyndsay's nor Pitscottie's report of their affair and its dramatic conclusion can be entirely accurate.

The records in question are as follows:

Et de xl li., in partem solutionis octuaginta librarum compositionis facte cum Magistro Patricio Lausoune pro respectuato sibi facto pro mutilatione Georgii Haldan, Willelmi Meldrum, et suorum compliciium et pro precogitata felonia in hujus modi mutilatione commissa, ac pro arte et parte ejusdem; et sic restant xl li. onerande ut supra.
TA 5:107–08 (from section dated 17 January – 17 September 1517)

[And of £40 in partial payment of the £80 total agreed with Master Patrick Lawson with respect to his part in the mutilation of George Haldane, William Meldrum, and their companions, and for the malice aforethought with which this mutilation was carried out, and for art and part of the same; and thus £40 remains owing, as stated above.][75]

. . . the lady of Glennegas be put at fredom and have hir free will to pas quher scho plesis best, and that [neither] William Meldrum allegit to be hir spous, Maister James nor Maister Patrik Lausone mak hir na trouble nor impediment thairintill as thai will answer to my Lordis Regentis and Consell tharapon.
Acta Dom. Con. MS. Vol. 30:31 [dated 20 June 1517]

The historical "lady of Glennegas" (Gleneagles) in 1517 was indeed Marjorie Lawson, who had married Sir John Haldane of Gleneagles in 1508. They had two sons before he was

---

[74] Marjorie's two legitimate sons with Sir John Haldane may have caused confusion here.

[75] Translation mine. "Art and part" is a Scottish legal phrase covering the various means of participating in a crime, from instigating or encouraging it to actually committing it.

killed at Flodden in September 1513.[76] Both Haldanes and Lawsons were prominent families and there is ample documentation to confirm not only their marriage and Marjorie's subsequent possession of the Gleneagles estates, but also to fill out her family background (see the family trees in the Appendix). Pitscottie is correct in identifying her as the daughter of Master Richard Lawson of High Riggs and Humbie, justice clerk and Provost of Edinburgh. The record also confirms a romantic liaison with Meldrum in its description of him as one who was "allegit to be hir spous." But in place of Lyndsay's anonymous "cruell knicht" or Pitscottie's Luke Stirling and the laird of Keir, it names two of Marjorie's own brothers, Masters James and Patrick Lawson. More surprisingly still for those familiar with the Lyndsay or Pitscottie version of events, it orders both them *and* Meldrum to leave Marjorie alone. This record is clearly related to the one from the *Treasurer's Accounts* recording partial payment of a substantial fine imposed on Master Patrick Lawson for the mutilation of William Meldrum, George Haldane, and companions; the weight of the fine is explained by the "malice aforethought in the way in which this injury was committed." Unfortunately there is no exact date for this record, so we cannot be certain that the "restraining order" was issued after the vicious attack on Meldrum, but it does reconfirm that the primary attacker in the eyes of the law was Marjorie's own brother Patrick. It also names George Haldane as co-victim with Meldrum. This is almost certainly George Haldane of Kippen, an uncle to Marjorie's deceased husband who would later act as one of the tutors of Marjorie's son, James Haldane. The prominent naming of Haldane as co-victim incidentally casts doubt on the story of Meldrum's magnificent solo stand, backed by only a handful of nameless underlings.

A complex picture of family rivalries is emerging from these two brief records. An affair evidently took place between William Meldrum and the wealthy widow Marjorie Lawson, and her brothers appear to have been implacably opposed to it, although Meldrum seems to have had support from some members of Marjorie's deceased husband's family.[77] But the affair seems to have gone sour by June 1517, when the Lords of Council ordered Meldrum along with Marjorie's brothers to "mak hir na trouble nor impediment." It is tempting to imagine that Marjorie, by this point, regretted the affair and wanted rid of the whole lot of them, although it is also possible that the inclusion of Meldrum in this "restraining order"

---

[76] They married sometime between 28 May 1508 and 20 January 1508/09, the respective dates of a charter for Haldane which makes no mention of a wife (*Reg. Mag. Sig.* 2:691, no. 3236), and one citing "Johanni Haldane, et Marjorie Lawsoun ejus sponse" (*Reg. Mag. Sig.* 2:702–03, no. 3288). For further joint legal arrangements, see NRS GD198/71–74 of 29 January 1508/09, and *TA* 4:387 (for 1512). That Haldane was killed at the disastrous battle of Flodden (9 September 1513) is confirmed by a special retour of 29 November 1513, in favor of his son James Haldane as heir of his lands in the baronies of Gleneagles and Haldane: "said James being declared to be of legitimate age by reason of dispensation of late king in favour of heirs of those killed at Twischilhaugh, (excepting lands of Rusky [Ruskie] and Lanrik [Lanrick] in stewartry of Menteth) [Menteith], said lands having been in king's hands since death of said Sir John on field of battle with deceased king in Northumberland, guarding person of king, ten weeks ago or thereabout" (NRS GD198/122–123). Haldane lists a second son, Archibald (*Haldanes of Gleneagles*, pp. 35–36).

[77] This accords with Lyndsay's passing mention of how the affair often obliged Meldrum to fight, thanks to the "jelousie and fals invie" of others (lines 1185–90). If Meldrum and Marjorie were unable to marry thanks to Meldrum's distant kinship with her deceased husband's family (as Lyndsay and Pitscottie claim), this may explain George Haldane's support for him.

was not her idea. Either way, Meldrum lost any support he once had as Marjorie's lover. Lyndsay then claims that she was married "aganis hir will" (line 1465) — to whom he does not say.

Pitscottie does not mention her marriage, but he does claim that the attack was made by the laird of Keir on behalf of his uncle Luke Stirling, who supposedly hoped to marry Marjorie himself. This claim is arresting because Marjorie did in fact marry Luke Stirling of Keir.[78] The date of the marriage is unknown, but in an instrument of resignation transferring lands to her son James Haldane, dated 9 December 1526, she is identified as "relict [widow] of John Haldene of Glenneges, and of Luke Striviling [Stirling]."[79] Was he involved in the Meldrum ambush, or does the story of his involvement only spring up as a consequence of her later marriage to him? Either way, it rather spoils Lyndsay's claim that she mourned the loss of Meldrum forever after (lines 1465–79). She may even have married a third time within Meldrum's lifetime, this time to Robert Menteith of Wester Kerse (perhaps a kinsman of her first husband through his grandmother, Agnes Menteith).[80] This may be the same Robert Menteith who appears among the witnesses of a retour of 19 March 1547, which names Marjorie's grandson John Haldane as heir of his father's lands in Gleneagles.[81] Assuming he was of an age with Marjorie, he may also be the Robert Menteith to whom Marjorie's son James Haldane had directed a precept of sasine relating to some Haldane lands back in March 1518. This was drawn up with the consent of James' tutors (he cannot have been older than nine at the time), and one of those so named is George Haldane of Kippen, the same man who was badly injured by Marjorie's brother Patrick in the attack on Meldrum only the previous year.[82] These were tight-knit family circles.

To return to the potential involvement of the Stirlings of Keir in the separation of Marjorie and Meldrum, Hamer remarks guardedly that "all the accounts of Stirling's attack on Meldrum, wherever they appear, have only two authorities, Lindsay and Pitscottie,"and he is inclined to dismiss Pitscottie's allegations against Luke Stirling.[83] He also exonerates Sir John Stirling of having any interest in marrying Marjorie himself on the grounds that he was already married to Margaret Forrester, daughter of Sir Walter Forrester of Torwood, but Sir John is not let off the hook.[84] Lyndsay states that the anonymous "cruell knicht" was

---

[78] Fraser theorized that Meldrum's appearance on the scene had overturned some sort of previous agreement between Marjorie and Luke Stirling (*Stirlings of Keir*, pp. 33–34).

[79] NRS GD198/126.

[80] Haldane, *Haldanes of Gleneagles*, p. 35, citing a document of 11 August 1549 from the *Protocol Books* of Stirling.

[81] NRS GD198/117 and GD198/127.

[82] NRS GD430/60; the precept is described as being by "John Haldane of Gleneagles," but the date (1518) and the fact that it is in favor of Margaret Erskine indicates that it must be by Marjorie's son James Haldane, who was contracted to marry Margaret Erskine in that same year. See NRS GD124/3/4 (14 December 1518).

[83] *Works*, 3:212, and see 3:211–14 for his detailed if inconclusive discussion of evidence for Stirling's involvement.

[84] They were married by 13 July 1513: Hamer (*Works*, 3:214) cites Fraser, *Stirlings of Keir*, p. 34 (itself citing the *Keir Inventory*, p. 25). See also a letter of reversion (i.e., the right to redeem heritable lands upon payment of a debt) of 18 July 1513, in which Forrester refers to Stirling as "my gude sone in law" (transcribed by Fraser, *Stirlings of Keir*, p. 297, item 89). They were still married on 8 October

eventually murdered on Stirling Bridge (lines 1495–99), and Sir John Stirling would indeed be murdered in 1539, perhaps near Stirling where the subsequent trial was held, something which seems to link Lyndsay's and Pitscottie's accounts.[85] Hamer argues that "the records of his land-dealings prove him to have been a brutal, relentless persecutor," but the only evidence he provides comes not from contemporary documents but from a tale recounted in an eighteenth-century history of the house of Buchanan.[86] This claims that Sir John Stirling of Keir had obtained superiority over half of the Lenny estate of Walter Buchanan of Lenny, but when he failed to evict Buchanan from the premises, he persuaded David Shaw to do it for him, in the event by murder. Shaw was then supposedly overcome by remorse for disinheriting the widow and daughters of Buchanan, which "put him upon the resolution of expiating Lenny's murder by that of Keir, which he accordingly performed by killing of Keir, as he met him occasionally near Stirling."[87] Unsurprisingly, there is no contemporary evidence for Shaw's remorse, although there is plenty to substantiate his extensive career of violence: he and George Dreghorne, his accomplice in Stirling's murder, were the subject of a letter of respite (i.e., a delay granted in court proceedings) on 4 November 1542 not only for the murder of Stirling, but for "all utheris slauchteris, mutilationis, actionis, transgressionis, crimes and offensis quhatsumevir committit in ony tyme bigane."[88] The fact that Stirling was sheriff of Perth from 1516 until at least 1519 may have given him an alternative reason to take an interest in affairs at Gleneagles, although it tells us nothing of what kind of interest.[89] In sum, there is no contemporary evidence to link the Stirlings to the attack on Meldrum, but Pitscottie is so specific in accusing members of this prominent local family that the possibility of such a link is difficult to dismiss altogether. We will never know for certain unless other records come to light.

What does become apparent in the combing of contemporary records is just how interconnected all of these families were long before — and after — the affair between Marjorie and Meldrum took place, something which tells a rather different story to Lyndsay's. Significantly, these connections extend even to the audience for Lyndsay's poem (see "Audience" below). Lyndsay describes the start of the affair as if it were an episode in a romance: the returning hero Meldrum is traveling through Strathearn one evening when he spots a castle and decides to take shelter. Its mistress is charmed by her unexpected

---

1530 (see *Reg. Sec. Sig.* 2:95, no. 751), "Preceptum Carte Confirmationis Johnannis Striuiling de Keire, militis, et Margarete Forestar ejus sponse . . ." and *Reg. Mag. Sig.* 3:212 (no. 969).

[85] Hamer cites a charter of 22 May 1539 in which Sir John Stirling is alive (citing Fraser, *Stirlings of Keir*, p. 361, charter no. 14, 22), and a letter of 10 June 1539 in which he is listed as "umquhill Johne Striueling of the Keir, knycht" in *Reg. Sec. Sig.* 2.451 (no. 3052: see also nos. 3102 and 3133 of 31 July and 31 August respectively, dealing with the inheritance of his father's properties by "James Striueling, sone and are of the umquhill Johnne Striueling of the Keyre, knycht"). The trial was held in Stirling in 1542–43; see Pitcairn, *Criminal Trials*, 1.1:327 (5 January 1542–43).

[86] Hamer, *Works*, 3:211. Buchanan, *Historical and Genealogical Essay*, p. 90. No dates or supporting documents are cited in this account.

[87] Buchanan, *Historical and Genealogical Essay*, p. 249.

[88] *Reg. Sec. Sig.* 2:753, no. 4968 (4 November 1542).

[89] Fraser dates his tenure of this post from 1516 (*Stirlings of Keir*, p. 29); see also an instrument of sasine dated 5 October 1519, citing a precept issued by "John Steirling of the Keir, kt, sheriff of Perth" (NRS GD26/3/1030).

visitor and they fall more or less immediately in love. In reality, the Meldrum and Lawson families appear to have known each other for years; when Sir John Haldane was making arrangements for his new bride Marjorie in 1508–09 with infeftments in their joint names, the witnesses to one of the instruments of sasine included "Archibald Meldrum of Bynnis [Binns]" — probably the squire's father — and "George Haldene, uncle of John Haldene [Haldane] of Glennegas [Gleneagles], kt," the man with whom Squire Meldrum would later be caught in the fatal ambush.[90] Meanwhile, a contract of marriage drawn up in 1518 between Margaret Erskine and Marjorie's young son James Haldane (a union which did eventually take place) was approved by Haldane's tutors, among whom was "George Haldane of Kippane," and witnessed by "Sir Walter Forrester of the Torwood," already by this point Sir John Stirling's father-in-law.[91] The Stirlings and Lawsons also knew each other: Marjorie's brother Master James Lawson (one of Meldrum's attackers in 1517) would agree to act as one of the arbiters in a dispute between Sir John Stirling of Keir and Alexander Drummond on 14 October 1529.[92] The Lawsons and Haldanes themselves go back well before Marjorie's marriage. In 1490, her father Master Richard Lawson was involved, as king's justice clerk, in settling the dispute over the Lennox inheritance in which Sir John Haldane's grandfather (also John) was one of the claimants; Richard Lawson and Sir John Haldane (grandfather to Marjorie's husband) were also joint witnesses to an instrument of resignation relating to some Fife lands back in 1481.[93] Ties remained strong in the decades after the Meldrum affair: when an instrument of sasine was drawn up in 1539 for Marjorie's nephew James Lawson (son of her eldest brother Robert), the witnesses included her son "James Haldane of Glennagis," along with his son and heir John Haldane; in 1542, the cousins witnessed another document together.[94]

Lyndsay's account of the love-affair and the attack on Meldrum is thus deliberately inaccurate in some key particulars. When this fact is combined with the comic disparity between the charming young Meldrum of the *Historie* and the incorrigibly boastful old Meldrum of the *Testament*, it helps to cast doubt on the accuracy of some other episodes in this biography. It raises the question, for example, of whether the otherwise untraceable English champion "Talbart" (see note to the *Historie*, lines 265–71) might be intended to

---

[90] NRS GD198/75–77 (following on from GD198/71). Another document in this series of arrangements, a precept of chancery dated 29 January 1508/09 (NRS GD198/74), was witnessed by "Sheriffs of Perth in that part; Laurence Haldan [Haldane], William Meldrum and Archibald Lindesay." If this refers to the young Squire Meldrum rather than a member of one of the many other branches of Meldrums, Lyndsay omitted this phase entirely from his biography. See also NRS GD198/225, a summons against John Thayne by Sir John Haldane of Gleneagles relating to lands in Strathearn, executed by "William Meldrome [Meldrum], sheriff in that part," dated 25 January 1508/09. One of the witnesses is "Robert Lausone," probably Marjorie's eldest brother.

[91] Historical Manuscripts Commission, *Report on the Manuscripts*, p. 9.

[92] NRS GD17/86.

[93] See NRS GD430/82, dated 18 May 1490, and *Cal. Laing Charters*, p. 47, no. 184, dated 26 November 1481.

[94] *Protocol Books*, eds. Beveridge and Russell, pp. 37–38, no. 194, dated 19 April 1539; and NRS GD158/248, letters of reversion by Adam Boithwell witnessed by "James Halden of Glennagas" and "James Lausoun of Hie Riggis," as well as "Archibald Halden," who may be James' younger brother (4 May 1542).

represent *the* most important Talbot of Henry VIII's army, i.e., George Talbot, Earl of Shrewsbury, chivalric idol and lieutenant of the English vanguard — someone whom Meldrum is extremely unlikely to have engaged in individual combat. Lyndsay would thus not be recording historical events so much as Meldrum's great propensity for exaggeration in reporting the events of his life. The same might apply to Meldrum's capture of the English warship, so suspiciously similar to events in Hary's *Wallace* (see notes to lines 710 ff.) and indeed any episode in which Meldrum displays the extraordinary qualities of a knight of romance. While this allows the text to operate as a critique of medieval romance and the simplistic ideals which this genre often portrayed, as Riddy so convincingly argued, it also offers wry comment on those — such as the elderly Meldrum of the *Testament* — who wished to present *themselves* through the restrictive prism of romance values. Such a dynamic may not be immediately apparent to modern readers with nothing but the relationship between the *Historie* and *Testament* to go on, but it must have been very clear, and a source of some amusement, to an audience with first-hand knowledge of the mismatch between Meldrum's life and Lyndsay's romanticized version of it, as Lyndsay's original audience appears to have been.

AUDIENCE

All the evidence suggests that the *Meldrum* poems were written for private consumption in the immediate social circle of the Lords Lindsay of the Byres. Part of this impression comes from the poems themselves: apart from the fact that the Meldrum of the *Testament* chooses "My freind Sir David Lyndsay of the Mont" to direct his funeral (lines 92–93), he calls upon "David Erll of Craufuird" another member of the extended Lindsay clan, as well as his own patron "Johne Lord Lindesay, my maister speciall" (lines 22–23) to be his executors, and he bids farewell not only to Lord Lindsay but to his unnamed lady and daughters, and sons Patrick and Norman (see note to lines 205–09), names that would mean little to a wider audience. Further evidence for an intimate initial audience comes from the atypical publication history of the *Meldrum* poems. Several of Lyndsay's poems were printed within a year or two of composition, which suggests that he tended to write for wider public consumption even when a poem happened to be addressed familiarly to the king.[95] Those works not printed (or known to have been printed) in Lyndsay's lifetime appeared soon after it in the collections of his *Warkis* published from 1558 onwards, which were later "augmentit with sindrie warkis" (including the *Answer to the Kingis Flyting*) from 1568.[96] But there is no evidence for any print of the *Meldrum* poems before c. 1580, and no actual surviving witness until the 1594 Charteris print on which the present edition is based. This suggests that the *Meldrum* poems, unlike his other works, remained in private hands for a generation, despite the fame of their author.

A key point about this intimate first audience for the *Historie* and *Testament* is that they were personally acquainted, not only with Meldrum himself, but with some of the other

---

[95] Hamer (*Works*, 4:15–23) cites probable lost Scottish editions of *The Dreme* c. 1528–30, *The Complaynt*, c. 1529–30, *Papyngo* 1530, *The Deploration of the Death of Queen Magdalene* 1537 (the year of her death), *The Tragedie of the Cardinall* 1547 (the year after Beaton's death, followed by an extant London edition of 1548), and the extant 1554 edition of *Ane Dialog betuix Experience and the Courteour*.

[96] See discussion of the 1568 *Warkis* in the Introduction to the *Answer to the Kingis Flyting*.

participants (or potential participants) in the story of Meldrum's disastrous love-affair. A retour of 8 March 1525–26 confirming John Lindsay (the future fifth Lord Lindsay of the Byres) as heir to his father lists among the jurors "John Stirling of Keir, knight" and "George Haldane of Kippen"; if the former's involvement in Meldrum's affair with the Lady of Gleneagles is uncertain, the latter's is beyond doubt.[97] It is thus likely that the audience at Struthers had independent knowledge of Meldrum's real history already, and were able to amuse themselves by comparing it to Lyndsay's version, just as they could compare Lyndsay's dramatized portrayal of Meldrum in the *Testament* to the real article. They enjoyed a ready-made dramatic irony to which modern readers will never be privy. Lyndsay thus had no need to seed the poems with the usual textual markers of irony or authorial intervention. This dynamic relationship between the *Meldrum* poems and Lyndsay's original audience also has a bearing on the date of composition.

DATE

Although most previous editors date the poems to c. 1550, this needs re-examination. It does not at first seem controversial: the *Historie* ends by recording the death of its subject — "Thus at the Struther into Fyfe, / This nobill squyer loist his lyfe" (lines 1589–90) — and the historical Meldrum disappears from the records after July 1550. The *Testament* refers to his old flame Marjorie Lawson as if she were still alive, which would seem to date it to before her death in 1553 (see above, "The *Historie* and History"). Lyndsay himself died early in 1555, providing an absolute *terminus ad quem*. Hamer accordingly suggests composition in 1550–53, although he adds that "whether the poem which describes his early adventures [i.e., the *Historie*] was written before or after his death is a matter for individual opinion."[98] A dating of 1550–53 would accord nicely with the assumption that the *Meldrum* poems were written to honor the life of a much-missed old friend, but one detail in the *Testament* suggests an alternative dating, and this has an important bearing on the interpretation of the poems themselves.

In the *Testament*, the dramatized Meldrum appoints for himself three executors (lines 22–28). The first two are unproblematic: they are David Lindsay, ninth earl of Crawford, and his own employer John Lindsay, fifth Lord Lindsay of the Byres, both of whom outlived Meldrum and indeed Lyndsay himself (see note to lines 22 and 23). But the third is Sir Walter Lindsay, preceptor of Tophichen Priory and head of the Scottish chapter of the knights of St. John of Jerusalem, and Sir Walter was dead by March 1547 (see note to lines 26–27). The head of the Order of St. John for Scotland was a prominent public figure and there is no way that Lyndsay or his audience could *not* have known of the death of Sir Walter and the accession of James Sandilands. This means that either Lyndsay has Meldrum appoint himself an executor whom everybody knows to be dead already, or the *Meldrum* poems were written before March 1547, and therefore while Meldrum himself was still alive and probably resident at Struthers. Hamer could not bring himself to accept the latter conclusion, with all of its implications for tone and authorial intent:

---

[97] Fraser, *Memorials of the Earls of Haddington* 2: 250. Longer-standing connections are suggested by the fact that Lord John's grandfather Patrick — Meldrum's original employer — and Marjorie's father Mr. Richard Lawson are listed together as lords of council in an extract decreet of 18 November 1500 (NRS GD124/1/544).

[98] *Works*, 3:182.

> I think, therefore, that either Sir Walter must have resigned the preceptorship in 1547, or
> else Sir James Sandilands had received the assurance that he would be elected preceptor
> after the death of Sir Walter. Both things may have happened, in fact . . . . I do not think we
> are entitled either to assume that the poem was written before Meldrum's death, or after Sir
> Walter's, if this took place in 1547, on account of Lindsay's honesty in historical fact.[99]

Setting aside that last wistful claim, this position depends on an assumption that Sir Walter's death in 1547 had been reported in error: "The report just quoted from [*Historical MSS Commission*, Second Report, 196] does not reproduce the documents," Hamer adds hopefully. But the documents have since been reexamined and are incontestable (see note to the *Testament*, lines 26–27). Could Lyndsay have assigned Meldrum two living and one dead executor, even in jest? It is hard to think of any possible motivation, and it does not make a good joke. The inescapable conclusion is that the poems — despite the *Historie*'s solemn report of Meldrum's death — were written while Meldrum was still alive. This much is hinted at by the fact that the dramatized Meldrum of the *Testament* advises his audience to "go reid the legend of my life" (line 72), a text apparently already available, although "Meldrum" still stands before them.

The reinterpretation that such a revised dating demands is dramatic, but can nonetheless be briefly set out. If Meldrum were alive at the point of composition, he would almost certainly have been a member of that original, knowledgeable audience for the poems. The *Testament*'s dramatic monologue by a "Meldrum" who boasts of his female conquests and orders up a funeral fit for a king may thus have been performed *for* Meldrum, along with the thrilling *Historie* (now much more obviously a work of semi-fiction, since it claims to mourn the death of a member of the immediate audience). This brings the tone of the *Meldrum* poems far closer than previously imagined to that of a work like the *Answer to the Kingis Flyting* — a text that amuses and flatters its subject but also teases him, and not always gently. Lyndsay is unlikely to have felt as constrained in teasing Meldrum as he was with his sovereign. If the flattering *Historie* is a gift to Meldrum, the *Testament* is more like a mischievous roasting which, in addition, contrives to turn the *Historie* into an entertaining example of the squire's own wishful thinking, or boasting. This does not negate earlier readings of the *Historie* as a critique of romance and medieval chivalric values; nor does it mean that Meldrum and Lyndsay could not have been friends, as has always been assumed. But it does require a less naïve reading of the *Historie* as biography, and an even greater recognition of the subtlety and ironic layering of the poems as a pair.

"Before 1547" is a much less satisfactory dating than c. 1550 or c. 1550–53, but it can probably be narrowed down somewhat. Although the information provided by the poems themselves is to be treated with caution, they would not be nearly so effective if the real Meldrum were *not* an older man inclined to nostalgic exaggeration of the exploits of his youth. If Meldrum were born by 1485 (see above, "Squire of Cleish and Binns"), he would have been in his later fifties by the time he witnessed two legal documents for Lyndsay and his wife in 1541/42, the point by which we can prove that he and the poet were personally acquainted. It has been suggested that the funeral of James V on 8 January 1543 — which Lyndsay had organized — provided inspiration for some of Meldrum's own requests in the *Testament*, an impression bolstered by the fact that Meldrum specifies Lyndsay as his own

---

[99] *Works*, 3:228.

funeral-director.[100] Would Lyndsay, close to the king throughout the latter's life, have found it funny to model Meldrum's mock-funeral on James' real one? This is not a question that can be answered merely by referring to modern sensibilities of what constitutes 'good taste,' but it does at least give pause for thought: Lyndsay need not have run James' funeral already to know how a spectacular chivalric funeral should go. On balance, the most likely window for composition seems to be c. 1540–47, a period when Lyndsay was most often in residence in Fife and his acquaintanceship with Meldrum is certain.

THE *MELDRUM* POEMS: PRE-1700 PRINTS

- **C** Edinburgh: Henrie Charteris, 1594 (STC 2nd ed. 15679)
  The Historie of ane nobil and wailzeand Squyer, William Meldrum, vmquhyle Laird of Cleische and Bynnis. Compylit be Sir Dauid Lyndesay of the Mont, alias, Lyoun King of Armes. (H C) *The Testament of the said Williame Meldrum Squyer. Compylit alswa be Sir Dauid Lyndesay, &c.* Imprentit at Edinburgh be Henrie Charteris. Anno M.D.XCIIII. Cum Priuilegio Regali.

Quarto volume; 56 pages; 35 lines per page. Printed in blackletter, but — as is usual in early prints of vernacular material — with the running headers and most of the title page printed in Roman typeface. Roman typeface is also used for names of classical gods in the *Historie* — see "Mars" (line 390), "Phoebus" (lines 712, 932), and "Venus" (line 906) — but the *Testament* prints such names in blackletter, reserving Roman typeface for the Latin phrases of the final macaronic stanza. Running header: "THE SQVYER [sometimes SQWYER] / OF THE BYNNIS [sometimes BINNIS]" (for both texts).
Collation: A–C[8] (for the *Historie*); D[4] (for the *Testament*).

The title page contains two Latin epigraphs which would seem to have been supplied by Charteris rather than Lyndsay, since they also appear, with another two quotations from Cicero, on the title pages of Charteris' 1594 print of Hary's *Wallace*, for which their sentiments are more appropriate:

> Cicero Philip. 14.
> Proprium sapientis est, grata eorum virtutem memoria prosequi, qui pro Patria vitam profuderunt.[101]

> ["It is most appropriate for the wise to follow with grateful memory the valor of those who have given their lives for their country's sake."]

> Ovid.2. Fast.
> Et memorem famam, qui bene gessit habet.[102]

> ["He who has won the day possesses an eternal fame."]

---

[100] Thomas, *Princelie Majestie*, pp. 213–15.

[101] From *Philippic 14*, 11.31. Meldrum did not die for his country of course, but Charteris evidently felt that the general tone was appropriate.

[102] From *Fasti*, 2.380.

Extant Copies

1. Edinburgh, National Library of Scotland, H.29.c.23(2). Pages c. 184 x 140mm. Bound together with Charteris' print of Lyndsay's *Warkis* of 1592, which lists the *Meldrum* poems in its Table of Contents but does not itself contain them. Damage to the foot of the last few pages of the *Historie* and all of the *Testament*, although the wide margins mean that only the final two lines of each page are affected.

2. San Marino, CA, Henry E. Huntington Library and Art Gallery, 62229. This copy was filmed for *Early English Books Online* (*EEBO*).

3. London, British Library, C.39.d.23. Inscribed on title page: "Tho: Arrowsmyth seruant to Henry Bowes Esquire. Empt: in Edenbr: Marche ij° 1597. prᵗ xxx d. Scottish."[103]
The *English Short Title Catalogue* (*ESTC*) also lists a copy within Aberdeen Library and Information Services, but current staff report that they are unable to trace this volume or any record of it in their holdings, and they suspect a cataloguing error. Laing also recorded a copy in private hands, bound up with the *Warkis* of 1592.[104]

Hamer demonstrates that this 1594 print is probably a paginary reprint of a lost edition of c. 1580, printed in Edinburgh by John Ross for Henry Charteris and intended to accompany his edition of the *Warkis of . . . Schir Dauid Lyndesay of the Mont* printed the same year (STC 2nd ed. 15661).[105] Although both of the surviving copies of the c. 1580 *Warkis* are damaged, lacking both date and the last few items of the Table of Contents, the volume was reissued by Charteris in 1582 with a new title page and preliminaries, and there the Table of Contents is rounded off with "The Historie of the Squyer William Meldrum of the Benis, neuer befoir Imprentit" and "The Testament of the said Squyer."[106] (See the Introduction to the *Answer to the Kingis Flyting* for a description of this edition of the *Warkis*.) Further evidence of the existence of a separate print of the *Meldrum* poems by the early 1580s is provided by the will of bookbinder Robert Gourlay or Gourlaw, who died of plague on 6 September 1585 (the will was registered 22 April 1586): "Item, the Squyer of Meldrum, blak, sax, at xij d. the peice — summa vj s." (i.e., six copies printed in black letter at twelve pence each, in total six shillings).[107] Gregory Kratzmann argues that Charteris may have known of the *Meldrum* poems as early as 1568 when he compiled his enlarged *Warkis*, since he refers in the "Preface to the Reidar" to Lyndsay's "frutefull and commodious Historyis, baith humane and divine, baith recent and ancient."[108] Kratzmann theorizes that *Meldrum* was omitted in 1568 because Charteris "could not accommodate it within a *Warkis* which was to

---

[103] Description of this witness quoted in Hamer, *Works*, 4:64.

[104] *Poetical Works*, 3:285.

[105] See Hamer, *Works*, 4:54.

[106] Hamer, *Works*, 4:54–57.

[107] Laing, Scott, and Thomson, eds., "Wills of Thomas Bassadyne and Other Printers," p. 214. Charteris' own will (dated 16 April 1598) listed "Item, xl Squyres of Meldrum, at ij s. the pece — summa, iiij l." (p. 224). Presumably these were copies of his 1594 print. It is notable that they are twice the price of the *Meldrum* copies in Gourlaw's will.

[108] Kratzmann, "Sixteenth-Century Poetry," p. 109.

support the cause of reform,"[109] but several of the comic poems in the 1568 *Warkis* offer equally little to "the cause of reform," such as the *Answer to the Kingis Flyting*, the "Complaynt and Confessioun of Bagsche, the kingis auld hound" or "The Justing betuix James Watsone, and Johne Barbour." But many of the poems published in the 1568 *Warkis* deal with relatively recent people and events, such as "The Tragedie of the Cardinall" (about Cardinal David Beaton, assassinated in 1546), or the description of the realm and complaint of the Commonweal in *The Dreme*. It seems more likely that these are the "recent histories" extolled by Charteris in the volume's Preface.[110]

- **L**   Edinburgh: Printed [by T. Finlason][111] for Richard Lawson, 1610 (STC 2nd ed. 15680).
  THE HISTORIE OF A NOBLE AND VALIANT SQVYER VViliam Meldrum, VM-quhile Laird of Cleish and Binnes. Compyled be Sir David Lindesay of the Mount, aliâs, Lyon King of Armes. The testament of the said William Meldrum squyer. Compyled alswa be Sir David Lindesay, &c.

Quarto volume; 56 pages; 35 lines per page. Printed in blackletter, with Roman typeface for the title page, running headers, and many personal names and places within the texts (not just for classical gods' names, as in C).
A paginary reprint of C, and retaining C's Latin epigraphs on the title page.
Running header: *"The Squyer of the Binnes / The Squyer of the Binnes"* (for both *Historie* and *Testament*).
Collation: A–C^8 (for the *Historie*); D^4 (for the *Testament*).

Extant Copy: San Marino, CA, Henry E. Huntington Library and Art Gallery, 31527, where it is bound together with T. Finlason's print of the *The VVorks of . . . Sir David Lyndesay* (Edinburgh, 1610), STC 2nd ed. 15665. Consulted on *EEBO*.

Hamer lists an additional copy in the "Library of the Earl of Crawford and Balcarres. Formerly Laing's copy. Laing Sale Catalogue, 1.1872, bought by Quaritch, £22, 10s."[112]

- **H**   Edinburgh: heires of Andrew Hart, Decemb. 27. 1634 (STC 2nd ed. 15680.5)
  THE HISTORIE OF A NOBLE AND VA-/liant Squyer WILLIAM MELDRUM, Vmquile Laird of Cleish and Binnes. Also the Testament of the said William Meldrum, Compiled by Sir DAVID LINDESAY of the Mount: alias, Lyon King of Armes.

---

[109] Kratzmann, "Sixteenth-Century Poetry," p. 109, quoting from Charteris' 1568 "Preface to the Reidar," p. 1.

[110] Kratzmann also notes the surprising absence of the *Meldrum* poems from "that other great literary monument of 1568, the Bannatyne manuscript," which does contain excerpts from Lyndsay's *Ane Satyre of the Thrie Estaitis*. He suggests that George Bannatyne may have known of Charteris' new expanded *Warkis* and thus felt no need to copy Lyndsay's poems himself ("Sixteenth-Century Poetry," p. 109). Bannatyne may well have omitted Lyndsay's other works from his manuscript because they were already circulating widely in print form, but this tells us nothing about whether the *Meldrum* poems were among them.

[111] Hamer (*Works*, 4:78) notes that G4^b contains the initials and device of Thomas Finlason.

[112] Hamer, *Works*, 4:78.

Octavo volume, 64 pages, 31 lines per page. Printed in blackletter with Roman typeface for title page, running headers, and most names and places within the text. The title page bears a clumsy woodcut portrait labeled "S. DAVID LYNDSAY" in which he is shown wearing a badge of the royal coat of arms (presumably denoting his status as Lyon King of Arms) and a rather worried expression. (This portrait also appears in Hart's *Workes* of the same year.) On the verso of the title page are the arms of James VI and Anne of Denmark. The "heires" of Andrew or Andro Hart were his wife, Jonet Keene, and sons Samuel and John, who ran the business from Hart's death in 1621 until 1639.[113]
Running header: "The Historie of / Squyer Meldrum"
Collation: A–[D⁸]

Extant Copy: Edinburgh, Central Library, Class Y, Z.152.H32.[114] 152 x 95mm. A–C⁸ is mistakenly followed by a second copy of B¹⁻⁸: D¹⁻⁸ is missing. Text of *Historie* breaks off after line 1422, "And sent him backwart to Dunbar" (where C reads "And send him backward to Dumbar").

- **S**   Glasgow: Robert Sanders, 1669. (Wing L2321A)
  The HISTORY OF THE NOBLE and valiant Squyer WILLIAM MELDRUM, umwhile Laird of Cleish and Bins. As also the Testament of the said WILLIAM MELDRUM. Compyled by Sir DAVID LINDSAY of the Mount: Alias, Lyon King of Arms. GLASGOW, by ROBERT SANDERS, Printer to the Town, and are to be sold in his Shop. 1669.

Duodecimo volume; 48 pages; 42 lines per page. Printed in blackletter with Roman typeface for title page etc.
Collation: A⁴B²C⁴D²E⁴F²G⁴H²

Extant Copy: London, British Library C.57.aa.44(2). Approximately 124 x75 mm. This tiny brown half-bound volume, with *Miscellaneous Poems 1667–69* stamped on its spine, contains: Alexander Montgomerie's *Cherrie and the Slae* (missing its first 36 pages and imprint); the *Meldrum* poems; *The Frier and the Boy*, "Very delectable, though unpleasant to all Stepmothers" (Glasgow, 1668); *The History of Adam Bell, Clim of the Clough and William of Cloudesly* (Glasgow: Robert Sanders, 1668); *Scottish Proverbs . . . gathered together by David Ferguson, sometime Minister at Dumfermline* (printed 1667); *The History of Sir Eger, Sir Grahame and Sir Gray-Steel* (Glasgow: Robert Sanders, 1669). This textual company gives a good sense of the later reception of the *Meldrum* poems.[115]

---

[113] See entry for "Hart, Andro" in the *Scottish Book Trade Index*.

[114] Described briefly by Cowan, "An Edition of Sir David Lyndsay's *Squyer Meldrum*, 1634," pp. 103–04.

[115] A copy of both *Meldrum* poems would again keep company with *The History of Sir Eger, Sir Grahame and Sir Gray-Steel* (also known as *Eger and Grime*) in Oxford, Bodleian Library, Douce R 267. Both were printed in 1711 (printer and place unknown) while the third text of Douce R 267, *Beuis of Hampton*, has lost its date but was printed in Aberdeen by James Nicol; it appears to use the same type as the *Meldrum* poems and *Sir Eger* so all three texts may be Aberdeen productions by Nicol.

- **A**   Edinburgh: Heir of Andrew Anderson, 1683. (Wing L2322)
  The HISTORY of the NOBLE and valiant Squyer WILLIAM MELDRUM, umwhile Laird of Cleish and Bins. As also the Testament of the said WILLIAM MELDRVM Compyled by Sir DAVID LINDSAY of the Mount: Alias, Lyon King of Arms. EDINBVRGH, Printed by the Heir of Andrew Anderson. Printer to the Kings most Sacred Majesty, and are be sold at his shop. Anno. 1683.

Duodecimo volume; 48 pages; 42 lines per page. Roman typeface throughout (the earliest extant *Meldrum* print to abandon blackletter). Contains a woodcut on the verso of the title page of an Elizabethan man smoking a pipe.
Running header: "*The History / of Squyer* Meldrum"

Extant Copies
1. Oxford, Bodleian Library, Malone 954. Incomplete: missing title page and the whole of sheet D, which contained the final six lines of the *Historie* and the whole of the *Testament*.

2. London, British Library, C.34.a.29. Wing suggested the imprint "Glasgow: Robert Sanders, 1683" (2nd ed., L2322), presumably on the basis of the incomplete Malone print, and this was followed by both the *ESTC* (citation no. R31700) and *EEBO*, which filmed Malone with its missing title page and sheet D. The British Library catalogue currently describes its complete copy as "Edinburgh, 1683" but offers no publisher or additional description, which is supplied here from Hamer.[116] The printer Andrew Anderson died in 1676; his wife Agnes and son James continued the business, initially under the imprint "Heir of Andrew Anderson" (used 1676–94). They were often involved in legal wrangles with other Scottish printers, including the Robert Sanders to whom the incomplete Malone copy of this print was erroneously attributed by Wing, *ESTC*, and *EEBO*.[117]

Richard Heber's sale catalogue from 1836 lists as item 854: "Lyndsay. The Historie of a Noble and Valiant William Meldrum Squyer, Umqle Laird of Cleish and bins. Compilled by Sir D. Lindesay. *Written by James Clark*, 1635. *Glasgow. Russia.*"[118] This lost witness is the only recorded manuscript copy of the *Meldrum* poems. Hamer notes that it had been bought by Heber from Pinkerton's library in 1812, and was sold in 1836 to an untraceable "J. Bohn."[119] Earlier, Pinkerton had written of this manuscript:

> The editor [i.e., Pinkerton himself] has a correct and well-written MS. of it in 12mo [i.e., duodecimo, a tiny format], *Glasgow, written be James Clark, 1635*. This would seem copied from another MS.; for the transcriber, had he seen any of the printed copies, would hardly have taken this trouble with a fix-penny pamphlet. This piece is the very best of all Lindsay's works; being descriptive of real manners and incidents: tho' it has somewhat too much *spice*, as the French call it, being very free in a passage or two. This has prevented the Scottish booksellers from reprinting it, lest it should offend their godly customers.[120]

---

[116] *Works*, 4:91.

[117] See entry for "Anderson, Andrew, Heirs and Successors of" in the *Scottish Book Trade Index*.

[118] *Bibliotheca Heberiana*, p. 88, no. 854.

[119] *Works*, 4:12. Hamer misprinted the squire's forename as "Willam."

[120] *The Edinburgh Magazine, or Literary miscellany*, 5:335. Italics Pinkerton's.

On a lost print of c. 1580, see the discussion of C above. A final early print — a miniscule octodecimo edition — was listed by Laing as: "Glasgow, printed by Robert Sanders, one of His Majesties Printers, &c. 1696," but is now untraceable.[121]

PREVIOUS EDITIONS

These are listed by the abbreviations used in the Notes.

Bawcutt and Riddy: *Longer Scottish Poems, Vol. 1: 1375-1650*. Eds. Priscilla Bawcutt and Felicity Riddy. Edinburgh: Scottish Academic Press, 1987. It contains only the *Historie*, lines 840–1516.

Chalmers: *The Poetic Works of Sir David Lyndsay of the Mount*. Ed. George Chalmers. 3 vols. London: Longman, Hurst, Rees and Orme, 1806. This was the first serious attempt at a scholarly edition.

Hadley Williams: *Sir David Lyndsay: Selected Poems*. Ed. Janet Hadley Williams. Glasgow: Association for Scottish Literary Studies, 2000. The most recent edition of the *Meldrum* poems and the *Answer to the Kingis Flyting*, with much new scholarship in the notes as well as on-page glossing.

Hamer: *The Works of Sir David Lindsay of the Mount, 1490-1555*. Ed. Douglas Hamer. 4 vols. STS 3rd series 1, 2, 6, 8. Edinburgh: William Blackwood and Sons, 1931–36. Still an invaluable edition, Hamer provides by far the fullest account of the printing history of Lyndsay's works and an extremely comprehensive documentation of the lives of Lyndsay, Meldrum, and other relevant figures, most of which is quoted in full.

Kinsley: *Squyer Meldrum*. Ed. James Kinsley. London and Edinburgh: Thomas Nelson and Sons, 1959.

Laing: *The Poetical Works of Sir David Lyndsay*. Ed. David Laing. 3 vols. Edinburgh: William Paterson, 1879.

Small and Hall: *Sir David Lyndesay's Works*. Eds. J. Small, J. and F. Hall. EETS o.s. 11, 19, 35, 37, 47. London, 1865–71. This edition offers no substantial annotation and has not been consulted here.

THIS EDITION

The copy-text for the present edition is C, which dates from 1594 and is the earliest surviving witness to the text: there are no manuscript witnesses to any of the Lyndsay poems edited for this volume. Richard Lawson's print of 1610 (L) was also consulted, as were the later, more anglicized prints H (Edinburgh, 1634) and A (Edinburgh, 1683). These witnesses are mentioned occasionally in the explanatory notes, but they have not been

---

[121] Laing, *Poetical Works*, 3:294; Hamer, *Works*, 4:93.

collated with C since they rarely differ from it except in spelling, and where they do differ, C almost invariably offers the superior reading. At lines 22–23 of the *Historie*, for example, Charteris' strongly alliterative and metrically regular phrase "squyeris . . . / That wounders wrocht in weirlie weidis" becomes in L "squyers . . . / That wonderouslie wrocht into their weeds" (H and A clearly follow L with "wond[e]rously wrought in their weed[e]s"). For more substantive differences, see the notes to the *Historie*, lines 122 and 1259, or line 5 of the *Testament*.

In accordance with METS editorial policy, the letters þ (thorn, letter-form identical with printed y) and ȝ (yogh) have been transcribed with their modern equivalents *th* and *y* (the latter is always the value for yogh intended in these texts); the distribution of *u/v* has been normalized according to modern spelling practice; article *the* and pronoun *thee* have been differentiated by the addition of an extra *e* to the latter; and accented final *-e* has been marked. Punctuation, capitalization, and word-division have been modernized. Manicules or paraph-marks indicating section-breaks have been rendered as indentation and an additional space between lines.[122]

---

[122] Manicules appear in C's *Historie* at lines 65, 601, 431, 851, 1455, 1481, and 1519; a single paraph is used at line 1183, and double paraphs at line 245. C's *Testament* has a manicule at line 15.

THE HISTORIE OF ANE NOBIL AND VAILYEAND SQUYER, WILLIAM MELDRUM, UMQUHYLE LAIRD OF CLEISCHE AND BYNNIS

Compylit be Sir David Lyndesay of the Mont, alias, Lyoun, King of Armes.

	Quho that antique stories reidis,	*old-fashioned*
	Considder may the famous deidis	
	Of our nobill progenitouris,	*ancestors*
	Quhilk suld to us be richt mirrouris,	
5	Thair verteous deidis to ensew,	*take as a model*
	And vicious leving to eschew.	*living; avoid*
	Sic men bene put in memorie	
	That deith suld not confound thair glorie.	*cast down*
	Howbeit thair bodie bene absent,	*Although*
10	Thair verteous deidis bene present.	
	Poetis, thair honour to avance,	
	Hes put thame in rememberance.	*Have*
	Sum wryt of preclair conquerouris,	*illustrious*
	And sum of vailyeand empriouris,	*valorous emperors*
15	And sum of nobill michtie kingis	
	That royallie did reull thair ringis;	*rule; realms*
	And sum of campiounis, and of knichtis	*champions*
	That bauldlie did defend thair richtis,	*boldly*
	Quhilk vailyeandlie did stand in stour	*valiantly; battle*
20	For the defence of thair honour;	
	And sum of squyeris douchtie deidis,	*squires' valiant*
	That wounders wrocht in weirlie weidis.	*warlike attire (i.e., armor)*
	Sum wryt of deidis amorous,	
	As Chauceir wrait of Troilus,	*wrote*
25	How that he luiffit Cressida;	*loved*
	Of Jason and of Medea.	
	With help of Cleo I intend —	
	Sa Minerve wald me sapience send —	*Providing that*
	Ane nobill squyer to discryfe	*tell of*
30	Quhais douchtines during his lyfe	*Whose valor*
	I knaw my self: thairof I wryte,	
	And all his deidis I dar indyte,	*venture to write of*
	And secreitis that I did not knaw,	
	That nobill squyer did me schaw.	
35	Sa I intend, the best I can,	
	Descryve the deidis and the man,	*[To] write of*

	Quhais youth did occupie in lufe,	*[He] whose; spend; love*
	Full plesantlie without reprufe;	*disgrace*
	Quhilk did as monie douchtie deidis	*Who*
40	As monie ane that men of reidis	*As many a man that people read about*
	Quhilkis poetis puttis in memorie	*Whom; memorialize (pl.)*
	For the exalting of thair glorie.	
	Quhairfoir I think, sa God me saif,	*God save me*
	He suld have place amangis the laif,	*among the rest*
45	That his hie honour suld not smure,	*be extinguished*
	Considering quhat he did indure	
	Oft times for his ladeis sake.	
	I wait Sir Lancelote du Lake,	*I am sure*
	Quhen he did lufe King Arthuris wyfe,	*love*
50	Faucht never better with sword nor knyfe	*Fought*
	For his ladie in no battell,	
	Nor had not half so just querrell.	*cause*
	The veritie, quha list declair,	*to state it plainly*
	His lufe was ane adulterair	*adulteress*
55	And durst not cum into hir sicht,	*[he] did not dare*
	Bot lyke ane houlet on the nicht.	*Except; owl in*
	With this squyer it stude not so:	*was not the case*
	His ladie luifit him and no mo.	*loved; other*
	Husband nor lemman had scho none,	*lover*
60	And so he had hir lufe alone.	
	I think it is no happie lyfe,	
	Ane man to jaip his maisteris wyfe	*seduce*
	As did Lancelote: this I conclude,	
	Of sic amour culd cum na gude.	*such love*
65	Now to my purpois will I pas,	
	And shaw yow how the squyer was	
	Ane gentilman of Scotland borne;	
	So was his father him beforne,	*before him*
	Of nobilnes lineallie discendit,	*nobility directly*
70	Quhilks thair gude fame hes ever defendit.	*Who (pl.); reputation*
	Gude Williame Meldrum he was namit	
	Quhilk in his honour was never defamit,	
	Stalwart and stout in everie stryfe,	
	And borne within the schyre of Fyfe;	*shire of Fife*
75	To Cleische and Bynnis richt heritour,	*heir*
	Quhilk stude for lufe in monie stour	*defended; many battles*
	He was bot twentie yeiris of age,	
	Quhen he began his vassalage:	*displays of prowess*
	Proportionat weill; of mid stature;	*medium height*
80	Feirie and wicht and micht indure;	*Nimble; bold*
	Ovirset with travell both nicht and day;	*Oppressed by hardship*
	Richt hardie baith in ernist and play;	

	Blyith in countenance; right fair of face;	*Cheerful*
	And stude weill ay in his ladies grace,	
85	For he was wounder amiabill,	*attractive*
	And in all deidis honorabill,	
	And ay his honour did avance,	*always*
	In Ingland first, and syne in France,	
	And thair his manheid did assaill,	*test*
90	Under the kingis greit admirall	
	Quhen the greit navie of Scotland,	
	Passit to the sey aganis Ingland.	*sea*
	And as thay passit be Ireland coist,	*coast*
	The admirall gart land his oist	*had his host land*
95	And set Craigfergus into fyre,	*Carrickfergus on*
	And saifit nouther barne nor byre.	*saved; barn; cow-shed*
	It was greit pietie for to heir	
	Of the pepill the bailfull cheir,	*wretched mourning*
	And how the land folk wer spuilyeit;	*robbed*
100	Fair wemen underfute wer fuilyeit.	*defiled*
	Bot this young squyer, bauld and wicht,	*strong*
	Savit all wemen quhair he micht;	*wherever*
	All preistis and freiris he did save,	*priests and friars*
	Till at the last he did persave	*notice*
105	Behind ane garding amiabill	*pleasant garden*
	Ane womanis voce richt lamentabill,	*voice; sorrowful*
	And on that voce he followit fast,	
	Till he did see hir at the last,	
	Spuilyeit, naikit as scho was borne.	*Robbed; naked*
110	Twa men of weir wer hir beforne	*men of war (i.e., soldiers)*
	Quhilk wer richt cruell men and kene,	*fierce*
	Partand the spuilyie thame betwene.	*Dividing the booty*
	Ane fairer woman nor scho wes	*than*
	He had not sene in onie place.	
115	Befoir him on hir kneis scho fell,	
	Sayand: "For him that heryit Hell,	*ravaged*
	Help me, sweit Sir — I am ane mayd!"	*virgin*
	Than softlie to the men he said:	
	"I pray yow give againe hir sark,	*chemise*
120	And tak to yow all uther wark."	
	Hir kirtill was of scarlot reid,	*gown*
	Of gold, ane garland of hir heid,	
	Decorit with enamelyne,	*enamelling*
	Belt and brochis of silver fyne.	*brooches*
125	Of yallow taftais wes hir sark,	*yellow taffeta; chemise*
	Begaryit all with browderit wark	*Striped; embroidered*
	Richt craftelie, with gold and silk.	
	Than said the ladie quhyte as milk,	*white*
	"Except my sark, no thing I crave:	

130	Let thame go hence with all the lave."	*rest*
	Quod thay to hir, "Be Sanct Fillane,	*Saint Fáelán*
	Of this ye get nathing agane!"	
	Than said the squyer courteslie,	
	"Gude freindis, I pray yow hartfullie,	*sincerely*
135	Gif ye be worthie men of weir,	*If; soldiers*
	Restoir to hir agane hir geir	*things (i.e., clothes and other possessions)*
	Or, be greit God that all hes wrocht,	
	That spuilyie sal be ful deir bocht!"	*plunder*
	Quod thay to him, "We thee defy!"	
140	And drew thair swordis haistely,	
	And straik at him with sa greit ire	
	That from his harnes flew the fyre.	*sparks*
	With duntis sa darflie on him dang,	*blows; violently; struck*
	That he was never in sic ane thrang.	*danger*
145	Bot he him manfullie defendit,	
	And with ane bolt on thame he bendit	*sudden spring; leapt*
	And hat the ane upon the heid,	*hit*
	That to the ground he fell doun deid,	
	For to the teith he did him cleif:	*teeth; cleave*
150	Lat him ly thair with ane mischeif.	*with a curse*
	Than with the uther hand for hand,	*at close quarters*
	He beit him with his birneist brand:	*burnished sword*
	The uther was baith stout and strang,	
	And on the squyer darflie dang,	*violently struck*
155	And than the squyer wrocht greit wonder,	
	Ay till his sword did shaik in sunder.	*shatter to pieces*
	Than drew he furth ane sharp dagair	*dagger*
	And did him cleik be the collair,	*catch*
	And evin in at the collerbane,	
160	At the first straik he hes him slane:	*killed*
	He founderit fordward to the ground.	*collapsed forward*
	Yit was the squyer haill and sound,	
	Forquhy he was sa weill enarmit,	*Because; armed (and armored)*
	He did escaip fra thame unharmit.	
165	And quhen he saw thay wer baith slane,	
	He to that ladie past agane	
	Quhair scho stude nakit on the bent,	*grass*
	And said, "Take your abulyement,"	*clothing*
	And scho him thankit full humillie,	*humbly*
170	And put hir claithis on spedilie.	
	Than kissit he that ladie fair,	
	And tuik his leif at hir but mair.	*And took his leave of her without more delay*
	Be that the taburne and trumpet blew	*Then; drum*
	And everie man to shipburd drew.	
175	That ladie was dolent in hart	*mournful*
	From tyme scho saw he wald depart	

	That hir relevit from hir harmes,	*rescued; injury*
	And hint the squyer in hir armes	*took*
	And said, "Will ye byde in this land,	*If you will stay*
180	I sall yow tak to my husband:	
	Thocht I be cassin now in cair,	*fallen; into distress*
	I am," quod scho, "my fatheris air,	*heir*
	The quhilk may spend of pennies round	
	Of yeirlie rent ane thowsand pound."	
185	With that hartlie scho did him kis.	*heartily*
	"Are ye," quod scho, "content of this?"	
	"Of that," quod he, "I wald be fane	*delighted*
	Gif I micht in this realme remane,	
	Bot I mon first pas into France.	*must*
190	Sa quhen I cum agane, perchance,	
	And efter that the peice be maid,	*peace*
	To marie yow I will be glaid.	
	Fairwell, I may no langer tarie:	
	I pray God keip yow, and sweit Sanct Marie."	
195	Than gaif scho him ane lufe taking,	*love token*
	Ane riche rubie set in ane ring.	
	"I am," quod scho, "at your command,	
	With yow to pas into Scotland."	
	"I thank yow hartfullie," quod he,	*sincerely*
200	"Ye are ovir young to saill the see,	*too young*
	And speciallie with men of weir."	
	"Of that," quod scho, "tak ye na feir,[1]	
	I sall me cleith in mennis clais,	*clothe; clothes*
	And ga with yow quhair evir ye pleis:	
205	Suld I not lufe him paramour,	*take him as a lover*
	That saifit my lyfe and my honour?"	
	"Ladie, I say yow in certane,	
	Ye sall have lufe for lufe agane,	
	Trewlie, unto my lyfis end!	
210	Fairweill: to God I yow commend."	
	With that into his boit he past,	*boat*
	And to the ship he rowit fast.	
	Thay weyit thair ankeris and maid saill,	*weighed their anchors*
	This navie with the admirall,	
215	And landit in bauld Brytane.	*Brittany*
	This admirall was erle of Arrane,	
	Quhilk was baith wyse and vailyeand,	*valiant*
	Of the blude royall of Scotland,	
	Accompanyit with monie ane knight	
220	Quhilk wer richt worthie men and wicht.	*bold*

---

[1] *"In that case," said she, "if you will not take a spouse"*

Amang the laif, this young squyar   *rest*
Was with him richt familiar,
And throw his verteous diligence,
Of that lord he gat sic credence   *earned such a good name*
225   That quhen he did his courage ken,   *make known*
Gaif him cure of fyve hundreth men   *care*
Quhilkis wer to him obedient,
Reddie at his commandement.
It wer to lang for to declair
230   The douchtie deidis that he did thair.
Becaus he was sa courageous,
Ladies of him wes amorous.   *were in love with him*
He was an munyeoun for ane dame: *darling*
Meik in chalmer lyk ane lame,   *chamber; lamb*
235   Bot in the feild ane campioun,   *champion*
Rampand lyke ane wyld lyoun,   *Rampaging*
Weill practikit with speir and scheild,
And with the formest in the feild.   *foremost*
No chiftane was amangis thame all
240   In expensis mair liberall.   *more generous*
In everilk play he wan the pryse,   *every fight; was victorious*
With that he was verteous and wyse,
And so, becaus he was weill pruifit,   *tried and tested*
With everie man he was weill luifit.   *By; loved*

245   Hary the aucht, king of Ingland,   *Henry VIII*
That tyme at Caleis wes lyand   *Calais; stationed*
With his trimphant ordinance,   *host*
Makand weir on the realme of France.
The King of France his greit armie
250   Lay neir hand by in Picardie,
Quhair aither uther did assaill,   *each the other*
Howbeit thair was na set battaill,   *Although*
Bot thair wes daylie skirmishing,
Quhair men of armis brak monie sting.   *many a staff*
255   Quhen to the squyer Meldrum
Wer tauld thir nouellis all and sum,   *these tidings*
He thocht he wald vesie the weiris,   *go to see; fighting*
And waillit furth ane hundreth speiris,   *chose; spearmen*
And futemen quhilk wer bauld and stout,   *foot soldiers*
260   The maist worthie of all his rout.   *armed band*
            Quhen he come to the king of France,   *came*
He wes sone put in ordinance;   *marshaled*
Richt so was all his companie
That on him waitit continuallie.   *attended to him*
265   Thair was into the Inglis oist   *among; armed forces*
Ane campioun that blew greit boist.   *spoke very arrogantly*

	He was ane stout man and ane strang,	
	Quhilk oist wald with his conduct gang	*Whose company would; leadership*
	Outthrow the greit armie of France,	*Throughout*
270	His valiantnes for to avance,	
	And Maister Talbart was his name,	
	Of Scottis and Frenche quhilk spak disdane,	*spoke scornfully*
	And on his bonnet usit to beir	
	Of silver fyne takinnis of weir.	*badges of war*
275	And proclamatiounis he gart mak	*had made*
	That he wald, for his ladies saik,	
	With any gentilman of France	
	To fecht with him with speir or lance:	*fight*
	Bot no Frenche man in all that land	
280	With him durst batteil hand for hand.	*at close quarters*
	Than, lyke ane weiriour vailyeand,	
	He enterit in the Scottis band:	
	And quhen the squyer Meldrum	
	Hard tell this campioun wes cum,	*Heard; had come*
285	Richt haistelie he past him till,	*went to him*
	Demanding him quhat was his will.	
	"Forsuith, I can find none," quod he,	
	"On hors nor fute dar fecht with me."	*who dares to fight*
	Than said he, "It wer greit schame	
290	Without battell ye suld pas hame:	
	Thairfoir to God I mak ane vow,	
	The morne my self sall fecht with yow,	
	Outher on horsbak or on fute —	*Either*
	Your crakkis I count thame not ane cute.[1]	*(see note)*
295	I sall be fund into the feild,	*found in*
	Armit on hors with speir and scheild."	
	Maister Talbart said, "My gude chyld,	
	It wer maist lik that thow wer wyld.	*You seem to be crazy*
	Thow ar to young, and hes no might	
300	To fecht with me that is so wicht.	*powerful*
	To speik to me thow suld have feir,	
	For I have sic practik in weir	*professional skill*
	That I wald not effeirit be	*frightened*
	To mak debait aganis sic thre,	*contest with*
305	For I have stand in manie stour	*stood; many a battle*
	And ay defendit my honour.	
	Thairfoir, my barne, I counsell thee,	*child*
	Sic interprysis to let be."	*enterprises*
	Than said this squyer to the knight:	
310	"I grant ye ar baith greit and wicht.	*powerful*

---

[1] *I couldn't care less about your loud boasts*

Young David was far les than I
Quhen he with Golias manfullie
Withouttin outher speir or scheild   *either*
He faucht and slew him in the feild.
315   I traist that God salbe my gyde
And give me grace to stanche thy pryde.   *quell*
Thocht thow be greit, like Gowmakmorne,   *(see note)*
Traist weill I sall yow meit the morne   *tomorrow morning*
Beside Montruill, upon the grene,
320   Befoir ten houris I salbe sene.   *ten o'clock*
And gif ye wyn me in the feild,   *overcome*
Baith hors and geir I sall yow yeild,   *armor*
Sa that siclyke ye do to me."   *If; the same*
"That I sall do, be God!" quod he,
325   "And thairto I give thee my hand."
And swa betwene thame maid an band   *thus; agreement*
That thay suld meit upon the morne.   *the next morning*
Bot Talbart maid at him bot scorne,   *just mocked him*
Lychtlyand him with wordis of pryde,   *Disdaining*
330   Syne hamewart to his oist culd ryde,   *homewards; army; did ride*
And shew the brethren of his land   *told; fellow men*
How ane young Scot had tane on hand   *taken it upon himself*
To fecht with him beside Montruill,   *fight*
"Bot I traist he sall prufe the fuill."   *trust; prove the fool*
335   Quod thay: "The morne that sall we ken: *know*
The Scottis ar haldin hardie men."   *are thought to be*
Quod he, "I compt thame not ane cute:
He sall returne upon his fute   *on foot*
And leif with me his armour bricht,
340   For weill I wait he hes no micht   *I know full well*
On hors nor fute to fecht with me.
Quod thay: "The morne that sall we se."   *Tomorrow morning*
Quhan to Monsour de Obenie
Reportit was the veritie,   *truth of the matter*
345   How that the squyer had tane on hand   *taken it upon himself*
To fecht with Talbart hand for hand,   *at close quarters*
His greit courage he did commend,
Sine haistelie did for him send.   *Then hurriedly*
And quhen he come befoir the lord,
350   The veritie he did record —   *truth*
How for the honour of Scotland,
That battell he had tane on hand: *taken*
"And sen it givis me in my hart,   *since*
Get I ane hors to tak my part,   *If I could get*
355   My traist is sa in Goddis grace,   *trust*
To leif him lyand in the place.   *lying in the field*
Howbeit he stalwart be and stout,   *Although*

	My lord, of him I have no dout."	*fear*
	Than send the lord out throw the land,	
360	And gat ane hundreth hors fra hand:	*immediately*
	To his presence he brocht in haist,	
	And bad the squyer cheis him the best.	*invited; choose*
	Of that the squyer was rejoisit,	*delighted*
	And cheisit the best as he suppoisit,	
365	And lap on him delyverlie.	*leapt upon; nimbly*
	Was never hors ran mair plesantlie	
	With speir and sword at his command,	
	And was the best of all the land.	
	He tuik his leif and went to rest,	*took his leave*
370	Syne airlie in the morne him drest	
	Wantonlie, in his weirlyke weid,	*Lightheartedly; armor*
	All weill enarmit saif the heid.	*except*
	He lap upon his cursour wicht,	*leapt; powerful war-horse*
	And straucht him in his stirroppis richt.	*immediately; directly*
375	His speir and scheild and helme wes borne	
	With squyeris that raid him beforne:	
	Ane velvot cap on heid he bair,	*velvet*
	Ane quaif of gold to heild his hair.	*skull-cap; hold*
	This lord of him taik sa greit joy,	*took*
380	That he himself wald him convoy;	*escort*
	With him ane hundreth men of armes,	*fighting men*
	That thair suld no man do him harmes.	
	The squyer buir into his scheild	*bore upon*
	Ane otter in ane silver feild.	*(see note)*
385	His hors was bairdit full richelie,	*caparisoned*
	Coverit with satyne cramesie.	*crimson satin*
	Than fordward raid this campioun,	*champion*
	With sound of trumpet and clarioun,	*(shrill) trumpet*
	And spedilie spurrit ovir the bent	*field*
390	Lyke Mars the god armipotent.	*mighty in arms*
	Thus leif we rydand our squyar,	*riding*
	And speik of maister Talbart mair,	
	Quhilk gat up airlie in the morrow,	
	And no maner of geir to borrow —	
395	Hors, harnes, speir nor scheild —	
	Bot was ay reddie for the feild,	
	And had sic practik into weir,	*experience in warfare*
	Of our squyer he tuik na feir,	*had no fear*
	And said unto his companyeoun,	
400	Or he come furth of his pavilyeoun:	*Before; tent*
	"This nicht I saw into my dreame	
	Quhilk to reheirs I think greit shame.	*Something that; rehearse (i.e., say again)*
	Me thocht I saw cum fra the see	*sea*
	Ane greit otter rydand to me,	

405	The quhilk was blak with ane lang taill,	*Which*
	And cruellie did me assaill	
	And bait me till he gart me bleid,	*bit; made me bleed*
	And drew me backwart fra my steid.	
	Quhat this suld mene I can not say	
410	Bot I was never in sic ane fray."	*have never been so frightened*
	His fellow said: "Think ye not schame	
	For to gif credence till ane dreame?	
	Ye knaw it is aganis our faith!	
	Thairfoir go dres yow in your graith,	*prepare yourself; armor*
415	And think weill throw your hie courage	
	This day ye sall wyn vassalage."	*honor in battle*
	Than drest he him into his geir	
	Wantounlie, like ane man of weir	*Jovially*
	Quhilk had baith hardines and fors,	
420	And lichtlie lap upon his hors.	*leapt*
	His hors was bairdit full bravelie,	*caparisoned; splendidly*
	And coverit wes richt courtfullie	*elegantly*
	With browderit wark and velvot grene;	*embroidered; velvet*
	Sanct Georges croce thair micht be sene	*cross*
425	On hors, harnes and all his geir.	
	Than raid he furth withouttin weir,	*without doubt*
	Convoyit with his capitane,	*Escorted by*
	And with monie ane Inglisman	
	Arrayit all with armes bricht:	
430	Micht no man see ane fairer sicht.	
	Than clariounis and trumpettis blew	
	And weiriouris monie hither drew.	*warriors; many*
	On everie side come monie man	
	To behald quha the battell wan.	*who*
435	The feild wes in the medow grene,	*battle ground*
	Quhair everie man micht weill be sene:	
	The heraldis put thame sa in ordour	*organized them so well*
	That no man passit within the bordour,	*boundary*
	Nor preissit to cum within the grene,	
440	Bot heraldis and the campiounis kene.	
	The ordour and the circumstance	*organization; details*
	Wer lang to put in remembrance.	
	Quhen thir twa nobill men of weir	*these*
	Weir weill accowterit in thair geir,	*equipped*
445	And in thair handis strang burdounis,	*strong spears*
	Than trumpotis blew and clariounis,	
	And heraldis cryit hie on hicht:	
	"Now let thame go: God shaw the richt!"	*May God reveal [who has] the just cause*
	Than spedilie thay spurrit thair hors,	
450	And ran to uther with sic fors	

That baith thair speiris in sindrie flaw.   *shattered into pieces*
Than said they all that stude on raw,   *abreast*
Ane better cours than they twa ran   *charge (on horseback)*
Was not sene sen the warld began.   *since*
455   Than baith the parties wer rejoisit;
The campiounis ane quhyle repoisit   *rested*
Till thay had gottin speiris new.
Than with triumph the trumpettis blew
And they, with all the force they can,
460   Wounder rudelie at aither ran,   *fiercely; each other*
And straik at uther with sa greit ire
That fra thair harnes flew the fyre.   *sparks*
Thair speiris war sa teuch and strang   *tough*
That aither uther to eirth doun dang,   *each the other; struck*
465   Baith hors and man with speir and scheild,
That flatlingis lay into the feild.   *prostrate; on*
Than maister Talbart was eschamit: *ashamed*
"Forsuith, forever I am defamit!"   *Indeed; disgraced*
And said this: "I had rather die,
470   Without that I revengit be."   *Unless*
Our young squyer, sic was his hap,   *luck*
Was first on fute, and on he lap   *leapt*
Upon his hors without support.
Of that the Scottis tuke gude comfort
475   Quhen thay saw him sa feirelie   *nimbly*
Loup on his hors sa galyeardlie.   *Leap; gallantly*
The squyer liftit his visair
Ane lytill space to take the air.   *For a little while*
Thay bad him wyne, and he it drank   *offered*
480   And humillie he did thame thank.
Be that, Talbart on hors mountit,   *By that [time]*
And of our squyer lytill countit,
And cryit gif he durst undertak   *agree*
To ryn anis for his ladies saik.   *have one encounter*
485   The squyer answerit hie on hight: *loudly*
"That sall I do, be Marie bricht!
I am content all day to ryn,   *joust*
Till ane of us the honour wyn."
Of that Talbart was weill content,
490   And ane greit speir in hand he hent.   *took*
The squyer in his hand he thrang   *gripped*
His speir, quhilk was baith greit and lang,
With ane sharp heid of grundin steill,   *ground (i.e., sharpened) steel*
Of quhilk he was appleisit weill.   *With which; pleased*
495   That plesand feild was lang and braid,

Quhair gay ordour and rowme was maid,[1]
And everie man micht have gude sicht,
And thair was monie weirlyke knicht.   *warlike*
Sum man of everie natioun
500   Was in that congregatioun.
Than trumpettis blew triumphantlie,
And thay twa campiounis egeirlie
Thay spurrit thair hors with speir on breist,
Pertlie to preif their pith thay preist.[2]
505   That round rinkroume wes at utterance,[3]
Bot Talbartis hors with ane mischance,   *bad luck*
He outterit, and to ryn was laith,   *swerved; run; reluctant; (see note)*
Quhairof Talbart was wonder wraith.   *furious*
The squyer furth his rink he ran,   *course*
510   Commendit weill with everie man,
And him dischargit of his speir
Honestlie, lyke an man of weir.
Becaus that rink thay ran in vane,   *round (of jousting); in vain*
Than Talbart wald not ryn agane
515   Till he had gottin ane better steid,
Quhilk was brocht to him with gude speid,
Quhairon he lap, and tuik his speir,   *leapt*
As brym as he had bene ane beir,   *fierce; bear*
And bowtit fordwart with ane bend,   *darted; leap*
520   And ran on to the rinkis end,   *tournament-ground's*
And saw his hors was at command.   *obedient*
Than wes he blyith, I understand,   *happy*
Traistand na mair to ryn in vane.   *Trusting*
Than all the trumpettis blew agane:
525   Be that, with all the force they can,
Thay richt rudelie at uther ran.   *fiercely; each other*
Of that meiting ilk man thocht wounder,
Quhilk soundit lyke ane crak of thunder,
And nane of thame thair marrow mist.   *neither; opponent*
530   Sir Talbartis speir in sunder brist,   *burst into pieces*
Bot the squyer with his burdoun   *spear*
Sir Talbart to the eirth dang down.   *struck*
That straik was with sic micht and fors   *stroke*
That on the ground lay man and hors,
535   And throw the brydell hand him bair,
And in the breist ane span and mair.[4]

---

[1] *Where splendid arrangements were made and space cleared*

[2] *They pressed (assailed) boldly to prove their vigor*

[3] *That round jousting area was used to the utmost*

[4] Lines 535–36: *And through the bridle hand [he] bore [it] / And in [his] breist more than a span*

	Throw curras and throw gluifis of plait,	*cuirass (breastplate); plate gloves*
	That Talbart micht mak na debait.	*make no defense*
	The trencheour of the squyeris speir	*point*
540	Stak still into Sir Talbartis geir.	*armor*
	Than everie man into that steid	*in that place*
	Did all beleve that he was deid.	
	The squyer lap richt haistelie	
	From his cursour deliverlie,	*lightly*
545	And to Sir Talbart maid support,	
	And humillie did him comfort.	
	Quhen Talbart saw into his scheild,	*upon*
	Ane otter in ane silver feild,	
	"This race," said he "I may sair rew,	*encounter; sorely regret*
550	For I see weill my dreame wes trew.	
	Me thocht yone otter gart me bleid,	*that; made me*
	And buir me backwart from my steid.	*bore*
	Bot heir I vow to God soverane,	
	That I sall never just agane."	
555	And sweitlie to the squyer said,	
	"Thow knawis the cunnand that we maid:	*agreement*
	Quhilk of us twa suld tyne the feild,	*Whichever; lose*
	He suld baith hors and armour yeild.	
	Till him that wan, quhairfoir, I will	*therefore*
560	My hors and harnes geve thee till."	*give to you*
	Than said the squyer courteouslie:	
	"Brother, I thank yow hartfullie —	*sincerely*
	Of yow forsuith nathing I crave,	*in truth*
	For I have gottin that I wald have."	
565	With everie man he was commendit,	
	Sa vailyeandlie he him defendit.	
	The capitane of the Inglis band	
	Tuke the young squyer be the hand	
	And led him to the pailyeoun,	*pavilion*
570	And gart him mak collatioun.	*had him take refreshment*
	Quhen Talbartis woundis wes bund up fast,	
	The Inglis capitane to him past	
	And prudentlie did him comfort,	
	Syne said: "Brother, I yow exhort	
575	To tak the squyer be the hand."	
	And sa he did at his command,	
	And said: "This bene bot chance of armes."[1]	
	With that he braisit him in his armes,	*embraced*
	Sayand: "Hartlie I yow forgeve,"	*Sincerely*
580	And than the squyer tuik his leve,	

---

[1] *And said: "This is just the fortunes of war"*

Commendit weill with everie man.
Than wichtlie on his hors he wan,   *energetically; mounted*
With monie ane nobill man convoyit: *escorted*
Leve we thair Talbart sair annoyit.   *distressed*
585   Sum sayis of that discomfitour,   *defeat*
He thocht sic schame and dishonour
That he departit of that land,
And never wes sene into Ingland.
Bot our squyer did still remane
590   Efter the weir, quhill peice was tane.   *until peace was agreed*
All capitanes of the kingis gairdis
Gaif to the squyer riche rewairdis;
Becaus he had sa weill debaitit,   *fought*
With everie nobill he wes weill traitit.
595   Efter the weir he tuke licence,   *took his leave*
Syne did returne with diligence   *Then*
From Pycardie to Normandie,
And thair ane space remanit he,
Becaus the navie of Scotland
600   Wes still upon the coist lyand.   *lying off the coast*

Quhen he ane quhyle had sojornit,   *stayed*
He to the court of France returnit
For to decore his vassalege,   *embellish his martial reputation*
From Bartanye tuke his veyage   *Brittany set out*
605   With aucht scoir in his companie   *eight-score (i.e., 160)*
Of waillit wicht men and hardie,   *selected; brave*
Enarmit weill lyke men of weir
With hakbut, culvering, pik and speir,   *(see note)*
And passit up throw Normandie
610   Till Ambiance in Pycardie,   *Amiens*
Quhair nobill Lowes, the king of France,   *Louis XII*
Wes lyand with his ordinance   *stationed; army*
With monie ane prince and worthie man.
And in the court of France wes than
615   Ane mervellous congregatioun
Of monie ane divers natioun;
Of Ingland monie ane prudent lord
Efter the weir makand record.   *accord*
Thair wes than ane ambassadour,
620   Ane lord, ane man of greit honour:
With him was monie nobill knicht
Of Scotland, to defend thair richt,
Quhilk guydit thame sa honestlie,   *conducted themselves*
Inglismen had thame at invie   *envy*
625   And purposit to mak thame cummer,   *trouble*
Becaus they wer of greiter number.

	And sa, quhairever thay with thame met,	
	Upon the Scottis thay maid onset,	*attacked*
	And lyke wyld lyounis furious,	
630	Thay layd ane seige about the hous	
	Thame to destroy, sa thay intendit.	
	Our worthie Scottis thame weill defendit:	
	The Sutheroun wes ay fyve for ane,[1]	
	Sa on ilk syde thair wes men slane.	
635	The Inglismen grew in greit ire,	
	And cryit, "Swyith — set the hous in fyre!"	*Quick*
	Be that the squyer Meldrum	*At that point*
	Into the market streit wes cum	
	With his folkis in gude array,	
640	And saw the toun wes in ane fray.	*uproar*
	He did inquyre the occasioun:	
	Quod thay, "The Scottis are all put doune	*overcome*
	Be Inglismen into thair innis."	*at their lodgings*
	Quod he: "I wald gif all the Bynnis,	
645	That I micht cum or thay departit!"	*If; before*
	With that he grew sa cruell hartit,	
	That he was like ane wyld lyoun,	
	And rudelie ran outthrow the toun	*fiercely*
	With all his companie weill arrayit,	*armed*
650	And with baner ful braid displayit.	
	And quhen thay saw the Inglis rout,	*crowd*
	Thay set upon thame with ane schout;	
	With reird sa rudelie on thame ruschit,	*a loud cry; fiercely*
	That fiftie to the eirth thay duschit.	*battered down*
655	Thair was nocht ellis bot tak and slay.[2]	
	This squyer wounder did that day,	
	And stoutlie stoppit in the stour,	*stood firm in battle*
	And dang on thame with dintis dour.	*struck; heavy blows*
	Wes never man buir better hand;	
660	Thair micht na buckler byde his brand,[3]	
	For it was weill sevin quarter lang.	*seven ells*
	With that sa derflie on thame dang	*hardily; struck*
	That, lyke ane worthie campioun,	*champion*
	Ay at ane straik he dang ane doun.	*struck one down*
665	Sum wes evill hurt, and sum wes slane;	*badly*
	Sum fel quhilk rais not yit agane.	*did not get up again*
	Quhen that the Sutheroun saw his micht,	
	Effrayitlie thay tuke the flicht	*In fright; fled*

---

[1] *The Southern (i.e., English) were always five (Englishmen) to one (Scotsman)*

[2] *It was all (i.e., there was nothing else except) capturing and killing*

[3] Lines 659–60: *No man ever gave better support; / There might (be) no shield (able to) withstand his sword*

And wist not quhair to flie for haist,   *did not know where*
670 Thus throw the toun he hes thame chaist.
Wer not Frenchemen come to the redding,[1]
Thair had bene mekill mair blude shedding.   *much more*
        Of this journey I mak an end,   *day's performance*
Quhilk everie nobill did commend.
675 Quhen to the king the cace wes knawin,
And all the suith unto him shawin,   *truth*
How this squyer sa manfullie
On Sutheroun wan the victorie,
He put him into ordinance.   *military service*
680 And sa he did remane in France
Ane certane tyme for his plesour,
Weill estemit in greit honour,
Quhair he did monie ane nobill deid.
With that, richt wantoun in his weid,   *extravagant in his clothes*
685 Quhen ladies knew his hie courage,   *manly spirit*
He was desyrit in mariage
Be ane ladie of greit rent,   *income*
Bot youth maid him sa insolent   *disdainful*
That he in France wald not remane,
690 Bot come to Scotland hame agane.
Thocht Frenche ladies did for him murne,   *Although*
The Scottis wer glaid of his returne.
At everie lord he tuke his leve,
Bot his departing did thame greive,
695 For he was luifit with all wichtis   *people*
Quhilk had him sene defend his richtis.
Scottis capitanes did him convoy,   *escort*
Thocht his departing did thame noy.   *grieve*
At Deip he maid him for the saill,[2]
700 Quhair he furnischit ane gay veschaill   *ship*
For his self and his men of weir
With artailyie, hakbut, bow, and speir,   *artillery; guns*
And furneist hir with gude victuaill,   *her (i.e., the ship); food*
With the best wyne that he culd waill.   *choose*
705 And quhen the schip was reddie maid,
He lay bot ane day in the raid   *anchorage*
Quhill he gat wind of the southeist.   *Until*
Than thay thair ankeris weyit on haist,   *in haste*
And syne maid saill, and fordwart past
710 Ane day at morne, till at the last,
Of ane greit saill thay gat ane sicht,

---

[1] *Had not the Frenchmen come to separate them*

[2] *At Dieppe he prepared himself for a journey by sea*

	And Phoebus schew his bemis bricht	*Phoebus Apollo (i.e., the sun) displayed*
	Into the morning richt airlie.	
	Than past the skipper richt spedelie	
715	Up to the top with richt greit feir,	*platform up on mast*
	And saw it wes ane man of weir,	*man-of-war (i.e., a fighting ship)*
	And cryit: "I see nocht ellis, perdie,	
	Bot we mon outher fecht or fle."[1]	
	The squyer wes in his bed lyand,	
720	Quhen he hard tell this new tydand.	*news*
	Be this, the Inglis artailye	*At that point; artillery*
	Lyke hailschot maid on thame assailye,	*an attack*
	And sloppit throw thair fechting saillis,	*made holes; fighting*
	And divers dang out ovir the waillis.	*struck; gunwales*
725	The Scottis agane, with all thair micht	
	Of gunnis than thay leit fle ane flicht.	*let fly; round (of gunfire)*
	Thar thay micht weill see quhair they wair:	
	Heidis and armes flew in the air.	
	The Scottis schip scho wes sa law,	*low (in the water)*
730	That monie gunnis out ovir hir flaw[2]	
	Quhilk far beyond thame lichtit doun,	*landed*
	Bot the Inglis greit galyeoun	
	Fornent thame stude lyke ane strang castell,	*In front of*
	That the Scottis gunnis micht na way faill,	
735	Bot hat hir ay on the richt syde	*always hit her*
	With monie ane slop, for all hir pryde,	*hole*
	That monie ane beft wer on thair bakkis.	*were beaten backwards*
	Than rais the reik with uglie crakkis,	*rose the smoke*
	Quhilk on the sey maid sic ane sound	*sea*
740	That in the air it did redound,	*resound*
	That men micht weill wit on the land,	*know*
	That shippis wer on the sey fechtand.	*fighting at sea*
	Be this thegyder straik the shippis	*Then together ran*
	And ather on uther laid thair clippis,	*each; grappling hooks*
745	And than began the strang battell —	
	Ilk man his marrow did assaill.	*opponent*
	Sa rudelie thay did rushe togidder,	*violently*
	That nane micht hald thair feit for slidder,[3]	
	Sum with halbert and sum with speir,	
750	Bot hakbuttis did the greitest deir.	*harm*
	Out of the top the grundin dartis	*From the top platform; sharpened*
	Did divers peirs out throw the hartis.	*pierce many through the heart*
	Everie man did his diligence	*tried his hardest*

---

[1] Lines 717–18: *And cried: "I see no other option, by God, / But that we must either fight or flee"*

[2] *That many missiles flew over her [i.e., the ship]*

[3] *That none might stay on their feet for the slipperiness*

	Upon his fo to wirk vengence,	
755	Ruschand on uther routtis rude,	*Inflicting violent blows on others*
	That ovir the waillis ran the blude.	*gunwales*
	The Inglis capitane cryit hie:	
	"Swyith yeild, yow doggis, or ye sall die!	*Surrender immediately*
	And do ye not, I mak ane vow	*if you do not*
760	That Scotland sal be quyte of yow."	*rid*
	That peirtlie answerit the squyer,	*unflinchingly*
	And said, "O tratour tavernar —	*traitorous taverner*
	I lat thee wit, thow hes na micht	*I'll have you know*
	This day to put us to the flight."	
765	Thay derflie ay at uther dang;	*boldly*
	The squyer thristit throw the thrang	*pushed through the crowd*
	And in the Inglis schip he lap,	*leapt*
	And hat the capitane sic ane flap	*hit; blow*
	Upon his heid till he fell doun,	
770	Welterand intill ane deidlie swoun.	*Tumbling into a deathly faint*
	And quhen the Scottis saw the squyer	
	Had strikkin doun that rank rever,	*foul pirate*
	They left thair awin schip standand waist	*standing empty*
	And in the Inglis schip in haist	
775	They followit all thair capitane,	
	And sone wes all the Sutheroun slane.	
	Howbeit thay wer of greiter number,	*Although*
	The Scottismen put thame in sic cummer	*caused them such distress*
	That thay wer fane to leif the feild,	*eager to leave*
780	Cryand mercie, than did thame yeild.	
	Yit wes the squyer straikand fast	
	At the capitane, till at the last,	
	Quhen he persavit no remeid,	*alternative*
	Outher to yeild or to be deid,	*Either*
785	He said: "O gentill capitane,	
	Thoill me not for to be slane —	*Do not allow me to be slain*
	My lyfe to yow sal be mair pryse	*will be worth more*
	Nor sall my deith ane thowsand syse!	*Than; times*
	For ye may get, as I suppois,	
790	Thrie thowsand nobillis of the rois	*(see note)*
	Of me, and of my companie.	
	Thairfoir I cry yow loud mercie.	
	Except my lyfe, nothing I craif:	*desire*
	Tak yow the schip and all the laif.	*rest*
795	I yeild to yow baith sword and knyfe —	
	Thairfoir, gud maister, save my lyfe!"	
	The squyer tuik him be the hand,	
	And on his feit he gart him stand,	*made him stand*
	And treittit him richt tenderly,	
800	And syne unto his men did cry,	

	And gaif to thame richt strait command	
	To straik no moir, bot hald thair hand.	
	Than baith the capitanes ran and red,	
	And so thair wes na mair blude shed.	
805	Than all the laif thay did thame yeild,	*remainder*
	And to the Scottis gaif sword and scheild.	
	Ane nobill leiche the squyer had —	*physician*
	Quhairof the Inglismen wes full glaid —	
	To quhome the squyer gaif command	
810	The woundit men to tak on hand,	
	And so he did with diligence,	
	Quhairof he gat gude recompence.	
	Than quhen the woundit men wer drest,	
	And all the deand men confest,	*dying*
815	And deid men cassin in the see,	*cast*
	Quhilk to behald wes greit pietie,	
	Thair was slane of Inglis band	
	Fyve score of men, I understand,	*(i.e., 100 men)*
	The quhilk wer cruell men and kene,	
820	And of the Scottis wer slane fyftene.	
	And quhen the Inglis capitane	
	Saw how his men wer tane and slane,	*overcome*
	And how the Scottis, sa few in number,	
	Had put thame in sa greit ane cummer,	*Had caused them such great distress*
825	He grew intill ane frenesy,	*into a frenzy*
	Sayand, "Fals Fortoun, I the defy!	
	For I belevit this day at morne,	
	That he was not in Scotland borne	
	That durst have met me hand for hand	
830	Within the boundis of my brand."	*Within reach of my sword*
	The squyer bad him mak gude cheir,	
	And said, "It wes bot chance of weir:	
	Greit conquerouris, I yow assure,	
	Hes hapnit siclike adventure.	
835	Thairfoir mak mirrie and go dyne,	
	And let us preif the michtie wyne!"	*try; potent*
	Sum drank wyne and sum drank aill,	
	Syne put the shippis under saill,	*Then*
	And waillit furth of the Inglis band	*picked out*
840	Twa hundreth men, and put on land	
	Quyetlie on the coist of Kent:	
	The laif in Scotland with him went.	*rest*
	The Inglis capitane, as I ges,	
	He wairdit him in the Blaknes,	*imprisoned*
845	And treitit him richt honestlie,	
	Togither with his companie,	
	And held thame in that garnisoun	*garrison*

	Till thay had payit thair ransoun.	*ransom*
	Out throw the land than sprang the fame	*news*
850	That squyer Meldrum wes cum hame.	

	Quhen they hard tell how he debaitit,	*fought*
	With everie man he was sa treitit,	*treated*
	That quhen he travellit throw the land,	
	Thay bankettit him fra hand to hand[1]	
855	With greit solace, till at the last	*joy*
	Out throw Straitherne the squyer past,	
	And as it did approch the nicht,	
	Of ane castell he gat ane sicht,	
	Beside ane montane in ane vaill,	*valley*
860	And than, efter his greit travaill,	
	He purpoisit him to repois	*decided to rest*
	Quhair ilk man did of him rejois.	*each*
	Of this trimphant plesant place,	
	Ane lustie ladie wes maistres	*delightful*
865	Quhais lord was deid schort tyme befoir,	
	Quhairthrow hir dolour wes the moir.	*so that; more*
	Bot yit scho tuke sum comforting	
	To heir the plesant dulce talking	*gentle speech*
	Of this young squyer of his chance,	*fortunes*
870	And how it fortunit him in France.	*things went for him*
	This squyer and the ladie gent	
	Did wesche, and then to supper went.	*wash*
	During that nicht thair was nocht ellis	*nothing else*
	Bot for to heir of his novelis.	*news (stories)*
875	Eneas, quhen he fled from Troy,	
	Did not Quene Dido greiter joy	
	Quhen he in Carthage did arryve,	
	And did the seige of Troy discryve.	*describe*
	The wonderis that he did reheirs	
880	Wer langsum for to put in vers,	*tedious*
	Of quhilk this ladie did rejois.	
	Thay drank, and syne went to repois.	*rest*
	He fand his chalmer weill arrayit,	*found; chamber; arranged*
	With dornik work on buird displayit.	*fine linen; table*
885	Of venisoun he had his waill,	*choice*
	Gude aquavite, wyne and aill,	*whisky; ale*
	With nobill confeittis, bran and geill,[2]	
	And swa the squyer fuir richt weill.	*fared*
	Sa, to heir mair of his narratioun,	

---

[1] *They laid on banquets for him from one place to another*

[2] *With excellent sweetmeats, meat (brawn) and jelly*

890	This ladie come to his collatioun,	*late supper*
	Sayand he was richt welcum hame.	
	"Grandmercie than," quod he, "Madame."	
	Thay past the time with ches and tabill,	*tables (a board game)*
	For he to everie game was abill.	
895	Than unto bed drew everie wicht:	*person*
	To chalmer went this ladie bricht,	
	The quhilk this squyer did convoy,	*Whom; escort*
	Syne till his bed he went with joy.	*Then*
	That nicht he sleipit never ane wink,	
900	Bot still did on the ladie think.	
	Cupido with his fyrie dart	
	Did peirs him so outthrow the hart,	*pierce; through*
	Sa all that nicht he did bot murnit,	*just lamented*
	Sumtyme sat up, and sumtyme turnit,	
905	Sichand with monie gant and grane,	*Sighing; gape; groan*
	To fair Venus makand his mane,	*making his complaint*
	Sayand, "Ladie, quhat may this mene?	
	I was ane fre man lait yistrene,	*yesterday evening*
	And now ane cative, bound and thrall,	*captive; enslaved*
910	For ane that I think flour of all.	
	I pray God, sen scho knew my mynd,	*grant that*
	How for hir saik I am sa pynd	*in such torment*
	Wald God I had bene yit in France	
	Or I had hapnit sic mischance:	*Before I had suffered such misfortune*
915	To be subject or serviture	*servant*
	Till ane quhilk takis of me na cure!"	*To one who cares nothing for me*
	This ladie ludgit neirhand by,	*stayed*
	And hard the squyer prively,	*heard*
	With dreidfull hart makand his mone,	*fearful; complaint*
920	With monie cairfull gant and grone.	*With many an unhappy gape and groan*
	Hir hart, fulfillit with pietie,	
	Thocht scho wald haif of him mercie,	
	And said: "Howbeit I suld be slane,	
	He sall have lufe for lufe agane.	
925	Wald God I micht with my honour,	
	Have him to be my paramour!"	*lover*
	This wes the mirrie tyme of May,	
	Quhen this fair ladie, freshe and gay,	
	Start up to take the hailsum air,	*wholesome*
930	With pantonis on hir feit ane pair,	*slippers*
	Airlie into ane cleir morning	
	Befoir fair Phoebus uprysing,	*Phoebus Apollo (i.e., the sun)*
	Kirtill alone, withouttin clok,	*Gown*
	And saw the squyeris dure unlok.	*door*
935	Scho slippit in or ever he wist,	*before he was aware of it*
	And fenyeitlie past till ane kist,	*pretending; chest*

And with her keyis oppinnit the lokkis
And maid hir to take furth ane boxe —
Bot that was not hir erand thair.
940   With that, this lustie young squyar   *hearty*
Saw this ladie so plesantlie
Cum to his chalmer quyetlie,   *chamber*
In kyrtill of fine damais broun,   *patterned silk*
Hir goldin traissis hingand doun.   *tresses hanging*
945   Hir pappis wer hard, round and quhyte,   *breasts; firm*
Quhome to behald wes greit delyte.
Lyke the quhyte lyllie wes hir lyre;   *lily; flesh*
Hir hair was like the reid gold wyre,
Hir schankis quhyte, withouttin hois,   *legs; hose*
950   Quhairat the squyer did rejois,
And said than, "Now, vailye quod vailye,   *come what may*
Upon the ladie thow mak ane sailye!"   *advance*
Hir courtlyke kirtill was unlaist,   *elegant; unlaced*
And sone into his armis hir braist   *clasped*
955   And said to hir: "Madame, gude morne —
Help me, your man that is forlorne.
Without ye mak me sum remeid,   *Unless; remedy*
Withouttin dout, I am bot deid,
Quhairfoir ye mon releif my harmes."   *So you must relieve my suffering*
960   With that he hint hir in his armes,   *took*
And talkit with hir on the flure,   *floor*
Syne quyetlie did bar the dure.   *lock the door*
"Squyer," quod scho, "quhat is your will?
Think ye my womanheid to spill?   *ruin*
965   Na, God forbid, it wer greit syn!
My lord and ye wes neir of kyn.
Quhairfoir I mak yow supplicatioun:
Pas and seik ane dispensatioun.
Than sall I wed yow with ane ring;
970   Than may ye leif at your lyking,   *live as you wish*
For ye ar young, lustie and fair,   *lovely*
And als ye ar your fatheris air.   *heir*
Thair is na ladie in all this land
May yow refuse to hir husband.
975   And gif ye lufe me as ye say,
Haist to dispens the best ye may,   *Hurry to arrange things*
And thair to yow I geve my hand —
I sall yow take to my husband."
Quod he: "Quhill that I may indure,   *last*
980   I vow to be your serviture,   *servant*
Bot I think greit vexatioun
To tarie upon dispensation —"   *delay for*
Than in his armis he did hir thrist,   *clasp tightly*

	And aither uther sweitlie kist,	*each the other*
985	And wame for wame thay uther braissit;	*belly to belly; embraced*
	With that hir kirtill wes unlaissit.	*gown; unlaced*
	Than Cupido, with his fyrie dartis,	
	Inflammit sa thir luiferis hartis,	*these lovers'*
	Thay micht na maner of way dissever,	*in no way separate*
990	Nor ane micht not part fra ane uther,	
	Bot like wodbind thay wer baith wrappit.	*woodbine*
	Thair tenderlie he hes hir happit	*tucked*
	Full softlie up intill his bed —	
	Judge ye gif he hir schankis shed.	*parted her legs*
995	"Allace," quod scho, "quhat may this mene?"	
	And with hir hair scho dicht hir ene.	*(see note)*
	I can not tell how thay did play,	
	Bot I beleve scho said not nay.	
	He pleisit hir sa, as I hard sane,	*said*
1000	That he was welcum ay agane.	
	Scho rais and tendirlie him kist,	*rose*
	And on his hand ane ring scho thrist,	*pushed*
	And he gaif hir ane lufe drowrie —	*love-token*
	Ane ring set with ane riche rubie,	
1005	In takin that thair lufe for ever	*As a sign*
	Suld never from thir twa dissever.	*these two separate*
	And than scho passit unto hir chalmer,	
	And fand hir madinnis sweit as lammer	*found; ambergris (see note)*
	Sleipand full sound, and nothing wist	*unaware*
1010	How that thair ladie past to the kist.	
	Quod thay: "Madame, quhair have ye bene?"	
	Quod scho: "Into my gardine grene,	
	To heir thir mirrie birdis sang.	*these*
	I lat yow wit, I thocht not lang,	
1015	Thocht I had taryit thair quhill none."[1]	
	Quod thai: "Quhair wes your hois and schone?	*hose and shoes*
	Quhy yeid ye with your bellie bair?"	*went*
	Quod scho: "The morning wes sa fair,	
	For be him that deir Jesus sauld,	*sold (i.e., Judas Iscariot)*
1020	I felt na wayis ony maner of cauld."	*cold*
	Quod thay: "Madame, me think ye sweit."	*sweat*
	Quod scho: "Ye see I sufferit heit:	
	The dew did sa on flouris fleit	*flow (collect)*
	That baith my lymmis ar maid weit.	*legs*
1025	Thairfoir ane quhyle I will heir ly,	
	Till this dulce dew be fra me dry.	*soft*
	Ryse and gar mak our denner reddie."	*have made; dinner*

---

[1] Lines 1014–15: *"I tell you, I wouldn't have tired of it / Even if I'd dawdled there until noon"*

       "That sal be done," quod thay, "My ladie."

       Efter that scho had tane hir rest,

1030 Sho rais and in hir chalmer hir drest,

       And efter mes to denner went.   *mass*

       Than wes the squyer diligent

       To declair monie sindrie storie   *many different*

       Worthie to put in memorie.

1035   Quhat sall we of thir luiferis say?   *these lovers*

       Bot all this tyme of lustie May,   *lovely*

       They past the tyme with joy and blis,

       Full quyetlie with monie ane kis.

       Thair was na creature that knew

1040 Yit of thir luiferis chalmer glew,   *lit. "bedroom sport"*

       And sa he levit plesandlie

       Ane certane time with his ladie,

       Sum time with halking and hunting,   *hawking*

       Sum time with wantoun hors rinning,   *spirited; riding*

1045 And sum time, like ane man of weir,

       Full galyardlie wald ryn ane speir.   *valiantly; i.e., joust*

       He wan the pryse abone thame all,   *above*

       Baith at the buttis and the futeball;   *archery-targets*

       Till everie solace he was abill,   *At; pastime*

1050 At cartis and dyce, at ches and tabill;   *cards; dice; board-games*

       And gif ye list, I sall yow tell   *wish*

       How that he seigit ane castell.   *besieged*

       Ane messinger come spedilie

       From the Lennox to that ladie,

1055 And schew how that Makfagon —   *(see note)*

       And with him monie bauld baron —

       Hir castell had tane perfors   *seized by force*

       And nouther left hir kow nor hors,   *neither; cow*

       And heryit all that land about,   *ravaged*

1060 Quhairof the ladie had greit dout.   *was greatly alarmed*

       Till hir squyer scho passit in haist,

       And schew him how scho wes opprest,   *explained to him*

       And how he waistit monie ane myle   *laid waste*

       Betwix Dunbartane and Argyle.   *Dumbarton*

1065 And quhen the squyer Meldrum

       Had hard thir novellis all and sum,   *these tidings*

       Intill his hart thair grew sic ire   *Within*

       That all his bodie brint in fyre,   *burned*

       And swoir it suld be full deir sald,   *very dearly paid for*

1070 Gif he micht find him in that hald.   *stronghold*

       He and his men did them addres   *attire*

       Richt haistelie in thair harnes,   *armor*

       Sum with bow and sum with speir,

       And he, like Mars the god of weir,

1075	Come to the ladie and tuke his leif,	
	And scho gaif him hir richt hand gluif,	*glove*
	The quhilk he on his basnet bure	*bore on his helmet*
	And said: "Madame, I yow assure	
	That worthie Lancelot du laik,	
1080	Did never mair for his ladies saik	
	Nor I sall do, or ellis de,	*Than; die*
	Without that ye revengit be."	*Unless*
	Than in hir armes scho him braist,	*embraced*
	And he his leif did take in haist,	*leave*
1085	And raid that day and all the nicht,	*rode*
	Till on the morne he gat ane sicht	*gained sight*
	Of that castell baith fair and strang.	
	Than, in the middis his men amang,	*amidst his men*
	To michtie Mars his vow he maid,	
1090	That he suld never in hart be glaid,	
	Nor yit returne furth of that land	
	Quhill that strenth wer at his command.[1]	
	All the tennentis of that ladie	
	Come to the squyer haistelie,	
1095	And maid aith of fidelitie	*an oath*
	That they suld never fra him flie.	
	Quhen to Makferland, wicht and bauld,	*hardy*
	The veritie all haill wes tauld	*The whole truth*
	How the young squyer Meldrum	
1100	Wes now into the cuntrie cum,	
	Purpoisand to seige that place,	*Intending; besiege*
	Than vittaillit he that fortres	*provisioned*
	And swoir he suld that place defend	
	Bauldlie untill his lyfis end.	*Boldly*
1105	Be this, the squyer wes arrayit,	*armed*
	With his baner bricht displayit,	
	With culvering, hakbut, bow and speir.	
	Of Makfarland he tuke na feir,	*had no fear*
	And like ane campioun courageous,	
1110	He cryit and said, "Gif ovir the hous!"	*Surrender*
	The capitane answerit heighly	*haughtily*
	And said: "Tratour, we thee defy!	
	We sall remane this hous within,	
	Into despyte of all thy kyn."	*Despite*
1115	With that the archeris bauld and wicht	*bold and brave*
	Of braid arrowis let fle ane flicht	*broad arrows*
	Amang the squyers companie,	
	And thay agane richt manfullie	

---

[1] *For as long as he had military strength at his command*

	With hakbute, bow and culveryne,	*With guns, arrows and gunshot*
1120	Quhilk put Makferlandis men to pyne,	*made; suffer*
	And on thair colleris laid full sikker,	*collars assailed fiercely*
	And thair began ane bailfull bikker.	*dire encounter*
	Thair was bot schot and schot agane,	
	Till on ilk side thair wes men slane.	*each*
1125	Than cryit the squyer couragious:	
	"Swyith, lay the ledderis to the house!"	*Quickly; ladders*
	And sa thay did, and clam belyfe	*climbed swiftly*
	As busie beis dois to thair hyfe.	*bees; hive*
	Howbeit thair wes slane monie man,	*Although*
1130	Yit wichtlie ovir the wallis they wan.	*bravely; got*
	The squyer, formest of them all,	*foremost*
	Plantit the baner ovir the wall,	
	And than began the mortall fray —	
	Thair wes not ellis bot tak and slay.	*capture and strike down*
1135	Than Makferland, that maid the prais,	*pressed the attack*
	From time he saw the squyeris face,	*When*
	Upon his kneis he did him yeild,	
	Deliverand him baith speir and scheild.	
	The squyer hartlie him ressavit,	*cordially; received*
1140	Commandand that he suld be savit,	
	And sa did slaik that mortall feid,	*end; enmity*
	Sa that na man wes put to deid.	*death*
	In fre waird was Makferland seisit,	*(see note)*
	And leit the laif gang quhair they pleisit.	*let the rest go*
1145	And sa this squyer amorous	
	Seigit and wan the ladies hous,	*Besieged*
	And left thairin ane capitane,	
	Syne to Stratherne returnit agane,	*Strathearn*
	Quhair that he with his fair ladie	
1150	Ressavit wes full plesantlie,	*Received*
	And to tak rest did him convoy.	*lead*
	Judge ye gif thair wes mirth and joy:	
	Howbeit the chalmer dure wes cloisit,	*Although; chamber door*
	They did bot kis, as I suppoisit.	
1155	Gif uther thing wes them betwene,	
	Let them discover that luiferis bene,	*lovers*
	For I am not in lufe expart	
	And never studyit in that art.	
	Thus they remainit in merines,	
1160	Beleifand never to have distres.	*Believing*
	In that meine time this ladie fair	*mean*
	Ane douchter to the squyer bair:	*daughter; gave birth*
	Nane fund was fairer of visage.	*None found*
	Than tuke the squyer sic courage,	

1165	Agane the mirrie time of May, [1]
	Threttie he put in his luferay	*Thirty; livery*
	In scarlot fyne and of hew grene,
	Quhilk wes ane semelie sicht to sene.
	The gentilmen in all that land
1170	Wer glaid with him to mak ane band,
	And he wald plainelie take thair partis,	*publicly*
	And not desyring bot thair hartis.	*And desiring only their hearts [in return]*
	Thus levit the squyer plesandlie,	*lived*
	With musick and with menstralie.	*minstrelsy*
1175	Of this ladie he wes sa glaid,
	Thair micht na sorrow mak him sad.
	Ilk ane did uther consolatioun,
	Taryand upon dispensatioun.	*Waiting for*
	Had it cum hame, he had hir bruikit, [2]
1180	Bot or it come, it wes miscuikit,	*before; mismanaged*
	And all this game he bocht ful deir,
	As ye at lenth sall efter heir.
	Of warldlie joy it wes weill kend	*known*
	That sorrow bene the fatall end,
1185	For jelousie and fals invie
	Did him persew richt cruellie.
	I mervell not thocht it be so,	*though*
	For they wer ever luiferis fo,	*lovers' enemies*
	Quhairthrow he stude in monie ane stour, [3]
1190	And ay defendit his honour.
	Ane cruell knicht dwelt neir hand by
	Quhilk at this squyer had invy,	*Who felt malice towards this squire*
	Imaginand intill his hart	*in*
	How he thir luiferis micht depart,	*these lovers; separate*
1195	And wald have had hir maryand	*marrying*
	Ane gentilman within his land
	The quhilk to him wes not in blude.	*Who; unrelated*
	Bot finallie, for to conclude,
	Thairto scho wald never assent.
1200	Quhairfoir the knicht set his intent
	This nobill squyer for to destroy,
	And swore he suld never have joy
	Intill his hart, without remeid,	*In; relief (cure)*
	Till ane of thame wer left for deid.

---

[1] Lines 1164–65: *Then the squire resolved, / In preparation for the merry season of May*

[2] *If it [i.e., the dispensation] had come from abroad, he would have enjoyed possession of her [i.e., in marriage]*

[3] *On account of which he fought in many a battle*

1205	This vailyeand squyer manfully	
	In ernist or play did him defy,	
	Offerand himself for to assaill	
	Bodie for bodie in battaill;	
	The knicht thairto not condiscendit,	*would not assent*
1210	Bot to betrais him ay intendit.	*betray; ever*
	Sa it fell anis upon ane day	*once*
	In Edinburgh, as I hard say:	
	This squyer and the ladie trew	
	Was thair, just matteris to persew.	*lawful*
1215	That cruell knight, full of invy,	
	Gart hald on them ane secreit spy	*Set*
	Quhen thai suld pas furth of the toun,	*out*
	For this squyeris confusioun,	*downfall*
	Quhilk traistit no man suld him greive	*believed; harm*
1220	Nor of tressoun had no beleive,	*treachery; expectation*
	And tuik his licence from his oist	*leave; the landlord*
	And liberallie did pay his coist	*expenses*
	And sa departit blyith and mirrie,	
	With purpois to pas ovir the ferrie.	
1225	He wes bot auchtsum in his rout,	*He was one of only eight men in his band*
	For of danger he had no dout.	*fear*
	The spy come to the knicht anone,	*straight away*
	And him informit how they wer gone.	
	Than gadderit he his men in hy	*in haste*
1230	With thrie scoir in his company,	*three score (i.e., 60 men)*
	Accowterit weill in feir of weir,	*Well equipped in warlike array*
	Sum with bow and sum with speir,	
	And on the squyer followit fast,	
	Till thay did see him at the last,	
1235	With all his men richt weill arrayit,	*in order*
	With cruell men nathing effrayit.	*By; not at all alarmed*
	And quhen the ladie saw the rout,	*band [of men]*
	Got wait gif scho stude in greit dout.	*God knows; fear*
	Quod scho: "Your enemeis I see —	
1240	Thairfoir, sweit hart, I reid yow fle.	*suggest; escape*
	In the cuntrey I will be kend;	*(see note)*
	Ye ar na partie to defend.	*You are in no position to defend yourself*
	Ye knaw yone knichtis crueltie,	*that (yonder)*
	That in his hart hes no mercie:	
1245	It is bot ane that thay wald have.	*just one [person]*
	Thairfoir, deir hart, yourself ye save —	
	Howbeit thay tak me with this trane,	*Although; trap*
	I sal be sone at yow agane —	*with*

	For ye war never sa hard staid."[1]	
1250	"Madame," quod he, "be ye not raid,	*afraid*
	For be the halie Trinitie,	
	This day ane fute I will not fle!"	*i.e., not one foot*
	And be he had endit this word,	*And as soon as he had finished this speech*
	He drew ane lang twa-handit sword,	
1255	And put his aucht men in array,	*eight; battle-formation*
	And bad that thay suld take na fray.	*not take fright*
	Than to the squyer cryit the knicht,	
	And said: "Send me the ladie bricht!	
	Do ye not sa, be Goddis corce,	*If you don't; body*
1260	I sall hir tak away perforce!"	*by force*
	The squyer said: "Be thow ane knicht,	
	Cum furth to me and shaw the richt,	
	Bot hand for hand, without redding,[2]	
	That thair be na mair blude shedding.	
1265	And gif thow winnis me in the feild,	*overcome*
	I sall my ladie to the yeild."	
	The knicht durst not for all his land	
	Fecht with this squyer hand for hand.	
	The squyer than saw no remeid,	*alternative*
1270	Bot outher to fecht or to be deid.	*either*
	To hevin he liftit up his visage,	
	Cryand to God with hie courage:	
	"To thee my querrell I do commend."	
	Syne bowtit fordwart with ane bend,	*Then [he] sprang forward with a leap*
1275	With countenance baith bauld and stout,	
	He rudelie rushit in that rout,	*violently; crowd*
	With him his litill companie,	
	Quhilk them defendit manfullie.	*themselves*
	The squyer with his birneist brand	*polished sword*
1280	Amang his famen maid sic hand	*Among his enemies he showed such valor*
	That Gaudefer, as sayis the letter,	*i.e., book*
	At Gadderis Ferrie faucht no better.	
	His sword he swappit sa about,	*whirled*
	That he greit round maid in the rout,	*That he cut a great circle in the crowd*
1285	And like ane man that was dispairit,	
	His wapoun sa on thame he wairit,	*waged war*
	Quhome ever he hit, as I hard say,	
	Thay did him na mair deir that day.	*harm*
	Quha ever come within his boundis,	
1290	He chaipit not but mortall woundis.	*escaped not without*
	Sum mutilate wer, and sum wer slane,	*struck down or killed*

---

[1] *For you have never been so hard-pressed*

[2] *But hand-to-hand, without anyone separating us*

Sum fled and come not yit agane.

He hat the knicht abone the breis   *struck; above; eyebrows*

That he fel fordwart on his kneis: *forward*

1295   Wer not Thome Giffard did him save,   *Were it not that*

The knicht had sone bene in his grave.

Bot than the squyer with his brand

Hat Thomas Giffard on the hand: *Struck*

From that time furth during his lyfe,

1300   He never weildit sword nor knyfe.

Than come ane sort as brim as beiris,   *band as fierce as bears*

And in him festnit fyftene speiris   *planted*

In purpois to have borne him doun,

Bot he, as forcie campioun,   *powerful champion*

1305   Amang thai wicht men wrocht greit wounder,   *hardy*

For all thai speiris he schure in sunder.   *those; sliced to pieces*

Nane durst com neir him hand for hand,

Within the boundis of his brand.   *reach; sword*

This worthie squyer courageous

1310   Micht be compairit to Tydeus

Quhilk faucht for to defend his richtis,

And slew of Thebes fyftie knichtis.

Rolland with Brandwell, his bricht brand,

Faucht neuer better hand for hand,

1315   Nor Gawin aganis Golibras,

Nor Olyver with Pharambras.

I wait he faucht that day alse weill   *know*

As did Sir Gryme aganis Graysteille,

And I dar say, he was als abill,

1320   As onie knicht of the Round Tabill,

And did his honour mair avance,

Nor onie of thay knichtis perchance,   *Than; those*

The quhilk I offer me to preif   *offer myself as witness*

Gif that ye pleis, sirs, with your leif.   *permission*

1325   Amang thay knichts wes maid ane band   *agreement*

That they suld fecht bot hand for hand,   *fight only*

Assurit that thair suld cum no mo.   *Confident*

With this squyer it stude not so:

His stalwart stour quha wald discryfe,   *valiant battle; describe*

1330   Aganis ane man thair come ay fyfe.   *always*

Quhen that this cruell tyrane knicht   *wicked*

Saw the squyer sa wounder wicht,   *astonishingly hardy*

And had no micht him to destroy,

Into his hart thair grew sic noy   *vexation*

1335   That he was abill for to rage   *on the point of*

That no man micht his ire asswage.[1]
"Fy on us," said he to his men:
"Ay aganis ane sen we ar ten!   *since*
Chaip he away, we are eschamit —[2]
1340   Like cowertis we sal be defamit.   *cowards; disgraced*
I had rather be in hellis pane
Or he suld chaip fra us unslane."   *Than; escape; unslain*
And callit thrie of his companie,
Said: "Pas behind him quyetlie."
1345   And sa thay did richt secreitlie,
And come behind him cowartlie,
And hackit on his hochis and theis   *houghs; thighs*
Till that he fell upon his kneis.
Yit quhen his schankis wer schorne in sunder,   *shins*
1350   Upon his kneis he wrocht greit wounder,
Sweipand his sword round about,
Not haifand of the deith na dout.   *any fear*
Durst nane approche within his boundis,   *within his reach*
Till that his cruell mortall woundis
1355   Bled sa, that he did swap in swoun: *drop; a faint*
Perforce behuifit him than fall doun.   *he was forced to*
And quhen he lay upon the ground,
They gaif him monie cruell wound
That men on far micht heir the knokkis,   *far away*
1360   Like boucheouris hakkand on their stokks.   *butchers; blocks*
And finallie, without remeid,   *relief*
They left him lyand thair for deid   *lying*
With ma woundis of sword and knyfe   *many*
Nor ever had man that keipit lyfe.   *Than; remained alive*
1365   Quhat suld I of thir tratouris say?   *these*
Quhen they had done they fled away.
Bot than this lustie ladie fair,   *lovely*
With dolent hart scho maid sic cair,   *grieving; such lamentation*
Quhilk wes greit pietie for to reheirs   *repeat*
1370   And langsum for to put in vers.   *overlong (tedious)*
With teiris scho wuische his bludie face,   *washed*
Sichand with manie loud "allace."   *Sighing*
"Allace," quod scho, "that I was borne —
In my querrell thow art forlorne!   *ruined*
1375   Sall never man efter this hour
Of my bodie have mair plesour,
For thow was gem of gentilnes,
And verie well of worthines."

---

[1] Lines 1335–36: *On the point of raging so [much] / that no man might calm his anger*

[2] *Should he escape, we'll be dishonored*

	That to the eirth scho rushit doun	*tumbled*
1380	And lay intill ane deidlie swoun.	*in a deadly faint*
	Be that the regent of the land	*Then*
	Fra Edinburgh come fast rydand:	
	Sir Anthonie Darsie wes his name,	
	Ane knicht of France and man of fame,	
1385	Quhilk had the guiding haillilie	
	Under Johne, Duke of Albanie,	
	Quhilk wes to our young king tutour,	
	And of all Scotland governour.	
	Our king was bot fyve yeiris of age,	
1390	That time quhen done wes the outrage.	
	Quhen this gude knicht the squyer saw	
	Thus lyand intill his deid thraw,	*in his death throes*
	"Wo is me," quod he, "to see this sicht	
	On thee, quhilk worthie wes and wicht!	*who; hardy*
1395	Wald God that I had bene with thee	
	As thow in France was anis with me	*once*
	Into the land of Picardy,	
	Quhair Inglis men had greit invy	*desire*
	To have me slane, sa they intendit,	
1400	Bot manfullie thow me defendit	
	And vailyeandlie did save my lyfe.	
	Was never man with sword nor knyfe —	
	Nocht Hercules, I dar weill say —	
	That ever faucht better for ane day,	
1405	Defendand me within ane stound:	*an instant*
	Thow dang seir sutheroun to the ground.	*struck many*
	I may thee mak no help, allace,	
	Bot I sall follow on the chace	
	Richt spedilie, baith day and nicht,	
1410	Till I may get that cruell knicht.	
	I mak ane vow: gif I may get him,	
	In till ane presoun I sall set him,	*prison*
	And quhen I heir that thow beis deid,	
	Than sall my handis straik of his heid."	
1415	With that he gave his hors the spurris,	
	And spedelie flaw ovir the furris.	*flew; furrows*
	He and his gaird with all thair micht	
	They ran till thai ovirtuik the knicht.	
	Quhen he approchit, he lichtit doun,	
1420	And like ane vailyeand campioun,	
	He tuik the tyrane presonar,	*villain prisoner*
	And send him backward to Dumbar,	*back*
	And thair remainit in presoun	
	Ane certane time in that dungeoun.	
1425	Let him ly thair with mekill cair,	

	And speik we of our heynd squyar,	*gentle*
	Of quhome we can not speik bot gude.	
	Quhen he lay bathand in his blude,	
	His freindis and his ladie fair,	
1430	They maid for him sic dule and cair	*sorrow and grief*
	Quhilk wer greit pietie to deploir:	*lament*
	Of that matter I speik no moir.	
	Thay send for leiches haistelie,	*physicians*
	Syne buir his bodie tenderlie	*carried*
1435	To ludge into ane fair ludgyne,	*lodge; lodging*
	Quhair he ressavit medicyne.	
	The greitest leichis of the land	*physicians*
	Come all to him without command,	*without being asked*
	And all practikis on him provit,	*And exercised all [their] skills on him*
1440	Becaus he was sa weill belovit.	
	Thay tuik on hand his life to save,	*tried*
	And he thame gaif quhat they wald have.	
	Bot he sa lang lay into pane,	*in*
	He turnit to be ane chirurgiane,	*surgeon*
1445	And als be his naturall ingyne,	*innate ability*
	He lernit the art of medicyne.	
	He saw thame on his bodie wrocht,	
	Quhairfoir the science wes deir bocht.	*knowledge*
	Bot efterward quhen he was haill,	*healed*
1450	He spairit na coist nor yit travaill	*effort*
	To preif his practikis on the pure,	*exercise; skills; poor*
	And on thame previt monie ane cure	*brought about*
	On his expensis, without rewaird —	
	Of money he tuik na regaird.	*had no care*

	Yit sum thing will we commoun mair	*discuss*
1455	Of this ladie quhilk maid greit cair,	
	Quhilk to the squyer wes mair pane	
	Nor all his woundis, in certane.	*Than*
	And than hir freindis did conclude,	
1460	Becaus scho micht to him na gude	
	That scho suld take hir leif and go	*leave*
	Till hir cuntrie, and scho did so.	
	Bot thir luiferis met never agane,	*these lovers*
	Quhilk wes to thame ane lestand pane,	*lasting pain*
1465	For scho aganis hir will wes maryit,	*married*
	Quhairthrow hir weird scho daylie waryit.[1]	
	Howbeit hir bodie wes absent,	*Although*
	Hir tender hart wes ay present	

---

[1] *On account of which she cursed her fate daily*

	Baith nicht and day with hir squyar:	
1470	Wes never creature that maid sic cair.	
	Penelope for Ulisses,	
	I wait, had never mair distres,	*I am sure*
	Nor Cresseid for trew Troylus	
	Wes not tent part sa dolorous.	*a tenth part*
1475	I wait it wes aganis hir hart	
	That scho did from hir lufe depart.	
	Helene had not sa mekill noy	*distress*
	Quhen scho perforce wes brocht to Troy.	
	I leif hir than with hart full sore,	*leave*
1480	And speik now of this squyer more.	

	Quhen this squyer wes haill and sound,	
	And softlie micht gang on the ground,	*slowly*
	To the regent he did complane.	
	Bot he, allace, wes richt sone slane	*i.e., the regent*
1485	Be David Hume of Wedderburne,	
	The quhilk gart monie Frenchemen murne,	*Which caused*
	For thair was nane mair nobill knicht,	
	Mair vailyeand, mair wys, mair wicht,	*valiant*
	And sone efter that crueltie,	
1490	The knicht was put to libertie,	
	The quhilk the squyer had opprest:	
	Sa wes his matter left undrest	*unresolved*
	Becaus the king was young of age,	
	Than tyrannis rang into thair rage,[1]	
1495	Bot efterward, as I hard say,	
	On Striviling brig upon ane day,	*Stirling bridge*
	This knight wes slane with crueltie,	
	And that day gat na mair mercie	
	Nor he gaif to the young squyar.	*Than*
1500	I say na mair, let him ly thair:	
	For cruell men, ye may weill see,	
	They end ofttimes with crueltie.	
	For Christ to Peter said this word:	
	"Quha ever straikis with ane sword,	
1505	That man sal be with ane sword slane."	
	That saw is suith, I tell yow plane.	*saying is true; honestly*
	He menis, quha straikis cruellie	
	Aganis the law without mercie,	
	Bot this squyer to nane offendit,	
1510	Bot manfullie himself defendit.	
	Wes never man with sword nor knyfe	

---

[1] *The cruel men prevailed in their violence*

Micht saif thair honour and thair lyfe
As did the squyer all his dayis,
With monie terribill effrayis.   *With many awe-inspiring assaults*
1515   Wald I at lenth his lyfe declair,   *Were I to; describe*
I micht weill writ ane uther quair.   *book*
Bot at this time I may not mend it,   *rectify this*
Bot shaw yow how the squyer endit.

Thair dwelt in Fyfe ane agit lord   *elderly*
1520   That of this squyer hard record,   *heard [an] account*
And did desire richt hartfullie   *sincerely*
To have him in his companie,
And send for him with diligence,   *assiduously*
And he come with obedience,
1525   And lang time did with him remane,
Of quhome this agit lord was fane.   *With; delighted*
Wyse men desiris commounlie
Wyse men into thair companie,
For he had bene in monie ane land —
1530   In Flanderis, France and in Ingland —
Quhairfoir the lord gaif him the cure   *running*
Of his houshald, I yow assure,
And in his hall cheif merschall,   *marshal*
And auditour of his comptis all.   *accounts*
1535   He was ane richt courticiane,   *courtier*
And in the law ane practiciane,   *practitioner*
Quhairfoir during this lordis lyfe,
Tchyref depute he wes in Fyfe,   *Sheriff-Depute*
To everie man ane equall judge,
1540   And of the pure he wes refuge,   *poor*
And with justice did thame support,
And curit thair sairis with greit comfort.   *afflictions*
For as I did reheirs before,
Of medicine he tuke the lore   *learned the art*
1545   Quhen he saw the chirurgience   *physicians*
Upon him do thair diligence.   *practice their art*
Experience maid him perfyte,   *fully versed*
And of the science tuke sic delyte
That he did monie thriftie cure,   *successful*
1550   And speciallie upon the pure,   *poor*
Without rewaird for his expensis,
Without regaird or recompencis.   *payment*
To gold, to silver, or to rent,   *income*
This nobill squyer tuke litill tent.   *paid little heed*
1555   Of all this warld na mair he craifit,   *desired*
Sa that his honour micht be saifit.   *So long as; preserved*
And ilk yeir for his ladies saik,   *every*

Ane banket royall wald he maik,
And that he maid on the Sonday
1560 Precedand to Asch Wednisday,
With wyld foull, venisoun and wyne;
With tairt, and flaun, and frutage fyne;   *tart; flawn (see note); fruit*
Of bran and geill thair wes na skant,[1]
And ipocras he wald not want.   *spiced sweetened wine*
1565 I have sene sittand at his tabill   *sitting*
Lordis and lairdis honorabill,
With knichtis and monie ane gay squyar
Quhilk wer to lang for to declair,   *Which would take too long to describe*
With mirth, musick and menstrallie.   *minstrelsy*
1570 All this he did for his ladie,
And for hir saik during his lyfe
Wald never be weddit to ane wyfe.
And quhen he did declyne to age,
He faillit never of his courage.
1575 Of ancient storyis for to tell,
Abone all uther he did precell,   *He did surpass all others*
Sa that everilk creature   *every person*
To heir him speik thay tuke plesure.
Bot all his deidis honorabill,
1580 For to descryve I am not abill.   *set down*
Of everie man he was commendit,   *By; praised*
And as he leivit, sa he endit,   *lived*
Plesandlie till he micht indure,   *as long as; go on*
Till dolent deith come to his dure,   *distressing; death; door*
1585 And cruellie with his mortall dart,
He straik the squyer throw the hart.
His saull with joy angelicall,   *soul*
Past to the hevin imperiall:
Thus at the Struther into Fyfe,
1590 This nobill squyer loist his lyfe.
I pray to Christ for to convoy   *lead*
All sic trew luiferis to his joy.   *such; lovers*
Say ye Amen, for cheritie:
Adew! Ye sall get na mair of me.   *Adieu (Fr. farewell)*

FINIS.

---

[1] *Of meat ("brawn") and jelly there was no lack*

THE TESTAMENT OF THE NOBILL AND VAILYEAND
SQUYER WILLIAME MELDRUM OF THE BYNNIS

Compylit be Sir David Lyndesay of the Mont etc.

	The holie man Job, ground of pacience,	*essence*
	In his greit trubill trewlie did report	
	Quhilk I persave now be experience:	*That which*
	That mennis lyfe in eirth bene wounder short.	
5	My youth is gane, and eild now dois resort;	*settle in*
	My time is gane; I think it bot ane dreame,	
	Yit efter deith remane sall my gude fame.	*reputation*

	I persave shortlie that I man pay my det:	*must; debt*
	To me in eirth no place bene permanent.	
10	My hart on it no mair now will I set,	
	Bot with the help of God omnipotent,	
	With resolute mind go mak my testament,	
	And tak my leif at cuntriemen, and kyn,	*take my leave of*
	And all the warld: and thus I will begyn.	

15	Thrie lordis to me sal be executouris,	
	Lindesayis all thrie, in surname of renoun.	
	Of my testament thay sall have hail the cure,	*the whole responsibility*
	To put my mind till executioun.	*To execute my wishes*
	That surname failyeit never to the croun:	*failed*
20	Na mair will thay to me, I am richt sure,	
	Quhilk is the caus that I give them the cure.	*responsibility*

	First, David Erll of Craufuird, wise and wicht,	*brave (strong)*
	And Johne Lord Lindesay, my maister speciall.	
	The thrid sal be ane nobill travellit knicht,	*well-traveled*
25	Quhilk knawis the coistis of feistis funeral;	*Who; funeral ceremonies*
	The wise Sir Walter Lindesay they him cal,	
	Lord of St Johne, and knicht of Torfichane,	
	Be sey and land ane vailyeand capitane.	*sea; valiant*

	Thocht age hes maid my bodie impotent,	*Although*
30	Yit in my hart hie courage doeth precell,	*great; is pre-eminent*
	Quhairfoir I leif to God with gude intent	*For which reason*
	My spreit, the quhilk he hes maid immortall,	*Which*

219

Intill his court perpetuallie to dwell,   *In*
And nevir moir to steir furth of the steid,   *go forth from that place*
35   Till Christ discend and judge baith quick and deid.   *living and dead*

I yow beseik, my lordis executouris,
My geir geve till the nixt of my kynrent.[1]
It is weill kend, I never tuik na cures   *known; cared about*
Of conquessing of riches nor of rent: *Acquiring; revenue*
40   Dispone as ye think maist expedient.   *Deal with it*
I never tuik cure of gold more than of glas —   *cared; glass*
Without honour, fy fy upon riches!

I yow requeist, my freindis ane and all,   *request; friends*
And nobill men of quhome I am descendit,
45   Faill not to be at my feist funerall,   *funeral ceremony*
Quhilk throw the warld I traist sal be commendit.   *praised*
Ye knaw how that my fame I have defendit   *reputation*
During my life unto this latter hour,
Quhilk suld to yow be infinit plesour.

50   First, of my bowellis clenge my bodie clene,   *bowels cleanse*
Within and out, syne wesche it weill with wyne,   *Inside and out*
Bot honestie see that nothing be sene;[2]
Syne clois it in ane coistlie carvit schryne   *Then enclose; coffin*
Of ceder treis, or of cyper fyne.   *cedar; cypress*
55   Anoynt my corps with balme delicious,
With cynamome and spycis precious.   *cinnamon*

In twa caissis of gold and precious stanis   *receptacles*
Inclois my hart and toung richt craftelie;   *skillfully*
My sepulture, syne, gar mak for my banis   *have made; bones*
60   Into the tempill of Mars triumphandlie,   *In*
Of marbill stanis carvit richt curiouslie,   *exquisitely*
Quhairin my kist and banis ye sall clois   *coffin; enclose*
In that triumphand tempill to repois.   *rest*

Mars, Venus and Mercurius, all thre
65   Gave me my natural inclinatiounis,
Quhilk rang the day of my nativitie,   *Who were dominant*
And sa thair hevinlie constellatiounis   *planetary influences*
Did me support in monie natiounis.
Mars maid me hardie like an feirs lyoun,   *fierce lion*
70   Quhairthrow I conqueist honour and renoun.   *gained*

---

[1] *Give my possessions to my next of kin*

[2] *Ensure that nothing except that which is respectable be seen*

Quho list to knaw the actis bellical,   *wishes; war-like acts*
Let thame go reid the legend of my life.
Thair sall thai find the deidis martiall,
How I have stand in monie stalwart strife   *stood; valiant*
75   Victoriouslie, with speir, sheild, sword and knife:
Quhairfoir to Mars, the god armipotent,   *So; powerful in arms*
My corps incloisit ye do till him present.   *enclosed body; to*

Mak offering of my toung rhetoricall   *tongue*
Till Mercurius, quhilk gaif me eloquence,
80   In his tempill to hing perpetuall: *hang forever*
I can mak him na better recompence,
For quhen I was brocht to the presence
Of kings in Scotland, Ingland and in France,
My ornate toung my honour did avance.

85   To fresche Venus my hart ye sall present,
Quhilk hes to me bene ay comfortabill,   *pleasant*
And in my face sic grace scho did imprent,
All creatures did think me amiabill.   *attractive*
Wemen to me scho maid sa favorabill,
90   Wes never ladie that luikit in my face,   *looked*
Bot honestlie I did obtene her grace.

My freind Sir David Lyndsay of the Mont
Sall put in ordour my processioun.
I will that thair pas formest in the front   *first*
95   To beir my penseil ane wicht campioun;   *[a small pennon]; brave champion*
With him ane band of Mars his religioun —[1]
That is to say, in steid of monkis and freiris —
In gude ordour ane thowsand hagbutteris.   *(see note)*

Nixt them, ane thowsand futemen in ane rout   *After; in a troop*
100 With speir and sheild, with buckler, bow and brand,   *sword*
In ane luferay, young stalwart men and stout.   *In the same livery*
Thridlie in ordour thair sall cum ane band
Of nobill men, abill to wraik thair harmes,   *avenge their wrongs*
Thair capitane with my standart in his hand,
105 On bairdit hors ane hundreth men of armes.   *caparisoned horses*
Amang that band my baner sal be borne
Of silver schene, thrie otteris into sabill,   *bright; in black*
With tabroun, trumpet, clarioun and horne,   *tabor (drum)*
For men of armes verie convenabill.   *appropriate*

---

[1] *With him a band of those of Mars' religion*

110   Nixt efter them, ane campioun honorabill
        Sall beir my basnet with my funerall;   *helm*
        Syne efter him, in ordour triumphall,

        My arming sword, my gluifis of plait and sheild,
        Borne be ane forcie campioun or ane knicht,   *powerful*
115   Quhilk did me serve in monie dangerous feild.
        Nixt efter him, ane man in armour bricht
        Upon ane jonet or ane cursour wicht,   *Spanish horse*
        The quhilk sal be ane man of greit honour,
        Upon ane speir to beir my coit armour.   *coat of arms*

120   Syne nixt my beir sall cum my corspresent —
        My bairdit hors, my harnes, and my speir —   *caparisoned horse; armor*
        With sum greit man of my awin kynrent,   *own family*
        As I wes wont on my bodie to beir
        During my time quhen I went to the weir,
125   Quhilk sal be offerit with ane gay garment
        To Mars his preist at my interrement.

        Duill weidis I think hypocrisie and scorne,   *Mourning attire*
        With huidis heklit doun ovirthort thair ene: *(see note)*
        With men of armes my bodie sal be borne.
130   Into that band see that no blak be sene: *Within*
        My luferay sal be reid, blew, and grene;   *livery*
        The reid for Mars, the grene for freshe Venus,
        The blew for lufe of god Mercurius.

        About my beir sall ryde ane multitude   *bier (coffin)*
135   All of ane luferay of my cullouris thrie —
        Erles and lordis, knichtis and men of gude,   *men of substance*
        Ilk barroun beirand in his hand on hie   *carrying; high*
        Ane lawrer branche in signe of victorie,   *laurel*
        Because I fled never out of the feild,
140   Nor yit as presoner unto my fois me yeild.   *foes*

        Agane that day faill not to warne and call   *In preparation for*
        All men of musick and of menstrallie,   *minstrelsy*
        About my beir with mirthis musicall,
        To dance and sing with hevinlie harmonie,
145   Quhais plesant sound redound sall in the sky.   *echo*
        My spreit I wait sal be with mirth and joy: *soul; know*
        Quhairfoir with mirth my corps ye sal convoy.   *Thus; escort*

        This beand done and all thing reulit richt,   *being; conducted properly*
        Than plesantlie mak your progressioun,
150   Quhilk I beleif sal be ane plesant sicht.

Se that ye thoill na preist in my processioun   *allow*
Without he be of Venus professioun,   *Unless*
Quhairfoir gar warne al Venus chapel clarks   *do summon*
Quhilk hes bene most exercit in hir warkis.[1]

155   With ane bischop of that religioun,
Solemnitlie gar thame sing my saull mes;[2]
With organe, timpane, trumpet and clarion   *drum or tambourine*
To shaw thair musick, dewlie them addres.
I will that day be hard no hevines: *heard*
160   I will na service of the requiem
Bot "Alleluya," with melodie and game.

Efter the evangell and the offertour,   *Gospel; offertory*
Throw all the tempill gar proclame silence:
Than to the pulpet gar ane oratour   *have*
165   Pas up, and schaw in oppin audience,   *declaim publicly*
Solempnitlie, with ornate eloquence,
At greit laser the legend of my life,   *leisure*
How I have stand in monie stalwart strife.   *stood; valiant*

Quhen he hes red my buik fra end till end,
170   And of my life maid trew narratioun,
All creature, I wait, will me commend,   *I know*
And pray to God for my salvatioun.
Than efter this solempnizatioun
Of service, and all brocht to end,
175   With gravitie than with my bodie wend,   *travel*

And clois it up into my sepulture,
Thair to repois till the greit judgement,
The quhilk may not corrupt, I yow assure,   *Which*
Be vertew of the precious oyntment
180   Of balme, and uther spyces redolent.
Let not be rung for me that day saull knellis,
Bot greit cannounis gar them crak for bellis.

Ane thousand hakbuttis gar schute al at anis,
With swesche talburnis and trumpettis awfullie:[3]
185   Lat never spair the poulder, nor the stanis,   *(gun)powder; missiles*
Quhais thundring sound redound sall in the sky,   *Whose; shall echo*

---

[1] *Who have been most diligent in her works*

[2] *Solemnly have them sing my soul's mass*

[3] Lines 183–84: *Have a thousand hakbuts [portable guns] shoot all at once, / With Swiss tabors [i.e., a type of drum] and trumpets awe-inspiringly*

That Mars may heir quhair he triumphandlie
Abone Phebus is situate full evin,   *Above; directly*
Maist awfull god under the sternie hevin.   *starry*

190 And syne hing up above my sepulture   *hang*
My bricht harnes, my scheild and als my speir,   *armor*
Togidder with my courtlie coit armour,   *coat of arms*
Quhilk I wes wont upon my bodie beir
In France, in Ingland being at the weir;
195 My baner, basnet, with my temperall,   *helm*
As bene the use of feistis funerall.   *funeral ceremonies*

This beand done, I pray yow tak the pane   *being; trouble*
My epitaphe to writ upon this wyis,   *in this way*
Abone my grave in goldin letteris fyne: *Above*
200 "The maist invincibill weiriour heir lyis,
During his time quhilk wan sic laud and pryis   *praise and esteem*
That throw the hevinis sprang his nobil fame:
Victorious William Meldrum wes his name."

Adew my lordis, I may na langer tarie.
205 My Lord Lindesay, adew abone all uther:
I pray to God and to the Virgine Marie,
With your lady to leif lang in the Struther;
Maister Patrik with young Normand, your brother;
With my ladies, your sisteris al, adew —
210 My departing I wait weill ye will rew.   *regret*

Bot maist of all, the fair ladies of France,
Quhen thai heir tell but dout that I am deid,   *for certain*
Extreme dolour wil change thair countenance,
And for my saik will weir the murning weid.   *mourning attire*
215 Quhen thir novellis dois into Ingland spreide,   *these tidings*
Of Londoun than the lustie ladies cleir   *merry; beautiful*
Will for my saik mak dule and drerie cheir.   *mourn and grieve*

Of Craigfergus, my dayis darling, adew —   *Carrickfergus*
In all Ireland of feminine the flour.   *womankind*
220 In your querrell twa men of weir I slew   *soldiers*
Quhilk purposit to do yow dishonour.   *intended*
Ye suld have bene my spous and paramour,   *lover*
With rent and riches for my recompence,   *income; my reward*
Quhilk I refusit throw youth and insolence.

225 Fairweill ye lemant lampis of lustines   *shining lamps of loveliness*
Of fair Scotland, adew my ladies all:
During my youth, with ardent besines   *diligence*

Ye knaw how I was in your service thrall.   *enslaved*
Ten thowsand times adew, abone thame all,   *above*
230   Sterne of Stratherne, my ladie soverane   *Star of Strathearn*
For quhom I sched my blud with mekill pane.   *great suffering*

Yit wald my ladie luke at evin and morrow
On my legend at lenth, scho wald not mis
How for hir saik I sufferit mekill sorrow.   *great*
235   Yit give I micht at this time get my wis,   *Yet if; wish*
Of hir sweit mouth, deir God, I had ane kis: *I would have*
I wis in vane. Allace, we will dissever.   *wish; part*
I say na mair, sweit hart — adew for ever.

Brether in armes, adew in generall;   *Brothers*
240   For me I wait your hartis bene full soir.
All trew companyeounis into speciall,   *in particular*
I say to yow adew for evermoir,
Till that we meit agane with God in gloir.
Sir Curat, now gif me incontinent   *Sir Priest; right away*
245   My crysme with the holie sacrament.

My spreit hartlie I recommend   *earnestly*
In manus tuas, Domine.   *Into your hands, Lord*
My hoip to the is till ascend,   *hope*
Rex, quia redemisti me,   *King, because you have redeemed me*
250   Fra syn *resurrexisti me,*   *From sin you have restored me*
Or ellis my saull had bene forlorne.
With sapience *docuisti me,*   *With wisdom you have taught me*
Blist be the hour that thow wes borne.

FINIS.

ABBREVIATIONS: **A**: Edinburgh, Heir of Andrew Anderson, 1683 (Wing L2322); *Acts of Council (Public Affairs)*: *Acts of the Lords of Council in Public Affairs*; **AN**: Anglo-Norman; *AND*: *Anglo-Norman Dictionary*; **Bawcutt and Riddy**: *Longer Scottish Poems Vol. 1*, ed. Bawcutt and Riddy; *Bruce*: Barbour, *The Bruce*, ed. McDiarmid and Stevenson; **C**: Edinburgh: Henrie Charteris, 1594 (STC [2nd ed.] 15679); *Cal. State Papers (Venice)*: *Calendar of State Papers and Manuscripts relating to English Affairs*; *Clariodus*: *Clariodus; A Metrical Romance*, ed. Irving; **CT**: Chaucer, *The Canterbury Tales*, ed. Benson; *DOST*: *Dictionary of the Older Scottish Tongue*; **EETS**: Early English Text Society; *ER*: *The Exchequer Rolls of Scotland*; **Hadley Williams**: Lyndsay, *Sir David Lyndsay: Selected Poems*, ed. Hadley Williams; **Hamer**: Lyndsay, *The Works of Sir David Lindsay*, ed. Hamer; *Hary's Wallace*: Hary, *The Wallace*, ed. McDiarmid; **L**: Edinburgh: Richard Lawson, 1610 (STC [2nd ed.] 15680); *LP Henry VIII*: *Letters and Papers, Foreign and Domestic, of the Reign of Henry VIII*; *MdnE*: Modern English; **ME**: Middle English; *MED*: *Middle English Dictionary*; *NIMEV*: *New Index of Middle English Verse*; **NLS**: Edinburgh, National Library of Scotland; **NRS**: National Records of Scotland; *ODNB*: *Oxford Dictionary of National Biography*; **OE**: Old English; *OED*: *Oxford English Dictionary*; **OF**: Old French; *PH*: Douglas, *Palis of Honoure*, ed. Parkinson; *Poems*: Dunbar, *Poems of William Dunbar*, ed. Bawcutt; *Reg. Mag. Sig.*: *Registrum Magni Sigilli Regum Scotorum (Register of the Great Seal of Scotland)*; *Reg. Sec. Sig.*: *Registrum Secreti Sigilli Regum Scotorum (Register of the Privy Seal of Scotland)*; **RPS**: Records of the Parliament of Scotland; **S**: Glasgow: Robert Sanders, 1683 (Wing L2322); *STC*: *A Short-Title Catalogue of Books Printed in England, Scotland and Ireland and English Books Printed Abroad 1473–1640*, ed. Pollard and Redgrave; **STS**: Scottish Text Society; *TA*: *Accounts of the Lord High Treasurer of Scotland*, ed. Dickson and Paul; *TC*: Chaucer, *Troilus and Criseyde*, ed. Benson; *Testament*: *Testament of Squyer Meldrum*; **Whiting**: Whiting, *Proverbs, Sentences and Proverbial Sayings from English Writings Before 1500*; **Wing**: Wing, *Short-Title Catalogue of Books Printed in England, Scotland and Ireland, Wales and British America and of English Books Printed in Other Countries 1641–1700*.

Textual notes are so few that they have been included here rather than listed separately. All translations are mine unless otherwise specified.

4   *Quhilk suld to us be richt mirrouris.* The injunction to emulate the noble deeds of ancestors is a common way to open any romance, epic, or chivalry biography which purports to tell of historical personages, as with these lines from *Florimond of Albany*:

        Quha blythlie will of elderris reid
        And tak exemple of þair gude deid,

> He may greitlie avansit be
> Give he will follov þair bounte
> (ed. Purdie, lines 5–9, p. 87)

or the more admonitory opening lines of *Hary's Wallace*:

> Our antecessowris that we suld of reide
> And hald in mynde, thar nobille worthi deid
> We lat ourslide throw werray sleuthfulnes,
> And castis ws euir till vthir besynes.
> (1.1–4)

"To make a mirror of the falling of another," meanwhile, was proverbial (see Whiting M581). "Now maik ōour merour be me, all maner of man" laments the shamed owl in Richard Holland's fifteenth-century Scots *Buke of the Howlat* (line 970). A variant of this sentiment is the injunction to look into one's own mirror for the self-knowledge that might help to avoid sin, as when the hideous ghost of Guinevere's mother warns her daughter to "Muse on þi mirrour" in the *Awntyrs off Arthure at the Terne Wathelyn* (line 167). The use of the phrase by the heroic leader Golagros after he has been defeated by Gawain combines the strength to be derived from self-reflection with the warning example of his own misfortune:

> Ilk man my kyth be his cure ["recognise through his study"]
> Baith knyght, king, and empriour,
> And muse in his myrrour,
> And mater maist mine is. ["and mine is the greatest example"]
> (lines 1232–35)

Meldrum, too, will eventually suffer a terrible reversal of fortune in battle.

13–22   *Sum wryt of . . . . in weirlie weidis.* The types of hero are listed in careful order of precedence: conquerors, emperors; kings, champions, and knights; and finally unknighted squires such as Meldrum. Although this might seem to belittle Meldrum's status, the later Middle Ages saw more than one squire who was greatly respected for his martial prowess but nevertheless remained unknighted, whether to avoid the considerable expense involved or simply because they saw the title of squire as sufficiently prestigious (see Keen, *Chivalry*, pp. 144–45). Stevenson gives the Scottish example of Patrick Crichton of Cranstonriddel, who became keeper of Edinburgh Castle in 1495, held a number of royal offices, and sat in parliament in 1513 (*Chivalry and Knighthood in Scotland*, p. 39). Wyntoun's *Original Chronicle*, describing the siege of Norham in 1355, notes:

> Twa gud sqwyaris, for suyth I heicht,
> Off Scottis men deit in þat feicht:
> Ane was Iohun of Haliburton*e*,
> A nobil sqwyar of gret ranowne;
> Iames Turnbuyl þe toþir wes.
> Þar saulis to Paradise mot passe.
> (Cotton MS, 6:209, 8.6571–76)

On the other hand, it was still quite common practice for kings or military leaders to knight followers who had performed the kind of exemplary military service that Meldrum apparently did in France. It is also unusual for a romance — the literary paradigm followed in this passage — to have a squire rather than a knight as its hero, although one famous example is the late fifteenth-century English romance *The Squire of Low Degree*: for later allusions to this romance, see notes to lines 907–26 below.

24–26   *As Chauceir wrait . . . . and of Medea*. Lyndsay follows in the tradition of Scottish poets such as Henryson, Dunbar, and Douglas with this implicit invitation to compare his poetry to Chaucer's, which was held up as the gold standard of elegant "Inglis" verse: see Henryson, *Testament of Cresseid*, line 41; Dunbar, *Goldyn Targe*, lines 253–61; *PH*, lines 919–20. *Troilus and Criseyde* was Chaucer's most admired work in the late medieval period.

Neither of the pairs of lovers cited here bodes well: Troilus is forsaken by his love Cressida, while Jason abandons Medea after using her to win the golden fleece. Chaucer stops his version of the tale there in his "Legend of Medea" (*Legend of Good Women*, ed. Benson, lines 1580–1679) but Gower's more gripping version includes Medea's terrible revenge of burning Jason's new wife Creusa to death and murdering the two sons of their own union (*Confessio Amantis*, ed. Peck, 5.3247–4222).

27   *Cleo*. Clio is the muse of History and is therefore appropriate here: she was famously invoked by Chaucer in *TC* (2.8–14). Douglas writes in the *Palis of Honoure* of "Lady Cleo, quhilk craftely dois set / Historiis ald lyk as thay wer present" (lines 854–55), but Dunbar associates her with the writing of poetry more generally: "My Lady Cleo, that help of makaris bene" (*Goldyn Targe*, *Poems*, 1:186, line 77). In another poem roughly contemporary with the *Historie*, Lyndsay — no longer in playful mode — rejects all classical gods or muses as sources of inspiration in favor of God alone. He promises to write:

> Withoute ony vaine inuocatioun
> To Minerua or to Melpominee.
> Nor ōitt wyll I mak supplicatioun,
> For help, to Cleo nor Caliopee:
> Sick marde Musis may mak me no supplee   *[confounded; assistance]*
> (*Ane Dialogue betuix Experience and ane Courteour*, ed. Hamer, 1:204, lines 216–20)

28   *Minerve*. Minerva is the goddess of wisdom. In James I's *Kingis Quair*, the narrator is led to her by the personification "Good Hope" after he has visited Venus (lines 778 ff.). In Douglas' *Palis of Honoure*, the first procession seen by the narrator is that of Minerva, surrounded by mainly classical and biblical figures of prophecy, learning, and wisdom: "Yone is the Quene of Sapience, but dout, / Lady Minerve" (lines 241–42).

30–34   *Quhais douchtines during . . . . did me schaw*. Lyndsay's assurance that he can personally attest to the squire's levels of valor is combined with the revelation that Meldrum himself has supplied all the details that Lyndsay "did not knaw."

On the one hand, this invokes the great authority of eyewitness testimony. On the other, Lyndsay thereby reveals that, for at least some of this history, there is no authority other than Meldrum's own word. Meldrum's tendency to sing his own praises will be vividly dramatized in the *Testament*.

36   *Descryve the deidis and the man*. A glancing allusion to the opening phrase of Virgil's *Aeneid*, *Arma virumque cano* ("I sing of arms and the man . . ."), translated by Gavin Douglas in his *Eneados* of 1513 as "The batalis and the man I wil discrive" (2:19, line 1). This reference to the empire-founding Aeneas (and indirectly also to the brilliance of Virgil's poetry) makes lines 37–38 something of an anti-climax: Meldrum "spent his youth in love most pleasantly, without [incurring] disgrace," although Lyndsay does then add that he performed "douchtie deidis" too (line 39). See note to lines 875–80 below for a more direct comparison of Meldrum to Aeneas.

48–64   *Sir Lancelote du Lake . . . . cum na gude*. The story of Lancelot and Guinevere's affair was clearly well known in Lyndsay's Scotland. The *Complaynt of Scotland* of c. 1550 cites a "lancelot du lac" (ed. Stewart, p. 50 [fol. 50v]) which may or may not refer to the fifteenth-century Older Scots *Lancelot of the Laik*. This romance, incomplete in its only extant copy, is based on material from the OF non-cyclical *Lancelot du Lac* and it recounts some of Lancelot's youthful exploits and the early stages of his affair with Guinevere — appropriately enough for this comparison to the young Meldrum. Although Lancelot is a positive figure in the Older Scots *Lancelot*, Cooper argues that the relative dearth of Lancelot material in medieval *English* literature before Malory may indicate a populace for whom "Lancelot, if they had heard of him at all, was merely one of the minor knights; and to whom any ideas of Arthur's incest and Lancelot's adultery with Guinevere were either unknown, or else regarded as slanderous French fictions" ("The *Lancelot-Grail Cycle* in England," p. 153). Lyndsay's dig at Lancelot foreshadows Roger Ascham's famous condemnation of Malory's *Morte Darthur* as a danger to the young and the gullible (though an appropriate source of amusement for the wise): "the whole pleasure of which booke standeth in two speciall poyntes, in open mans slaughter, and bold bawdrye: In which booke those be counted the noblest Knightes, that do kill most men without any quarell, and commit fowlest aduoulteries by subtlest shiftes: as Sir *Launcelote*, with the wife of king *Arthure* his master . . . This is good stuffe, for wise men to laughe at, or honest men to take pleasure at" (*The Scholemaster*, ed. Wright, p. 231).

50   *sword nor knyfe*. See lines 156–60 where Meldrum dispatches his opponent with a dagger once his sword has shattered. The phrase itself is conventional and recurs here at lines 795, 1300, 1363, 1402, 1511. Compare the *Bruce*: "Yai seruyt yaim on sa gret wane / With scherand swerdis and with knyffis / Yat weile ner all left ye lyvys" ("They served them so plentifully with slicing swords and with knives that almost all lost their lives"; 16.458–60).

67–69   *Ane gentilman of . . . . nobilnes lineallie discendit*. Hamer notes that "the marriage of Meldrum daughters with nobility was not uncommon throughout their history" (3:189). In his *History of Greater Britain* of 1521, the Scottish Unionist scholar John Major remarked of the Scots that "they take inordinate pleasure in noble birth, and . . . delight in hearing themselves spoken of as come of noble blood" (p. 45). Nevertheless, while late medieval English society tended to distinguish between nobility and mere gentry, social demarcations in Scotland seem to have been less rigid (see Wormald, "Lords and Lairds in Fifteenth-Century Scotland," pp. 181–200). See further note to line 1566 below.

75   *Cleische and Bynnis.* On squire Meldrum's estates, see the Introduction, "Squire of Cleish and Binns."

79   *Proportionat weill; of mid stature.* Compare Barbour's description of Thomas Randolph, earl of Moray: "He wes off mesurabill [medium] statur / And weile porturat at mesur [fashioned proportionately]" (*Bruce*, 10.285–86). The *Buik of King Alexander the Conquerour* attributed to Gilbert Hay includes a lengthy disquisition on "phisnomye," or how to assess men by the details of their appearance (ed. Cartwright, 3:22–31, lines 10108–483), and it speaks approvingly of the man who "haldis gude mesure in all his proportioun, / Off hede, of body, of lymmes vp and doun" and is "Nor hie nor law, nor fatt nor lene alsua," because "In mydlin way þe wertew is evir neist [most present]" (ed. Cartwright, 3:29–30, lines 10408–09, 10421, and 10433).

Nevertheless, it is more common for heroes to be described as tall and broad. Hary says of Wallace that "Ix quartaris large he was in lenth indeid. / Thryd part that lenth in schuldrys braid was he" (*Hary's Wallace*, 10.1224–25: McDiarmid notes that this would make Wallace about seven feet tall, 2:256n1224).

88   *In Ingland first.* It is not entirely clear whether this reference to Meldrum's exercise of prowess "[i]n Ingland first" is meant to refer to the raid on Carrickfergus (an English-held town in Ireland, see lines 91 ff.), or if Lyndsay is alluding to events in Meldrum's past which are not narrated here. The latter is implied by Meldrum's extravagant farewell to the "lustie ladies cleir" of London in the *Testament*, line 216, but Meldrum's reliability as a "witness" to his own life has been called into question by that point.

90 ff.   *the kingis greit admirall.* James Hamilton, first earl of Arran (1475?–1529) was made commander of the Scottish fleet — thus "the kingis greit admirall" — in July 1513; he is named as the earl of Arran here in line 216 (see *ODNB*, "Hamilton, James, first earl of Arran (1475?–1529)" for details). The Scottish Navy left Leith on 25 July 1513 to sail for France in order to assist the French against Henry VIII, who had sailed for Calais in June 1513 (Macdougall, *James IV*, pp. 268–69). They took the longer route counter-clockwise around the island of Britain, apparently stopping in Ireland to bombard the English stronghold of Carrickfergus ("Craigfergus," line 95). It is not clear whether James IV had intended them to attack Carrickfergus along the way (Pitscottie assumed Arran was disobeying orders in hopes of private gain; *Historie and Cronicles*, ed. Mackay, 1:256–58, but see discussion in Macdougall, *James IV*, pp. 268–69), or if they were simply taking the longer route to avoid the English navy, who were lying in wait for them off the coast of Kent. Certainly the English navy had hoped to intercept them: *Hall's Chronicle*, a contemporary English chronicle written in the 1530s, records the English admiral Howard's disappointment that "he hadde

soughte the Scottyshe Nauye, then beynge on the sea, but he coulde not mete with theim, because they were fledde into Fraunce, be the coste of Irelande" (p. 558).

102–03   *Savit all wemen . . . . all preistis and freiris.* A chivalric obligation to protect women is cited in numerous manuals of chivalry, implied in numerous romances, and given explicit expression by Malory in the "Pentecostal oath" sworn by the knights of the Round Table at the end of "The Wedding of King Arthur": "allwayes to do ladyes, damesels, and jantilwomen and wydowes soccour, strengthe hem in hir ryghtes, and never to enforce them, uppon payne of dethe" (*Le Morte Darthur,* ed. Field, 1:97, lines 31–33). Malory shows little concern for protecting men of the Church, but the fifteenth-century Scottish translator of various chivalric treatises, Sir Gilbert Hay, is careful to include them in his *Buke of the Ordre of Knychthede* (a translation of a French version of Ramon Llull's *Llibre de l'orde de cavalleria*):

> Alssua be vertu of fayth and gude custumes / knychtis defendis the clerkis and
> kirk men fra wikkit tyrane men / the quhilk agaynis the faith / and for default
> of faith schapis thame to derob and our'thraw bathe clerkis and kirkmen.
> (Chapter 7, *Prose Works,* ed. Glenn, 3:40, lines 32–36)

The immediate model for Lyndsay may be Hary's Wallace, who similarly refuses to slay "wemen and barnys" or "preystis als that war nocht in the feild [i.e., who did not fight]" when skirmishing in France (*Hary's Wallace,* 9.647–52).

109   *naikit as scho was borne.* The squire's later demand that the soldiers return her "sark" shows that this is meant literally (see note to line 119 below).

119   *sark.* This is a "chemise." That the men have taken her "sark" is proof that she really is naked (line 109), since this is the item worn next to the skin, over top of which would go a "kirtill" (line 121). Compare Henryson's *The Garmont of Gud Ladeis*: "Hir sark suld be hir body nixt / Of chestetie so quhyt" (ed. Fox, p. 162, lines 9–10).

120   *And tak to yow all uther wark.* As Hamer notes, Meldrum here "allows the men their proper share of plunder," taking "wark" in the sense of "pieces of workmanship," i.e., the lady's costly outer clothing and jewelry (see *DOST wark* (n.), sense 7).

122   *ane garland of hir heid.* L's "ane garland on her head" seems at first glance to be the sensible reading here, but the maiden is at this point "naikit as scho was borne" (line 109), so the enameled gold garland "of" (i.e., "from") her head is evidently amongst the spoils that her attackers have stolen from her.

128   *quhyte as milk.* The tradition of describing a beautiful woman's skin as "white as milk" goes back at least as far as Geoffrey of Vinsauf's influential early thirteenth-century guide to writing elegant poetry, the *Poetria Nova* (trans. Nims, p. 37). See note to lines 944–49 below.

131   *Sanct Fillane.* St. Fáelán was an early Scottish confessor-saint whom an early Irish martyrology connects with Strathearn, the area of Perthshire to which Meldrum

himself will return in triumph after his career in France. Although his legend became conflated with Irish saints of the same name, St. Fillan's cult was well established in western Perthshire by the ninth century and his popularity was greatly enhanced in later medieval Scotland through Robert Bruce's devotion to him: later generations of Scots could evoke the spirit of Robert Bruce by swearing by him. See Taylor, "The Cult of St Fillan in Scotland." The fact that the maiden's attackers swear by St. Fillan indicates that they are not, in fact, enemy English soldiers, but Irish or (most probably) some of Meldrum's fellow Scots.

142   *from his harnes flew the fyre*. The image of blows so ferocious that they strike sparks from weapons or armor was conventional and presumably also realistic. See line 462 and *MED* "fir" (n.), sense 4b, for further examples.

195–96   *Ane lufe taking, / Ane riche rubie set in ane ring*. Rings as love tokens are a staple of medieval romance, often (though not always) magical. In *Ywain and Gawain*, the Middle English version of Chrétien's *Yvain*, Alundyne presents Ywain with a magical ring which he later loses (ed. Braswell, lines 1527–44); in *Perceval of Galles* the hero helps himself to a ring as love-token from the maiden in the tent (ed. Braswell, lines 471–76); in *Sir Gawain and the Green Knight*, Gawain refuses a ruby ring pressed upon him by Bertilak's amorous wife (ed. Tolkien and Gordon, lines 1817–23). Meldrum himself will accept another ruby ring love-token from the Lady of Gleneagles. See lines 1002–06.

205–06   *Suld I not . . . . and my honour*. It is hardly necessary to comment on the irony of the lady's wish to become Meldrum's lover (to "lufe him paramour") out of gratitude for his saving her "honour." The trope of an insistent maiden disappointed in her pursuit of the hero is a commonplace of romance: it will be repeated after the squire's military triumphs in France (lines 685–91) and once again invites comparison of Meldrum to Lancelot, although the unattached Meldrum has no particular reason for refusing these ladies. This creates a build-up for his great affair with the lady of Gleneagles, whose advances he will not refuse, but the implied parallel with Guinevere also hints at her part in his tragic fall. See note to lines 863–65 below.

216   *erle of Arrane*. See note to line 90 ff.

233   *munyeoun*. "darling, favourite, lover." From the French *mignon*, it is not recorded until the very end of the fifteenth century by *DOST* or the *OED*. The term is (though not always) used in a derogatory sense, whence ME "minion."

234   *Meik . . . lyk ane lame*. The description of a martial hero as being "meek like a lamb" off of the battlefield, contrasted with the ferocity of a lion on it (as at line 236), is more conventional than it might first appear. In the earlier twelfth century it was applied by St. Bernard of Clairvaux to the fledgling order of the Knights Templar in his *In Praise of the New Knighthood* (*De laude novae militae*), addressed to one of the order's founders, Hugh de Payens:

> Thus in a wondrous and unique manner they appear gentler than lambs, yet fiercer than lions. I do not know if it would be more appropriate to refer to them as monks or as soldiers, unless perhaps it would be better to recognize them as being both. (Clairvaux, *In Praise of the New Knighthood*, p. 48)

243   *pruifit.* C: *pruift.* L: *proued.* Although this word may well have been pronounced
        as a single syllable as Charteris spells it, the weak participial ending is otherwise
        spelled *-it* as if it were syllabic (as in the rhyme-pair "luifit," line 244) so this is
        almost certainly a simple error on Charteris' part.

245–53 *Hary the aught . . . . was daylie skirmishing.* Henry VIII had landed at Calais on 30
        June 1513, but the Scottish fleet only arrived off the French coast in
        mid-September. Henry celebrated his capture of the town of Thérouanne in late
        August and Tournai in late September of that year. He apparently received news
        of the English victory at Flodden while at Tournai before returning to Dover in
        late October 1513, undisturbed by the Franco-Scottish navy which meant to
        intercept him. This allows for a window of perhaps a month for Meldrum to
        have performed the "douchtie deidis" (line 230) that establish his reputation, up
        to and including his great battle against the English champion Talbart. On
        Henry's movements, see Scarisbrick, *Henry VIII*, pp. 35–38; the diary of John
        Taylor, clerk of the Parliament (*LP Henry VIII*, 1:626–27). On Scottish
        preparations for war, see Macdougall, *James IV*, pp. 264–76. On the
        Franco-Scottish navy, see Spont, *Letters and Papers*, pp. xliv, 185–89.

249   *The King of France his greit armie.* The king of France is Louis XII (d. 1 Jan
        1514/15). For the grammar of this phrase, see *DOST he* (pron.), sense 3c, *his*
        "substituted for the inflection *-is*."

265–71 *Thair was into . . . . for to avance.* Hamer suggests that "Maister Talbart" might be
        one Sir Humphrey Talbot, eldest son of Sir Gilbert Talbot who was then
        lieutenant or deputy of Calais, adding that "[h]is eldest son, Sir Humphrey, is
        not recorded in the State Papers, but he was known as "the Giant." He died on
        a pilgrimage to the Holy Land." Hadley Williams, uneasily registering Hamer's
        lack of support for this statement, points to the episode's similarity to the
        common romance trope of a fight with a giant, as does Kinsley. An outstanding
        example of giant-slaying on behalf of one's country is *Guy of Warwick*'s defeat of
        the Danish giant Colbrand for the grateful King Athelstan of England. In
        addition to the Middle English versions of Guy of Warwick, a separate ballad of
        Guy and Colebrande was in existence by the fifteenth century (see Purdie,
        Anglicising Romance, pp. 193–94).

        Hamer's unreferenced label of "the giant" for Sir Humphrey Talbot appears to
        derive from a 1569 visitation of officers of the College of Arms to Worcestershire.
        The section on "Talbot of Lacock" lists "Sir Gilbart Talbott . . . Lord Deputy of
        Callis" as having three children, the eldest of whom is listed as "Henrey Talbott
        fil[s] ob. s.p. [i.e., "died without issue"] (Sir Humphrey Talbott surnamed the
        Giant died in the Holy Land)" (*The Visitation*, ed. Phillimore, pp. 133–34). While
        this must be Hamer's source, it does not in itself cite any source for the
        information and there is no other record of this Henry or Humphrey Talbot's
        service in France. There are occasional references in *LP Henry VIII* to a son of
        Sir Gilbert Talbot serving in France, but they do not give a forename and seem
        likely to refer instead to his son Sir Gilbert "of Grafton" (see for example no.
        1692, *LP Henry VIII* 1:775–76), who may be the "Sir Gilbert Talbot the younger"

listed amongst the captains of the vanguard led by the earl of Shrewsbury (*LP Henry VIII*, 1:608, no. 4253 [16 June 1513]).

The most famous Talbot fighting in France is of course the earl of Shrewsbury himself, George Talbot. As well as being lieutenant of the vanguard in France in 1513, Shrewsbury was steward or master of the king's house, and was therefore occasionally referred to as "master Talbot," as for example in a blackletter pamphlet describing the meeting of Henry VIII with the French king Francis I at the Field of the Cloth of Gold in June 1520 (*LP Henry VIII* 3:303–06, no. 869 [11 June 1520]). The chivalric prestige of George, and of the Talbot earls of Shrewsbury more generally, is indicated by the Venetian ambassador Andrea Badoer in a letter of 1512 in which he describes him as being "of a noble and ancient family named Talbot, and to this day in France they still their babes by threatening them when they cry with the coming of the Talbots" (*Cal. State Papers (Venice)*, 2:75, no. 185). If either Meldrum or Lyndsay himself wished to exaggerate Meldrum's record of fighting in France, this "master Talbot" would be an ideal choice.

273–74   *And on his bonnet usit to beir / Of silver fyne takinnis of weir.* A "bonnet" often referred to a steel hat in this period: see Dunbar's description of the followers of Ire dressed "In iakkis and stryppis and bonettis of steill" ("in padded leather jerkins, steel splints and steel hats"; "Off Februar the fyiftene nycht," line 37, *Poems*, 1:150), or a 1539 certificate of the muster for Newcastle-upon-Tyne, which lists dozens of men equipped with "a steill bonnet," variously spelled, sometimes along with a "cot of playt" (Welford, *History of Newcastle and Gateshead*, pp. 174–94 [see pp. 186–92]). But it is difficult to imagine how such a bonnet might have borne silver "takinnis of weir," and Hadley Williams argues that Talbart is instead wearing "a fashionable bonnet decorated with jewels or Italian-inspired cap badges." A contemporary portrait of Sir Nicholas Carew in full jousting armor by Hans Holbein the Younger (1532–33) shows him wearing just such an elaborate cloth bonnet, complete with decorative pin (Hans, Younger Holbein, "Portrait"), and it might be noted that Meldrum sets out the next day wearing only "ane velvot cap" (line 377).

It is not clear what the silver "takinnis of weir" themselves are; they may be badges of his own arms and/or of St. George's cross (on the use of St. George's cross in the English army, see note to lines 424–45). Hadley Williams suggests they are the "spoils of war, or badges appropriate to his martial calling"; Hamer (3:195n271) notes only that they imply high status.

294   *Your crakkis I count thame not ane cute.* "I couldn't care less about your loud boasts." *DOST* traces the common expression "not ane cute" to the Middle Dutch *cote* ("ankle bone") as used in playing games, and notes that Dutch also uses the phrase *niet ene cote*.

297   *My gude chyld. DOST* cites this line under sense 2 of *child* (n.), "A lad or boy, a young fellow." The *OED* entry for *child* includes a more specific sense of "A young man of noble or gentle birth" (sense 3), and some of the citations from *DOST*'s sense 2 are listed there. Talbart's condescension is nevertheless clear

from his use of the familiar "thow" where Meldrum had used the formal "ye," and it is underlined at line 307 when he addresses Meldrum unambiguously as "my barne" (my child).

311–14 *David . . . . Golias*. The Biblical David's defeat of the Philistine Goliath (1 Kings 17:4–51) inspired his inclusion in the list of those models of chivalric virtue known collectively as the Nine Worthies. See the *Balletis of the Nine Nobles* in the present volume, "David slew michti Golias" (line 25), and the Introduction to that poem. The boastful coward "Fynlaw of the Fute Band" in Lyndsay's "Proclamatioun maid in Cowpar of Fyffe" (a preface to a 1552 performance in Cupar of his *Satyre of the Thrie Estaitis*, written especially for this local audience) also claims that "War golias in to this steid / I dowt nocht to stryk of his heid" (Hamer 2:30, lines 240–41).

317   *Gowmakmorne*. Goll mac Morna was one of the fearsome mythical warriors of the Ulster Fenian Cycle, and an enemy of the hero Fionn mac Cumhaill (see MacKillop, *Dictionary of Celtic Mythology*, pp. 228–29). Both figures were well known in the late medieval Scots-speaking world. In Barbour's *Bruce*, when Bruce and his small retinue escape from the superior forces of the Lord of Lorne, the latter resentfully observes, "Rycht as Golmakmorn was wone / To haiff fra [Fyn] all his megne, / Rycht swa all his fra ws has he" (3.68–70: "Just as Goll mac Morna used to get all his retinue away from Finn, so he [Bruce] got his away from us"). The narrator of Gavin Douglas' c. 1501 *Palis of Honoure* sees "Gret Gowmakmorne and Fyn Makcoull, and how / Thay suld be goddis in Ireland, as thay say" (lines 1715–16). The boastful Fynlaw of Lyndsay's Proclamatioun maid in Cowpar of Fyffe" is put to flight by what he believes to be "grit Gowmakmorne" (line 257). See note to lines 311–14 above.

319   *Montruill*. Kinsley thinks Lyndsay refers to Montreuil-sur-Mer in the Pas-de-Calais; Hamer thinks Montreuil-sur-Seine near Paris, over 200 km to the south (presumably because we are told that Henry's troops are in *Picardie* [line 250]). Montreuil-sur-Mer seems the most likely, given its proximity to Calais (see line 246) and the towns of Thérouanne and Tournai, which Henry VIII captured in August and September.

337   See note to line 294 above.

343   *Monsour de Obenie*. Robert Stewart (c. 1470–1544), latterly "d'Aubigny," was a younger son of the tenth or first earl of Lennox who served in Louis XII's army under his Franko-Scottish cousin, the Sir "Barnard Stewart" eulogized by Dunbar (*Poems* 1:177, and see note to the *Testament*, line 64). Robert inherited Bernard's seigneurie of Aubigny upon the latter's death in 1508, and was made captain of Louis XII's Scots guards in October 1512 (*ODNB*).

353   *it givis me in my hart*. *DOST* cites this line mistakenly under the basic sense of "give," but "to have misgivings" is clearly the sense intended, for which the *MED* offers two examples (*yēven* [v.], sense 26a). Kinsley notes a similar usage in *Bruce*, 19.97–98: "Myne hart giffis me no mor to be / With ōow duelland in this cuntre."

373–74   *He lap upon . . . his stirroppis richt.* A hero who leaps fully armed into the saddle is a common romance trope: see *Bevis of Hampton*, "Into the sadel a lippte, / That no stirop he ne drippte" (ed. Herzman et al., lines 1945–46) or, for a Scottish example, *Florimond of Albany*, "he but sturep on him sprang" (ed. Purdie, p. 102, line 474). Talbart does likewise at line 420: Meldrum will do it again at lines 472–76, explicitly "without support" and to the great delight of the Scottish spectators. It may not be a mere romance exaggeration; the biography of Jean le Maingre, marechal of France (d. 1421), records that as part of Jean's knightly training he would leap *sanz mettre le pié en l'estrief sus un coursier, armé de toutes pieces* ("fully armed onto a warhorse, without putting his foot in the stirrup") (*Jehan le Maingre*, ed. Lalande, p. 25).

          DOST does not record this reflexive sense of the verb *richt*, "sit/stand up straight," but see *MED righten* (v.), sense 1b.

384   *Ane otter in ane silver feild.* "An otter on a silver background." Meldrum's arms are also mentioned at lines 548–51 (when Meldrum and Talbart meet in battle) and — slightly different in detail — in the *Testament* (line 107). The silver background or "field" described at lines 384 and 548 may also be implied in Talbart's dream of a large black otter coming "fra the see" (line 403): the late fifteenth-century heraldic manual *The Deidis of Armorie* describes heraldic silver or white as being "lik to þe wattir, quhilk is ane of þe clerast and quhittast / and mast clene elementis þat is" (ed. Houwen, 1:11). McAndrew notes that the family of Meldrum of Fyvie (Aberdeenshire) are "surprisingly little researched genealogically and agreeably varied heraldically," and arms are also recorded for a branch of the family from Seggie in Fife (*Scotland's Historic Heraldry*, p. 449). All show some variant of a black otter, or otters, on a silver background, sometimes emerging from the sea. Closest to the squire's arms in the *Historie* are those of Meldrum of Fyvie: "Argent, a demi-otter sable issuant from a fess wavy azure, or Argent, a demi-otter sable issuant from the waves of the sea" (i.e., a silver background on which a black otter emerges either from a wavy blue bar across the middle of the shield — the "fess wavy azure" — or from blue and white wavy lines representing the sea; *Scotland's Historic Heraldry*, p. 449). These arms are recorded for the Meldrums of Fyvie by Sir David Lyndsay himself in the *Armorial* he compiled in 1542 as Lyon King of Arms (see McAndrew, *Scotland's Historic Heraldry*, p. 272). Meanwhile, the banner of "Of silver schene, thrie otteris into sabill" that Meldrum describes for himself in the *Testament* (line 107) is closest to that recorded elsewhere for the Meldrums of Seggie in Fife: "Argent, three otters (2,1) passant sable" (i.e., a silver background with three horizontal black otters, two above one; McAndrew, *Scotland's Historic Heraldry*, p. 449).

390   *Lyke Mars the god armipotent.* I.e., "powerful in arms." See also the *Testament*, line 76. The earliest recorded English example of this particular epithet for Mars, the god of war, is in Chaucer's "Knight's Tale" (*CT* 1[A]1982, 2441), but it seems to have been popular amongst Older Scots poets when writing in an aureate style: see Dunbar's *The Goldyn Targe*, lines 112 and 152; Gavin Douglas' description of the kingly figure in the *Palis of Honoure*, line 1921, and see

Parkinson's note on manuscript variants here; the eponymous hero of the sixteenth-century romance *Clariodus* is frequently compared to Mars and once described as "armipotent"(ed. Irving, 5.2262). Meldrum will be compared to Mars again at line 1074, and Meldrum associates himself with Mars in the *Testament* lines 69–70, 94–97, 126, 132, 187.

401–10   *This nicht I saw . . . . in sic ane fray.* The animal imagery in this prophetic dream echoes King Arthur's terrifying dream of a dragon defeating a bear on the eve of his battle against the giant of Mont Saint-Michel, although in this case it is the giant-like Talbart himself (see note to lines 311–14) whose dream foretells his defeat by the young Meldrum. The dragon-bear dream occurs in Geoffrey of Monmouth's *History of the Kings of Britain* and its immediate derivatives (Wace's *Roman de Brut*, Layamon's *Brut*), as well as in the Middle English *Alliterative Morte Arthure* (lines 760–806), a text almost certainly known in Scotland. See Purdie, "Search for Scottishness," p. 99.

420   *lap upon his hors.* See Meldrum's parallel feat and note to lines 373–74 above.

424–25   *Sanct Georges croce . . . . all his geir.* The English army had worn the cross of St. George since the fourteenth century. Richard II's Ordinances of War of 1385 decreed that everyone of whatever estate should wear a large cross of St. George on their front and back. See Keen, "Richard II's Ordinances of War of 1385," pp. 39–41. The sixteenth-century chronicler Edward Hall notes that when Henry VIII was received at Calais in June 1513, "ouer his riuett [light armor] he had a garment of white cloth of gold with a redde cross," and when the Emperor Maximilian joined Henry's forces, "Themperour as the kynges soldiours ware a Crosse of saynTe George with a Rose" (*Hall's Chronicle*, p. 539).

437–38   *The heraldis put thame . . . . within the bordour.* By the later Middle Ages, heralds played an important part in both tournaments and genuine battles. They organized the pageantry of tournaments; they had "neutral" status in battle and so performed a vital role as messengers and diplomats, as well as being able to identify opponents by their arms. In both tournament and battle, they judged and recorded feats of prowess. See Keen, *Chivalry*, pp. 134–42.

444   *accowterit.* "equipped." C has *accowntterit*, L *accountered* and A *accounted*, all errors for *accowterit* from the French *accoutrer*. *DOST* records a similar spelling error of *accomptirit* in the 1552 Register of the Privy Council (*accouterit* [p.p.]).

445   *burdounis.* The basic meaning of *burdoun* is "staff," as in a pilgrim's staff, or cudgel, but here and at line 531 it is clearly used as a synonym for "lance" or "spear." See *OED bourdon* (n.1), sense 2, which cites this line and Douglas' *Eneados*, ed. Coldwell, 3:95, lines 69–70: "He with a burdon of ane lang stif tre, / The poynt scharpit and brynt a litill we [a little bit]."

448   *God shaw the richt.* "May God reveal [who has] the just cause." The phrase recurs at line 1262. This was part of the ritual of judicial combat, and Kinsley notes its appearance in Alexander Scott's roughly contemporary comic poem *The Justing and Debait up at the Drum*: "The harraldis cryd: 'God schaw the rycht!'" (line 63, ed. Bawcutt and Riddy, pp. 269–78).

472–76   *on he lap . . . . hors sa galyeardlie*. See note to lines 373–74 above.

483–84   *And cryit gif . . . . for his ladies saik*. The notion that a knight was improved by fighting in the name of (or in hopes of impressing) his lady was ingrained in the ideology of chivalry, and Talbart has already offered to fight "for his ladies saik" at line 276. For a review of medieval literature on the idea, see Jaeger, *Ennobling Love*, pp. 198–213. The ultimate model of the knight who performs great feats "for his ladies saik" is Lancelot, on whom see Lyndsay's disparaging remarks at lines 48–64 and note above. Meldrum will nevertheless promise the Lady of Gleneagles to do at least as much for her as ever Lancelot did for Guinevere (lines 1079–82).

504   *Pertlie to preif their pith thay preist*. Compare the fifteenth-century Scots romance *Ralph the Collier*: "Thay preis furth properly thair pithis to prufe" (line 863, *Three Middle English Charlemagne Romances*, ed. Lupack).

507   *He outterit*. L: *He vttered*. A: *Vttered*. *DOST*, citing this line, defines "outer" as "to swerve aside or refuse the encounter" (*outer* [v.1]). The *OED* is more specific in defining it as "to go out of the lists or course at a tournament" (again citing the line, and identifying it as a rare Scots usage: *utter* [v.1], sense 4). Both also cite Pitscottie: "Schir Patrickis horse wtterit witht him and wald on nowayis reconter his marrow" (i.e., "Sir Patrick's horse carried him out of the lists and refused to meet his opponent"; *Historie and Cronicles*, ed. Mackay, 1:234, lines 26–27). This is clearly what has happened to Talbart, who demands a new mount and tests it carefully before resuming the tournament (lines 515–23): this time, "name of thame thair marrow mist" (line 529).

556   *cunnand*. C: *cunning*. L: *cunning*. A: *cuning*. Charteris' *cunning* is listed in *DOST* as an error unique to this poem for *cunnand*, itself a reduced form of *convenant*, "agreement." Neither the *MED* nor *OED* list this variant at all, so the text has been emended here.

577   *This bene bot chance of armes*. "This is just the fortunes of war." Meldrum will repeat a version of this remark to another opponent later. See note to line 832–34.

577–78   *armes . . . . armes*. A rare example of *rime riche* in Lyndsay, pairing *armes* (warfare) with *armes* (arms, in the literal sense of limbs).

585–88   *Sum sayis . . . . never wes sene into Ingland*. This description would fit with Hamer's identification of "Talbart" with the Sir Humphrey Talbot who was reputed to have died in the Holy Land, although see note to lines 265–71 above on the problems with this. Alternatively, it could explain why no one else has heard of this supposedly famous champion. Or again, if George Talbot earl of Shrewsbury were jokingly meant (i.e., if Meldrum has exaggerated his own exploits somewhat), the claim that he "never wes sene into Ingland" would be amusingly ironic for the original Scottish audience: Shrewsbury was later appointed lieutenant-general in the turbulent Scottish borders (*ODNB*, "Talbot, George").

589–90   *Bot our squyer did still remane / Efter the weir, quhill peice was tane*. Lyndsay's (or Meldrum's) chronology becomes vague here. Louis XII of France agreed a preliminary truce with Henry VIII in March 1514 (which included his allies the Scots, although they had not actually been consulted), and a formal peace treaty was signed in August 1514 (Scarisbrick, *Henry VIII*, pp. 50–56; Emond, "Minority of King James V," pp. 12–13). This would indicate that Meldrum remained in France in 1514, but at lines 599–600 we are told that "the navie of Scotland / Wes still upon the coist lyand." In October 1513, the combined Franco-Scottish fleet was meant to intercept Henry VIII on his return to England, but they were scattered by storm and most of the Scottish fleet limped home at the beginning of November 1513, leaving only the largest ships behind in French pay (Governor Albany eventually sold the flagship *St Michael* to Louis XII in April 1514 [see *ER* 14:cxxxvi]). On 13 November 1513, Lord Dacre reported to Henry that "Th' Erl of Aren, admirall of Scotland, is commen home with the shippes of Scotland . . . which hath brought writings and credence from the French king and the Duke of Albany . . . The Scottische soldiours which be commen home make ill reaport of the French king, sayng thei were not well entreated there" (Spont, *Letters and Papers*, pp. 188–89, nos. 95, 96; see also pp. xliv–xlvi). This contrasts markedly with Meldrum's reported experience at the French court.

Lyndsay could conceivably have intended the "peice" of line 590 to refer to the lull following Henry's capture of Tournai and the simultaneous disastrous news from Flodden (i.e., late September until the end of October 1513), but the description of ambassadors crowding the court of Louis XII at lines 614–18 suggests rather the formal peace negotiations of 1514. Lyndsay (or Meldrum) seems thus to be telescoping events from late 1513 and 1514.

591   *the kingis gairdis*. This refers to Louis XII's Scots Guards, led by D'Aubigny. See note to line 343 above.

597–600 *From Pycardie . . . .the coist lyand*. On dating the Scottish fleet's movements (and therefore Meldrum's) see note to lines 589–90 above.

608   *hakbut, culvering, pik and speir*. Hackbuts and culverins were early portable guns, used in early sixteenth-century warfare alongside the pikes and spears listed here.

619   *ane ambassadour*. None of the candidates for this description are entirely satisfactory, and Lyndsay's vagueness here may be deliberate. Hamer suggests John Stewart, Duke of Albany, the French-born acting regent of Scotland who was detained by the French crown until 1515 (Hamer, see also note to lines 1380–87 below). The official Scottish ambassador was Andrew Forman, Bishop of Moray, but his later reputation in some quarters as the architect of James IV's ruin would seem to preclude seeing him as the "man of greit honour" here (line 620, see Macdougall, *James IV*, pp. 297–98). Yet another candidate is Antoine d'Arces, Seigneur de la Bastie, who would later become acting regent of Scotland. See note to lines 1395–1406 below.

629   *lyke wyld lyounis furious*. The villainous English setting upon the Scots "lyke wyld lyounis furious" is a caution against seeing Meldrum's earlier description, "Rampand lyke ane wyld lyoun" (line 236), as an allusion to the lion rampant on the royal arms of Scotland.

633   *Sutheroun.* The sudden introduction of this term, literally "Southerners," for the people Lyndsay has so far described merely as "Inglis" (see lines 265, 428, 567, 572), is reminiscent of the diction of *Hary's Wallace,* where the term is frequent.

661   *sevin quarter lang.* A "quarter" was a fourth of an ell: the *OED* gives a Scottish ell as 37.2 inches (*ell* [n.1], sense 1.a). This would make Meldrum's sword about five and half feet long, a substantial weapon. He is later described as wielding a formidable two-handed sword (see note to line 1254 below).

691–98   *Thocht Frenche ladies . . . . did thame noy.* The lamenting at Meldrum's departure is vaguely reminiscent of Wallace's departure from France, where "Lordys and ladyis wepyt wondyr fast" (*Hary's Wallace,* 12.319). But where Meldrum departs simply because "he in France wald not remane" (line 689), Wallace is anxious to return and defend his beleaguered country: "Till help his awn he had a mar plesance / Than thar to byd with all the welth off France" (*Hary's Wallace,* 12.299–300).

710–848   *Ane day . . . . payit thair ransoun.* This sea-battle has distinct echoes of the "Red Reiver" episode of *Hary's Wallace,* 9.184–391, and fainter ones of Wallace's second sea-battle with John of Lynn, 11.809–906.

730   *monie gunnis out ovir hir flaw.* "many missiles flew right over her [i.e., the ship]." *DOST* does not record examples of *gun* used in reference to the missiles fired, but the *OED* lists two, from Chaucer's *Legend of Good Women* and the *Avowing of King Arthur*: see *gun* (n.) sense 4. The Scottish ship is so much smaller and lower in the water that the English guns are finding it difficult to aim low enough to hit her, whereas the Scottish guns are finding the tall English ship an easy target. In *Hary's Wallace,* the ship of the English pirate John of Lynn is far better armed and similarly "mar off hycht" than Wallace's (11.893–94).

749   *halbert.* The halberd was a variant of the pole-axe, with an axe-blade and pick on either side of the shaft and a spear-head at the tip. The *OED* records references to them from the very end of the fifteenth century, but *DOST* only from the sixteenth, so Lyndsay is describing modern weaponry.

751   *Out of the top.* The "top" or "top-castle" was a platform at the head of a mast in fighting ships, often used by archers (see *OED top* [n.], sense 3.9a).

758   *Swyith yeild, yow doggis, or ye sall die.* Compare the Red Reiver episode in *Hary's Wallace*: "On loude he cryit, 'Stryk, doggis! ōe sall de!'" (9.263).

762   *tratour tavernar.* Hamer thought this was intended as a slur on the English captain's social class; Kinsley thought he was calling him a "brawling tippler." Both are possible, but Hadley Williams' suggestion that this alludes to a proverb about empty boasts made in a tavern (Whiting T49) is the most convincing. Whiting's entry is based on the following lines from *Richard Coer de Lyon*:

> Whenne they sytten at the taverne,
> There they ben stoute and sterne,   *brave and daring*
> Bostfyl wurdes for to crake,   *speak*
> And of here dedes, yelpyng to make.   *boasting*
> Lytyl wurth they are and misprowde;   *haughty (arrogant)*

> Fyghte they cunne with wurdes lowde,   *are able*
> And telle no man is here pere;   *proclaim; equal*
> But whene they comen to the mystere,   *time of peril (show-down)*
> And see men begynne strokes dele,   *deliver*
> Anon they gynne to turne here hele . . .
> (ed. Larkin, lines 3853–62)

776   *And sone wes all the Sutheroun slane.* Hamer takes "slane" in its usual sense of
        "killed" and describes this line as "a slight exaggeration, since two hundred
        men, we are told later [lines 840–41], were put ashore on the coast of Kent."
        Hadley Williams objects that "The sense seems to be 'defeated,' given following
        events" and indeed there are men alive and begging for mercy at lines 779–80.
        DOST offers three examples of *sla* in this weaker sense of "to strike down" (*sla*,
        [v.], sense 1.1) and, although they speculate that these might actually belong to
        the more usual sense of "kill by striking" (sense 1.3), the *MED* actually records
        non-fatal striking as the first, well-evidenced sense for *slēn* (v.). It is possible that
        Lyndsay is using deliberately archaic terminology here, since the three *DOST*
        examples in question are from Barbour's *Bruce* (c. 1375) and Wyntoun's *Original
        Chronicle* (c. 1420). Another non-fatal sense of "slay" occurs at line 1134 below,
        and see line 149 of "The Unicornis Tale" elsewhere in this volume.

781–88 *Yit wes . . . . ane thowsand syse.* Either Lyndsay (or his informant, Meldrum) forgot
        that the squire had knocked the captain into "ane deidlie swoun" a moment
        earlier (line 770), or the squire's blow was less deadly than originally implied.

790   *Thrie thowsand nobillis of the rois.* The "rose noble" was the most valuable of the
        various types of English noble — a gold coin — in circulation. They were
        introduced by Edward IV in 1464 and stamped with the York rose, hence the
        name. An act of the Scottish Parliament of 12 October 1467, under James III,
        ordered the valuation of "the Eduarde with the rose to xxxij s[hillings] of our
        mone." In the squire's own era, an act of Parliament of 20 August 1524 valued
        the various English nobles thus: "The Ros noble of Weiht for xliiij s the Hary
        noble of Weiht for xl s, the Angell noble for xxx s." (Cochran-Patrick, *Records of
        the Coinage of Scotland*, 1:32 and 1:54).

803   *ran and red.* Kinsley refers back to "the redding" (i.e. the physical separation of
        combatants in a fight) of line 671, which fits the general sense here, but compare
        the phrase "[h]is erandis for to ryne and red" in Dunbar's "Complane I wald, wist
        I quhome till" (*Poems* 1:68, line 44) where it simply means to "go and do." Lyndsay
        might then be paraphrased "then both the captains did so," i.e., arranged for the
        fighting to cease, rather than wading back into the thick of it themselves.

832–34 *It wes but chance . . . . hapnit siclike adventure.* This is similar to what Meldrum says
        earlier to the defeated Talbart, assuring him it was "bot chance of armes" (line
        577), but it is closer still to the words of Wallace to the Red Reiver: "For chans
        off wer thou suld no murnyng mak. / As werd will wyrk thi fortoun mon thou
        tak" (*Hary's Wallace*, 9.371–72).

844   *the Blaknes.* The well fortified Blackness Castle, on the south side of the Firth of
        Forth near Linlithgow, was often used as a prison. Its earliest mention in the

Records of the Parliaments of Scotland in this capacity is from 1467 (Judicial Proceedings for 17 October), in reference to an Andro Johnson: "And for the contemption done to the kingis hienes, that his persoune be enterit in ward in the castel of the Blaknes lyk as wes decretit be the lordis of counsale of before" (RPS 1467/10/35).

848   *ransoun.* It was common practice to ransom such prisoners of war as seemed likely to be able to afford it; presumably this is the basis on which some of the English were "waillit furth" ("picked out," line 839). See Ambühl, *Prisoners of War in the Hundred Years War.*

856   *Straitherne.* Strathearn is a valley in Perthshire (along the river Earn) where it meets northwest Fife. Either Meldrum has traveled overland through Fife or sailed north and into the river Tay, past Dundee — either route is logical enough for a man with lands in Cleish, northwest Fife. In her note to this line, Hadley Williams notes that "Meldrum's route recalls Wallace's," at least as described in Hary's poem. If so, it makes an interesting contrast: where the squire is feasted everywhere, Wallace must sneak back into the country, evading capture by the English. Strathearn is not specifically named, though he does enter it: "Wallace the land has tane / At Ernys mouth and is till Elchok gane" (i.e., Elcho Castle on the river Tay, near the mouth of the river Earn) (*Hary's Wallace,* 12.329–30).

858   *ane castell.* This is Gleneagles Castle is in southeast Perthshire. The ruins of its grand fifteenth-century tower, just south of the famous modern golf course, are still standing (see https://canmore.org.uk/site/25906/gleneagles-castle).

863–65   *Ane lustie ladie . . . . wes the moir.* So much effort has gone into establishing who this "ladie" was in real life and what happened between her and Meldrum that it is easy now to miss the fact that Lyndsay himself never names her, nor tells us anything more than that she lives in a castle somewhere in Strathearn (line 856, and compare "Sterne of Stratherne" in the *Testament,* line 230); she owns another castle somewhere in the Lennox (see note to line 1057); her former husband was a relation of Meldrum's (line 966); and eventually, that "scho aganis hir will wes maryit" to a man who is likewise unnamed (line 1465). This anonymity helps to highlight instead the literary allusions to Virgil's *Aeneid* and the *Squire of Low Degree* (see notes to lines 875–80 below) as well as to invite the audience to compare and contrast the couple with Lancelot and Guinevere (see note to lines 205–06 above) although she is not married, she will be the unintentional cause of Meldrum's doom. Perhaps the anonymity was also intended to help Lyndsay avoid accusations of slander, should his poem reach a wider audience than that for which it was originally intended. Identification of the lady and her two husbands was unnecessary for Lyndsay's original private audience in Fife, who were already familiar with the dramatic story of Meldrum's affair with Marjorie Lawson, Lady of Gleneagles. See the Introduction, "The *Historie* and History" for discussion.

875–80   *Eneas . . . . put in vers.* The squire's storytelling is likened to that of Aeneas at Carthage in book 2 of Virgil's *Aeneid.* Dido, a young widow like Marjorie, falls helplessly in love with Aeneas as he recounts the harrowing story of the fall of Troy and his escape from it. Gavin Douglas completed his translation of the *Aeneid* into Scots (the *Eneados*) in 1513, so it was readily accessible to a sixteenth-century Scottish audience. The implicit comparison does not bode well for the squire and the lady: Aeneas resumes his quest to found a new empire while the abandoned Dido commits suicide. In fact, however, Meldrum's lady will go on to re-marry and indeed outlive the squire, while Meldrum will be permanently crippled in the vicious ambush described (lines 1211–1380). It is difficult to gauge how much irony Lyndsay intends here, or in his aside that the rest of the squire's tale was, unlike Aeneas', "langsum for to put in vers." The parallels with the *Aeneid* are again hinted at with Meldrum's otherwise conventional prayer to Venus at lines 906–16. Venus was Aeneas' mother and the instigator of his disastrous affair with Dido.

900 ff.   *Bot still did on the ladie think* . . . . Bawcutt and Riddy observe: "It is difficult to tell how far this episode is to be taken seriously and how far it contains elements of burlesque." C. S. Lewis insisted that "the humour is not burlesque," referring instead to its "wholesome sensuality" and "homely realism" (*English Literature in the Sixteenth Century*, p. 103). Bawcutt and Riddy point to James I's *Kingis Quair* (at lines 274–350, 435–41, 470–97) for examples of the serious deployment of many of the conventions touched on here, including the May setting, the lover's torments, the lover as the lady's prisoner and thrall, the lady's dawn walk, and the elaborate description of her beauty (on which see further note to lines 944–49 below).

901   *Cupido with his fyrie dart*. Ovid depicts Cupid, the god of Love, as a vengeful youngster who fires arrows tipped with gold or lead — causing love and revulsion respectively — in the tale of Apollo and Daphne (*Metamorphoses* 1.452–74). But the thirteenth-century French poem *The Romance of the Rose* by Guillaume de Lorris and Jean de Meun offered probably the most detailed and influential version of this extended metaphor for falling in and out of love: see trans. Dahlberg, pp. 42–44 (lines 865–984), for the arrows and pp. 54–69 (lines 1681–2764) for the narrator and the God of Love, here portrayed as an adult lord (ed. Langlois, lines 865–984 and 1681–2764). Chaucer, who made his own translation of a portion of *The Romance of the Rose*, imagines Troilus being shot by "the God of Love" in *TC* 1.206–10. In book 2 of Virgil's *Aeneid*, Venus sends her son Cupid to cause Dido to burn with love for Aeneas. See note to lines 875–80 above on other allusions to the *Aeneid*.

907–26   *Ladie* . . . . *be my paramour*. The overheard lover's complaint is a common trope of medieval courtly poetry. Famous examples include Pandarus overhearing Troilus' lament (*TC* 1.547–50 and 2.519–60) or Chaucer's narrator overhearing the Black Knight in *The Book of the Duchess* (ed. Benson, lines 458 ff.), but the closest analogue here is the late fifteenth-century English romance *The Squire of Low Degree*, a semi-comical romance extremely popular throughout the sixteenth century in England and told in the same racy octosyllabic couplets as Lyndsay's *Historie* (see further the notes to lines 923–24, 934, and 962 below). The eponymous squire falls in love with a princess of Hungary (neither lover is ever named) but feels unworthy of her: he laments his plight in a beautiful garden (ed. Kooper, lines 68–88), where the princess overhears him from her room and decides to take pity on him (see the suggestively similar lines below, note to lines 923–24). She gives him a list of instructions of how to win her father's consent, but a jealous steward — compare Lyndsay's unnamed "cruell knicht" of line 1191 — is determined to keep the couple apart, first by telling the king about their liaison (who, however, is comically unperturbed) and then by ambushing the unarmed squire with a large party of men when he tries to visit the princess. Here the stories diverge: the squire of low degree slays the steward despite the desperate odds and his lack of armor; a series of misunderstandings keeps the squire either in prison or in exile for seven years while the faithful princess mourns his apparent death. Rather gruesomely, she has the mutilated body of what she believes to be the squire embalmed and kept at her bedhead this whole time. Eventually the deception is revealed, the couple are married, and the squire is made the king's heir. The Hungarian princess' fierce loyalty to what she believes to be the mutilated body of her squire contrasts with the way the lady of Gleneagles will drop abruptly out of Meldrum's life after his own disfigurement in the ambush that ends their affair.

The Squire of Low Degree had been printed by Wynkyn de Worde as early as c. 1520 under the title *Undo Youre Dore* (see STC [2nd ed.] 23111.5). It had certainly found a market in Scotland by 1586, when a Scottish ship homeward bound from London was found to be carrying 50 copies of "Squire of low degre, Eng.," twice as many as any of the other 26 books listed on the inventory (see Robertson, "A Packet of Books for Scotland," p. 52).

923–24   *Howbeit . . . . agane.* Compare *Squire of Low Degree*: "Though I for thee should be slayne, / Squyer, I shall thee love agayne" (ed. Kooper, lines 153–54).

934, 962   *squyeris dure unlok; bar the dure.* This focus on the locking and unlocking of the squire's door is again reminiscent of the *Squire of Low Degree*, whose alternative title in some prints was *Vndo Your Dore* (see STC [2nd ed.] 23111.5, "Here begynneth vndo your dore" [London: Wynkyn de Worde, ?1520]). The squire, believing himself to be unobserved, creeps up to the princess' door: "'Your dore undo! / Undo,' he sayde, 'nowe, fayre lady!'"; "Undo thy dore, my worthy wyfe"; "Undo your dore, my lady swete"; "Undo thy dore, my frely floure" (ed. Kooper, lines 534–35, 539, 541, 545). The lady, not recognizing his voice, retorts: "I wyll not my dore undo / For no man that cometh therto" (lines 551–52). Eventually she realizes who he is and makes a fulsome speech of welcome, but this only serves to give the jealous steward's men enough time to attack. The squire kills the steward but is hauled away, while the steward's disfigured body is left for the lady to find (and mistake for the squire's) when she undoes her door at last. Meldrum's affair runs in almost inverse parallel to that in the *Squire of Low Degree*, with the lady creeping up to his door but finding the lock already undone; Meldrum locking the door himself with her on the inside, and finally — tragically — Meldrum himself being horribly mutilated by the "cruell knicht" who wants to separate the lovers (see lines 1215 ff.).

944–49   *His goldin traissis . . . . withouttin hois.* The early thirteenth-century writer Geoffrey of Vinsauf provided a much imitated (and satirized) model for how to describe a beautiful woman, recommending among other things that a poet should "let the colour of gold give a glow to her hair;" that her skin be so white that "lilies bloom high on her brow;" that "her breast, the image of snow, show side by side its twin virginal gems," and that "the border of her robe gleam with fine linen" (*Poetria Nova*, trans. Nims, pp. 36–37).

951   *vailye quod vailye.* This translates as "come what may" (from Latin *valeo*, "prevail"), a common expression that Lyndsay assigns elsewhere to a fat, overconfident parrot who is determined to climb to the top of a tree in *Testament of the Papyngo*: "'I wyll,' said scho, 'ascend, vailye quod vailye'" (line 161; she then falls and is fatally injured). For a more dignified example of the phrase in battle, see Barbour's *Bruce* 9.148. This scene evidently made a strong impression on at least one early eighteenth-century reader. George, 1st Earl of Cromartie, wrote to the Earl of Mar in 1707 that if he is forced to wait any longer for his salary, "I will study for as much to borrow as will cary [sic] my old bones up to complain, *vale que vale*, as Squire Meldrum said"; and again in 1708, to the same correspondent, "I now come to act in another scene, and to intreat for my freends, *vale que vale*, as old Squire Meldrum did sing in the dayes of yore" (Fraser, *The Earls of Cromartie*, 2:45 and 2:57, letters of 25 September 1707 and 17 January 1708).

953   *courtlyke.* C: *courlyke.* L: *curtlike.* The *OED* records adj. *courtlike* from the later sixteenth century, but no spellings without medial *t*. *DOST* cites only this line — likewise emended — for its entry for *cour[t]lyk* (adj.). A corrects to "courtly."

955–64   *Madame, gude morne . . . . my womanheid to spill.* If the squire's earlier lament recalled serious works in the courtly love tradition, this scene is far more reminiscent of fabliaux such as Chaucer's Miller's Tale in which — in a spoof of these same courtly conventions — the crafty young student Nicholas approaches his landlord's wife Alison:

> And prively he caughte hire by the queynte [private parts]
> And seyde, "Ywis, but if ich have me wille,
> For deerne [secret] love of thee, lemman, I spille [die].
> (*CT* 1[A]3276–78)

After a brief and unconvincing protest — "Do wey youre handes, for youre curteisye!" — Alison "hir love hym graunted atte laste" (*CT* 1[A]3287–90). Meldrum's lady is at least widowed when she makes her equally token objection.

963–66   Contemporary canon law imposed an extremely restrictive set of impediments to marriage based on kinship of either consanguinity or affinity, extending both to the fourth degree. This meant that marriage was prohibited, not only to a blood relative to within the fourth degree (i.e., someone with whom one shared a great-great-grandparent), but also to someone within four degrees of relation to one's former spouse (see Sellar, "The Family," pp. 98–99). The latter is clearly the case for Meldrum, although his relationship to the lady's former husband is never spelled out. The solution was to seek a dispensation from the Pope, but this was an expensive business and was often ignored by couples. The Archbishop of St Andrews protested to the Pope in a letter of 1 September 1554 that "such was the connexion between families in Scotland, that it was scarce possible to match two persons of good birth who should not come within the forbidden degrees; and on that account . . . many married without dispensation, promising to obtain it subsequent to marriage; but afterwards instead of doing so, sought for divorce, or put away their wives on the pretext of the want of dispensation and of the expense of procuring one" (*Liber Officialis Sancti Andree*, ed. Forbes and Innes, pp. xxv–xxvi and 164–65).

No blood connection between the Meldrums and the Haldanes can be traced in the scant surviving historical records, but we do not know the name of William Meldrum's mother or of his great-grandmother on his father's side (see the conjectural Meldrum family tree in the Introduction, "Squire of Cleish and Binns"), so there is plenty of scope for the connection to have been a close one, whether with the Haldanes directly, or via the family of Sir John Haldane's mother, Christian Grahame (named in a 1481 charter by his grandfather John, NRS GD198/16), or that of his grandmother, Agnes of Menteth (named in an instrument of resignation from 1472, NRS GD198/45, and a protest against a precept of chancery of 1473, NRS GD198/49).

987   *Cupido*. See note to line 901 above.

990–99   *Nor ane . . . . I hard sane*. Although references to sex are normally more coy than this in romances, such directness is not unknown. In the fifteenth-century Middle English *Partonope of Blois*, the heroine Melior has — like the lady here — engineered things so that she and her beloved are alone in a bedroom. When he puts an arm around her, she raises only a feeble objection, and:

> . . . . a-none ganne he
> In hys armes her faste to hy*m* brase.
> And fulle softely þen sho sayde: "Allas!"
> And her legges sho gan to knytte,
> And wy*th* hys knees he gan hem on-shote.
> And þer-wy*th*-all she sayde: "Syr, mercy!"
> He wolde not lefe ne be þer-by;
> For of her wordes toke he no hede;
> But þys a-way her maydenhede
> Haþe he þen rafte *and* geffe her hys.
> (ed. Bödtker, lines 1562–71)

The narrator's disingenuous claim to be unsure what happened is entirely traditional.

991   *wodbind*. This can refer to ivy or similar green climbing plants, or to climbing honeysuckle. Either way it is a common metaphor for lovers clinging to each other. See Marie de France's brief *lai* of *Chievrefoil*, telling of a secret tryst between Tristram and Isolde; *chievrefoil* translates as "goatleaf," or honeysuckle (*Lais*, ed. Rychner, pp. 151–54). See also Chaucer's description of Troilus and Criseyde when they finally get together:

> And as aboute a tree, with many a twiste,
> Bytrent and writh the swote wodebynde,
> Gan ech of hem in armes other wynde.
> (*TC* 3.1230–32)

996   *And with hir hair scho dicht hir ene.* Hamer, Kinsley: "and with her hair she covered her eyes." Bawcutt and Riddy object that "there seems to be no parallel for *dicht* in this sense," and they translate as "wiped" based on *DOST dicht*, (v.), sense 3b: "the lady may be wiping away a (false) tear or even feigning surprise by rubbing her eyes." But compare *MED dighten* (v.), sense 1b.b, which offers several examples of the sense "clothe, cover"; the exceptionally poor survival rate for Older Scots texts means that many usages attested in ME are likely to apply to Scots also, though they do not happen to be exemplified in the surviving corpus. Either way she is clearly feigning shame, much like the equally unrepentant Melior when she makes the token gestures of sighing "Allace!" and crossing her legs after luring Partonope into bed with her (see note to lines 990–99 above).

1002–06   *he gaif her . . . . thir twa dissever.* On the ruby ring love-token see note to lines 195–96.

1008   *lammer.* Although the OE plural form of "lamb" was *lambru, lambur*, and the description of sleeping maidens as being 'as sweet as lambs' would be appropriate ("lambs" is Hadley Williams', Bawcutt, and Riddy's preferred gloss), *DOST* (*lam, lamb(e* (n.)) notes that "The regular and only plur. forms known to Sc. are in *-is, -es*, unless we count some place-names in *Lammer-*." Lyndsay twice uses the expression "sweiter nor/than the lamber/lammer" elsewhere to describe women, in both cases rhymed with "chalmer" as here (*Ane Satyre*, line 531 and "Proclamatioun" line 152) and seeming to refer to "ambergris" as used in perfume. The terms *amber/lamber/lammer* were used interchangeably for ambergris and for the gemstone amber; see *OED amber* (n.1), sense A.I, and *DOST lammer* (n.).

1019   *be him that deir Jesus sauld.* Bawcutt and Riddy quip that "It is appropriate that in glibly lying to her maids the lady should swear by Judas" (i.e., Judas Iscariot).

1048   *the futeball.* Although not considered a noble pastime, football (or soccer) was enormously popular from the later Middle Ages onwards, not to mention violent (see Reeves, *Pleasures and Pastimes*, pp. 91–92.) It was banned by successive Scottish kings throughout the fifteenth century, evidently without the slightest success (see RPS James I, 1424/19; James II, 1458/3/7; James III, 1471/5/6; James IV, 1491/4/17). In 1497, students at the University of St Andrews were banned from playing *ad pilam pedalem* on pain of excommunication (Dunlop, *Acta Facultatis*, pp. 265–66). Meanwhile, however, the *Treasurer's Accounts* for that same year record a payment "to Jame Dog to by fut ballis to the King" (*TA* 1:330). The footballing students of rival colleges of St Andrews would go on to cause a serious breach of the peace in 1537 (*Acta Facultatis*, pp. cxxxii, 380–81 [19 February 1537]). I am grateful to Professor Roger Mason for drawing these records to my attention.

1054   *the Lennox.* See note to line 1057 below.

1055 *Makfagon*. So C and L. S: *Mackfarlon*. Bawcutt and Riddy emend to *Makfaron* to rhyme with *baron* (line 1066), although they admit that this is not otherwise recorded as a variant of the name otherwise rendered consistently as *Makferland* or *MacFarland* at lines 1097, 1108, 1120, 1135, and 1143. (On the MacFarlanes, see note to line 1057 below.) If *Makfagon* is Charteris' error, he may — as Hadley Williams notes — have been thinking of Hary's wicked (albeit fictional) Highlander *Makfadōan* in *Hary's Wallace* (7.623–868) who led a band of supposedly savage Irish and Hebridean men in a raid on Argyll, to be defeated by the combined forces of Wallace and Lord Campbell of Loch Awe (possibly inspired by the attack of a real Maurice MacFadyane on the bishop of Argyll in 1452). As Boardman remarks: "Hary visualised the confrontation between Wallace and Campbell's forces and MacFadzan's men as a straightforward struggle between 'civilisation' and 'savagery'" (*The Campbells*, p. 212). That the name "MacFadyan" became synonymous with Highland savagery for Lowland audiences is suggested by Dunbar's inclusion of a *Makfadōane* and his "Ersche" (i.e., Gaelic) followers in an infernal dance of the Seven Deadly Sins (*Poems* 1:152, lines 110, 116).

    As for what stood in Lyndsay's original text, neither *Makferlan(d)* nor *Makfagon* rhyme with line 1056's *baron*, so it may be that the lines originally rhymed *Makferland* with *brigand* or *tyran(d)*, which a distracted later copyist altered to the more common collocation of "bold baron." Compare lines 1420 and 1493, where *tyrane, tyrannis* is used in the general sense of "villain."

1057 *Hir castell*. This would seem to be Boturich Castle on the southeast bank of Loch Lomond in the Lennox, a region taking in much of present-day Dunbartonshire and west Stirlingshire. The current Boturich Castle is nineteenth-century country house built upon the ruins of the fifteenth-century castle. A charter of January 1508/9 includes "duas le Bothurches" — i.e., Boturich — among the lands consolidated into the barony of Haldane for John Haldane and Marjorie Lawson, who are both named in the charter (*Reg. Mag. Sig.* 2:702–03, no. 3288). On Haldane's involvement in the disputed inheritance of the lands and title of the earldom of Lennox, see Napier, *History of the Partition of the Lennox*, pp. 77–79. Although Fraser describes a raid on Boturich Castle by "the Macfarlanes of Arrochar," the only source he gives is Lyndsay's poem (Fraser, *Lennox* 1:155). James MacFarlane likewise highlights the MacFarlanes' general reputation as cattle-raiders and allies of the outlawed MacGregors and he likewise mentions this raid on the Haldane property of Boturich, but once again, Lyndsay's poem is the only cited source (*History of Clan MacFarlane*, p. 52). Doubts over the truth of this particular episode notwithstanding, the general unruliness of the MacFarlanes is a matter of historical record; Hadley Williams (in her note to line 1143) cites a statement in the Acts of the Lords of Council for 21 July 1518: "'the lardis of Bucquhannane and McFerlane wer takin and putt in warde for gret misreul maid be thaim in the cuntre,'" and the Council intended to consider how to deal with them so that the whole area including the Lennox "'may be putt to peax'" (*Acts of Council in (Public Affairs)*, p. 126).

1064   *Dunbartane and Argyle.* "Dumbarton and Argyll" in the west of Scotland. See note to line 1057 above on the extent of the lady's lands in the Lennox (which included Dumbarton), and note to line 1055 above on the association of the MakFadyans — here conflated with MacFarlanes — with Argyll.

1076–77   *scho gaif him . . . . his basnet bure.* On the practice of bearing a lady's token into tournament or battle, and the inspiration such practices drew from literary romance, see Keen, *Chivalry*, pp. 212–16.

1077–81   *That worthie Lancelot . . . . I sall do.* On Lancelot, about whom Lyndsay was earlier quite disparaging, see note to lines 48–64 above.

1088–92   *Than . . . . at his command.* From tournament and battlefield vows to more personal ones, vowing played a major part in chivalric culture. An influential literary precedent is the *Voeux du Paon* or "Vows upon the Peacock," an early fourteenth-century text incorporated into the Old French *Alexander* cycle which would be translated into Scots twice over the course of the fifteenth century, first as part of the *Buik of Alexander* and then as part of the *Buik of King Alexander the Conquerour*, associated with Gilbert Hay. Meldrum's vow that "he suld never in hart be glaid" recalls one in the Older Scots romance *King Orphius* (a version of the Middle English *Sir Orfeo*): when the regent-nephew is told that King Orphius lies dead and unburied somewhere, he exclaims: "I sall never gleid be / Quhill [until] þat body buryit be, / Nor ever ane horss ane [f]it [one foot] to ryd" (ed. Purdie, Laing text, lines 60–62). On the culture of chivalric vows generally, see Keen, *Chivalry*, pp. 212–15.

1107   *culvering, hakbut.* See note to line 608 above.

1116   *braid arrowis.* See *DOST brade* (adj.), sense 2.b.1, for other examples of this epithet applied to arrows. MacFarlane's troops do not appear to have any artillery with which to answer the squire's "hakbute" or "culveryne" fire.

1134   *tak and slay.* On the sense of "slay" as to "strike down" rather than to kill, see note to line 776 above.

1143   *In fre waird . . . . was Makferland seisit.* I.e., he is technically Meldrum's prisoner, but will not actually be imprisoned; see *DOST ward* (n.1), sense 4b.

1155–58   *Gif uther thing . . . . in that art.* Lyndsay makes the same claims to ignorance about love (perhaps equally tongue in cheek) in the *Answer to the Kingis Flyting*, lines 12–13. An influential model is Chaucer's narrator in *TC* 1.15–21; 2.12–21 (as well as the narrators of his *Book of the Duchess* and *The Parliament of Fowls*).

1162   *Ane douchter to the squyer bair.* Pitscottie says she bore him two children (*Historie and Cronicles*, ed. Mackay, 1:299), although it is hard to see how he would know more about it than Lyndsay (Mackay gives Pitscottie's approximate date of birth as 1532, decades after the events in question). The historical record offers no other hint of any children from the union, but Marjorie did have two sons with her first husband, Sir John Haldane, so it is possible that there is some conflation here. See further discussion in the Introduction, "The *Historie* and History."

1167–68 *In scarlot fyne . . . . sicht to sene.* Bawcutt and Riddy note that "scarlot" was a rich cloth but not necessarily red in color; in this case, it is green. See *OED scarlet* (n.), sense 1a. On the distribution of green liveries for "Maying" celebrations, see Crane, *The Performance of Self*, pp. 39–72.

1169–70 *The gentilmen . . . . mak ane band.* This sounds like the bond of "manrent," a practice common in late-medieval Scotland in which the bonded man offered life-long service in return for a lord's protection, without any exchange of land-rights. See Wormald, *Lords and Men in Scotland*, pp. 14–33.

1178 *dispensatioun.* See note to lines 966–68 above.

1183–84 *Of warldlie joy . . . . the fatall end.* A very common proverbial saying. For English examples see Whiting J58; for Older Scots ones, see Whiting, "Proverbs and Proverbial Sayings from Scottish Writings," Part 1:194–95, "Joy."

1189–90 *Quhairthrow he stude . . . . defendit his honour.* This passing allusion to more widespread friction caused by the squire's liaison with the lady of Gleneagles (leading him to fight in "monie ane stour") is, unlike some other aspects of Lyndsay's tale, borne out by the historical record; see Introduction, "The *Historie* and History."

1197 *not in blude.* Although all early prints read thus, Pinkerton (and following him Chalmers and Laing), emended to "neir in blude" in order to align the story more closely with the version recounted by Pitscottie, in which the "cruell knicht" (line 1191) is identified as Sir John Stirling of Keir, and is held to have organized the ambush on behalf of his uncle Luke Stirling (*Historie and Cronicles*, ed. Mackay, 1:299). Records show that Marjorie Lawson did marry Luke Stirling, but other aspects of both Lyndsay's and Pitscottie's account of this ambush are difficult to square with the few historical documents relating to it. See the Introduction, "The *Historie* and History."

1221 *tuik his licence from his oist.* "[O]ist" can be translated either as "armed company" (as Hadley Williams glosses it) or "landlord, host." But the more domestic scene of paying the bill at their inn seems more likely. Had they felt the need to travel with an armed host in the first place, it seems unlikely that they would dismiss it for the journey home.

1224 *ovir the ferrie.* There were various ferry-points across the Firth of Forth, but this is almost certainly referring to south Queensferry near Edinburgh. *DOST* (*ferry* (n.), sense a) notes that the name *Queneferie* occurs from c. 1295.

1241 *kend.* The usual sense of this word is "known," as Bawcutt and Riddy gloss it; taken thus, she could be reassuring the squire that she is too well known to come to harm if she continues on alone. Another shade of meaning is "guided, shown the way" (see *DOST ken* (v.), sense 4b), the sense in which Kinsley takes it in order to paraphrase the line as "I shall be helped home."

1244 *no.* C is generally a very accurate copy, but in this line the letter *u* was substituted for *n*. It has been corrected in L.

1254   *ane lang twa-handit sword.* The sixteenth-century Italian writer Giacomo de Grassi writes of the powerful two-handed sword:

> One may with it, as a Galleon among many Gallies, resist many swords and other weapons . . . And because its weight and bigness require great strength, therefore those only are allotted to the handling thereof which are mighty and big to behold, great and strong in body and of stout and valiant courage (quoted in Oakeshott, *European Weapons and Armour*, p. 148).

Compare lines 1351–53, where Meldrum is described as "sweipand his sword round about . . . Durst nane approche within his boundis."

1259   *be Goddis corce.* This probably means "by the body of God," although as Bawcutt and Riddy point out, "by God's cross" (with metathesis of *r*) is also possible. The latter is certainly what L understood, since he printed "be Gods Croce," followed by A with "by God his Cross."

1262   *shaw the richt.* Meldrum uses the language of judicial combat here (see note to line 448 above) to underscore the injustice of the "cruell knicht['s]" attack.

1281–82   *Gaudefer . . . . At Gadderis Ferrie.* Gaudifer is one of the main heroes of one of the branches of the OF Alexander cycle known as the *Fuerre de Gadres*, or "Foray of Gaza." It was translated into Scots as part of the early fifteenth-century *Buik of Alexander* and again in the mid-fifteenth century *Buik of King Alexander the Conquerour* associated with Gilbert Hay. Gaudifer, fighting against Charlemagne's men, earned their profound admiration when he defended the retreat of Duke Betys of Gaza's forces against terrible odds. His name became a by-word for extreme courage and prowess, and Barbour accordingly likens Robert Bruce to him when he defends his own followers' escape from the far more numerous forces of John of Lorne (*Bruce* 3.67–92). Hamer, Kinsley, and Bawcutt and Riddy all describe line 1282's "Gadderis Ferrie" as Lyndsay's own mistranscription of *The Forray of Gadderis*, but it seems unlikely that Scotland's chief herald would not recognize such an element of chivalric vocabulary. If it is an error, it seems more likely to be a scribe's or printer's (both L and A retain "Ferrie/Ferry"). Otherwise, it might be noted that the *MED* records a late-medieval spelling of *ferray* in the Towneley Plays for "foray" (see *forrai* (n.)), while Anglo-Norman offers the related term *fereis*, "attack" (see *AND*).

1295, 1298   *Thome; Thomas Giffard.* Thomas Giffard, or Gifford, is named twice here although so many other characters go unnamed, including the "cruell knicht" leading the attack. This may be the "Thomas Giffert," messenger-at-arms, who is listed among several colleagues called to account for fermes [land rents] of barony of Strathavane (Strathaven, Lanarkshire) on 24 May 1530 (*ER* 16, p. 524); he may or may not be the same "late Thomas Giffert" whose Dalkeith lands are the subject of an instrument of sasine of 28 May 1546 (*Cal. Laing Charters*, pp. 135–36, no. 517). The messengers-at-arms were official couriers who also acted as "sheriffs in that part" — executing royal summonses and other writs, and issuing (and collecting) fines and other penalties, a potentially dangerous job in early modern Scotland which would have required robust officers. Thomas Giffert was thus exactly the kind of person whom Lyndsay's "cruell knicht" was likely to have called upon to assist in his ambush of the squire. More importantly, the messengers-at-arms were under the control of the Lyon King of Arms by 1510 at the latest (see *DOST messinger* (n.), sense 1b). David Lyndsay would not hold this office until later in the 1530s (see Biography of Sir David Lyndsay); he was a herald by 1530 and is thus likely to have known Giffert personally.

1310–12　*Tydeus . . . . fyftie knichtis.* A hero of the OF *Roman de Thèbes* (itself based on Statius' Latin *Thebaid*), Tydeus was another medieval by-word for displays of courage and prowess against terrible odds. While traveling alone as a messenger for Polynices, he fought his way out of a 50-man ambush arranged by Polynices' brother and rival Ethiocles (*Roman de Thèbes*, ed. Petit, lines 1483–1820; Statius, *Thebaid*, book 2). Barbour engages in a bit of one-upmanship by disingenuously comparing Tydeus' solo defeat of 50 men to Bruce's defense of a narrow pass against 200 comers (*Bruce*, 6.181–270). The "richtis" which Lyndsay describes Tydeus as defending may, as Hadley Williams notes, refer simply to "those of just conditions of combat," since Tydeus was in fact representing Polynices' claim to the Theban throne.

1313　*Rolland with Brandwell.* Roland was the most famous of Charlemagne's *douzeperes* — the Frankish equivalent of the knights of the Round Table — alongside Oliver (on whom see note to line 1316 below). In the OF *Chanson de Roland* of c. 1100, Roland dies fighting the Saracens at Roncevaux, too proud to call for reinforcements until it is too late. When he realizes he is about to die, he addresses a eulogy to his sword Durendal and tries to break it to prevent it from falling into enemy hands, but it slices the rocks instead (ed. Bédier, lines 2300–54 [laisses 171–73]). In the OF *Otinel* and its ME descendants (*Otuel and Roland*, *Otuel a Knight*, and *Duke Rowland and Sir Ottuel of Spayne*), Roland battles with — and eventually brings about the conversion of — the noble Saracen champion Otinel/Otuel. An uncharacteristically restrained Roland also features in the fifteenth-century Older Scots comic romance *Rauf Coilyear*.

Roland's sword is still named Durendal, Durindale, or Durnedale in the ME romances of *Otuel a Knight*, *Roland and Vernagu*, and *The Sowdone of Babylone* respectively, so Lyndsay's "Brandwell" remains unexplained. In his Additional Notes (Hamer, 3:495–96), Hamer tries to argue that "Brandwell" is instead the name of Roland's opponent. Finding no one of such a name in the tales of Charlemagne, he suggests rather wildly that it might be a corruption of "Brandelis," a character who fights Gawain in the entirely unrelated thirteenth-century OF Lancelot-Grail Cycle. In fact Brandelis first appears in the First Continuation of *Perceval*, which coincidentally supplied the raw material for *Golagros and Gawane* (on which see note to line 1315 below). "Brandwell" remains unexplained.

1315　*Gawin aganis Golibras.* This refers to the fifteenth-century Older Scots romance *Golagros and Gawane* (or *The Knightly Tale of Gologras and Gawain* in Hahn's METS edition) in which Arthur sends Gawain into battle against the proudly independent Golagros, who has refused Arthur's demands for homage. Gawain is victorious, but gallantly feigns defeat so that Golagros can consult his own followers over whether to die (his preference) or submit to Arthur, and whether they would like to be released from his service first if so. His men refuse to either abandon their lord or see him die, and Arthur in turn is so impressed by Golagros' prowess and nobility of conduct that he releases him from all feudal obligations. Much of the narrative has been culled from the OF First Continuation of Chrétien de Troyes' *Perceval*, but the name "Golagros" is unique to the Older Scots romance.

1316   *Olyver wyth Pharambras*. Oliver was the most famous of Charlemagne's *douzeperes* after Roland (see note to line 1313 above). In the OF *Fierabras*, the AN *Fierenbras*, and the ME derivatives *Sir Firumbras* and *Sir Ferumbras*, Oliver converts the eponymous Saracen champion by defeating him in single combat. That the story was well known in Scotland is demostrated by the fact that Barbour has Bruce cheer his men up during their flight across Loch Lomond by recounting the tale of "Ferambrace" (*Bruce*, 3.435–62).

1318   *Sir Gryme aganis Graysteille*. This refers to the Older Scots romance of *Eger and Grime*, in which Grime avenges the defeat of his friend Eger by the mysterious and terrifying Graysteill. Some version of it was in existence by 1497, when a payment was recorded in James IV's *Treasurer's Accounts* for two fiddlers "that sang Graysteil to the King" (*TA* 1:330, 19 April 1497). Its continued popularity in Lyndsay's day is demonstrated by the inclusion of "syr egeir and syr gryme" in a list of contemporary romances and tales given in the c. 1550 *Complaynt of Scotland* (p. 50). The earliest extant texts, however, date from the seventeenth century.

1320   *As onie knicht of the Round Tabill*. Meldrum has of course been compared to (or rather contrasted with) Lancelot, one of the chief knights of Arthur's Round Table, earlier in the poem. See note to lines 48–64 above.

1325–27   *Amang thay knichts . . . . cum no mo*. This clearly does not apply to the men attacking the squire, who are presumably not all knights in any case. It seems instead to refer to the knights "of the Round Tabill," regarding whom Bawcutt and Riddy quote the "Pentecostal oath" described in Malory's *Morte Darthur*:

> the kynge . . . charged them never to do outerage nothir mourthir, and
> allwayes to fle treson, and to gyff mercy unto hym that askith mercy, uppon
> payne of forfiture of theire worship . . . . Also that no man take no batayles in
> a wrongefull quarell for no love ne for no worldis goodis.
> (ed. Field, 1:97, lines 27–35)

1347   *hochis and theis*. Houghs are the "backs of the knees and thighs." See *OED hough* (n.), sense 2. To "hoch" someone is to hamstring them. Hamer (thanking earlier editors) notes the similarity to the fate of Wetherington in the sixteenth-century ballad *The Hunting of the Cheviot*: "For when both his leggis were hewyne in to, / yet he knyled and fought on hys kny" (stanza 54), or the more flippant account in the seventeenth-century Percy Folio ballad of *Chevy Chase*: "For Witherington needs must I wayle / as one in dolefull dumps, / For when his leggs were smitten of, / he fought vpon his stumpes" (stanza 50). For both texts, see *English and Scottish Popular Ballads*, ed. Child, 3:303–15 (ballad 162). Another parallel can be found in the brawl-scene of the Older Scots comic poem *Chrystis Kirk of the Grene*. The miller is a powerful, well-built man whom even ten men fear to take on: nevertheless, "Syne tratourly behind his bak / They hewit him on the howis / behind" (ed. Ritchie, 3:262–68, lines 160–61). See the Introduction, "The *Historie* and History," for Pitscottie's even more graphic description of Meldrum's injuries.

1375–76　*Sall never man . . . . have mair plesour*. The real "ladie," Marjorie Lawson, went on to marry again at least once, possibly twice (see Introduction, "The *Historie* and History"), although Lyndsay does claim at line 1465 that this was "aganis hir will."

1381–88　*the regent . . . . of all Scotland governour*. The regent of Scotland in 1517 was John Stewart, Duke of Albany. Son of Alexander Stewart, the rebellious younger brother of James III, Albany had been brought up in exile in France and built a career serving the French king, but he was sent for by the General Council of Scotland in September 1513 after the loss of James IV at Flodden. Louis XII was reluctant to release him, however, so Albany sent Antoine d'Arces ("Sir Anthonie Darsie"), Seigneur de la Bastie, to the Scottish Council in his stead in October 1513. Albany would not come to Scotland in person until May 1515 (Emond, "Minority of James V," pp. 4–6). On de la Bastie, see note to lines 1395–1406 below.

1389–90　*Our king . . . . wes the outrage*. James V was born 10 April 1512 and crowned 21 September 1513, so these events took place during his minority in 1517. See note to lines 1484–85, below, on de la Bastie's murder that same year, which would have dated Meldrum's ambush readily for a contemporary audience even without this additional clue. Here, and again at lines 1492–94, Lyndsay is careful to stress that the lawlessness of this period was not the young king James' fault.

1391　*this gude knicht*. I.e., Antoine D'Arces, Seigneur de la Bastie.

1395–1406　*Wald God . . . . to the ground*. Previous editors are divided over whether this is a reference to Meldrum's rescue of the besieged Scots at Amiens as described at lines 619–79. Hadley Williams assumes it is (p. 293n619–22); Hamer thinks "probably"; Kinsley "perhaps," while Bawcutt and Riddy state firmly that "the incident to which de la Bastie refers is not included by Lindsay in the earlier part of the poem." De la Bastie's reference to the "sutheroun" attackers (line 1406) certainly helps to recall this incident (see note to line 633 above), but there is no mention of the famous de la Bastie or any other Frenchman in that earlier account; see note to line 619, above, on the difficulties of identifying the unnamed "ambassador" with the Scots at Amiens.

If the historical accuracy of this tale cannot be ascertained, the intended effect of this enthusiastic praise for the squire from de la Bastie is clear. Long before he was appointed Albany's lieutenant regent in Scotland, de la Bastie (as he was most commonly called in Scottish records) was celebrated as an international star of the jousting lists and battlefields of Europe. Sometimes glamorously nicknamed "the White Knight" (see for example the 1514 letter from the Florentine ambassador in France [*Cal. State Papers (Venice)*, 2:157, no. 370]), he was also "the Franch knight" whose lavish jousting contest with "the Lord Hamiltoun" was recorded in the Scottish *Treasurer's Accounts* for 26 November 1506 (*TA* 3:xli–xlii). This "Lord Hamiltoun" is the earl of Arran who was admiral of the Scottish fleet in 1513. De la Bastie is thus the kind of real-life chivalric icon whom Meldrum aspires to be. His status as lieutenant Regent for Albany at the time of Meldrum's attack makes his involvement in bringing Meldrum's attackers to justice entirely plausible.

1403   *Hercules*. This figure was clearly well known in Lyndsay's Scotland. In *The Sex Werkdays and Agis*, a brief "universal history" copied into the Asloan manuscript c. 1513–30, there is mentioned "Hercules þat slewe *and* wencust [vanquished] / þe monyest giand*is* and cruellest monsto*uris* of ony / þat evir we reid" (ed. Houwen, p. 40, lines 316–18). The c. 1550 *Complaynt of Scotland* lists "the tayl quhou Hercules sleu the serpent hidra that hed vij heydis" ("the tale [of] how Hercules slew the serpent Hydra that had seven heads"; ed. Stewart, p. 50).

1422   *Dumbar*. Dunbar Castle was used as prison in this period. More importantly, it was held by de la Bastie on behalf of the Duke of Albany, to whom it had been returned as an inducement to bring him back to Scotland. See *Acts of Council (Public Affairs)*, pp. 27–28, 20 November 1514.

1443–46   *Bot he . . . . art of medicyne*. Bawcutt and Riddy note that "[t]he former knight who gives up combat to become a doctor is familiar in chivalric romance," and they point to the example of Malory's Sir Baldwin of Brittany in "The Fair Maiden of Ascolat" (*Le Morte Darthur*, ed. Field, 1:812–25). For a historical example see the life of John of Arderne, who served with Henry Plantagenet and John of Gaunt in battle, then learned how to repair wounds and wrote medical treatises. See *ODNB*, "Arderne, John (b. 1307/8, d. in or after 1377)" and Peck, "Gower and Science," p. 193n54.

1455–62   *Yit sum thing . . . . scho did so*. See the Introduction, "The *Historie* and History." on the disparity between at least one contemporary document and Lyndsay's description of the lady staying and doting on Meldrum as he recovers, before finally being persuaded by friends to give up.

1471   *Penelope for Ulisses*. Penelope's chaste twenty-year wait for Ulysses' return from the siege of Troy made her one of the medieval ideals of wifehood. The first letter of Ovid's widely circulated and translated *Heroides* was from Penelope to Ulysses, begging him to return. Lydgate highlights Penelope's tears and distress in his *Troy Book*:

> For his absence, bothe eve and morwe,
> Was deth to hir and inportable sorwe.   *unbearable*
> And ay in sothe for joie or any game,   *truth in all circumstances*
> Whan it fel she herd Hectoris name,   *happened*
> In any place anoon she fil aswowne   *at once; in a faint*
> And gan hirsilf al in teris drowne . . .
> (ed. Edwards, 5.2173–78)

One contemporary reader of a late fifteenth or early sixteenth-century manuscript containing Lydgate's *Troy Book* and fragments of the *Scottish Troy Book* (Cambridge, University Library MS KK.5.30) quotes lines 5–6 from the *Heroides* 1 in the margin (fol. 274v: see Wingfield, *Trojan Legend*, p. 117).

1473 *Cresseid for trew Troylus*. Cresseid, with her famous betrayal of "trew Troylus," is an ambiguous figure with whom to compare the lady of Gleneagles. On the other hand, both Chaucer and Henryson highlight her distress in *Troilus and Criseyde* and the *Testament of Cresseid*, and sympathy for her is implied by the reference to her "saikles slander" in the earlier sixteenth-century Scottish romance of *Clariodus*, ed. Irving, 5.70. Hadley Williams suggests that "the underlying sense is that the lady's subsequent actions were not wholly within her own control," as is also the case for Helen of Troy (p. 305n1477–78; see also note for lines 1475–77 below).

1475 *it wes*. C: *is wes*. C's rare typo is corrected in L.

1477–78 *Helene . . . . brocht to Troy*. Helen of Troy, the wife of Menelaus whose abduction by (and adultery with) Paris sparked the Trojan war, is another potentially ambiguous comparison, although Bawcutt and Riddy note that Guido delle Colonne's influential *Historia destructionis Troiae* portrays her grief as genuine and bitter (ed. Griffin, p. 76). See also the reference to the "teeris of Eleyne" in Chaucer's Man of Law's Prologue (*CT* II[B[1]]70).

1484–85 *Bot he . . . . David Hume of Wedderburne*. Antoine d'Arces, Seigneur de la Bastie, was murdered by David Home of Wedderburn on 17 September 1517, an event shocking enough to be noted in the *Treasurer's Accounts* with the note "obiit Labastye" (*TA* 5:149). For a detailed discussion of the murder, Home's motives, and the aftermath, see Emond, "Minority of King James V," pp. 172–81 and 192.

1496–99 *On Striviling brig . . . . the young squyar*. On this allusion to the much later murder of Meldrum's enemy, and the assumption that he was Sir John Stirling of Keir, see the Introduction, "*The Historie* and History."

1504–05 *Quha ever straikis . . . . ane sword slane*. Compare Matthew 26:52 as quoted from two contemporary English translations: "For all that take the swerde, shal perish with the swerde," in Miles Coverdale's *Biblia, the Bible*, STC (2nd ed.) 2063; or "For all that ley hond on the swearde shall perisshe with the swearde," in William Tyndale's *New Testament*, STC (2nd ed.) 2828a.

1519 *ane agit lord*. This is Patrick, fourth Lord Lindsay of the Byres, who served as sheriff of Fife from 1514 (see Dickinson, *Sheriff Court Book of Fife*, p. 205). Upon his death in 1526 he was succeeded by his grandson John, fifth Lord Lindsay of the Byres, for whom Meldrum continued to work. A retour of 8 March 1525–26 confirms "John Lindesay" as heir to his late father "Sir John Lindesay of Pitcruvy," with frank-tenement of the lands reserved "to Patrick, Lord Lindsay, grandfather of John Lindesay" (Fraser, *Memorials of the Earls of Haddington*, 2:250); an instrument of sasine of 10 February 1526/27 for lands in Calder is made in favor of "John, Lord Lindsay of the Byres" (NRS GD1/1088/5).

1538   *Tchyref depute*. Sheriff-deputes were appointed by the county sheriff — in Meldrum's case, Patrick Lord Lindsay of the Byres — to serve under them and act in their stead in the sheriff courts: Meldrum seems to have been one of two Fife sheriff-deputes in 1522, with Thomas Grundistoun the other (Dickinson, *Sheriff Court Book of Fife*, pp. 250, 255, 258, etc.) and they were still in post as of March of 1527–28 (*Reg. Mag. Sig.* 3:125, no. 565 [21 March]). "All schireffs sall have gud and sufficient deputes or baillies, for quhom thay sall answere . . . and generallie it is trew that ilk scheriff and uther ordinar judge salbe halden to answer for their deputes, as themselves," writes Skene in *De Verborum Significatione* (quoted in Dickinson, p. lv). Evidently it was a position of trust. Dickinson notes that while some fought for the right to be a sheriff-depute, others complained of the expenses incurred (p. liv note 3). There was no salary attached to the post, so a depute "probably looked to his 'perquisites' to bring him in no inconsiderable return." In other words, his income would be very much dependent on his honesty and decency (pp. lviii–lix). This offers some context for the many comments Lyndsay makes about the squire's lack of interest in riches or payment (lines 1548–54), and Meldrum's own insistence on the same in the *Testament* (lines 38–42) although he goes on to order a fantastically lavish funeral for himself.

1552   *regaird*. C: *regaitd*. L, S: *regard(e)*. For the definition, *DOST* hazards a guess of "? A payment" (*regard* (n.), sense 7) though it cites only this example and another from the sixteenth-century works of Alexander Scott. In fact, support for *DOST*'s suggestion can be found in Anglo-Norman usage; the *AND* offers several examples of the sense "remuneration" or "reward" for *regard* (n.), sense 9.

1559–60 *the Sonday . . . . Asch Wednisday*. This is Quinquagesima, the last Sunday before the lean season of Lent begins and a day on which last-minute feasting might be expected.

1562   *flaun*. C: *flam*. L, S: *flame*. A "flaun" is a kind of custard or cheese cake, see *OED flawn* (n.); see also *MED* and *AND flaun* (n.). The dishes of this feast in the lady's honor recall the supper she laid out for him when he first arrived at her castle (lines 885–87). This line is the only example recorded by *DOST* (*flam* (n.2)) of any reference to this item in Older Scots, and they label the prints' spelling here a "var. of (or error for) ME. *flaun*." None of the *MED*, *OED*, or *AND* offer examples of spellings with *-m*, so it has been treated as a typo and corrected here.

1566   *Lordis and lairdis*. Both terms derive from OE *hlāford* and they were initially interchangeable, but from the earlier fifteenth century in Scotland, "laird" came to refer to "the 'smaller barons' or smaller landowners generally, as opposed to the greater or titled barons or 'lords'" (quoting from *DOST lard* (n.), sense 3). All lords and lairds were landowners, but over the course of the fourteenth and fifteenth centuries, the titles held by many lords became gradually dissociated from actual territories. The term *lord* came to denote a peer or a "parliamentary lord" who claimed a status similar to that of a peer and could expect to be personally summoned to parliament (such as Meldrum's employers, the Lords Lindsay of the Byres). See Grant, "The Development of the Scottish Peerage."

"By contrast," writes Wormald, "it was still their landed estates which gave the lairds their dignity and title; a laird had to be laird of somewhere" ("Lords and Lairds in Fifteenth-Century Scotland," p. 187).

1589   *the Struther into Fyfe*. Struthers castle — "the Struther" or sometimes "Ochterotherstruther" in contemporary documents (see Fraser, *Memorials of the Earls of Haddington*, 2:261, no. 363) — was in northeast Fife, just west of Ceres and south of Cupar, within five miles of Sir David Lyndsay's own estate at the Mount.

EXPLANATORY NOTES TO *TESTAMENT OF SQUYER MELDRUM*

ABBREVIATIONS: *Acts of Council (Public Affairs)*: *Acts of the Lords of Council in Public Affairs*; *AND*: *Anglo-Norman Dictionary*; **C**: Edinburgh: Henrie Charteris, 1594 (STC [2nd ed.] 15679); *Cal. State Papers (Venice)*: *Calendar of State Papers and Manuscripts relating to English Affairs*; *DOST*: *Dictionary of the Older Scottish Tongue;* **EETS**: Early English Text Society; *ER*: *The Exchequer Rolls of Scotland*; **Hadley Williams**: Lyndsay, *Sir David Lyndsay: Selected Poems*, ed. Hadley Williams; **Hamer**: Lyndsay, *The Works of Sir David Lindsay*, ed. Hamer; **Kinsley**: *Squyer Meldrum*, ed. Kinsley; **L**: Edinburgh: Richard Lawson, 1610 (STC [2nd ed.] 15680); *LP Henry VIII*: *Letters and Papers, Foreign and Domestic, of the Reign of Henry VIII*; **MdnE**: Modern English; **ME**: Middle English; *MED*: *Middle English Dictionary*; *NIMEV*: *New Index of Middle English Verse*; **NLS**: Edinburgh, National Library of Scotland; **NRS**: National Records of Scotland; **OE**: Old English; *OED*: *Oxford English Dictionary*; **OF**: Old French; *Poems*: Dunbar, *Poems of William Dunbar*, ed. Bawcutt; **Reg. Mag. Sig.**: *Registrum Magni Sigilii Regum Scotorum (Register of the Great Seal of Scotland)*; **Reg. Sec. Sig.**: *Registrum Secreti Sigilli Regum Scotorum (Register of the Privy Seal of Scotland)*; **STC**: *A Short-Title Catalogue of Books Printed in England, Scotland and Ireland and English Books Printed Abroad 1473–1640*, ed. Pollard and Redgrave; **STS**: Scottish Text Society; *TA*: *Accounts of the Lord High Treasurer of Scotland*, ed. Dickson and Paul; *TC*: Chaucer, *Troilus and Criseyde*, ed. Benson; **Whiting**: Whiting, *Proverbs, Sentences and Proverbial Sayings from English Writings Before 1500*; **Wing**: Wing, *Short-Title Catalogue of Books Printed in England, Scotland and Ireland, Wales and British America and of English Books Printed in Other Countries 1641–1700*.

1–4 *holie man Job . . . . bene wounder short.* Although the Biblical Job is famous for his suffering and patience, the more specific allusion here may be to the Office of the Dead. Fein observes that "the Matins of the Office of the Dead, also called the Nine Lessons of the Dirge, was a long-established sequence of verses drawn from Job's speeches to God" (Introduction to *Pety Job*, ed. Fein, p. 289). See also the note to lines 246–53 below. Job's question to God — *Quid est homo, quia magnificas eum?* ("What is a man that thou shouldst magnify him?" Job 7:17) — could be seen to underlie Lyndsay's *Meldrum* poems as a whole.

5 *My youth is gane, and eild now dois resort.* So C. L: *My by past time was spent in weir & sport.* It is unusual for L to differ substantively from C like this. Given how much more in keeping C's line is with the sentiments represented by the book of Job as cited in line 1, L's line would seem to be the result of faulty transmission.

22 *David Erll of Craufuird.* Hamer identifies this person as David Lindsay, ninth earl of Crawford, who died in 1558.

23   *Johne Lord Lindesay.* John, fifth Lord Lindsay of the Byres, was the grandson and
          heir of Patrick, fourth Lord Lindsay, the "agit lord" who had originally hired
          Meldrum and died in 1526 (see note to line 1519 of the *Historie*). Meldrum
          seems to have remained at Struthers (see the *Historie*, note to line 1589) with
          John for the rest of his life. John died in 1563 (see Hamer 3:229–30).

25   *feistis funerall*. Compare to Lyndsay's *Testament of the Papyngo* in which the
          "papyngo" (parrot) laments that the nightingale, jay, blackbird or turtledove
          "My obsequees and feistis funerall / Ordour thay wald" (lines 726–27), if only
          they were present. The term recurs at lines 45, 196.

26–27   *Sir Walter Lindsay . . . . knicht of Torfichane.* Sir Walter Lindsay was preceptor of
          Torphichen priory, the Scottish headquarters of the order of the knights of St.
          John of Jerusalem, or the "Hospitallers." He thus used the title "Lord of St
          Johne" and would have traveled abroad frequently ("ane nobill travellit knicht,"
          line 24). On 30 April 1544, both he and Lyndsay — in his role as Lyon King of
          Arms — were commissioned on behalf of the infant Mary, Queen of Scots, to
          return James V's insignia of the Order of the Golden Fleece to the emperor
          Charles V, although it does not look as if Lyndsay actually went; further letters
          cite only Sir Walter as the bearer (*LP Henry VIII*, 19.272–73, nos. 434, 435, 436).
          See also the "protectioun, saufgard and respitt" issued to Walter, his tenants,
          and his servants while he was "furth of the realme," registered at Edinburgh on
          24 April 1544 (*Reg. Sec. Sig.* 3:108, no. 716).

          Walter was certainly dead by March 1547, when the grand master of the order
          at Malta conferred on James Sandilands the preceptory of Torphichen, "vacant
          by death of brother Walter Lindsay" (*Knights of St John*, ed. Cowan et al., p. 184,
          no. 101 [dated Malta, 29 March 1547; Cod. 421, fol. 162r–v]). Cowan, Mackay,
          and Macquarrie also provide a transcription of a notarial instrument dated at
          Edinburgh, 23 June 1547 which refers to the "quondam [i.e., deceased] nobilis
          domini Walteri domini sancti Johannis militis preceptoris de torphichen"
          (*Knights of St John*, ed. Cowan et al., pp. 133–36, quoted at p. 134 [NRS RH
          6/1408]). See the *Squyer Meldrum* Introduction for the complications this
          introduces to the dating of the *Meldrum* poems.

41   *gold more than of glas*. The collocation of gold and glass has a proverbial ring to
          it; compare Dunbar, *The Tretis of the twa mariit wemen and the wedo*: "He had the
          glemyng of gold and wes bot glase fundin" (*Poems*, 1:46, line 202). Meldrum's
          claim to care nothing for money is tacitly contrasted with the tremendous
          expense of the funeral he demands for himself.

50–56   *First . . . . and spycis precious*. Embalming was necessary to preserve the body of
          one whose funeral would require lengthy planning, or whose body was to be
          transported a long way to its resting place, e.g., that of a noble who had been on
          pilgrimage (Gittings, *Death, Burial and the Individual*, p. 166). Meldrum later
          notes that his body will not decay in its tomb thanks to the embalming (lines
          178–80). Compare the embalming of Bruce's body in Barbour's *Bruce*: "And he
          debowailyt wes clenly, / And bawmyt syne richly" (ed. McDiarmid and Stevenson,

20.295–96); or that of Alexander in the mid-fifteenth century *Buik of King Alexander the Conquerour* associated with Gilbert Hay:

> They vncled him of all his vestamentis,
> And him anoyntit with precious oyntmentis,
> Syne bowelleit him and spyiceit him in þe cors
> (ed. Cartwright, 3.18, 532–34)

In Lyndsay's own time, separate burial of entrails took place for both Henry VIII of England and Francis I of France, both in 1547, and probably for James V of Scotland in 1543 (Thomas, *Princelie Majestie*, p. 215; Gittings, *Death, Burial and the Individual*, p. 216; and Giesey, *The Royal Funeral Ceremony*, p. 2).

54   *ceder treis . . . syper fyne*. Cedar and cypress are both scented, decay-resistant woods; both would almost certainly have to be imported to Scotland in the sixteenth century. Hadley Williams notes that the cypress "often was associated with death and mourning" (compare Douglas, *Eneados*, ed. Coldwell, 2:112, lines 120–22).

57–85   *In twa caissis. . . . ye sall present*. Separate burial of the heart, enclosed in a casket, is recorded for the Scottish kings Alexander III, Robert Bruce, James I, and perhaps Alexander II. See Dean, "Crowns, Wedding Rings, and Processions," pp. 39–42. The further adventures of Robert Bruce's heart (apparently taken on crusade by his loyal follower William Douglas) are narrated by Barbour in *The Bruce* (ed. McDiarmid and Stevenson, 20.182–253, 313–497, 603–11) as well as by Richard Holland (with some variations) in the *Buke of the Howlat*, ed. Hanna, pp. 70–73, lines 436–546. Brown discusses the medieval tradition amongst royal families of separate burials for body, heart, and/or entrails ("Death and the Human Body," pp. 228–33 and 258–65). This is the practice Meldrum has in mind when he wishes his bones to be interred in the temple of Mars, his tongue in that of Mercury, and his heart in that of Venus.

64   *Mars, Venus and Mercurius*. Allusions to the influence of the planetary gods were common in formal poetry of the Middle Ages, although Meldrum's instructions for the burial of various organs in pagan temples turn his otherwise plausible — if inappropriately grand — funeral arrangements into an amusing fantasy. As Kinsley notes, Meldrum's choice for himself of Mars, Venus, and Mercury may be modeled on encomia such as Dunbar's "[B]allade of . . . Barnard Stewart, lord of Aubigny," in which he describes Stewart as being favored by Mars, Saturn, Venus, Mercury, and Fortuna major (*Poems*, 1:179, lines 73–80).

71–75   *Quho list to knaw . . . . sword and knife*. Ariès, describing French noble practice, remarks: "In the sixteenth, seventeenth and eighteenth centuries, it very often happens that the epitaph is a true biographical account intended to glorify the deceased, something like the notice in a dictionary of celebrities, with special emphasis placed on military citations . . . very often devoted to the brilliant feats and outstanding services of men of war . . . The inscriptions that cover the floors and walls of churches and cemeteries are like the pages of a dictionary of famous people, a kind of *Who's Who* laid open for the perusal of passersby" (*The Hour of Our Death*, p. 223). Slightly closer to home, the lavish funeral in 1524 of the

English victor at the battle of Flodden, Thomas Howard, second Duke of Norfolk (the Earl of Surrey as was), included a recitation of his noble deeds by the Carlisle herald (Gittings, *Death, Burial and the Individual*, p. 37). Francis Blomefield records an inscription of over 3,000 words detailing the triumphs of Howard's career attached to his monument (*An Essay towards a Topographical History of the County of Norfolk*, 2:119–25). In Meldrum's case, we suddenly realize that this legend is the *Historie* we have just read. He refers to his legend again at lines 167 and 233.

79   *Mercurius.* Lyndsay elsewhere describes Mercury as he whom "poetis callis god of eloquence" (*Dreme*, line 394). Meldrum's description of advancing his honor through "his ornate toung" could simply mean that he spoke well — this is the straightforward significance of Dunbar's praise for Barnard Stewart: "On the Marcurius furtheyet his eloquence" (*Poems*, 1:179, line 78). On the other hand, we were also told that many of the details in the *Historie* were supplied to Lyndsay by Meldrum himself (*Historie*, lines 33–34), so the trustworthiness of his "tongue" becomes an issue. An ambivalent attitude to the "toung rhetoricall" is apparent in Lyndsay's *Testament of the Papyngo*, in which the chagrined dying parrot bequeaths her "Eloquence and toung rethoricall" (line 78) to the goose (lines 1104–05).

In addition to eloquence, Mercury was also the god of commerce, cheats, and thieves, some additional associations which Walter Kennedy may have had in mind when he referred to Dunbar as a "monstir maid be god Mercurius" in their famous *Flyting* (*Poems*, 1:216, line 490). In Gower's widely-circulated *Confessio Amantis*, one born under the sign of Mercury is described as:

. . . slouh and lustles to travaile	*sluggish*
In thing which elles myhte availe:	*prosper (be sufficient)*
He loveth ese, he loveth reste,	
So is he noght the worthieste;	
Bot yit with somdiel besinesse	*diligence (industry)*
His herte is set upon richesse.	
(ed. Peck, 7.761–66)	

In his note to these lines, Peck discusses the medieval antecedents for this association of Mercury's children with commence, theft, and the eager pursuit of riches. In Meldrum's case, they might make readers suspicious of his repeated claims to care nothing for riches. See lines 37–39, 41–42, less directly lines 222–24, and the *Historie*, lines 1551–56.

93   *my processioun.* Chivalric funerals such as the one Meldrum describes here would have been organized by a herald. As Scotland's chief herald, Lyon King of Arms, Lyndsay was eminently well qualified for the job; he would also direct the funeral of James V (whether or not this had already taken place depends on the date assigned to this poem; see the *Squyer Meldrum* Introduction). Pre-Reformation English heraldic funerals that are similar to what Meldrum outlines here (though generally less lavish) are described by Houlbrooke, *Death, Religion, and the Family in England*, pp. 258–64.

95   *my penseil*. This is a small pennon (a streamer-shaped flag). The seventeenth-century guidelines drawn up by Lord Lyon Sir James Balfour of Denmiln state that "Ane Esquyre is to have A pennon of his Armes, A Coate of Armes, Healme and crest," as indeed Meldrum does here (NLS MS Gen. Cat. 57, 32.2.14, quoted from Burnett, "Funeral Heraldry," p. 474).

98   *ane thowsand hagbutteris*. This figure might be compared to the mere 80 hagbutters (soldiers armed with an early precursor to the rifle) that Pitscottie says the Seigneur de la Bastie had at his command in 1517 when he was acting regent of Scotland (*Historie and Cronicles*, ed. Mackay, 1:299, line 2), or the 279 "hagbusshes" listed in the 1547 inventory of the garrison at Calais (Grummit, *Calais Garrison*, p. 123).

104   *standart*. The standard was a long narrow flag with split ends. In later Scottish codifications, standards were only permitted to those of baronial rank or above, though it is not clear how strictly such things were regulated in Meldrum's Scotland. See Innes, *Scots Heraldry*, pp. 43–44.

106   *baner*. The banner was either a square or an upright rectangular flag displaying arms. Innes asserts that "in actual mediaeval warfare none below knights-banneret and (feudal) barons displayed the square banner," but that other nobles and lairds might use the upright rectangular banner (Innes, *Scots Heraldry*, p. 42).

107   *Of silver schene, thrie otteris into sabill*. The syntax of this description of Meldrum's banner is ambiguous. The punctuation adopted here assumes that a banner of bright ("schene") silver with three otters in black ("sabill") is to be borne amongst the band of noble men. This lists the elements of his banner in the usual order for heraldic description, i.e., color of field ("silver"), followed by the charges ("otteris") and their color (sable, or black). An alternative reading suggested by Hadley Williams is that this is a specific funeral hatchment in which the charges — now silver otters — are shown on a black background, for which practice she cites Burnett, "Funeral Heraldry," pp. 490, 492 and illustrations on pp. 496–553. It is certainly true that Lyndsay does not stick to the formal heraldic ordering of elements when describing Meldrum's arms elsewhere in the *Historie* (compare "Ane otter in ane silver feild," lines 384 and 548). On the other hand, Burnett also observes that "there is not enough remaining evidence to show if this code was used on pre-Union hatchments but it was used consistently on Scottish hatchments after 1707" ("Funeral Heraldry," p. 490), so the question remains as to whether such funeral hatchments were in use as early as c. 1550. On Meldrum's arms, see note to line 384 of the *Historie*.

110–19 *Nixt efter them . . . . my coit armour*. Apart from the inflated numbers of followers, Meldrum's instructions for the items and ordering of this part of his funeral are very similar to the instructions for directing a heraldic funeral as copied by John Scrymgeour of Myres in a manuscript of the first half of the sixteenth century: "Item þe secund offerand sould be þe heallme" (this is equivalent to Meldrum's basnet); "Item þe thrid offerand should be þe swerd"; "Item þe ferd offerand of a horss coverit with þe armes of þe deid And a gentillman salbe vpon him or a freind of þe deid quhilk sall beir his baner or be þe bachileir his pennon And he salbe cumpanit with tua noble men þe maist vailliant and þe maist of renown to be capitanes"; "Item þe fyft offrand salbe siclyck of ane horss coverit with his loveray [i.e., livery] and a man aboue" (NLS, Advocates MS 31.5.2, transcribed in Dean, "Crowns, Wedding Rings, and Processions," Appendix A, pp. 338–39).

113   *arming sword*. This is the standard short sword as used in knightly combat or worn with military harness. See Oakeshott, *European Weapons and Armour*, pp. 125–26.

117   *jonet . . . cursour*. The jennet was a small Spanish horse; the courser a more powerful horse appropriate for carrying armed knights (see *DOST jonet* (n.2) and *MED courser* (n.)).

120–26   *my corspresent . . . . at my interrement*. The "corspresent" was a payment or gift to the clergy, and for heraldic funerals it might be a horse and armor as Meldrum plans to offer here. That this was a traditional (if expensive) gift is suggested by the fact that Hugh Earl of Stafford, in his will of 1385, specifically forbade his executors to arrange for it: "I desire that no horse or arms be offered at my funeral, and that no prayers be said thereat excepting by ecclesiastical persons, my allies, and friends" (Nicolas, *Testamenta Vetusta*, 1:118).

125–26   *Quhilk sal . . . . at my interrement*. C accidentally inserts a space between these two lines, rather than at the end of the stanza after line 126.

128   *With huidis heklit doun ovirthort thair ene*. *DOST* defines *heklit* (adj. and ppl.) as "having a border or a fringe like a cock's hackle" (i.e., a cockerel's neck-feathers). Whatever the style intended, Meldrum means that the hoods hang low enough to almost cover their eyes.

151–61   *ye thoill na preist . . . . melodie and game*. Meldrum's refusal to admit clergy to his funeral procession other than those of "Venus professioun" and "Venus chapel clarks" (i.e., lovers and those who assist them) and his insistence on "melodie and game" recall the conclusion of Dunbar's satirical testament "I maister Andro Kennedy," in which the drunkard Andro insists:

> I will na preistis for me sing
> *Dies illa, dies ire* [that day, that day of wrath]
> Na ōit na bellis for me ring,
> *Sicut semper solet fieri*, [As always is the custom]
> Bot a bag pipe to play a spryng [dance-tune]
> *Et vnum* ail wosp *ante me* . . .
> [i.e., the bundle of straw marking an ale-house]
> (*Poems*, 1:92, lines 105–110; Latin trans. 2:332)

Meldrum likewise refuses to have the passing-bell rung for him, demanding instead that cannons and 1,000 hagbuts be fired for him as well as trumpets blown (lines 181–86).

154   *Quhilk hes bene most exercit in hir warkis*. C omits the stanza-break after this line, probably because it is the penultimate line on his page.

181–82   *Let not be rung . . . . crak for bellis*. See note to lines 151–61 above.

195   *temperall*. As Hadley Williams has shown, this is not "worldly goods" but a specific term for "coat-armor," the rich vest embroidered with heraldic devices as worn by heralds, or by knights over top of their armor. See *A Dictionarie of the French and English Tongues* which has "Temporalles. *Coat-armors; or Heraulds coats*" (ed. Cotgrave).

199–203   *Abone my grave . . . . wes his name*. A survey of the wills in Nicolas, *Testamenta Vetusta*, reveals that many of the testators specify marble tombstones, sometimes with an image of the deceased in brass or carved into the stone. The frequency with which the wording of an inscription is specified increases over the fifteenth and sixteenth centuries, but it generally remains a combination of the pious and the soberly biographical. One might compare the boastful epitaph desired by Meldrum to that on James V's tomb:

> ILLVSTRIS. SCOTORUM. REX. JACOBUS.
> EJUS. NO[MIN]IS. 5. ETATIS. SUE. ANNO. 31. REGNI.
> VERO. 30. MORTEM. OBJIT. IN. PALACIO. DE.
> FALKLAND. 14. DECEMBRIS. ANNO. D[OMI]NI. 1542.
> CUJUS. CORPUS. HIC. TRADITV[M]. EST. SEPULTURAE.

> [Illustrious James, King of the Scots, fifth of that name, aged 31, having reigned for thirty years, died in the palace of Falkland on 14 December, in the year of our Lord 1542, [and his] body was buried here.]
> (translation mine)

This inscription was copied into NLS Advocates MS 33.3.26 (Sibbaldi Caledonia) from the coffin plate in "'a vault in the south-east corner of ye Abby Church of Halyroodhouse, on the 24th of January 1683'" (Dunbar, *Scottish Kings: A Revised Chronology*, p. 240).

204   *Adew*. Meldrum's repeated "adew[s]" to those he believes will be inconsolable upon his death (lines 201, 202, 209, 218, 226, 238, 239, 242) recall the anaphoral oupouring of grief by Alexander's followers in Gilbert Hay's *Buik of King Alexander the Conquerour*, more evidence of Meldrum's comically high opinion of his own importance:

> Adew, fairveill, our confort and blyithnes,
> Adew," thay said, "our lyife, adew our dead,
> Adew, our wit, our counsall, and our read,
> Adew, fair-veill, our haill and our seik)ness,
> Adew, our warldis ioy and our solace,
> Adew, fair-weill . . .
> (ed. Cartwright, 3:237, lines 18597–603; there are a further six "Adew[s]")

205–09   *My Lord Lindesay . . . . your sisteris al*. On "My Lord Lindesay," i.e., John, fifth Lord Lindsay of the Byres, see note to line 23 above. His "lady" was Helen Stuart, daughter of the earl of Atholl. Their eldest son and the future sixth Lord Lindsay is the "Maister Patrik" named here; their third son is "Normand" (the second son John had died decades earlier). Patrick and Norman are both cited in a precept of sasine granting lands at Drem, Haddington, to Norman: it was dated at Ochterotherstruther (i.e., Struthers), 30 May 1550, and one of the witnesses was "William Meldrum of Bynnis" (Fraser, *Memorials of the Earls of Haddington*, 2:261, no. 363). The "sisteris al" of Patrick and Norman are the seven daughters of John and Helen who survived into adulthood, meticulously named by Hamer (3:229–30) as Isabel, Janet, Margaret, Marie, Helen, Catherine, and Elizabeth.

207   *the Struther*. Struthers Castle, the Fife seat of the Lords Lindsay. See note to line 1589 of the *Historie*.

211–14   *But maist of all . . . . the murning weid.* See the *Historie*, lines 685–91, on the eagerness of one nameless French lady to marry Meldrum and the general distress of the ladies of France upon his departure.

215–17   *Quhen thir novellis . . . . drerie cheir.* On Meldrum in England, see note to the *Historie*, line 88.

218–24   *Of Craigfergus . . . . youth and insolence.* The rescue of the maiden at Carrickfergus is the very first adventure narrated in the *Historie* (lines 104–72). She offers to stow away with the Scottish fleet as his paramour when he will not take her as his wife (lines 202–06). His remark about refusing her "throw youth and insolence" does not so much recall the Carrickfergus episode (in which he just seemed eager to escape the maiden's advances) as his refusal of a nameless French lady "of greit rent" [income] because "youth maid him sa insolent" (lines 686–88).

225   *lemant lampis of lustines.* Dunbar calls Margaret Tudor "Lodsteir and lamp of euery lustines" (*Poems*, 1:81, line 10), while the eponymous hero of the sixteenth-century Scots romance *Clariodus* addresses his beloved Meliades very similarly as "Lodstar of love, and lampe of lustieheid" (ed. Irving, 2.365), possibly in imitation of Dunbar's diction. On "lodstar," see note to line 230 below.

229–38   *Ten thousand times . . . . adew for ever.* This is the great love affair of his life, and its story takes up lines 863–1478 of the *Historie*. Marjorie Lawson, Lady of Gleneagles and the real person behind this story, is never named by Lyndsay in either poem; see the Introduction, "The Historie and History."

230   *Sterne of Stratherne.* Chaucer's Troilus twice calls Criseyde his "lode-sterre," i.e., guiding star (*TC* 5.232, 1392), and Meliades in the sixteenth-century Scots romance of *Clariodus* is several times called "lodstar" (ed. Irving, 2.365 and 1317, 3.584, 4.1202). See Wingfield, *Trojan Legend* (pp. 82–87) on *Clariodus'* debt to *Troilus and Criseyde*; both texts may have influenced Lyndsay's diction here.

245   *crysme.* Chrism is the mixture of oil and balm used in the administration of certain sacraments of the Church, such as the Last Rites.

246–53   *My spreit hartlie . . . . thow wes borne.* This final stanza abandons rhyme royal for a single eight-line stanza of four-stress lines rhyming *ababbcbc*, the same stanza employed by the influential satiric *lais* and *Testament* of the fifteenth-century French poet François Villon (see *Squyer Meldrum* Introduction) although it is not uncommon elsewhere. It begins by alternating Latin and English lines, but by the second half of the stanza, the two Latin lines actually begin in Scots. This change in stanza form is reminiscent of Dunbar's "I, Maister Andro Kennedy," in which he moves from an eight-line stanza of alternating Latin and English lines to a final stanza of twelve lines (see note to lines 151–61 above). C and L print the Latin lines in Roman typeface, to distinguish them from the blackletter used for the Scots.

The first two Latin lines echo Psalm 30:6: *In manus tuas commendo spiritum meum; redemisti me, Domine Deus veritatis* ["Into thy hands I commend my spirit: thou hast redeemed me, O lord, the God of truth"]. The association of this Psalm with the Office of the Dead is illustrated graphically in an earlier fifteenth-century manuscript, the "Grandes Heures de Rohan" (Bibliothèque Nationale de France, MS Lat. 9471, fol. 159), which may have been commissioned by the dauphin Charles, Duke of Berry. (It might be noted in passing that Charles' daughter-in-law was Margaret Stewart, daughter of James I of Scotland — a keen reader and writer herself, and the subject of the *Complaint for the Death of Margaret* edited elsewhere in this volume). The miniature on the opening page of the Office of the Dead depicts a naked corpse quoting Psalm 30:6, and Christ replying (in French) that the dead man will do penance for his sins, but will be reunited with him on Judgment Day. See Kinch, *Imago Mortis*, pp. 21–22. See the *Testament*'s earlier allusion to the Office of the Dead through references to Job at lines 1–4 above and note.

APPENDIX: THE LAWSON AND HALDANE FAMILY TREES

Documents supporting the Lawson and Haldane Family Trees:
These are in addition to documents cited in the Introduction to the *Meldrum* Poems, "The *Historie* and History." Note that the relative ages of the Lawson siblings are unknown apart from that of the eldest son and heir Robert, and there may have been more siblings than shown here.

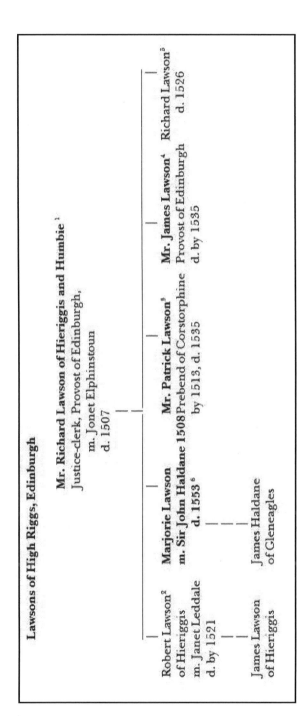

Lawsons of High Riggs, Edinburgh

Mr. Richard Lawson of Hieriggis and Humbie [1]
Justice-clerk, Provost of Edinburgh,
m. Jonet Elphinstoun
d. 1507

Robert Lawson [2]
of Hieriggis
m. Janet Leddale
d. by 1521

James Lawson
of Hieriggis

Marjorie Lawson
m. **Sir John Haldane 1508**
d. 1553 [6]

James Haldane
of Gleneagles

Mr. Patrick Lawson [3]
Prebend of Corstorphine
by 1513, d. 1535

Mr. James Lawson [4]
Provost of Edinburgh
d. by 1535

Richard Lawson [5]
d. 1526

271

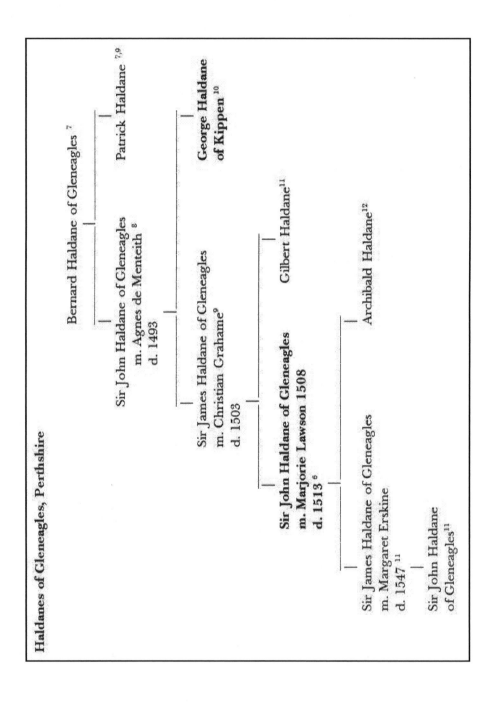

Haldanes of Gleneagles, Perthshire

Bernard Haldane of Gleneagles [7]

Patrick Haldane [7,9]

Sir John Haldane of Gleneagles
m. Agnes de Menteith [8]
d. 1493

George Haldane
of Kippen [10]

Sir James Haldane of Gleneagles
m. Christian Grahame [9]
d. 1503

Gilbert Haldane [11]

**Sir John Haldane of Gleneagles
m. Marjorie Lawson 1508
d. 1513** [6]

Archibald Haldane [12]

Sir James Haldane of Gleneagles
m. Margaret Erskine
d. 1547 [11]

Sir John Haldane
of Gleneagles [11]

1.   Listed as Provost of Edinburgh in May 1492 and January 1504/05 (see the Appendix to Marwick, *Extracts from the Records of the Burgh of Edinburgh*). See also an instrument of sasine dated 13 March 1492/93 citing "Mr. Richard Lauson of Hieriggis, clerk of the King's justiciary" and "his spouse Jonet Elphinstoun" (NRS GD103/1/19); their marriage is also confirmed in GD150/243 (16 March 1494/95), and the charter NRS GD120/3 (27 April 1500). For Master Richard's date of death, see note 2 below.

2.   *Reg.Mag.Sig.* 2:664, no. 3110, charter granted to "Jonet Liddale" and her spouse "Roberto Lawsoun, filio et heredi apparenti M. Ricardi L. de Hieriggis," issued 28 June 1507 and registered 2 July; evidently Robert was the eldest son. His father Richard seems to have died between these two dates, since the introductory clause describes him as "quondam familiaris regis" (a former intimate of the king's). Robert himself was dead by 9 May 1521, the date of a precept recognizing "James Lausoun as heir to deceased Robert L., his father" (NRS GD120/19).

3.   See NRS GD122/1/579, a resignation by Walter Zong dated 18 April 1513 and witnessed by "Robert Lawson, of Hierigg" and "Master Patrick Lawson, Prebend of Corstophin."

4.   A tack for the lands of Skiprig was issued to "Mr. James Lausoun, son of the deceased Mr. Richard Lausoun of the Hieriggis" on 19 February 1516/17. In a discharge of 6 June 1535, the land would be made over to "John and Patrick Lausoun, sons of the deceased Mr. James Lausoun, provost of Edinburgh," and at a later date still, these brothers died and the land went to a third brother George. For all three records, see *Report on Manuscripts in Various Collections*, 5:25–26.

5.   See NRS GD120/14, an instrument of sasine by "Mr. Richard Lausoun ex propriis manibus to Richard Lausoun, his son," dated 10 October 1504. This Richard was dead by 5 November 1526, when his nephew James Lawson of Hieriggis (son of Robert) issued a precept in favor of Mr. Patrick Lausoun as heir to deceased "Richard L., his brother" (NRS GD120/21).

6.   Her date of death is given as July 1553 in the action raised on 13 December 1555 by her grandson John, "Oy [grandson] and air to umquhile Johnne Haldane of Glennegas, quha wes slane at the feild of Flowdoun," and "umquhill Marioun [i.e., Marjorie] Lawsoun his spous, Gudame [grandmother] to the said John Haldane, now of Glennegas" (Hamer, *Works*, 3:203–04, quoting from *Acta Dom.Con.* MS. 12.343 as printed in Laing, *Poetical Works*, 1:324).

7.   NRS GD198/18: "Precept of sasine by John Halden [Haldane], son and heir of Bernard Halden [Haldane] of Gleneges [Gleneagles]," with one of the baillies named as "Patrick Halden [Haldane], brother of granter," dated 30 September 1472.

8.   NRS GD198/45: Instrument of resignation by "Agnes of Menteth [Menteith], spouse of John Haldan [Haldane] . . . for new infeftment in favour of James Haudane [Haldane], son and apparent heir of said Agnes and John," dated 6 April 1472. See also GD198/49, 23 July 1473.

9.   NRS GD198/16, Charter of 20 December 1481 by John Haldane "to James Halden [Haldane], his son and apparent heir, and Christian Grahame [Graham] his spouse"; baillies include "Patrick Haldane, brother of John Halden [Haldane] of Glennegas [Gleneagles]" (see associated precept of sasine, NRS GD198/17). Sir James' year of death is given in a retour of 1 July 1505 in favor of his heir John Haldane, the lands "having been in [the] king's hands for two years or thereby" (NRS GD198/67).

10.   NRS, GD198/65: Instrument of sasine in favor of "James Haudane [Haldane] of Glennegas [Gleneagles], kt.," witnessed by "George Haudane [Haldane], brother of the said James," dated 6 January 1501/02. NRS GD198/119–120: instrument of sasine witnessed by "George Haldene [Haldane], uncle of Sir John Haldane of Glenegas [Gleneagles]," dated 14 May 1513.

11.   NRS, GD198/124: Instrument of sasine of 12 January 1513/14 following a precept of 2 December 1513 "in favour of James Haudene [Haldane], son and heir of deceased John Haudene [Haldane] of Glenegas [Gleneagles], kt., in lands and barony of Glenegas and lands and barony of Haudene [Haldane], excepting lands of Rusky [Ruskie] and Lanrik [Lanrick] in stewartry of Menteth [Menteith] in hands of Margaret Lausone [error for Marjorie], spouse of said deceased Sir John, by reason of conjunct fee." Procurator is "Mr. Gilbert Haudene [Haldane], tutor testamentar and legal of James Haudene of Glenegas [Gleneagles]." (Haldane, *Haldanes of Gleneagles*, pp. xviii–xix has Gilbert as Sir John Haldane's brother and James' uncle). James died in February 1547: see the retour of 29 March 1547, in favor of his son John in the lands and baronies of Gleneagles and Haldane, excepting lands held by James' wife Margaret Erskine or mother Marjorie (misnamed "Marion"), both called "ladies of Gleneges" (NRS, GD198/127).

12.   According to Haldane, *Haldanes of Gleneagles*, pp. 35–36, this may be the "Archibald Halden" who witnessed a document of 4 May 1542 alongside "James Halden of Glennagas" and "James Lausoun of Hie Riggis" (NRS GD158/248; letters of reversion by Adam Boithwell and his mother Katherine Bellendene).

❧ BIBLIOGRAPHY

Accounts of the Lord High Treasurer of Scotland. Ed. James Balfour Paul and Thomas Dickson. 13 vols. Edinburgh: H. M. General Register House, 1877–1978.

Acta Dominorum Concilii: Acts of the Lords of Council in Civil Causes. Ed. T. Thomson, George Neilson, Henry Paton. 3 vols. Edinburgh: H. M. Stationary Office, 1839–1993.

Acta Facultatis Artium Universitatis Sanctiandree, 1413–1588. Ed. Annie I. Dunlop. Edinburgh: Oliver & Boyd for the University Court of the University of St Andrews, 1964.

Acts of the Lords of Council in Public Affairs 1501–1554: Selections from the Acta Dominorum Concilii Introductory to the Register of the Privy Council of Scotland. Ed. Robert Kerr Hannay. Edinburgh: H. M. General Register House, 1932.

Alexander, Flora. "Late Medieval Scottish Attitudes to the Figure of Arthur: A Reassessment." *Anglia* 93 (1975), 17–34.

Alliterative Morte Arthure. In *King Arthur's Death: The Middle English Stanzaic Morte Arthur and Alliterative Morte Arthure*. Ed. Larry D. Benson. Exeter: University of Exeter, 1986. Rpt. 1988. Rev. Edward E. Foster. Kalamazoo, MI: Medieval Institute Press, 1994.

An Alphabet of Tales: An English 15ᵗʰ Century Translation of the Alpabetum Narrationum *of Étienne de Besançon*. Ed. Mary Macleod Banks. 2 vols. EETS o.s. 126–27. London: Kegan Paul, Trench, Trübner & Co., Ltd, 1904–05.

Ambühl, Rémy. *Prisoners of War in the Hundred Years War: Ransom Culture in the Late Middle Ages*. Cambridge: Cambridge University Press, 2013.

Anderson, James Maitland, ed. *Early Records of the University of St. Andrews: The Graduation Roll 1413–1579 and the Matriculation Roll 1473–1579*. Scottish History Society. 3rd series 8. Edinburgh: T. and A. Constable for the Scottish History Society, 1926.

Anglo-Norman Dictionary. University of Aberystwyth and University of Swansea. Arts and Humanities Research Council of the United Kingdom, 2001. Online at http://www.anglo-norman.net/gate/.

Archibald, Elizabeth. "Declarations of 'Entente' in *Troilus and Criseyde*." *Chaucer Review* 25.3 (1991), 190–213.

Ariès, Philippe. *The Hour of Our Death*. Trans. Helen Weaver. Harmondsworth: Penguin, 1983.

Ascham, Roger. *English Works: Toxophilus, Report of the Affaires and State of Germany, The Scholemaster*. Ed. William Aldis Wright. Cambridge: Cambridge University Press, 1904.

Ashurst, David. "Alexander the Great." In *Heroes and Anti-Heroes in Medieval Romance*. Ed. Neil Cartlidge. Cambridge: D. S. Brewer, 2012. Pp. 27–41.

The Asloan Manuscript: A Miscellany in Prose and Verse. Ed. W. A. Craigie. 2 vols. STS 2nd series 14, 16. Edinburgh: Scottish Text Society, 1923–25.

Augustine, Saint. *City of God*. Ed. G. R. Evans. Trans. Henry Bettenson. London: Penguin, 2003.

The Awntyrs off Arthure at the Terne Wathelyn. Ed. Ralph Hanna III. Manchester: Manchester University Press, 1974.

Bach, Ulrich. *Das Testament als literarische Form: Versuch einer Gattungsbestimmung auf der Grundlage Englischer Texte*. Düsseldorf: Stern-Verl, 1977.

"Ane Ballet of the Nine Nobles." In *Early Popular Poetry of Scotland and the Northern Border*. Ed. David Laing. Revised by W. Carew Hazlitt. Vol. 1. London: Reeves and Turner, 1895. Pp. 300–03.

"The 'Ballet of the Nine Nobles.'" Ed. W. A. Craigie. *Anglia* 21 (1899), 359–65.

The Bannatyne Manuscript. Ed. W. Tod Ritchie. 4 vols. STS 2nd series 22, 23, 26; 3rd series 5. Edinburgh: Scottish Text Society, 1928–34.

The Bannatyne Miscellany: Containing Original Papers and Tracts, Chiefly Relating to the History and Literature of Scotland. Ed. W. Scott, D. Laing, and T. Thomson. 3 vols. Edinburgh: Bannatyne Club, 1827–55.

Barbé, Louis A. *Margaret of Scotland & the Dauphin Louis: An Historical Study.* Glasgow and Bombay: Blackie and Son, 1917.

Barbour, John. *Barbour's Bruce.* Ed. Matthew P. McDiarmid and James A. C. Stevenson. 3 vols. STS 4th series 12, 13, 15. Edinburgh: Scottish Text Society, 1980, 1981 and Edinburgh: Blackwood, Pillans, & Wilson Ltd., 1985.

Bath, Michael. *Renaissance Decorative Painting in Scotland.* Edinburgh: National Museums of Scotland Publishing, 2003.

Bawcutt, Priscilla. "Bear or Boar in *The Tales of the Five Beasts.*" *Scottish Literary Journal* Supplement 13 (1980), 11–12.

———. "The Art of Flyting." *Scottish Literary Journal* 10.2 (1983), 5–24.

———. "A Medieval Scottish Elegy and its French Original." *Scottish Literary Journal* 15.1 (1988), 5–13.

———. "A First-Line Index of Early Scottish Verse." *Studies in Scottish Literature* 26 (1991), 254–70.

———. "'My Bright Buke': Women and their Books in Medieval and Renaissance Scotland." In *Medieval Women: Texts and Contexts in Late Medieval Britain: Essays for Felicity Riddy.* Ed. Jocelyn Wogan-Browne, Roselynn Voaden, Arlyn Diamond, Ann Hutchison, Carol M. Meale, and Lesley Johnson. Turnhout: Brepols, 2000. Pp. 17–34.

———. "French Connections? From the *Grands Rhétoriqueurs* to Clément Marot." In *The European Sun.* Eds. Caie, et al. Pp. 119–28.

———. "The Contents of the Bannatyne Manuscript: New Sources and Analogues." *Journal of the Edinburgh Bibliographical Society* 3 (2008), 95–133.

Bawcutt, Priscilla, and Bridget Henisch. "Scots Abroad in the Fifteenth Century: The Princesses Margaret, Isabella and Eleanor." In *Women in Scotland c. 1100–c. 1750.* Eds. Ewan and Meikle. Pp. 45–55.

Bawcutt, Priscilla, and Felicity Riddy, eds. *Longer Scottish Poems, Vol. 1: 1375–1650.* Edinburgh: Scottish Academic Press, 1987.

Bellenden, John, trans. *The Chronicles of Scotland Compiled by Hector Boece.* Ed. Walter Seton, R. W. Chambers, and Edith C. Batho. 2 vols. STS 3rd series 10, 15. Edinburgh: Scottish Text Society, 1938–41.

Bellon-Méguelle, Hélène. *Du Temple de Mars à la Chambre de Vénus: Le Beau Jeu Courtois dans les Vœux du Paon.* Paris: Honoré Champion, 2008.

Benoît de Sainte-Maure. *Le Roman de Troie.* Ed. Léopold Constans. 6 vols. Paris: Librairie de Firmin-Didot et Cie, 1904–12.

Benson, C. David. "Prudence, Othea and Lydgate's Death of Hector." *The American Benedictine Review* 26.1 (1975), 115–23.

Bernard of Clairvaux. *In Praise of the New Knighthood: A Treatise on the Knights Templar and the Holy Places of Jerusalem.* Trans. M. Conrad Greenia. Kalamazoo, MI: Cistercian Publications, 2000.

Beveridge, James and James Russell, eds. *Protocol Books of Dominus Thomas Johnsoun, 1528–1578.* Edinburgh: J. Skinner & Co., 1920.

Bibliotheca Heberiana: Catalogue of the Library of the late Richard Heber, Esq. Part the Eleventh. Manuscripts. London, 1836.

The Binns Papers 1320–1864: Part I — 1329–1685. Ed. Sir James Bruce Wilkie Dalyell and James Beveridge. Edinburgh: J. Skinner and Company for the Scottish Record Society, 1936.

Blaeu, Joan. *Blaeu Atlas of Scotland, 1654.* Trans. Ian Cunningham. National Library of Scotland. Accessed November 2017. Online at http://maps.nls.uk/atlas/blaeu/atlas_index.html.

Blomefield, Francis, and Charles Parkin. *An Essay Towards a Topographical History of the County of Norfolk.* 11 vols. London: Miller, 1805–10.

Boardman, Stephen. *The Campbells 1250–1513.* Edinburgh: John Donald, 2006.

Boece, Hector. *Chronicle of Scotland*. Amsterdam: Theatrum Orbis Terrarum, 1977.

Boffey, Julia. "Lydgate, Henryson, and the Literary Testament." *Modern Language Quarterly* 53.1 (1992), 41–56.

Bouwmeester, Gerard. "The Nine Worthies in Middle Dutch Miscellanies." *The Dynamics of the Medieval Manuscript*. Accessed November 2017. Online at https://dynamicsofthemedieval manuscript.eu/wp-content/uploads/sites/297/2017/09/Bouwmeester_Nine_Worthies.pdf.

Bower, Walter. *Scotichronicon*. Gen. Ed. Donald Watt. 9 vols. Aberdeen: Aberdeen University Press, 1987–1998.

Breeze, Andrew. "Dunbar's *Brylyoun, Carrybald, Cawanderis, Slawsy, Strekouris*, and *Traikit*." *Notes & Queries* 54.2 (2007), 125–28.

Brown, Elizabeth A. R. "Death and the Human Body in the Later Middle Ages: The Legislation of Boniface VIII on the Division of the Corpse." *Viator* 12 (1981), 221–70.

Brown, Michael H. "'The Stock that I am a Branch of': Patrons and Kin of Sir Gilbert Hay." In *Fresche Fontanis*. Eds. Hadley Williams and McClure. Pp. 17–30.

Bryce, William Moir. *The Scottish Grey Friars*. 2 vols. Edinburgh: William Green and Sons, 1909.

Buchanan, William, of Auchmar. *Historical and Genealogical Essay upon the Family and Surname of Buchanan: To which is added a brief inquiry into the genealogy and present state of ancient Scottish surnames, and more particularly of the Highland clans*. Glasgow: William Duncan, 1723. Rpt. Cincinnati: J. A. and U. P. James, 1849.

The Buik of Alexander, or the Buik of the Most Noble and Valiant Conquerour Alexander the Grit [The Octosyllabic Alexander]. Ed. R. L. Græme Ritchie. 4 vols. STS 2nd series 12, 17, 21, 25. Edinburgh: Scottish Text Society, 1921–29.

The Buke of the Chess: Edited from the Asloan Manuscript (NLS MS 16500). Ed. Catherine van Buuren. STS 4th series 27. Edinburgh: Scottish Text Society, 1997.

The Buke of the Sevyne Sagis: A Middle Scots Version of the Seven Sages of Rome edited from the Asloan Manuscript (NLS Acc. 4233), c. 1515. Ed. Catherine van Buuren. Leiden: Leiden University Press, 1982.

Burnett, C. J. "Funeral Heraldry in Scotland with Particular Reference to Hatchments." *Proceedings of the Society of Antiquaries of Scotland* 116 (1986), 473–559.

Caie, Graham, Roderick J. Lyall, Sally Mapstone, and Kenneth Simpson, eds. *The European Sun: Proceedings of the Seventh International Conference on Medieval and Renaissance Scottish Language and Literature*. East Linton: Tuckwell Press, 2001.

Calendar of the Laing Charters, A.D. 854–1837 belonging to the University of Edinburgh. Ed. Rev. John Anderson. Edinburgh: J. Thin, 1899.

Calendar of Scottish Supplications to Rome. Ed. Edward Reginald Lindsay, Annie I. Dunlop, Ian Borthwick Cowan, David MacLauchlan, James Kirk, Roland J. Tanner, and Alan Macquarrie. 3 vols. Scottish History Society 3rd series 23, 48, 4th series 7. Edinburgh: T. & A. Constable, 1934, 1956, 1970.

Calendar of State Papers and Manuscripts Relating to English Affairs, Existing in the Archives and Collections of Venice, and in Other libraries of northern Italy. Vol. 2. Ed. Rawdon Brown. London: Longman Green, 1867.

Calin, William. *The Lily and the Thistle: The French Tradition and the Older Literature of Scotland — Essays in Criticism*. Toronto: University of Toronto Press, 2014.

Cameron, Jamie. *James V: The Personal Rule, 1528–1542*. Ed. Norman Macdougall. Edinburgh: Tuckwell Press, 1998.

Cary, George. *The Medieval Alexander*. Ed. D. J. A. Ross. Cambridge: Cambridge University Press, 1956.

Caughey, Anna, and Emily Wingfield. "Conquest and Imperialism: Medieval Scottish Contexts for Alexander's 'Journey to Paradise.'" In *Les Voyages d'Alexandre au Paradis: Orient et Occident, Regards Croisés*. Ed. Catherine Gaullier-Bougassas and Margaret Bridges. Turnhout: Brepols, 2013. Pp. 463–84.

Champion, Pierre. *La Dauphine Mélancolique*. Paris: Marcelle Lesage, 1927.

———. *Louis XI*. 2 vols. Paris: H. Champion, 1927.

Chanson de Roland. Ed. Joseph Bédier. Paris: l'édition d'art H. Piazza, 1937. Rpt. 1966.

Chaucer, Geoffrey. *The Riverside Chaucer*. Third edition. Gen. Ed. Larry D. Benson. Boston: Hougton Mifflin, 1987.

The Chester Mystery Cycle. Ed. R. M. Lumiansky and David Mills. 2 vols. EETS s.s. 3, 9. London: Oxford University Press, 1974–1986.

Child, F. J. *The English and Scottish Popular Ballads*. 5 vols. New York: Dover, 1965.

Cicero. *Philippics 7–14*. Ed. and trans. D. R. Shackleton Bailey. Rev. John T. Ramsey and Gesine Manuwald. Cambridge, MA: Harvard University Press, 2010.

Clariodus; A Metrical Romance: Printed from a Manuscript of the Sixteenth Century. Ed. D. Irving. Edinburgh: Maitland Club, 1830. Rpt. New York: AMS Press Inc., 1973.

Clewett, Richard M., Jr. "Rhetorical Strategy and Structure in Three of Sir David Lindsay's Poems." *Studies in English Literature, 1500–1900* 16.1 (1976), 3–14.

Cochran-Patrick, R. W. *Records of the Coinage of Scotland: From the Earliest Period to the Union*. 2 vols. Edinburgh: Edmonston and Douglas, 1876.

Colkelbie Sow and The Talis of the Fyve Bestes. Ed. Gregory Kratzmann. New York and London: Garland, 1983.

The Commissariot Record of Edinburgh. Register of Testaments. Part 1: Volumes 1 to 35 1514–1600. Ed. Francis J. Grant. Edinburgh: Scottish Record Society, 1897.

The Commissariot Record of St Andrews. Register of Testaments, 1549–1800. Ed. Francis J. Grant. Edinburgh: Scottish Record Society, 1902.

Complainte pour la Mort de Madame Marguerite d'Escosse, daulphine de Viennoys. In Thiry, "Recherches sur la Déploration Funèbre Française à la Prérenaissance." 2:9–23.

The Complaynt of Scotland (c. 1550). Ed. A. M. Stewart. STS 4th series 11. Edinburgh: Scottish Text Society, 1979.

Concise Scots Dictionary. Gen. ed. Mairi Robinson. Aberdeen: Aberdeen University Press, 1985.

Cooper, Helen. "The *Lancelot-Grail Cycle* in England: Malory and his Predecessors." In *A Companion to the Lancelot-Grail Cycle*. Ed. Carol Dover. Cambridge: D. S. Brewer, 2003. Pp. 147–62.

———. *The English Romance in Time: Transforming Motifs from Geoffrey of Monmouth to the Death of Shakespeare*. Oxford: Oxford University Press, 2004.

Corbett, John, J. Derrick McClure, and Jane Stuart-Smith. "A Brief History of Scots." In *The Edinburgh Companion to Scots*. Ed. John Corbett, J. Derrick McClure, and Jane Stuart-Smith. Edinburgh: Edinburgh University Press, 2003. Pp. 1–16.

Coverdale, Miles. *Biblia. The Bible, that is, the holy Scripture of the Olde and New Testament, faithfully and truly translated out of Douche and Latyn in to Englishe*. Cologne: E. Cervicornus and J. Soter, 1535.

Cowan, Edward J., and Lizanne Henderson, eds. *A History of Everyday Life in Medieval Scotland, 1000–1600*. Edinburgh: Edinburgh University Press, 2011.

Cowan, Ian B., P. H. R. Mackay, and Alan Macquarrie, eds. *The Knights of St John of Jerusalem in Scotland*. Scottish History Society 4th series 19. Edinburgh: Clark Constable, 1983.

Cowan, William. "An Edition of Sir David Lyndsay's *Squyer Meldrum*, 1634." *Papers of the Edinburgh Bibliographical Society* 6 (1906), 103–04.

Crane, Susan. *The Performance of Self: Ritual, Clothing and Identity During the Hundred Years War*. Philadelphia: University of Pennsylvania Press, 2002.

Cropp, Glynnis M. "Les Vers Sur Les Neuf Preux." *Romania* 120 (2002), 449–82.

Cunningham, I. C. "The Asloan Manuscript." In *The Renaissance in Scotland: Studies in Literature, Religion, History and Culture Offered to John Durkan*. Ed. A. A. MacDonald, Michael Lynch, and Ian B. Cowan. Leiden: Brill, 1994. Pp. 107–35.

Daniell, Christopher. *Death and Burial in Medieval England 1066–1550*. London: Routledge, 1997.

Dean, Lucinda Hazel Stewart. "Crowns, Wedding Rings, and Processions: Continuity and Change in the Representations of Scottish Royal Authority in State Ceremony, c. 1214–c. 1603." D. Phil. Thesis: University of Stirling, 2013.

"The Declaration of Arbroath." Ed. and trans. Sir James Fergusson and Alan Borthwick. *National Archives of Scotland* (2005). Accessed October 2017. Online at https://www.nrscotland. gov.uk/files /research/declaration-of-arbroath/declaration-of-arbroath-transcription-and-translation.pdf.

The Deidis of Armorie: A Heraldic Treatise and Bestiary. Ed. L. A. J. R. Houwen. 2 vols. STS 4th series 22, 23. Edinburgh: Scottish Text Society, 1994.

Delisle, Léopold V. *Le Cabinet des Manuscrits de la Bibliothèque Impériale [Nationale]: Étude sur la Formation de ce Dépôt*. 3 vols. Paris: Imprimerie Impériale, 1868–81.

Dent, Arthur. *The Plain Man's Pathway to Heaven*. Belfast: North of Ireland Book and Tract Depository, 1859.

Devotional Pieces in Verse and Prose: From MS. Arundel 285 and MS. Harleian 6919. Ed. J. A. W. Bennett. STS 3rd series 23. Edinburgh: Scottish Text Society, 1955.

A Dictionarie of the French and English Tongues. Ed. Randle Cotgrave. London: Adam Islip, 1611.

Dictionary of the Scots Language. Ed. William A. Craigie. Online at http://www.dsl.ac.uk.

Dickinson, William Croft, ed. *The Sheriff Court Book of Fife 1515–1522*. Scottish History Society 3rd series 12. Edinburgh: T. and A. Constable, 1928.

Dineen, P. S. *Foclóir Gaedhilge agus Béarla: An Irish-English Dictionary*. Dublin: Elo Press, 1996.

Douglas, Gavin. [*Eneados*] *Virgil's Aeneid*. Ed. David F. C. Coldwell. 4 vols. STS 3rd series 25, 27, 28, 30. Edinburgh: Scottish Text Society, 1951–60.

———. *The Palis of Honoure*. Ed. David J. Parkinson. Kalamazoo, MI: Medieval Institute Publications, 1992.

———. *The Shorter Poems of Gavin Douglas*. Ed. Priscilla Bawcutt. Second edition. STS 5th series 2. Edinburgh: Scottish Text Society, 2003.

Drexler, Marjorie. "The Extant Abridgements of Walter Bower's 'Scotichronicon'." *The Scottish Historical Review* 61.171 (1982), 62–67.

Du Fresne de Beaucort, Gaston. *Histoire de Charles VII. Vol. 4: L'Expansion de la Royauté 1444–1449*. Paris: Librarie de la Société Bibliographique, 1888.

Duclos, Charles P. *Histoire de Louis XI*. Vol. 3. Amsterdam: 1746.

Dunbar, Sir Archibald H. *Scottish Kings: A Revised Chronology of Scottish History 1005-1625*. Second edition. Edinburgh: David Douglas, 1906.

Dunbar, William. *The Poems of William Dunbar*. Ed. W. Mackay Mackenzie. London: Faber & Faber, 1932. Rpt. 1970.

———. *The Poems of William Dunbar*. Ed. Priscilla Bawcutt. 2 vols. Glasgow: The Association for Scottish Literary Studies, 1997–98.

———. *The Complete Works*. Ed. John Conlee. Kalamazoo, MI: Medieval Institute Publications, 2004.

Durkan, John. "Education in the Century of the Reformation." In *Essays on the Scottish Reformation: 1513–1625*. Ed. David McRoberts. Glasgow: Burns, 1962. Pp. 145–68.

———. "St Andrews in the John Law Chronicle." *Innes Review* 25 (1974), 49–62.

Early English Books Online. ProQuest, 2003–17. Online at http://eebo.chadwyck.com/home.

Easting, Robert. *Annotated Bibliographies of Old and Middle English Literature, Vol. III: Visions of the Other World in Middle English*. Cambridge: D. S. Brewer, 1977.

The Edinburgh Magazine, or, Literary Miscellany. Vol. 5. Edinburgh: J. Sibbald, 1787.

Edington, Carol. *Court and Culture in Renaissance Scotland: Sir David Lindsay of the Mount*. Amherst: University of Massachusetts Press, 1994.

———. "Paragons and Patriots: National Identity and the Chivalric Ideal in Late-Medieval Scotland." In *Image and Identity: The Making and Re-making of Scotland Through the Ages*. Ed. Dauvit Broun, R. J. Finlay and Michael Lynch. Edinburgh: John Donald, 1998. Pp. 69–81.

Emond, William Kevin. "The Minority of King James V, 1513–1528." D. Phil. Thesis: University of St Andrews, 1989.

Ewan, Elizabeth. "'For Whatever Ales Ye': Women as Producers in Late Medieval Scottish Towns." In *Women in Scotland, c. 1100–1750*. Eds. Ewan and Meikle. Pp. 125–35.

————. "'Many Injurious Words': Defamation and Gender in Late Medieval Scotland." In *History, Literature, and Music in Scotland, 700–1560.* Ed. R. Andrew McDonald. Toronto: University of Toronto Press, 2002. Pp. 163–86.

Ewan, Elizabeth, and Maureen M. Meikle, eds. *Women in Scotland c. 1100–c. 1750.* East Linton: Tuckwell Press, 1999.

The Exchequer Rolls of Scotland; Rotuli Scaccarii Regum Scotorum. Eds. J. Stuart, G. Burnett, A. J. G. Mackay, and G. P. McNeill. Edinburgh: H. M. General Register House, 1878–1908.

Fein, Susanna Greer, ed. *Moral Love Songs and Laments.* Kalamazoo, MI: Medieval Institute Publications, 1998.

Fifae Paris Orientalis [The East Part of Fife]. In Blaeu, *Blaeu Atlas of Scotland, 1654.* Online at http://maps.nls.uk/view/00000450.

Fisher, Keely. "The Contemporary Humour in William Stewart's *The Flytting betuix þe Sowtar and the Tailōour.*" In *Literature, Letters and the Canonical.* Eds. Van Heijnsbergen and Royan. Pp. 1–21.

Fleming, David Hay. *The Register of the Privy Seal of Scotland. Vol. 2: 1529–1542.* Edinburgh: General Register House, 1921.

Flynn, Caitlin, and Christy Mitchell. "'It may be verifyit that thy wit is thin': Interpreting Older Scots Flyting through Hip Hop Aesthetics." *Oral Tradition* 29.1 (2014), 69–86.

Fraser, William. *The Stirlings of Keir, and Their Family Papers.* Edinburgh, 1858.

————. *The Lennox. Vol. 1: Memoirs.* Edinburgh: T. & A. Constable, 1874.

————. *The Earls of Cromartie: Their Kindred, Country, and Correspondence.* 2 vols. Edinburgh, 1876.

————. *Memorials of the Earls of Haddington.* 2 vols. Edinburgh, 1889.

Furrow, Melissa M., ed. *Ten Bourdes.* Kalamazoo, MI: Medieval Institute Publications, 2013.

Geoffrey of Monmouth. *The History of the Kings of Britain: An Edition and Translation of De Gestis Britonum [Historia Regum Britanniae].* Ed. Michael D. Reeve. Trans. Neil Wright. Woodbridge: Boydell, 2007.

Geoffrey of Vinsauf. *Poetria Nova. Poetria Nova of Geoffrey of Vinsauf.* Trans. Margaret F. Nims. Toronto: Pontifical Institute of Mediaeval Studies, 1967.

Gesta Romanorum: The Early English Versions of the Gesta Romanorum. Ed. Sidney J. H. Herrtage. EETS e.s. 33. London: Oxford University Press, 1879.

Giesey, Ralph E. *The Royal Funeral Ceremony in Renaissance France.* Geneva: Droz, 1960.

Gittings, Clare. *Death, Burial and the Individual in Early Modern England.* London: Croom Helm, 1984.

Golagros and Gawane. Ed. Ralph Hanna. STS 5th series 7. Edinburgh: Scottish Text Society, 2008.

Goldstein, R. James. "'With Murth My Corps Ōe Sal Convoy': *Squyer Meldrum* and the Work of Mourning." In *Langage Cleir Illumynate: Scottish Poetry from Barbour to Drummond, 1375–1630.* Ed. Nicola Royan. New York: Rodopi, 2007. Pp. 145–63.

Gollancz, I., ed. "Appendix: Texts Illustrative of 'The Nine Worthies', Etc." In *Select Early English Poems.* Vol. 2. London: Humphrey Millford, Oxford University Press. 1915. N.p.

Göller, Karl Heinz. "King Arthur in the Scottish Chronicles." Trans. Edward D. Kennedy. In *King Arthur: A Casebook.* Ed. Edward D. Kennedy. New York: Garland Publishing, 1996. Pp. 173–84.

Gower, John. *Mirour de L'Omme.* Ed. G. C. Macaulay. In *The Complete Works of John Gower.* Vol. 1: *The French Works.* Oxford: Clarendon Press, 1899. Pp. 1–334.

————. *Confessio Amantis.* Second edition. Ed. Russell A. Peck. 3 vols. Kalamazoo, MI: Medieval Institute Publications, 2004–13.

Grant, Alexander. "The Development of the Scottish Peerage." *The Scottish Historical Review* 57.163 (1978), 1–27.

Gray, Douglas. *Robert Henryson.* Leiden: E. J. Brill, 1979.

————. "Rough Music: Some Early Invectives and Flytings." *Yearbook of English Studies* 14 (1984), 21–43.

————, ed. *The Oxford Book of Late Medieval Verse and Prose.* Oxford: Clarendon Press, 1985.

Green, Richard Firth. "An Epitaph for Richard, Duke of York." *Studies in Bibliography* 41 (1988), 218–24.

Grummitt, David. *The Calais Garrison: War and Military Service in England, 1436–1558*. Woodbridge: Boydell & Brewer, 2008.

Guido delle Colonne. *Historia destructionis Troiae*. Ed. Nathaniel Edward Griffin. Cambridge, MA: Mediaeval Academy of America, 1936.

Guillaume de Lorris and Jean de Meun. *Le Roman de la Rose*. Ed. Ernest Langlois. 5 vols. Vols. 1–2: Paris: Firmin-Didot. Vols. 3–5: Paris: Édouard Champion, 1914–24.

———. *The Romance of the Rose*. Trans. Charles Dahlberg. Hanover, NH: University Press of New England, 1983.

Hadley Williams, Janet. "'Thus euery man said for hym self': The Voices of Sir David Lyndsay's Poems." In *Bryght Lanternis*. Eds. McClure and Spiller. Pp. 258–72.

———. "The Earliest Surviving Text of Lyndsay's *Tragedie of the Cardinall*: An English Edition of a Scottish Poem." In *Literature, Letters and the Canonical*. Eds. Van Heijnsbergen and Royan. Pp. 22–34.

———, ed. *Stewart Style 1513–1542: Essays on the Court of James V*. East Linton: Tuckwell Press, 1996.

Hadley Williams, Janet, and J. Derrick McClure, eds. *Fresche Fontanis: Studies in the Culture of Medieval and Early Modern Scotland*. Newcastle: Cambridge Scholars Publishing, 2013.

Haldane, General Sir J. A. L. *The Haldanes of Gleneagles*. Edinburgh: W. Blackwood and Sons, 1929.

Hall, Edward. *Hall's Chronicle; Containing the History of England During the Reign of Henry the Fourth, and the Succeeding Monarchs, to the End of the Reign of Henry the Eighth, in which are Particularly Described the Manners and Customs of those Periods. Carefully Collated with the Editions of 1548 and 1550*. London: G. Woodfall for J. Johnson, F. C. and J. Rivington, T. Payne, Wilkie and Robinson, Longman, Hurst, Rees and Orme, Cadell and Davies, and J. Mawman, 1809.

Hammond, P. W., Anne F. Sutton, and Livia Visser-Fuchs. "The Reburial of Richard, Duke of York, 21–30 July 1476." *The Ricardian* 10.127 (1994), 122–65.

Hardman, Philipa, and Marianne Ailes. *The Legend of Charlemagne in Medieval England: The Matter of France in Middle English and Anglo-Norman Literature*. Cambridge: D. S. Brewer, 2017.

Hargreaves, Henry. "The Crathes Ceiling Inscriptions." In *Bryght Lanternis*. Eds. McClure and Spiller. Pp. 373–86.

Hary's Wallace [*Vita Nobilissimi Defensoris Scotie Wilelmi Wallace Militis*]. Ed. Matthew P. McDiarmid. 2 vols. STS 4th series 4, 5. Edinburgh: Scottish Text Society, 1968–69.

Hasler, Antony J. *Court Poetry in Late Medieval England and Scotland: Allegories of Authority*. Cambridge: Cambridge University Press, 2014.

Hay, Sir Gilbert. *The Buik of King Alexander the Conquerour*. Ed. John Cartwright. 2 vols. STS 4th series 16, 18. Edinburgh: Scottish Text Society, 1986 and Aberdeen: University of Aberdeen Press, 1990.

———. *The Prose Works of Sir Gilbert Hay* [including *The Buke of the Law of Armys*, *The Buke of the Ordre of Knychthede* and *The Buke of the Gouernaunce of Princis*]. Ed. Jonathan A. Glenn. 2 vols. STS 4th series 21; 5th series 3. Edinburgh: Scottish Text Society, 1993. Rpt. Chippenham: Antony Rowe Ltd., 2005.

Henisch, Bridget Ann. *The Medieval Cook*. Rochester, NY: Boydell Press, 2009.

Henryson, Robert. *The Poems of Robert Henryson*. Ed. Denton Fox. Oxford: Clarendon Press, 1981.

———. *Robert Henryson: The Complete Works*. Ed. David J. Parkinson. Kalamazoo, MI: Medieval Institute Publications, 2010.

Hesk, Jon. "Homeric Flyting and How to Read It: Performance and Intratext in *Iliad* 20.83–109 and 20.178–258." *Ramus: Critical Studies in Greek and Roman Literature* 35.1 (2006), 4–28.

Herzman, Ronald B., Graham Drake, and Eve Salisbury, eds. *Four Romances of England*. Kalamazoo, MI: Medieval Institute Publications, 1999.

Heywood, John. *Johan Johan the Husband*. Ed. G. R. Proudfoot and S. W. Wells. Oxford: Oxford University Press for the Malone Society, 1972.

Higgins, Paula. "Parisian Nobles, a Scottish Princess, and the Woman's Voice in Late Medieval Song." *Early Music History* 10 (1991), 145–200.

———. "The 'Other Minervas': Creative Women at the Court of Margaret of Scotland." In *Rediscovering the Muses: Women's Musical Traditions*. Ed. Kimberly Marshall. Boston: Northeastern University Press, 1993. Pp. 169–85.

Higgitt, John. "Manuscripts and Libraries in the Diocese of Glasgow Before the Reformation." In *Medieval Art and Architecture in the Diocese of Glasgow*. Ed. Richard Fawcett. Leeds: British Archaeological Association, 1988. Pp. 102–10.

———. "Decoration and Illustration." In Bower. *Scotichronicon*. Ed. Watt. 9:157–85.

Historic Environment Scotland. "Gleneagles Castle." Accessed November 2017. Online at https://canmore.org.uk/site/25906/gleneagles-castle.

Historical Manuscripts Commission. *Report on the Manuscripts of the Earl of Mar and Kellie Preserved at Alloa House, N.B.* Ed. Henry Paton. London: printed for H.M. Stationery Office by B. Johnson & Co., York, 1904.

Hoccleve, Thomas. *The Regiment of Princes*. Ed. Charles R. Blyth. Kalamazoo, MI: Medieval Institute Publications, 1999.

Holland, Richard. *The Buke of the Howlat*. Ed. Ralph Hanna. STS 5th series 12. Edinburgh: Scottish Text Society, 2014.

Höltgen, K. J. "Die 'Nine Worthies.'" *Anglia* 77 (1959), 279–309.

The Holy Bible: Douay-Rheims Version. Ed. Bishop Richard Challoner. Rockford, IL: Tan Books and Publishers, 1989. Originally published Baltimore: John Murphy, 1899. Available online at http://www.drbo.org/drl/index.htm.

Houlbrooke, Ralph. *Death, Religion, and the Family in England, 1480–1750*. Oxford: Clarendon Press, 1998.

Hue de Rotelande. *Ipomédon*. Ed. A. J. Holden. Paris: Klincksieck, 1979.

Inglis, Barbara, ed. *Une Nouvelle Collection de Poésies Lyriques et Courtoises du XVe Siècle: Le Manuscrit B.N. Nouv. Acq. Fr. 15771*. Geneva: Editions Slatkine, 1985.

Innes, Sir Thomas. *Scots Heraldry*. Second edition. London: Oliver and Boyd, 1956.

International Courtly Literature Society. "Branch Constitution." University of Warwick, 2000. Accessed November 2017. Online at https://www2.warwick.ac.uk/fac/arts/ren/icls/constitution.

Ireland, John. *The Meroure of Wyssdome, Composed for the use of James IV, King of Scots A.D. 1490, by Johannes de Irlandia*. Ed. Charles Macpherson, F. Quinn, and C. McDonald. 3 vols. STS 2nd series 19; 4th series 2, 19. Edinburgh: Scottish Text Society, 1926 and 1965, and Aberdeen: Aberdeen University Press, 1990.

Irvine Smith, J. "Criminal Procedure." In *An Introduction to Scottish Legal History*. Edinburgh: Stair Society, 1958. Pp. 426–48.

Irving, David. *The Lives of the Scottish Poets with Preliminary Dissertations on the Literary History of Scotland, and the Early Scotish Drama, in Two Volumes*. Vol 2. Edinburgh: Oliver & Boyd, 1810. Rpt. New York: Johnson Reprint Corporation, 1972.

Jaeger, C. Stephen. *Ennobling Love: In Search of a Lost Sensibility*. Philadelphia: University of Pennsylvania Press, 1999.

James I of Scotland. *The Kingis Quair*. Ed. John Norton-Smith. Oxford: Clarendon Press, 1971.

———. *The Kingis Quair*. In *The Kingis Quair and other Prison Poems*. Ed. Linne R. Mooney and Mary-Jo Arn. Kalamazoo, MI: Medieval Institute Publications, 2005. Pp. 17–112.

James VI of Scotland. *Ane Schort Treatise Conteining Some Reulis and Cautelis to be Observit and Eschewit in Scottis Poesie*. In *The Mercat Anthology of Early Scottish Literature 1375–1707*. Ed. R. D. S. Jack and P. A. T. Rozendaal. Edinburgh: Mercat Press, 1997. Pp. 460–47.

Le Jardin de Plaisance et Fleur de Rhethoricque. Paris: Antoine Vérard, 1502.

Kaeuper, Richard W. *Medieval Chivalry*. Cambridge: Cambridge University Press, 2016.

Keen, Maurice. *Chivalry*. New Haven: Yale University Press, 1984.

———. "Richard II's Ordinances of War of 1385." In *Rulers and Ruled in Late Medieval England: Essays Presented to Gerald Harriss*. Ed. Rowena E. Archer and Simon Walker. London: Hambledon, 1995. Pp. 33–48.

Kennedy, Walter. *The Poems of Walter Kennedy*. Ed. Nicole Meier. STS 5th series 6. Edinburgh: Scottish Text Society, 2008.

Ker, N. R. *Medieval Manuscripts in British Libraries: Abbotsford-Keele*. Vol. 2. Oxford: Clarendon Press, 1977.

Kinch, Ashby. *Imago Mortis: Mediating Images of Death in Late Medieval Culture*. Leiden: Brill, 2013.

Kitchin, George. *A Survey of Burlesque and Parody in English*. Edinburgh: Oliver and Boyd, 1931.

The Knightly Tale of Golagros and Gawane. In *Sir Gawain: Eleven Romances and Tales*. Ed. Thomas Hahn. Kalamazoo, MI: Medieval Institute Publications, 1995. Pp. 227–308.

Knox, John. *The Works of John Knox*. Ed. David Laing. 6 vols. Edinburgh: Thin, 1846–64.

Kooper, Erik, ed. *Sentimental and Humorous Romances: Floris and Blancheflour, Sir Degrevant, The Squire of Low Degree, The Tournament of Tottenham, and the Feast of Tottenham*. Kalamazoo, MI: Medieval Institute Publications, 2006.

Kratzmann, Gregory. *Anglo-Scottish Literary Relations, 1430–1550*. Cambridge: Cambridge University Press, 1980.

———. "Sixteenth-Century Secular Poetry." In *The History of Scottish Literature, Vol. 1: Origins to 1660 (Mediæval and Renaissance)*. Ed. R. D. S. Jack. Aberdeen: Aberdeen University Press, 1988. Pp. 105–24.

Laing, David. "De Cronicis Scotorum Brevia by John Law, Canon of St Andrews. 1521." In *Inquiries Respecting Some of the Early Historical Writers of Scotland*. Edinburgh: Neil & Co., 1878. Pp. 8–9.

Laing, David, Walter Scott, and Thomas Thomson, eds. "The Wills of Thomas Bassandyne, and Other Printers, &c. in Edinburgh, 1577–1687." In *The Bannatyne Miscellany*. Eds. Scott, Laing, and Thomson. 2:185–296.

Lancelot of the Laik and Sir Tristrem. Ed. Alan Lupack. Kalamazoo, MI: Medieval Institute Publications, 1994.

Lee, Maurice. *James Stewart, Earl of Moray: A Political Study of the Reformation in Scotland*. New York: Columbia University Press, 1953.

Legends of the Saints: In the Scottish Dialect of the Fourteenth Century. Ed. W. M. Metcalfe. 6 vols. STS 1st series 13, 18, 23, 25, 35, 37. Edinburgh and London: Scottish Text Society, 1887–95.

L'Estrange, Elizabeth. *Holy Motherhood: Gender, Dynasty and Visual Culture in the Later Middle Ages*. Manchester: Manchester University Press, 2008.

Letters and Papers, Foreign and Domestic, of the Reign of Henry VIII. Ed. J. S. Brewer, J. Gairdner and R. H. Brodie. 21 vols. London: Mackie & Co., 1862–1932.

Lewis, C. S. *English Literature in the Sixteenth Century, Excluding Drama*. Oxford: Clarendon Press, 1954.

Liber Conventus S. Katherine Senesis prope Edinburgum. Edinburgh: Abbotsford Club, 1841.

Liber Officialis Sancti Andree. Ed. J. H. Forbes and C. Innes. Edinburgh: Abbotsford Club, 1845.

Liber Pluscardensis. Ed. Felix J. H. Skene. 10 vols. Edinburgh: William Paterson. 1877–80.

Le Roux de Lincy, M. *Les Femmes Célèbres de l'Ancienne France*. Paris: Leroi, 1848.

Lindesay, Robert, of Pitscottie. *The Historie and Cronicles of Scotland from the Slaughter of King James the First to the Ane Thousande Fyve Hundreith Thrie Scoir Fyftein Zeir*. Ed. Æ. J. G. Mackay. 3 Vols. STS 1st series 42, 43, 60. Edinburgh: Scottish Text Society, 1899–1911.

Lindsay, Sir David. See Lyndsay, Sir David.

Le Livre des Fais du Bon Mesire Jehan le Maingre, Dit Bouciquaut, Mareschal de France et Gouverneur de Jennes. Ed. Denis Lalande. Geneva: Droz, 1985.

Lock, Peter. *The Routledge Companion to the Crusades*. London: Routledge, 2006.

Loomis, Roger Sherman. "Verses on the Nine Worthies." *Modern Philology* 15.4 (1917), 19–27.

Lupack, Alan, ed. *Three Middle English Charlemagne Romances: The Sultan of Babylon, The Siege of Milan, and Ralph the Collier*. Kalamazoo, MI: Medieval Institute Publications, 1990.

Lyall, R. J. "Politics and Poetry in Fifteenth and Sixteenth Century Scotland." *Scottish Literary Journal* 3.2 (1976), 5–29.

———. "The Court as a Cultural Centre." *History Today* 34.9 (1984), 27–33.

———. "Books and Book-Owners in Fifteenth-Century Scotland." In *Book Production and Publishing in Britain 1375–1475*. Ed. Jeremy Griffiths and Derek Pearsall. Cambridge: Cambridge University Press, 1989. Rpt. 2007. Pp. 239–56.

Lydgate, John. *Troy Book: Selections*. Ed. Robert R. Edwards. Kalamazoo, MI: Medieval Institute Publications, 1998.

Lyndsay, Sir David. *The Poetical Works of Sir David Lyndsay of the Mount, Lion King at Arms, Under James V*. Ed. George Chalmers. 3 vols. London: Longman, Hurst, Rees, and Orme, 1806.

———. *Fac-Simile of an Ancient Heraldic Manuscript: Emblazoned by Sir David Lyndsay of the Mount. Lyon king of armes 1542*. Ed. David Laing. Edinburgh: W. & D. Laing, 1822.

———. *Sir David Lyndesay's Works*. Ed. J. Small and Fitzedward Hall. EETS o.s. 11, 19, 35, 37, 47. London: N. Trübner and Co., 1865–71.

———. *The Poetical Works of Sir David Lyndsay*. Ed. David Laing. 3 vols. Edinburgh: William Paterson, 1879.

———. *The Works of Sir David Lindsay of the Mount, 1490–1555*. Ed. Douglas Hamer. 4 vols. STS 3rd series 1, 2, 6, 8. Edinburgh: Scottish Text Society, 1931–36.

———. *Squyer Meldrum*. Ed. James Kinsley. Edinburgh: Thomas Nelson and Sons, 1959.

———. *Ane Satyre of the Thrie Estaitis*. Ed. Roderick Lyall. Edinburgh: Canongate Press, 1989. Rpt. 1998.

———. *Sir David Lyndsay: Selected Poems*. Ed. Janet Hadley Williams. Glasgow: Association for Scottish Literary Studies, 2000.

Macafee, Caroline, and A. J. Aitken. "History of Scots to 1700." In *Dictionary of the Scots Language*. Accessed November 2017. Online at www.dsl.ac.uk/about-scots/history-of-scots/.

Macdougall, Norman. *James IV*. Edinburgh: John Donald, 1989. Rpt. 2015.

———. *James III*. Edinburgh: John Donald, 2009.

MacFarlane, James. *History of Clan MacFarlane*. Glasgow: Clan MacFarlane Society, 1922.

MacKechnie, John. *Catalogue of Gaelic Manuscripts in Selected Libraries in Great Britain and Ireland*. 2 vols. Boston: G. K. Hall & Co., 1973.

MacKillop, James. *Dictionary of Celtic Mythology*. Oxford: Oxford University Press, 1998.

Macquarrie, Alan. *Scotland and the Crusades, 1095–1560*. Edinburgh: John Donald, 1985.

MacQueen, John. "The Literature of Fifteenth-Century Scotland." In *Scottish Society in the Fifteenth Century*. Ed. Jennifer M. Brown. New York: St. Martin's Press, 1977. Pp. 184–208.

The Maitland Folio Manuscript. Ed. W. A. Craigie. 2 vols. STS 2nd series 7, 20. Edinburgh: Scottish Text Society, 1919–27.

Major, John. *A History of Greater Britain as well England as Scotland*. Ed. and trans. Archibald Constable. Scottish History Society. 1st series 10. Edinburgh: T. & A. Constable, 1892.

Malory, Sir Thomas. *Le Morte Darthur*. Ed. P. J. C. Field. 2 vols. Cambridge: D.S. Brewer, 2013.

Mann, Jill. *From Aesop to Reynard: Beast Literature in Medieval Britain*. Oxford: Oxford University Press, 2009.

Manuel, Don Juan. "Libro de Patronio." *Obras de Don Juan Manuel*. In *Biblioteca de Autores Espanōles* 51. Ed. Don Pascual de Gayangos. Madrid: Ediciones Atlas, 1860. Pp. 373–74.

Mapstone, Sally. "The Advice to Princes Tradition in Scottish Literature, 1450–1500." D. Phil. Thesis: University of Oxford, 1986.

———. "*The Talis of the Fyve Bestes* and the Advice to Princes Tradition." In *Scottish Language and Literature, Medieval and Renaissance: Fourth International Conference 1984, Proceedings*. Ed. Dietrich Strauss and Horst W. Drescher. Frankfurt am Main: Verlag Peter Lang, 1986. Pp. 239–54.

———. "Was there a Court Literature in Fifteenth-Century Scotland?" *Studies in Scottish Literature* 26.1 (1991), 410–22.

———. "The *Scotichronicon*'s First Readers." In *Church, Chronicle and Learning in Medieval and Early Renaissance Scotland*. Ed. Barbara E. Crawford. Edinburgh: Mercat Press, 1999. Pp. 31–55.

———. "Introduction: Older Scots Literature and the Sixteenth Century." In *Older Scots Literature*. Ed. Sally Mapstone. Edinburgh: John Donald, 2005. Pp. 175–88.

———. "The *Liber Pluscardensis* and *De Regimine Principum*." In *The Wisdom of Princes*. Forthcoming.

Marie de France. *Les Lais de Marie de France*. Ed. Jean Rychner. Paris: Honoré Champion, 1971.

Marshall, Susan. "Illegitimacy in Medieval Scotland, 1165–1500." D. Phil. Thesis: University of Aberdeen, 2013.

Marsland, Rebecca. "Complaint in Scotland c. 1424–c. 1500." D. Phil. Thesis: University of Oxford, 2014.

Martin, Joanna. *Kingship and Love in Scottish Poetry, 1424–1540*. Aldershot: Ashgate, 2008.

Martin, Joanna, and Emily Wingfield, eds. *Premodern Scotland: Literature and Governance 1420–1587: Essays for Sally Mapstone*. Oxford: Oxford University Press, 2017.

Marwick, J. D., ed. "Appendix: Lists of Provosts, Bailiffs and other Officers." In *Extracts From the Records of the Burgh of Edinburgh, 1403–1528*. Edinburgh: Scottish Burgh Records Society, 1869. Pp. 246–84. Accessed October 2017. Online at https://www.british-history.ac.uk/ edinburgh-burgh-records/1403-1528/pp246-284.

McAndrew, Bruce A. *Scotland's Historic Heraldry*. Woodbridge: Boydell & Brewer, 2006.

McClure, J. D. "Scottis, Inglis, Suddroun: Language Labels and Language Attitudes." In *Proceedings of the Third International Conference on Scottish Language and Literature (Medieval and Renaissance)*. Ed. Roderick J. Lyall and Felicity Riddy. Stirling and Glasgow: Universities of Stirling and Glasgow, 1981. Pp. 52–70.

McClure, J. Derrick, and Michael R. G. Spiller, eds. *Bryght Lanternis: Essays on the Language and Literature of Medieval and Renaissance Scotland*. Aberdeen: Aberdeen University Press, 1989.

McKitterick, Rosamond. *Charlemagne: The Formation of a European Identity*. Cambridge: Cambridge University Press, 2008.

McLaughlin, Martin L. "The Dispute between Poggio and Valla." In *Literary Imitation in the Italian Renaissance: The Theory and Practice of Literary Imitation in Italy from Dante to Bembo*. Oxford: Oxford University Press, 1995. Pp. 126–46.

Middle English Dictionary. Ann Arbor: University of Michigan Press, 2001–. Online at http://quod.lib.umich.edu/m/med/.

The Middle-English Versions of Partonope of Blois. Ed. A. Trampe Bödtker. EETS e.s. 109. Millwood, NY: Kraus Reprint Co., 1975. Originally published in London: Kegan Paul, Trench, Trübner & Co., 1911.

Miller, Sarah Alison. "Monstrous Sexuality: Variations on the Vagina Dentata." In *The Ashgate Companion to Monsters and the Monstrous*. Ed. Asa Simon Mittman and Peter J. Dendle. Burlington, VT: Ashgate, 2013. Pp. 311–28.

Montgomerie, Alexander. *Alexander Montgomerie: Poems*. Ed. David J. Parkinson. 2 vols. STS 4th series 28, 29. Edinburgh: Scottish Text Society, 2000.

Müller, Catherine. "Autour de Marguerite d'Écosse: Quelques Poétesses Méconnues du XVe Siècle." In *Contexts and Continuities: Proceedings of the IVth International Colloqium on Christine de Pizan (Glasgow 21–27 July 2000), published in honour of Liliane Dulac*. Ed. Angus J. Kennedy, Rosalind Brown-Grant, James C. Laidlaw, and Catherine M. Müller. Vol. 2. Glasgow: University of Glasgow Press, 2002. Pp. 603–19.

Napier, Mark. *History of the Partition of the Lennox*. Edinburgh: William Blackwood & Sons, 1835.

National Records of Scotland. Crown Copyright. Accessed November 2017. Online at https://www.nrscotland.gov.uk/.

Nesson, Pierre de. *Les Vigiles des Morts (XVeS)*. Ed. Alain Collet. Paris: Honoré Champion, 2002.

A New Index of Middle English Verse. Eds. Julia Boffey and A. S. G. Edwards. London: The British Library, 2005.

Nichols, John, and Richard Gough. *A Collection of All the Wills, Now Known to be Extant, of the Kings and Queens of England, Princes and Princesses of Wales, and Every Branch of the Blood Royal, From the Reign of William the Conqueror to that of Henry the Seventh exclusive: With explanatory notes, and a glossary*. London: Printed by J. Nichols, 1780.

Nicolas, Nicholas Harris. *Testamenta Vetusta: Being Illustrations from Wills, of Manners, Customs etc. as well as of the Descents and Possessions of Many Distinguished Families*. 2 vols. London: Nichols and Son, 1826.

Ninth Report of the Royal Commission on Historical Manuscripts. London: Eyre and Spottiswoode, 1883–84.

Norman, Joanne S. "William Dunbar: Grand Rhetoriqueur." In *Bryght Lanternis*. Eds. McClure and Spiller. Pp. 179–93.

Oakeshott, Ewart. *European Weapons and Armour: From the Renaissance to the Industrial Revolution*. Woodbridge: Boydell Press, 2000.

The Octosyllabic Alexander. In *The Buik of Alexander*. Ed. Ritchie.

Oram, Richard D. "Disease, Death and the Hereafter in Medieval Scotland." In *A History of Everyday Life in Medieval Scotland*. Eds. Cowan and Henderson. Pp. 196–225.

Ouy, Gilbert. "Charles d'Orléans and his Brother Jean d'Angoulême in England: What their Manuscripts Have to Tell." In *Charles d'Orléans in England (1415–1440)*. Ed. Mary-Jo Arn. Cambridge: D. S. Brewer, 2000. Pp. 47–60.

———. *La Librairie des Frères Captifs. Les Manuscrits de Charles d'Orléans et Jean d'Angoulême*. Turnhout: Brepols Publishers, 2007.

Ovid. *Fasti*. Trans. James G. Frazer. Rev. G. P. Goold. Cambridge, MA: Harvard University Press, 1931.

———. *Metamorphoses*. Ed. and trans. Frank Justus Miller. 2 vols. Cambridge, MA: Harvard University Press, 1916.

Owst, G. R. *Literature and Pulpit in Medieval England: A Neglected Chapter in the History of English Letters & of the English People*. Second edition. Oxford: Basil Blackwell, 1961.

Oxford Dictionary of National Biography. Oxford University Press, 2004–16. Accessed November 2017. Online at http://www.oxforddnb.com/.

The Oxford English Dictionary. Oxford University Press. Online at http://www.oed.com/.

Patch, Howard Rollin. *The Other World: According to Descriptions in Medieval Literature*. Cambridge, MA: Harvard University Press, 1950.

Peck, Russell. "Gower and Science." In *The Routledge Research Companion to John Gower*. Ed. Ana Sáez-Hidalgo, Brian Gastle, and R. F. Yeager. Abingdon and New York: Routledge, 2017. Pp. 172–96.

Penman, Michael. "The Bruce Dynasty, Becket and Scottish Pilgrimage to Canterbury, c. 1178–c. 1404." *Journal of Medieval History* 32.4 (2006), 346–70.

Phillimore, W. P. W., ed. *The Visitation of the County of Worcester Made in the Year 1569: With Other Pedigrees Relating to that County from Richard Mundy's Collection*. London: Harleian Society, 1888.

Pitcairn, Robert, ed. *Ancient Criminal Trials in Scotland*. 3 vols. Edinburgh: William Tait for the Bannatyne Club, 1833.

Pitscottie. See Lindesay, Robert, of Pitscottie.

The Place-Names of Fife. Ed. Simon Taylor and Gilbert Márkus. University of Glasgow. Accessed August 2017. Online at http:/fife-placenames.glasgow.ac.uk.

"Portrait of Sir Nicholas Carew 1532–33." In *Hans, the Younger Holbein: The Complete Works*. Accessed November 2017. Online at www.hans-holbein.org/Portrait-Of-Sir-Nicholas-Carew-1532-33.html.

The Pseudo-Turpin: Edited from Bibliothèque Nationale, Fonds Latin, MS. 17656. Ed. H. M. Smyser. Cambridge, MA: The Mediaeval Academy of America, 1937.

Purdie, Rhiannon. "The Search for Scottishness in *Golagros and Gawane*." In *The Scots and Medieval Arthurian Legend*. Eds. Purdie and Royan. Pp. 95–107.

———. *Anglicising Romance: Tail-Rhyme and Genre in Medieval English Literature*. Cambridge: D.S. Brewer, 2008.

———, ed. *Shorter Scottish Medieval Romances*. STS 5th series 11. Edinburgh: Scottish Text Society, 2013.

Purdie, Rhiannon, and Nicola Royan, eds. *The Scots and Medieval Arthurian Legend*. Cambridge: D.S. Brewer, 2005.

Rashdall, Hastings. *The Universities of Europe in the Middle Ages*. Rev. and ed. F. M. Powicke and A. B. Emden. 3 vols. Oxford: Oxford University Press, 1895. Rpt. 1997.

Ratis Raving and Other Early Scots Poems on Morals. Ed. Ritchie Girvan. STS 3rd series 11. Edinburgh: Scottish Text Society, 1939.

The Records of the Parliaments of Scotland to 1707. University of St Andrews, 2007. Accessed November 2017. Online at http://www.rps.ac.uk.

Reeves, Compton. *Pleasures and Pastimes in Medieval England*. Stroud: Alan Sutton, 1995. Rpt. New York: Oxford University Press, 1998.

Registrum de Dunfermelyn: Liber Cartarum Abbatie Benedictine S.S. Trinitatis et B. Margarete Regine de Dunfermelyn. Ed. Cosmo Nelson Innes. Edinburgh: Thomas Constable, 1842.

Registrum de Honoris de Morton: A Series of Ancient Charters of the Earldom of Morton with Other Original Papers in 2 Volumes. 2 vols. Ed. Cosmo Nelson Innes. Edinburgh: Thomas Constable, 1853.

Registrum Magni Sigilli Regum Scotorum. The Register of the Great Seal of Scotland [A.D. 1306–1668]. Ed. Thomas Thomson, J. M. Thomson, J. B. Paul, J. H. Stevenson, and W. K. Dickson. 11 vols. Edinburgh: H. M. General Register House, 1882–1914.

Registrum Secreti Sigilli Regum Scotorum. The Register of the Privy Seal of Scotland. Ed. Matthew Livingstone, David Hay Fleming, James Beveridge, and Gordon Donaldson. 8 vols. Edinburgh: H. M. General Register House, 1908–.

Report on Manuscripts in Various Collections: Vol. 5: the Manuscripts of Col. Mordaunt-Hay of Duns Castle, Sir Archibald Edmonstone of Duntreath, Sir John James Graham of Fintry, K. C. M. G. Hereford: H. M. Stationary Office, 1904.

Rice, Winthrop Huntington. *The European Ancestry of Villon's Satirical Testament*. New York: The Corporate Press, 1941.

Richard Coer de Lyon. Ed. Peter Larkin. Kalamazoo, MI: Medieval Institute Publications, 2015.

Riddy, Felicity J. "'Squyer Meldrum' and the Romance of Chivalry." *The Yearbook of English Studies* 4 (1974), 26–36.

———. "Dating *The Buke of the Howlat*." *The Review of English Studies* 37.145 (1986), 1–10.

Roberts, John Hawley. "The Nine Worthies." *Modern Philology* 19.3 (1922), 297–305.

Robertson, Donald. "A Packet of Books for Scotland." *Bibliotheck* 6.2 (1971), 52–53.

Rolland, John. *Ane Treatise Callit The Court of Venus: Deuidit into Four Buikis*. Ed. Walter Gregor. STS 1st series 3. Edinburgh: Scottish Text Society, 1884.

Le Roman de Thèbes. Ed and trans. Aimé Petit. Paris: Honoré Champion, 1991. Rpt. 2002.

Rondeaux et Autres Poésies du XVe Siècle. Ed. Gaston Raynaud. Paris: Firmin Didot, 1889.

Roswall and Lillian. In *Shorter Scottish Medieval Romances*. Ed. Purdie. Pp. 125–99.

Royan, Nicola. "'Na les vailyeant than ony uthir princis of Britane': Representations of Arthur in Scotland 1480–1540." *Scottish Studies Review* 3.1 (2002), 9–20.

———. "The Fine Art of Faint Praise in Older Scots Historiography." In *The Scots and Medieval Arthurian Legend*. Eds. Purdie and Royan. Pp. 43–54.

Runciman, Steven. *A History of the Crusades Vol. 1: The First Crusade and the Foundation of the Kingdom of Jerusalem*. Cambridge: Cambridge University Press, 1951. Rpt. 1962.

Saldanha, Kathryn. "*The Thewis of Gudwomen*: Middle Scots Moral Advice with European Connections?" In *The European Sun*. Eds. Caie, et al. Pp. 288–99.

Scarisbrick, J. J. *Henry VIII*. Berkeley and Los Angeles: University of California Press, 1968.

Schroeder, Horst. *Der Topos der Nine Worthies in Literatur und Bildender Kunst*. Göttingen: Vandenhoeck & Ruprecht, 1971.

———. "The Nine Worthies: A Supplement." *Archiv für das Studium der Neueren Sprachen und Literaturen* 218, Band 133 (1981), 330–40.

Scott, Sir Walter. *Marmion; a Tale of Flodden Field*. Ed. J. Howard B. Masterman. Cambridge: Cambridge University Press, 1928.

———. *Rob Roy*. Ed. Ian Duncan. Oxford and New York: Oxford University Press, 1998.

Scottish Book Trade Index. National Library of Scotland. Accessed June 2017. Online at http://www.nls.uk/catalogues/scottish-book-trade-index.

Sellar, David. "The Family." In *A History of Everyday Life in Medieval Scotland*. Eds. Cowan and Henderson. Pp. 89–108.

The Sex Werkdays and Agis: An Edition of a Late Medieval Scots Universal History from the Asloan Manuscript. Ed. L. A. J. R. Houwen. Groningen: Egbert Forsten, 1990.

Shakespeare, William. *Othello*. In *The Riverside Shakespeare*. Gen. Ed. G. Blakemore Evans. Boston: Houghton Mifflin, 1974. Pp. 1198–248.

Shepherd, Stephen H. A. "The Middle English *Pseudo-Turpin Chronicle*." *Medium Aevum* 65.1 (1996), 19–34.

A Short-Title Catalogue of Books Printed in England, Scotland and Ireland and English Books Printed Abroad 1473–1640. Ed. A. W. Pollard and G. R. Redgrave. Second edition. Rev. W. A. Jackson, F. S. Ferguson and K. F. Pantzer. 3 vols. London: Bibliographical Society, 1976–91. Online at http://estc.bl.uk.

Sibbald, Robert. *The History, Ancient and Modern, of the Sheriffdoms of Fife and Kinross*. Edinburgh: James Watson, 1710. Rev. Laurence Adamson. Cupar: Tullis, 1803.

Sir Gawain and the Green Knight. Ed. J. R. R. Tolkien and E. V. Gordon. Second edition. Rev. Norman Davis. Oxford: Oxford University Press, 1967.

Sir Perceval of Galles and Ywain and Gawain. Ed. Mary Flowers Braswell. Kalamazoo, MI: Medieval Institute Publications, 1995.

Smith, Janet M. *The French Background of Middle Scots Literature*. Edinburgh and London: Oliver and Boyd, 1934.

Smith, Jeremy J. *Older Scots: A Linguistic Reader*. STS 5th series 9. Edinburgh: Scottish Text Society, 2012.

Smyser, H. M. "Charlemagne Legends." In *A Manual of the Writings in Middle English 1050–1500*. Vol. 1. Ed. J. Burke-Severs. New Haven: Connecticut Academy of Arts and Sciences, 1967. Pp. 80–100.

Spearing, A. C. *The Medieval Poet as Voyeur: Looking and Listening in Medieval Love Narratives*. Cambridge: Cambridge University Press, 1993.

Speculum Stultorum. Ed. John H. Mozley and Robert R. Raymo. Berkeley: University of California Press, 1960.

Spence, Cathryn. *Women, Credit and Debt in Early Modern Scotland*. Manchester: Manchester University Press, 2016.

Spont, Alfred. *Letters and Papers Relating to the War with France, 1512–1513*. London: Navy Records Society, 1897.

Spottiswoode, John. *History of the Church of Scotland, Beginning the Year of our Lord 203, and Continued to the End of the Reign of King James VI*. 3 vols. Edinburgh: printed for the Spottiswoode Society, 1847–51.

State Papers Published under the Authority of His Majesty's Commission: King Henry VIII. 11 vols. London: J. Murray, 1830–52.

Statius. *Thebaid. Vol 1: Books 1–7*. Ed. and trans. D. R. Shackleton Bailey. Cambridge, MA: Harvard University Press, 2004.

Stauffer, Donald A. *English Biography Before 1700*. Cambridge, MA: Harvard University Press, 1930.

Stevenson, John Horne, and Marguerite Wood. *Scottish Heraldic Seals*. 3 vols. Glasgow: Robert Maclehose & Co., 1940.

Stevenson, Katie. *Chivalry and Knighthood in Scotland, 1424–1513*. Woodbridge: Boydell Press, 2006.

———. "Jurisdiction, Authority and Professionalisation: The Officers of Arms of Late Medieval Scotland." In *The Herald in Late Medieval Europe*. Ed. Katie Stevenson. Woodbridge: Boydell Press, 2009. Pp. 41–66.

Stewart, Alasdair M. "The Austrian Connection c. 1450–1483: Eleonora and the Intertextuality of *Pontus und Sidonia*." In *Bryght Lanternis*. Eds. McClure and Spiller. Pp. 129–49.

———. "The Final Folios of Adam Abell's 'Riot or Quheill of Tyme': An Obervantine Friar's Reflections on the 1520s and 30s." In *Stewart Style*. Ed. Hadley Williams. Pp. 227–53.

Stewart, Marion M. "Holland's 'Howlat' and the Fall of the Livingstones." *Innes Review* 26.2 (1975), 67–79.

Stone, Charles Russell. *From Tyrant to Philosopher-King: A Literary History of Alexander the Great in Medieval and Early Modern England*. Turnhout: Brepols, 2013.

A Summary Catalogue of Western Manuscripts in the Bodleian Library at Oxford. Ed. Richard W. Hunt, Falconer Madan, H. H. E. Craster, N. Denholm-Young, and P. D. Record. Vol. 2. Oxford: Oxford University Press, 1922.

Sutherland, Annie. *English Psalms in the Middle Ages, 1300–1450*. Oxford: Oxford University Press, 2015.

Swanson, Alan. "Scotia extranea: David Lyndsay in Danish." In *Rhetoric, Royalty, and Reality: Essays on the Literary Culture of Medieval and Early Modern Scotland*. Ed. Alasdair A. MacDonald and Kees Dekker. Leuven: Peeters, 2005. Pp. 137–49.

The Tale of Ralph the Collier. In *Three Middle English Charlemagne Romances: The Sultan of Babylon, The Siege of Milan, and Ralph the Collier*. Ed. Alan Lupack. Kalamazoo, MI: Medieval Institute Publications, 1990.

The Talis of the Fyue Bestis. In *Select Remains of the Ancient Popular and Romance Poetry of Scotland*. Ed. David Laing. Rev. John Small. Edinburgh and London: William Blackwood and Sons, 1885. Pp. 277–93.

———. In *Colkelbie Sow and The Talis of the Fyve Bestes*. Ed. Kratzmann. Pp. 87–103.

Taylor, Simon. "The Cult of St Fillan in Scotland." In *The North Sea World in the Middle Ages: Studies in the Cultural History of North-Western Europe*. Ed. Thomas R. Liszka and Lorna E. M. Walker. Dublin: Four Courts Press, 2001. Pp. 175–210.

Thiry, Claude. "Recherches sur la Déploration Funèbre Française à la Prérenaissance." 2 vols. D. Phil. Thesis: University of Liège, 1973.

Thomas, Andrea. *Princelie Majestie: The Court of James V of Scotland, 1528–1542*. Edinburgh: John Donald, 2005.

Thorndike, Lynn. "Nota de IX Paribus." *Speculum* 34.4 (1959), 640.

The Thre Prestis of Peblis: How Thai Tald Thar Talis, edited from the Asloan and Charteris Texts. Ed. T. D. Robb. STS 2nd series 8. Edinburgh and London: Scottish Text Society, 1920.

Tinkle, Theresa Lynn. *Medieval Venuses and Cupids: Sexuality, Hermeneutics, and English Poetry*. Stanford, CA: Stanford University Press, 1996.

Todd, Margo. *The Culture of Protestantism in Early Modern Scotland*. New Haven and London: Yale University Press, 2002.

Turville-Petre, Thorlac. "The Nine Worthies in the *Parliament of the Thre Ages*." *Poetica* 11 (1979), 28–45.

———. "A Poem on the Nine Worthies." *Nottingham Medieval Studies* 27 (1983), 79–84.

Tyndale, William. *The newe Testament, dylygently corrected and compared with the Greke by Willyam Tindale: and fynesshed in the yere of oure Lorde God A.M.D. and xxxv*. Antwerp: H. Peetersen van Middelburch, 1535.

Tyson, Diana. "Lament for a Dead King." *Journal of Medieval History* 30.4 (2004), 359–75.

Van Buuren, Catherine. "John Asloan, an Edinburgh Scribe." *English Studies* 47 (1966), 365–72.

———. "John Asloan and his Manuscript: An Edinburgh Notary and Scribe in the Days of James III, IV and V (c. 1470–c. 1530)." In *Stewart Style*. Ed. Hadley Williams. Pp. 15–51.

Van Buuren-Veenenbos, Catherine. See Van Buuren, Catherine.

Van den Gheyn, J. *Catalogue des Manuscrits de la Bibliothèque Royale de Belgique*. Vol. 7. Brussels: Henri Lamertin, 1907.

Van Dussen, Michael. "Three Verse Eulogies of Anne of Bohemia." *Medium Aevum* 78.2 (2009), 231–60.

Van Heijnsbergen, Theo, and Nicola Royan, eds. *Literature, Letters and the Canonical in Early Modern Scotland*. East Lothian: Tuckwell Press, 2002.

Villet de Viriville, Auguste. *Histoire de Charles VII Roi de France et de son Époque 1403–1461. Vol. 3: 1444–1461*. Paris: J. Renouard, 1865.

Les Voeux de Paon. In *The Buik of Alexander*. Ed. Ritchie.

Wallis, Faith, ed. *Medieval Medicine: A Reader*. Toronto: University of Toronto Press, 2010.

Welford, Richard, ed. *History of Newcastle and Gateshead. Vol. II: Sixteenth Century*. London: Walter Scott, 1885.

Whiting, Bartlett Jere. "Proverbs and Proverbial Sayings from Scottish Writings before 1600: Part One, A-L." *Mediaeval Studies* 11 (1949), 123–205.

———. "Proverbs and Proverbial Sayings from Scottish Writings before 1600: Part Two, M-Y." *Mediaeval Studies* 13 (1951), 87–164.

Whiting, Bartlett Jere and Helen Wescott Whiting, eds. *Proverbs, Sentences, and Proverbial Sayings from English Writings Mainly before 1500*. Cambridge, MA: Harvard University Press, 1968.

Williams, Gordon. *A Dictionary of Sexual Language and Imagery in Shakespearean and Stuart Literature*. 3 vols. London: Athlone Press, 1994.

Wilson, Edward. "*The Testament of the Buck* and the Sociology of the Text." *The Review of English Studies* 45.178 (1994), 157–84.

Wilson, S. C. "Scottish Canterbury Pilgrims." *The Scottish Historical Review* 24 (1926–27), 258–64.

Wingfield, Emily. "The Manuscript and Print Contexts of Older Scots Romance." D. Phil. Thesis: University of Oxford, 2010.

———. "'And He, That Did it Out of French Translait': *Cleriadus* in France, England and Scotland, c. 1440–1550." *Neophilologus* 95.4 (2011), 649–60.

———. "The Thewis off Gudwomen: Female Advice in *Lancelot of the Laik* and *The Buik of King Alexander the Conquerour*." In *Fresche Fontanis*. Eds. Hadley Williams and McClure. Pp. 85–96.

———. "Towards an Edition of the *Scottish Troy Book*." In *Probable Truth: Editing Medieval Texts from Britain in the Twenty-First Century*. Ed. Vincent Gillespie and Anne Hudson. Turnhout: Brepols, 2013. Pp. 326–43.

———. *The Trojan Legend in Medieval Scottish Literature*. Cambridge: D. S. Brewer, 2014.

———. *Reading and Writing Scotland's Queens c. 1424–1587*. Forthcoming.

Wormald, Jenny. *Lords and Men in Scotland: Bonds of Manrent 1442–1603*. Edinburgh: John Donald, 1985.

———. "Lords and Lairds in Fifteenth-Century Scotland: Nobles and Gentry?" In *Gentry and Lesser Nobility in Late Medieval Europe*. Ed. Michael Jones. Gloucester: Alan Sutton, 1986. Pp. 181–200.

Wyntoun, Andrew of. *The Original Chronicle of Andrew of Wyntoun*. Ed. F. J. Amours. 6 vols. STS 1st series 50, 53, 54, 56, 57, 63. Edinburgh: Scottish Text Society, 1903–14.

COMMENTARY SERIES

Haimo of Auxerre, *Commentary on the Book of Jonah*, translated with an introduction and notes by Deborah Everhart (1993)

Medieval Exegesis in Translation: Commentaries on the Book of Ruth, translated with an introduction and notes by Lesley Smith (1996)

Nicholas of Lyra's Apocalypse Commentary, translated with an introduction and notes by Philip D. W. Krey (1997)

Rabbi Ezra Ben Solomon of Gerona, *Commentary on the Song of Songs and Other Kabbalistic Commentaries*, selected, translated, and annotated by Seth Brody (1999)

John Wyclif, *On the Truth of Holy Scripture*, translated with an introduction and notes by Ian Christopher Levy (2001)

Second Thessalonians: Two Early Medieval Apocalyptic Commentaries, introduced and translated by Steven R. Cartwright and Kevin L. Hughes (2001)

The "Glossa Ordinaria" on the Song of Songs, translated with an introduction and notes by Mary Dove (2004)

The Seven Seals of the Apocalypse: Medieval Texts in Translation, translated with an introduction and notes by Francis X. Gumerlock (2009)

The "Glossa Ordinaria" on Romans, translated with an introduction and notes by Michael Scott Woodward (2011)

Nicholas of Lyra, Literal Commentary on Galatians, translated with an introduction and notes by Edward Arthur Naumann (2015)

Early Latin Commentaries on the Apocalypse, edited by Francis X. Gumerlock (2016)

Rabbi Eliezer of Beaugency: Commentaries on Amos and Jonah (with selections from Isaiah and Ezekiel), by Robert A. Harris (2018)

SECULAR COMMENTARY SERIES

Accessus ad auctores: Medieval Introduction to the Authors, edited and translated by Stephen M. Wheeler (2015)

The Vulgate Commentary on Ovid's Metamorphoses, *Book 1*, edited and translated by Frank Coulson (2015)

Brunetto Latini, La rettorica, edited and translated by Stefania D'Agata D'Ottavi (2016)

DOCUMENTS OF PRACTICE SERIES

Love and Marriage in Late Medieval London, selected, translated, and introduced by Shannon McSheffrey (1995)

Sources for the History of Medicine in Late Medieval England, selected, introduced, and translated by Carole Rawcliffe (1995)

A Slice of Life: Selected Documents of Medieval English Peasant Experience, edited, translated, and with an introduction by Edwin Brezette DeWindt (1996)

Regular Life: Monastic, Canonical, and Mendicant "Rules," selected and introduced by Douglas J. McMillan and Kathryn Smith Fladenmuller (1997); second edition, selected and introduced by Daniel Marcel La Corte and Douglas J. McMillan (2004)

Women and Monasticism in Medieval Europe: Sisters and Patrons of the Cistercian Reform, selected, translated, and with an introduction by Constance H. Berman (2002)

Medieval Notaries and Their Acts: The 1327–1328 Register of Jean Holanie, introduced, edited, and translated by Kathryn L. Reyerson and Debra A. Salata (2004)

John Stone's Chronicle: Christ Church Priory, Canterbury, 1417–1472, selected, translated, and introduced by Meriel Connor (2010)

Medieval Latin Liturgy in English Translation, edited by by Matthew Cheung Salisbury (2017)

Typeset in 10/13 New Baskerville
and Golden Cockerel Ornaments display

Medieval Institute Publications
College of Arts and Sciences
Western Michigan University
1903 W. Michigan Avenue
Kalamazoo, MI 49008-5432
http://www.wmich.edu/medievalpublications

 WESTERN MICHIGAN UNIVERSITY